1295

D0843579

Patients and Healers
in the
Context of Culture

Comparative Studies of Health Systems and Medical Care

NUMBER 3

COMPARATIVE STUDIES OF HEALTH SYSTEMS AND MEDICAL CARE

General Editor
Charles Leslie

Editorial Board
Fred Dunn, M.D., *University of California, San Francisco*
Renée Fox, *University of Pennsylvania*
Eliot Freidson, *New York University*
Edward Montgomery, *Washington University*
Yasuo Otsuka, M.D., *Yokohama City University Medical School*
Carl E. Taylor, M.D., *The Johns Hopkins University*
K. N. Udupa, M.S., F.R.C.S., *Banaras Hindu University*
Paul Unschuld, *University of Marburg*

Patients and Healers
in the
Context of Culture

**An Exploration of the Borderland between
Anthropology, Medicine, and Psychiatry**

Arthur Kleinman

UNIVERSITY OF CALIFORNIA PRESS
BERKELEY   LOS ANGELES   LONDON

University of California Press

Berkeley and Los Angeles, California

University of California Press, Ltd.

London, England

© 1980 by

The Regents of the University of California

First Paperback Printing 1981

ISBN 0-520-04511-4

Library of Congress Catalog Card Number: 78-57311

Printed in the United States of America

3 4 5 6 7 8 9

to Joan

Contents

Figures

Preface

Patients and Healers in the Context of Culture presents a theoretical framework for studying the relationship between medicine, psychiatry, and culture. That framework is principally illustrated by materials gathered in field research in Taiwan and, to a lesser extent, from materials gathered in similar research in Boston. The reader will find this book contains a dialectical tension between two reciprocally related orientations: it is both a cross-cultural (largely anthropological) perspective on the essential components of clinical care and a clinical perspective on anthropological studies of medicine and psychiatry. That dialectic is embodied in my own academic training and professional life, so that this book is a personal statement.

I am a psychiatrist trained in anthropology. I have worked in library, field, and clinic on problems concerning medicine and psychiatry in Chinese culture. I teach cross-cultural psychiatry and medical anthropology, but I also practice and teach consultation psychiatry and take a clinical approach to my major cross-cultural teaching and research involvements. The theoretical framework elaborated in this book has been applied to all of those areas; in turn, they are used to illustrate the theory. Both the theory and its application embody the same dialectic. The purpose of this book is to advance both poles of that dialectic: to demonstrate the critical role of social science (especially anthropology and cross-cultural studies) in clinical medicine and psychiatry and to encourage study of clinical problems by anthropologists and other investigators involved in cross-cultural research.

The book's origins may be of interest. In 1970 I returned to the United States after fourteen months of medical research in Taiwan and spent the next several years at Harvard reading my way through all the literature I could find concerned with medicine and psychiatry in different cultures. The body of literature I assembled was quite large, but extremely disparate, fragmented among a number of disciplinary and subspecialty approaches: medical and general anthropology, transcultural psychiatry, medical sociology, medical history, cross-cultural psychology, several medical and public health perspectives on international and social aspects of health care, area studies, studies of the health related aspects of modernization, and other fields.

The impact of reading through these varied materials, and my attempt to relate them to my field experience and to organize them within an overarching comparative framework that could make clinical sense, led to a predictable sense of confusion. Moreover, I found the empirical studies themselves to be confused and fragmented. They lacked discriminating theoretical frameworks and systematic methods. Even a shared problem-frame of questions considered worthy of systematic inquiry was missing. Nothing was available to integrate the different questions and research approaches abounding in this wide, unorganized, but extremely fascinating field.

Yet, after confronting these materials, I began to see a conceptual framework "naturally" emerge. I have outlined that theoretical orientation in a number of publications, and I have used it especially to organize our knowledge about medicine in Chinese culture (see references to Chapter 1), but this volume represents the most sustained elaboration of the theory. It is supported by materials from recent comparative field research aimed at testing certain of its hypotheses. In particular, I draw heavily from field studies I conducted in Taiwan from January through September, 1975. I also draw upon materials from similar research carried out in Boston in 1974. I discuss the research briefly in Chapter 1 but present relevant findings throughout the book. Intriguingly, the theoretical framework that I fashioned parallels and gains support from similar models proposed by other investigators working at the same time but independently in the anthropology of medicine and psychiatry. This eruption of theoretical interest testifies to the creative phase medical and psychiatric anthropology is passing through. Even more importantly, the striking parallels between the various models set forth are evidence of general agreement on what are now thought to be the major issues and relevant sources of knowledge.

Much of this book is concerned with illness and health care in Chinese culture. But my intention is not to make that the subject of the book, nor do I intend to present all of my field research findings from Chinese cultural areas. Rather, I use certain of these to illustrate and support cross-cultural generalizations and comparisons. This is not meant to be a complete medical and psychiatric ethnography of Taiwan, nor is it an exhaustive review of the cross-cultural literature. *Patients and Healers in the Context of Culture* is simply a report of my inquiries (theoretical and empirical) into various corners of this relatively new subject. I believe such a report will be instructive to others interested in this field as much for its limitations and failures as for its successes. The theory, though supported by considerable evidence (my own and others'), remains tentative and open, not closed and inviolate; it is presented in full in order to stimulate reaction, not to gain converts or stake out claims. We are still in the beginning stage of development in cross-cultural studies of medicine and psychiatry and in medical and psychiatric anthropology. Now is the time when most is to be gained from explorations of particular lines of investigation, such as this one, rather than from attempting to integrate most or all of what we know into a complete system, which simply cannot be done at present. Hence, it is especially valuable at this time to stimulate controversy and debate and to determine differences as well as similarities.

The approach presented here is interdisciplinary in almost every sense of the word. It includes ideas, methods, problem-frames, and solution-frames from social science and clinical science. I believe this is how we must proceed in cross-cultural studies of health care. Translation from social and behavioral sciences to clinical science, and the reverse, is specially important and in the past has been little and often poorly done. In exploring one line of inquiry into the unmarked borderland between medicine, psychiatry, anthropology, sociology, and public health, I do not seek to delimit the boundaries of medical anthropology and cross-cultural psychiatry or say what belongs to the health sciences and what to the social sciences. In fact, I wish to do the opposite by suggesting that this field requires mixing disciplines just as it requires sharing ideas and approaches.

Nonetheless, as a clinician I have found myself frequently disappointed by anthropological and cross-cultural studies of health care, because these studies often are so remote from or irrelevant to the chief interests of a clinician: the exigent and difficult reality of illness as a human experience and the core relationships and tasks of clinical care. Most anthropological and cross-cultural research on health care, even research by health scientists, has had little or nothing to say about these clinical issues. On the other hand, I entered medicine and remain in it because of my fascination with such matters; they are the chief interests behind my cross-cultural work and this book. But I do not think I have imposed an *a priori* clinical category on cross-cultural materials. Instead, I wish to advance the notion that clinical categories are intrinsic to all cultures and that their analysis and cross-cultural comparison are essential for understanding "medical systems." The problem is not one of importing a culture-specific suprastructure but rather is the result of failure to comprehend a universal aspect of social action—one that is grasped only through praxis. Comparisons of clinical categories and behaviors correct this lacuna in ethnomedical studies and, as I hope to show, yield concepts and findings more relevant for the application of such studies to the analysis and resolution of key problems in contemporary health care.

In following a clinical direction, however, I have tried to overcome the lack of interest in rigorous investigation of theoretical questions characteristic of many clinicians and, interestingly enough, of many medical anthropologists working in biomedicine as well. Clinicians tend to be simplistic about clinical practice. Their tendency toward positivistic scientism and atheoretical pragmatism discourages attempts to understand illness and care as embedded in the social and cultural world. Their reliance on "common sense" often masks ignorance of relevant behavioral and social science concepts that should be part of the foundation of clinical science and practice. This is the reason social science needs to be brought into medicine and psychiatry as a clinically applied science that systematically analyzes the clinically relevant effects of sociocultural determinants on sickness and care. The conceptual framework developed in this book seeks to do just that. It also attempts to contribute to theory in medical anthropology by examining the structure and functions of medical systems and by working out ways for more precisely defining and operationalizing *culture* as a variable in health-related research.

This framework has been used over the last several years at Harvard and the University of Washington to teach clinical social science to house officers and medical students, to teach social and cross-cultural psychiatry to psychiatrists, and to teach medical anthropology to anthropology undergraduates and graduate students. Furthermore, I have applied this framework directly to clinical work in psychiatric consultation in the general hospital setting, as the case illustrations in the book should amply demonstrate. It is with this clinical orientation in mind that I contend a cross-cultural approach forces us to rethink medicine and psychiatry. It is my hope this book will contribute to a much-needed general reassessment of the clinical field, a field that heretofore has failed to attract the sustained critical examination of its theoretical underpinnings that it so evidently deserves.

I am, of course, sensitive to the book's shortcomings. Among the most serious of these is my reliance on bi-cultural (Chinese and American) materials to support a framework that aims to be cross-cultural. But that framework is, in fact, supported by research from a wide range of cultures and different historical periods, as the content of these chapters and the bibliography will disclose. Another patent shortcoming is the wide range of questions examined, an examination that does not pretend to be complete and that rests upon a "logic" that more nearly reflects the author's special interests than the scope and major divisions of the subject. A model is as notable for what it excludes as for what it attends to. The expert may discover that I do not touch upon some questions he believes are central. This is a further caution that *Patients and Healers* should be read as a personal statement.

The ideas put forth here owe much to interaction with others. That is especially true for the reactions of my mentor, Leon Eisenberg, whom I thought of as my ideal reader while preparing the manuscript. That also includes reactions to my work from other teachers, colleagues, and friends, including: E. Russell Alexander, Everett Mendelsohn, John Pelzel, Nur Yalman, Byron Good, James Gale, Peter Kunstadter, Bernard Gallin, Dieter Koch-Weser, Thomas Hackett, Gerald Klerman, John Stoeckle, Charles Leslie, Barbara Rosenkrantz, Wen-shing Tseng, Tsung-yi Lin, Charles Keyes, Noel Chrisman, Nathan Sivin, Carl Eisdorfer, Theo Manschreck, and others. None of these individuals should be held responsible for the ideas developed in this book, which indeed run counter to those of several of the people I have mentioned and for which I alone accept full responsibility.

My work in Taiwan benefited from the support and help of the Department of Psychiatry, National Taiwan University Hospital, and the following individuals: Chen Chu-chang, Chen Kung-pei, Hwu Hai-gwo, Hsu Chen-chin, Li Yih-yuan, Ko Yung-ho, Rin Hsien, Wang Yao-tung, Wei Ping-yen, Yeh Eng-kung, Palmer Beasley, among others. I owe a large debt of thanks to a group of excellent research assistants: Marie Ao, Barbara Haines, Lok Chung-shan, and Lilias Ho Sung.

Grants and fellowships supported my work at various times and in many ways, allowing me to clear and travel along a very special path in medical anthropology and cross-cultural psychiatry. For that I am grateful to: the Geographic Medicine Branch, National Institute of Allergy and Infectious Diseases, National Institutes of Health (then directed by Howard Minners); the Commissioned Corps, United States Public Health Service; and the United States Naval Medical Research Unit #2, all of which enabled me to carry out research in Taiwan in 1969 and 1970; the National Science Foundation, which supported my work in comparative studies of medicine and psychiatry from 1970 through 1972; and the Dupont-Warren, Livingston, Milton, and Wellington Funds of the Harvard Medical School and Harvard University, the Foundations' Fund for Research in Psychiatry, the Harvard-Yenching Institute, and the Social Science Research Council, all of which have supported various aspects of my research from 1972 to 1976. I wish to acknowledge the support I received from the Massachusetts General Hospital (especially the Department of Psychiatry); the Harvard Medical School and Harvard University; and the Department of Psychiatry and Behavioral Sciences, University of

Washington. Support from the Fogarty International Center, N.I.H., made it possible to help organize, participate in, and edit the published proceedings of an international conference covering both health care in Chinese societies and comparative cross-cultural studies in medicine and psychiatry, where some of the ideas presented in this book were developed. Partial support for preparation of research materials for the book has been provided by the Biomedical Research Program of the National Institutes of Health (Grant 5-S07-RR-05432).

In teaching Harvard and, more recently, University of Washington undergraduates, graduate students, medical students, and house officers, I have had the opportunity repeatedly to work out and apply many of my ideas. I wish to thank them, and I especially wish to thank the Harvard students who participated in Anthropology 106 (Medical and Psychiatric Anthropology) and the predecessor seminars I gave, since in those seminars I first presented and had criticized the theoretical framework described in this book. I note with gratitude the benefit I derived from having had my theoretical ideas and empirical research discussed critically by members of the Harvard Faculty Seminar on "Cross-Cultural Studies of Illness and Clinical Care and Their Implications for Primary Health Care in the United States," supported by the Johnson Foundation and held fortnightly from October, 1975, through May, 1976; and from discussions with colleagues in the seminar on Anthropological and Cross-Cultural Aspects of Illness and Care, held monthly by the Division of Social and Cross-Cultural Psychiatry at the University of Washington, from August, 1976, through May, 1977.

Special appreciation goes in three directions: My work would not have been possible without the cooperation (often under difficult circumstances) of informants, patients, families, and practitioners (traditional and modern) in Boston and Taiwan. To them I am greatly obliged for their willingness to put up with me and my research, while teaching me most of what I have learned about illness and clinical care cross-culturally. I also wish to praise and express my deep gratitude to Charles Leslie for his several critical readings of the manuscript at different stages in its evolution and for his masterly editorial labor to shorten and improve it. And lastly, I wish to thank my wife, Joan, and our two children, Peter-John and Cici, for tolerating the many difficulties caused by almost a decade spent in pursuit of this elusive subject and for enabling and sustaining, with patience and grace, a not always easy and all too frequently self-absorbing quest. I hope this book will in part repay these debts.

1

Orientations 1:
The Problem, the Setting,
and the Approach

it is the substance, not the form, of structure which preoccupies experience. Every procedure, after all, is imperiled by our consciousness of it . . .

George Park, The Idea of Social Structure
(New York: Anchor Books, 1974), pp. 291—292.

PROLOGUE: A PHENOMENOLOGICAL FRAGMENT

In Taipei's old Lung-Shan district, which dates back to the Ch'ing Dynasty, there are several busy streets surrounding the spacious and ornate Lung Shan Temple that contain a remarkably large number of shops belonging to many different kinds of medical practitioners. These frequently stand next to each other. In one place, directly across from the high wall enclosing the temple, there are seven in a row. Within this conspicuously "medical" neighborhood, one sees: (1) the clinics of several Western-style and Chinese-style doctors, each of which bears a sign outside listing the kinds of medical problems the practitioner specializes in; (2) the offices of bone-setters, which display with somewhat mock ferocity the emblems of this ancient healing specialty—a large curved tin knife blade mounted on a pole and a mask with horrible features painted a hideous green and red; (3) several tiny shops run by specialists in the treatment of eye disorders, who are neither licensed to practice Western nor Chinese medicine, but whose antiquated and dirty equipment looks more like what might be found in much better condition in the offices of the former rather than in those of the latter; (4) several dental offices; (5) a number of pharmacies, some selling Chinese prescription medicines, others selling Western prescription medicines, and some selling patent medicines of both types; (6) the shop of a fortune-teller, who is also a geomancer, where people frequently come with questions about their illnesses or the fate of their health; and (7) numerous stores selling religious paraphernalia, where one can buy amulets to protect the health of a child or a pregnant mother. In those stores one also can purchase small carved wooden statues of various Buddhist and Taoist deities, several of whom are renowned for their healing powers, including Pao-sheng-ta-ti, the god of healers. Much of the incense and spirit money sold by these stores will be burned in religious ceremonies devoted to healing. Some of these stores also sell cheap paperback almanacs, which contain a considerable amount of information on how to prevent and treat illness in the metaphors of traditional Chinese beliefs about fate, the influence of macrocosmic forces on the microcosm of the family and the individual, and ancestor worship.

Also found in the neighborhood are tea shops that sell, besides the more common and popular teas, other teas famous for their medicinal qualities, such as "white tea" and "one hundred herbs tea." These are ingested to lower the internal hot energy or "fire" (*huo ch'i*),[1] believed to be "rising" and too "big" in certain kinds of illnesses coded into traditional Chinese medical theory and used as a popular term by patients and lay people generally to refer to a characteristic constellation of symptoms. Nearby, several street vendors sell coconuts, the juice of which is popularly reputed to have the same therapeutic effect. On these streets there are also the offices of for-

1. Chinese (the official language of Taiwan, where it is called *kuo-yü*, and the People's Republic of China, where it is called *p'u-t'ung-hua*) words are italicized. They are romanized in the Wade-Giles system. Hokkien words are romanized in the method of Douglas (1873) and Barclay (1923). Cantonese words are romanized following Meyer and Wempe (1947). Both Hokkien and Cantonese terms are underlined as well as italicized to distinguish them from Chinese terms. The words Mandarin, Peking dialect, and Chinese are used interchangeably.

tune-tellers, physiognomists, and geomancers, all of whom
advertise their skills in various matters, including health problems. Not far away is a fairly large charity hospital. Directly
across the street from the hospital is a traditional Chinese pharmacy, but built in an ultramodern style that makes the Japanese colonial hospital architecture seem terribly old-fashioned.
Some patients walk straight from the laboratories and specialty
clinics at the hospital across the street to consult two middle-
aged Chinese-style doctors, who see large numbers of patients
at their desks at the back of the pharmacy, from where they
can look almost directly across into the offices of their Western-
style medical "colleagues" at the hospital. Although they share
many patients, the practitioners in these two very different
health care facilities have neither formal nor informal relations
with each other.[2]

Outside, on the crowded and noisy streets, hawkers of foods
and drinks invoke the reputed medicinal properties of their
wares. Several blocks away, gaunt figures with shaved heads,
their fingers wrapped tightly around the bars of their windows,
stare out mutely, occasionally with silly smiles, at the active
street scene below. They are crowded into the second story of
a building that appears no different from those occupied by
commercial enterprises on either side of it, but that has a small
sign over the entrance announcing it is a private mental hospital.

In the spacious Lung Shan Temple itself, about half of the
people who come to pray and who use the divination blocks
to ask the temple's gods questions, ask about health-related
problems, usually their own illnesses or those of family members. Inside the central temple building an old man sits at one
of the counters to the side of the main entrance interpreting

2. By August 1978, three years after I recorded this Taipei street scene, the
modern Chinese pharmacy had moved, replaced by an impressive new
building for the charity hospital: a modernistic glass and steel high-rise. The
old hospital building was unoccupied. This change gave a predictably Western twist to the irony of medical modernization that I described. The symbolic
modernization of the traditional Chinese medicine facility had been superseded
by the very substantial modernization of the Western medical institution; the
largely symbolic integration of these very separate professional therapeutic
institutions owing to their propinquity and patient utilization had been can-
celled because of the bureaucratic and politicoeconomic "interests" which
evicted the pharmacy and built the new hospital.

ch'ien, or fortune papers, which people bring to him after they have obtained these from another counter where they are divided into two groups: those concerned with health questions and those concerned with all other questions. Some of the interpretations given by this *ch'ien* interpreter come directly from his much-thumbed-through book, used for analyzing the vague fragments of archaic poetry that are printed on the *ch'ien* paper. Other interpretations are remarkable for their psychological sophistication as well as for the striking fact that they bear little if any relation to what really is written on the *ch'ien* paper. The characters at the bottom of the *ch'ien* paper advise the sick person to go for treatment to the traditional Chinese pharmacy across from the charity hospital.

At certain hours, in other sections of the temple, one sees old and young women with infants strapped to their backs who have come to have a special healing ceremony performed that involves "calling back the soul" of the infants for a culturally defined disorder called "fright" by their mothers and grandmothers. "Fright" (*ching*, or "catch fright," *shou ching*) seems to include a variety of disorders. Pediatricians would classify them as measles, other childhood exanthems, symptoms caused by upper respiratory or gastrointestinal diseases, colic, and unexplained crying and irritability. Small red packets, (*hû-á*) are attached to strings around the necks of some of the infants. Inside these packets are charms to ward off illnesses and protect health. These same infants may have been given injections of antibiotics by Western-style doctors or pharmacists within the past hour.

To one side of this temple is a narrow alley containing ten tiny shops, eight of which specialize in selling local herbs. For the most part their owners are illiterate or just barely literate. They not only sell herbs, but also advise clients about which herbs to buy for specific symptoms or for particular illnesses. The herbs are all from Taiwan, mostly from mountainous rural areas surrounding the sprawling conurbation of Taipei. The herbs sold in the shops of the herbalists living in this alley do not resemble those sold in traditional Chinese pharmacies any more than do the herbalists' shops and the herbalists themselves resemble Chinese-style pharmacies and doctors. Most prescriptions prepared for patients in Chinese pharmacies are

4

Indigenous Treatment Settings

Offering prayers at a temple

Office of an unlicensed, "traditional" specialist in eye, skin and dental diseases

Bone-setter's clinic

Herbalists' stalls

mixtures compounded from many herbs (and sometimes containing animal and mineral substances) finely chopped or ground up and wrapped together into bulky paper packages. (Surprisingly, most still come from the China mainland.) In contrast, the herbalists' shops sell herbs as crude bundles of individual grasses, roots, or flowers (fresh or dried). The Chinese pharmacies tend to be much larger and more impressive than the herbalists' stores and are often richly decorated in traditional Chinese taste, containing, for example, beautifully designed wooden shelves with antique porcelain pots and rows of narrow drawers that hold the prepared herbs and other medicinal agents. Also found in these pharmacies are deer antlers, rhinoceros horns, dried lizards, pickled snakes, and sometimes barrels of aromatic herbs that strongly scent the air. At the back of the pharmacies, framed licenses of pharmacists and, frequently, of Chinese-style doctors hang on the walls, along with old scrolls and mounted calligraphy containing moral exhortations and testimonials from patients. Classical Chinese medical texts and other books often surround the Chinese-style doctor's desk, giving his office a scholarly appearance that contrasts sharply with the green-grocer ethos of the herbalists' shops. Yet people on the street will tell you that both kinds of practitioners' stores contain knowledge of "secret prescriptions" (mi-fang) essential for curing; many people are unable to explain what difference there is (besides cost) between the herbalist's herbs (ts'ao-yao) and the Chinese-style doctor's medicines (chung-yao).

Most Chinese pharmacies in this area tend to look like the picture I have sketched, but a few, like the one across from the hospital, are very modern in appearance, and at times are indistinguishable from Western-style pharmacies, except for the obvious differences in appearance of the medicines. Even that difference may be diminished by those Chinese-style pharmacies that prepare traditional Chinese medicine as powders or pills. Some pharmacies are quite literally split in half, with one side selling Chinese medicine and the other, Western medicine.

Across a market street from the alley of herbalists is a small temple, part of the local folk religion in which Taoist and Buddhist elements are syncretized. In that temple, on certain special occasions, a *tao-shih* (Taoist priest) conducts ceremonies for clients—most of whom come with problems that a Western medical observer would categorize as medical and psychiatric—to drive away ghosts and evil spirits or to placate gods held responsible for causing these problems. On other occasions, usually in the evenings, a shaman (*tâng-ki*) performs. Again, a substantial portion of his practice is made up of problems of a medical or psychiatric (or crisis intervention) character.

Out on the market street itself, one hears people trying to decide whether to buy a particular tonic to prevent or treat illness or special foods popularly alleged to be effective for certain kinds of disorders or ordinary foods according to whether they are culturally classified as "hot" or "cold" in the widely understood system of symbolic polarities. The last are used to treat putative imbalances of the hot and cold constituents of the body and similarly classified diseases. Other people in the same market street are purchasing vitamins, Western patent medicines, and foods they regard as possessing high nutrient value, again out of the same concern with their health status or because of specific symptoms they are experiencing. Indeed, the same individuals may do all of these things.

Some persons are asking other lay people (family and friends) for advice about their health problems. In return, they are receiving information about family prescriptions said to have been confirmed in actual experience as effective for the disorders they suffer from. Besides learning about specific family remedies, they are hearing about individual experiences with similar health problems. They hear the names used to label health problems, some of which have direct equivalents in English, while others are indigenous cultural categories that frequently do not possess lexical or even semantic equivalents in English or other languages. These individuals also hear the concrete details of how patients and families decided on a particular sickness label, which treatments were applied by them, how they chose a practitioner, what happened to them under that healer's care, and, if they were not cured, what decisions were made about recourse to other practitioners and other types of available health care. Included in these descriptions are the names of the medicines (Western or Chinese) held to have been effective and their cost. Certain people giving advice are listened to with special attention, because they are either family members, friends, or neighbors (usually old or middle-aged women) who are commonly believed to possess much knowledge about illness and treatment generally or who have had experience with the same problem affecting the listener.

Here we have a brief but graphic illustration of patients and healers in the context of culture. The argument presented in this book is that to understand patients and healers we must study them in particular cultural environments and then make cross-cultural comparisons to seek generalizations about these fundamental human experiences. In the example described here, the culture is, of course, a variant of Chinese culture in an urban setting in contemporary Taiwan. If, instead of Taipei, I had described from the same perspective a section of Boston, Bogota, Benares, or Benin, the description in each case would have been quite different. In each it would picture a distinct culture as well as a distinct assortment of health care practices and practitioners. In each city, the patients differ in the ways they think about, experience, and respond to their illnesses. They have differing institutions, patterns of institutional activities, and individual behaviors related to health and health care. Even if our descriptions were limited to Chinese cultures, they would be somewhat dissimilar, since health-related beliefs, behaviors, and institutions are not uniform in Taiwan, Hong Kong, Singapore, and overseas Chinese communities elsewhere in Asia and in the West. Obviously the dissimilarity would be greater if we added Peking to this comparison; it would be much less, though still significant, if we limited our sample to other (say, rural) areas of Taiwan.[3]

Regardless of which society we chose to examine, we would always find people we could identify (and more importantly, whom the local population would identify) as healers and patients. Despite the patent dissimilarities, we also would find some similarities (universals), not only in regard to these special social roles, but also with respect to how illness is construed and experienced and how treatment is selected and organized. Even where the specific content of health-related

3. Some descriptions of health care in the various Chinese settings mentioned in this paragraph have in fact been made; for several such descriptions, see relevant chapters in Kleinman et al. (1976) and in Leslie (1976b).

beliefs, behaviors, and institutions was strikingly unlike, their structural properties would reveal some surprising commonalities. This is so because we are dealing with a fundamental part of the social world, a part that belongs to every community and that is therefore important to compare cross culturally.

But how are we to understand these issues in the case of the particular illustration we have drawn from Chinese culture? How do we make sense of the large differences and equally impressive similarities that arise whenever we compare medical and psychiatric dimensions of different societies? Do these strange sights, which have been so hastily sketched, belong together, or are we lumping together things that should be kept separate? What significance do these concerns hold for studying patients and healers? And what can we learn from such a study that might contribute to a better understanding of sickness and healing in society and that might also have practical implications for clinical care?

The chief problem posed by the Taipei street scene is whether there is any means for moving beyond simple description toward an interpretation of this social reality. The introductory chapters that follow will set out what I take to be the best method for analyzing this cultural medical landscape. In order to fathom what is going on in the congested streets of this old section of Taipei or in analogous settings in other societies, we must work with some theoretical framework. After constructing such a conceptual apparatus, I focus on three interrelated subjects that constitute the core of this study: illness experiences, practitioner-patient transactions, and the healing process. For each I will present examples from Taiwan, compare them with related materials from other cultures, and, then, by relating these examples and comparisons to the theoretical framework, attempt to determine what is specific to the clinical domain in Chinese culture and what can be generalized as universal clinical processes. I will then examine two related questions: how culture affects core clinical activities and in what ways they constrain the cultural patterning of health care.

After setting out the theoretical constructs, I will return to the vivid scene of our cross-sectional slice through health care in Chinese culture and move from its surface details to its inner workings. The logic of that movement will take us from cultural beliefs and norms about sickness to the structural characteristics of lay health care-seeking and therapeutic relationships, from macro-analysis of the social organization of health care to micro-analysis of specific instances of sickness and healing. All will be examined through the lens of the theoretical constructs I discuss in the introductory chapters.

THE TAIWAN SETTING

Before discussing the theoretical framework, however, I shall draw a skeletal outline of Taiwan and of my research there to give the reader a sense of the context from which I have drawn much of my material, along with some understanding of how that material was obtained.

Taiwan is an island roughly 130 kilometers off the China mainland, across from the province of Fukien. It has been settled by Chinese in substantial numbers since the Ming Dynasty, mostly by people from Fukien, who speak the Hokkien dialect, and by the Hakka, who came via Kwangtung and speak the Hakka dialect. The island, which is almost 400 kilometers long and 144 kilometers broad at the widest point, has an area of 35,961 square kilometers (only one-third of which is arable), which would make it the smallest province of China. It is regarded as part of China by both the Nationalist Government, which has ruled it since its restoration from Japan in 1945 as the Republic of China, and the People's Republic of China, which claims it. There is an independence movement run from outside the country, with an unknown (but possibly large) amount of support inside Taiwan, that would like to see it become an independent nation. From 1895 to 1945 Taiwan was controlled by the Japanese, and Japanese culture has left its imprint on the population. Many people in Taiwan still maintain close relations with people and activities inside Japan.

In 1975 the island had a population of 16 million: 14 million Hokkien and Hakka speakers, referred to as Taiwanese, and almost 2 million mainlanders, most of whom came to Taiwan from the China mainland in the late 1940s with the retreat of the Nationalist Government. There are also a few hundred thousand aborigines, the original inhabitants of the island, most of whom now live in mountainous areas and are related ethnically and linguistically to Polynesians. The urban areas of Taiwan are among the most densely populated in the world.

The capital city, Taipei, which had a population of one million when I first resided in Taiwan in 1969–1970, now has a population of two million and is a sprawling, heavily industrialized, pollution-plagued, modern Asian city.

By all indices Taiwan is a rapidly industrializing developing society with a modern economy extensively engaged in foreign trade, principally with Japan and the United States. Four-fifths of the people over 15 years of age are said to have received some formal education, which is now compulsory at least through primary school. Average per capita income was the equivalent of $467 in 1973. Taiwan is well into the demographic transition from high death rate and birth rate to low death rate and birth rate, but population excess is a large problem, and there is an active if not entirely successful birth control program. It is estimated that in the 1980's the population will be greater than 20 million. Taiwan has already passed through the epidemiological transition from infectious disease being the chief cause of death to cancer and cerebrovascular disease being the chief causes of death, but tuberculosis remains an important public health problem. Taiwan has a modern system of public health and a national system of health care services that includes both public and private sectors, but no national health insurance.[4] The system of health care is not well integrated and is dominated by private practitioners engaged in a highly competitive marketplace economic practice.

The national health system is serviced entirely by Western-

4. For general statistics, see *China Yearbook 1974* (Taipei: China Publishing Co.); for general medical statistics, see *Health Statistics, Republic of China, 1974,* Vol. 1. General Health Statistics (National Health Administration, Republic of China). See Baker and Perlman (1967) for a detailed study of health manpower. For medical statistics concerning Taipei, see *Public Health in Taipei, 1973* (Taipei City Health Department). All health statistics for the three districts of Taipei City studied come from the Taipei City Health Department.

General historical, economic, and social essays about Taiwan are found in Paul Sih, ed., *Taiwan in Modern Times*. A very critical personal account of the political situation in Taiwan since 1945 is to be found in George Kerr, *Formosa Betrayed*. Since most American China anthropologists after 1949 turned to Taiwan for field research on Chinese culture, the village-based ethnographic literature about Taiwan is remarkably large, but only recently has attention turned to urban studies. Consult Ahern (1976), Gale (1976), Gould-Martin (1976), and Tseng (1976) for reports of anthropological, epidemiological, and clinical field research studies on various aspects of health care and healers in Taiwan.

style doctors, most of whom are graduates of one of Taiwan's seven medical schools. Taiwan exports doctors to the United States, and roughly three-fourths of the graduates of National Taiwan University Medical School over the past decade have emigrated to the United States. That prestigious medical school and hospital complex are quite comparable to smaller university medical centers in the United States with respect to quality of training of staff, level of health care services delivered, and research.

Taiwan in 1974 had 7,724 licensed Western-style doctors (*hsi-i-sheng*), 1,592 licensed Chinese-style doctors (*chung-i-sheng*), not including licensed bone-setters for whom no figure is available, 4,243 professional nurses, 2,510 modern midwives, and 4,141 Western-style, licensed pharmacists (Health Statistics, R.O.C., Vol. 1, 1974: 44–45). Public health services and government-sponsored health care services are dispensed from 346 rural township and urban district health stations, each of which is staffed by a medical team consisting of public health nurse, midwife, sanitation expert, and either full-time or part-time doctor. Besides licensed practitioners there are large numbers of unlicensed practitioners of both Western-style and Chinese-style medicine. Indeed, there are probably more unlicensed (and therefore illegal) than licensed practitioners of Chinese-style medicine. Both Western-style and Chinese-style doctors have their own licensing examinations, professional bureaucratic organizations, and systems of training; but only Western-style medicine receives direct financial support from the government.

In addition to these practitioners, there are all sorts of practitioners of secular and sacred folk medicine, including: herbalists, itinerant drug peddlers, unlicensed specialists in skin and eye disorders, experts in massage and systems of calisthenics (e.g., *kung-fu* and *t'ai chi ch'uan*), fortune-tellers, physiognomists, traditional midwives, priests of the local folk religion (a syncretic mixture of Taoism and Buddhism), shamans, temple-based interpreters of *ch'ien* (fortune papers) and ritual experts, and numerous other folk specialists. Most folk practitioners are unlicensed and illegal, but they had been tolerated by the authorities until September, 1975, when the government began to enforce some rules concerning medical practice.

Drugs are by law only to be distributed by doctors' prescriptions from licensed pharmacies. In fact, all Western and Chinese medicines, except narcotics, can be readily obtained from pharmacies and drug stores without prescriptions. Pharmacists frequently diagnose and prescribe—and at a lower fee than most doctors. Western and Chinese medicines are about equally expensive, and patent medicines of both kinds are widely available. There is no regulation of advertising. Billboards, signs on buses, radio, and television are filled with commercial advertising by all sorts of practitioners on behalf of every available type of therapy, especially medicinal agents. Medical legal suits, which are frequent, quite commonly involve Western-style doctors, rarely involve Chinese-style doctors, and almost never involve folk doctors. Medical fees vary greatly. But probably as much, if not more, is spent on diet, special foods, tonics, vitamins, massage, exercise, regulation of life-style, preventive ritual, and the like in the service of health maintenance as on the treatment of sickness.[5]

5. I mention financial aspects of clinical care in Taiwan throughout the book without providing any details. In brief, when a client sees a *ch'ien* interpreter, he pays only for incense he burns in order to pray (25¢ or 50¢) and for rituals he may need to perform (these may range from $1 up to as much as $5). (I am giving U.S. dollar equivalents; in 1975, when I gathered this information, the official exchange rate was NT $38 to one U.S. dollar.) The *ch'ien* interpreter receives no fee from the client but is paid by the temple. Visits to *tâng-ki*s (shamans) vary considerably in cost. There is the charge for burning incense and often a basic charge for asking the god questions (often 50¢ or 75¢), to which are added charges for charms and rituals. The client often spends $2 to $4, but poorer clients may give only $1 to $2. Visits to fortune-tellers and physiognomists range from $1 to $5, depending on what questions are asked. Chinese-style doctors' charges are based on the cost of the Chinese medicine prescribed; these, in turn, vary widely from less than $1 to quite large sums for special and difficult-to-obtain medication. Visits often average from $2 to $3, and frequent visits may be required for a single problem.

Visits to acupuncturists tend to be quite expensive, since they often involve payment for a series of treatments. This fee has escalated with the upswing in world popularity of acupuncture treatment. In the late 1960's it was not more expensive than herbal treatment. Private Western-style doctors often end up charging $2 to $5 depending on treatment given and economic status of the client. Visits to health station and government hospital clinics are less expensive. Visits to the large modern clinics catering to the elite approximate charges in the United States. The National Taiwan University Hospital sets

The research reported in this book was part of studies that I conducted in three districts of Taipei (Yen-Ping, Lung-Shan, and Shuang-Yüan). Most of the practitioners I describe practice in these three districts, which are the oldest in Taipei. They are noted for being inhabited primarily by Taiwanese, for being the most culturally traditional sections of the city, and for housing some of the poorest people in Taipei, along with middle-class residents. Shuang-Yüan, one of the poorest districts in Taipei, has many recent migrants from rural areas. The 1972 figures for population and *licensed* private medical practitioners in these three districts are summarized in Table 1. Note that Shuang Yüan has more than twice the population but substantially fewer Western-style and Chinese-style practitioners (counting bone-setters) than the other districts.

Only the poorest families in Taipei receive social welfare assistance and free medical care at local health stations. Some families, including most mainland families, have access to virtually free medical care at military hospitals and clinics. Some

---

different hospital charges based on class of room occupied (first, second, third, etc.). The basic charge on the psychiatric ward is $1.25 per day for food, $2 per day for room, and everything else, including medication, is extra. But this is still very inexpensive by United States standards. (By 1978, payment to shamans and other indigenous healers had increased only slightly, though prosperous clients sometimes donated large sums, but private Western medical practice fees for outpatient visits had increased by 25 to 50 percent.)

As for practitioner incomes, Western-style doctors in private practice in Taiwan are among the most affluent people in the population. They often own their own small hospitals and many have invested in real estate and business. But this situation appears to be changing for recent medical school graduates as competition increases. Payment of doctors in government hospitals is very low by United States standards. Consequently, these physicians, as well as physicians in research and teaching, engage in private practice. Chinese-style doctors usually make considerably less than Western-style doctors, but some have made large incomes based on advertising, local and national reputations, large numbers of patients, or ownership of a big pharmacy or drug factory. The incomes of folk practitioners are much harder to estimate, but I have seen *tâng-ki*s in Taipei make as much as $250 in a week and, in one case, in one night (this sum must be shared among assistants and the owner of temple), but these are extreme exceptions. The typical *tâng-ki* makes much less and usually remains at a lower-class or, for the more successful, lower middle-class income level.

14

Table 1
*Licensed Private Medical Practitioners
in Three Districts of Taipei*

	Yen-Ping District	Lung-Shan District	Shuang-Yüan District
Total population	58,263	67,933	142,961
Western pharmacists	68	76	84
Chinese pharmacy owners	86	39	37
Western patent drug stores	16	13	15
Chinese-style doctors	16	43	17
Bone-setters	7	4	0
Modern midwives (private)	8	8	13
Total Western-style doctors*	66	81	45
Pediatricians	6	6	2
Internists	35	56	36
Obstetrician-Gynecologists	3	3	2
Surgeons	11	4	2
Otolaryngologists	3	3	1
Ophthalmologists	2	2	0
Psychiatrists	0	0	2

Source: Table was compiled from data obtained from Taipei City Health Department in 1975.

*Specialities listed for practitioners do not reflect particular specialty training, since Western-style and Chinese-style doctors can advertise as specialists regardless of qualifications.

workers and government employees have health insurance, but most people do not. Each district has a health station, run by the Taipei City Health Department, in which public health work (vaccination, sanitation, etc.), medical education, and some health care services are provided. Health care services include treatment at relatively low cost of tuberculosis, hypertension, stroke, and a variety of maternal and child health problems. There are also public and private hospitals in each district. But the shops and shrines of traditional healers far outnumber the clinics of modern medical practitioners. It is also worth noting that only one district has private psychiatrists. In fact, these are not trained psychiatrists but general practitioners (licensed and unlicensed) who specialize in treating psychiatric disorders with drugs and ECT and who own and run their mental hospitals. These establishments are more like prisons or warehouses than hospitals, but the university and city psychiatric hospitals are comparable to their counterparts in developed countries. There is virtually no psychotherapy available in Taipei (or Taiwan). The psychiatric clinics of the National Taiwan University Hospital, the military hospitals, and the Taipei City Psychiatric Hospital are far from these three districts and only treat patients with the most severe psychiatric problems, especially former inpatients. Therefore, it comes as no surprise that traditional healing agencies provide most of the psychiatric care (at least for the less severe forms of mental illness) as well as a good deal of the general medical care in these areas. Since this care goes unrecorded, however, it is not reported in local or national statistics and is virtually disregarded in reports by public health officials, except where they make negative remarks about it. Obviously such reports and statistics, as in many other societies, seriously distort the true picture of health care.

One cautionary note is in order before we examine different types of medical practice in these three districts of Taipei. Although anthropologists rightly argue that Taiwan is a Chinese cultural area, from 1895 to 1945 it was controlled by the Japanese. For many of those years, especially since the 1930s, Taiwan was treated by the Japanese as if it were an integral part of Japan, and Japanese cultural values and language were imposed on the population. Since the 1930s, the Japanese systematically suppressed all signs of Chinese culture and language. Thus, for many middle-aged and older people, especially in Taipei, much of their secondary socialization was in Japanese culture, although their primary socialization experiences in the family were typically in the Hokkien dialect and Chinese cultural values. Nonetheless, one still encounters many Taiwanese who speak Japanese at home and cultivate Japanese aesthetic and culinary tastes. This may well influence their medical beliefs and practices.

As part of their suppression of things Chinese, the Japanese prohibited almost all folk medical practitioners, especially shamans and other temple-based healers. They severely limited the number of practitioners of Chinese-style medicine, and most Chinese-style doctors who practiced during the Japanese occupation did so illegally. Furthermore, medicine was one of the few professions the Japanese allowed Taiwanese to enter college to pursue, and consequently the current older generation of Taiwanese practitioners represents the educated elite of their generation and is active in many fields outside of medicine.

The vicissitudes of Chinese and Western medicine in China (and Taiwan) are reviewed by Croizier (1968) and in Kleinman et al. (1976). Both Chinese-style and Western-style medicine flourish in Taiwan at present (as does folk medicine). In the family-based surveys of health beliefs and attitudes I conducted, there was considerable sentiment in favor of integrating the two types of practice into one unified system, but there is no evidence that this will occur (cf. Gale 1976). The Western-style medical profession and the government health bureaucracy that it controls oppose this. Thus, the situations in Taiwan and the People's Republic are quite different.

THE RESEARCH PROJECT

I first went to Taiwan in 1969 as a National Institutes of Health research fellow to conduct biomedical research. During the 14 months my family and I lived in Taipei, I had the opportunity to meet many practitioners of both Western-style and Chinese-style medicine and to observe and compare them in actual clinical practice. I also had the opportunity to interview and treat patients (Taiwanese and mainlanders), and I informally discussed health beliefs and practices with several dozen informants in both urban and rural areas. With the exception of two small-scale community surveys about popular conceptions of and responses to leprosy and tuberculosis, I did not conduct systematic field research at this time. My observations and interviews were casual and haphazard. Hence, in preparing this book, I have not drawn upon materials collected in 1969 and 1970.

I mention this early experience because it was crucial to the field research I conducted in Taiwan five years later. It enabled me to immerse myself in a Chinese community and thereby to develop facility with the Chinese language, familiarity with Taiwanese culture, an overview of the local medical systems, and a network of friends and acquaintances (both lay and professional) that proved invaluable in planning and implementing the studies described. This early field experience served another purpose, one at least as important as those I have mentioned. In Taiwan I was confronted with clinical phenomena and engaged in clinical experiences that simply could not be adequately interpreted within the conceptual framework of the biomedical model.

My observations and experiences, though unsystematic and anthropologically "naive," forced me to recognize, not just that the biomedical model was freighted with Western cultural assumptions and saturated with a particular theoretical and value orientation, but that it had no means for taking into account patient and lay perspectives on a given sickness episode, to say nothing of alternative therapeutic formulations held by other healing systems. The biomedical model did not account for the meaning contexts of sickness, nor was it self-reflexive. If I can claim a single instance of inspired insight (albeit unoriginal and belated) in my professional development, this is it. Ever since, I have struggled with the same question: How can we elaborate an ethnomedical model that can systematically compare different culturally constituted frameworks for construing (and thereby, at least in part, socially constructing) sickness? What would such a model require to be able to provide both accurate *phenomenological* accounts of the way sickness is experienced in different cultural settings and valid *hermeneutic* accounts of divergent and perhaps conflicting interpretations of sickness? How would such a model enable us to make cross-cultural comparisons of the way therapeutic responses to the same type of sickness are differentially organized by various lay and practitioner perspectives? And how would an ethnomedical model determine which are the core clinical tasks of healers in different cultures?

Even before I departed from Taiwan in 1970, I had arrayed alongside these questions about the nature and uses of an ethnomedical model another set of questions engendered by just such a model, albeit rough and provisional, that would form the basis for my future research. What are the range of clinical phenomena in a society? How do they relate to systems of cultural meanings and norms on the one hand and to institutionalized social patterns of power relations on the other? How and to what extent do cultural conceptions about sickness influence the prevalence, morphology, and course of particular disorders? In what ways do differing cultural views of sickness and treatment affect clinical communication between patient, family, and practitioners? What are the culture-specific and universal characteristics of the healing process?

Initially these concerns led me into formal training in medical and psychiatric anthropology. Eventually I was able to put together a series of separate field studies as part of an overall comparative research project aimed at operationalizing these questions in different cultural settings in America and Taiwan.

In 1973 and 1974, I collaborated with Dr. Albert Gaw, a Chinese-American psychiatrist at Tufts University Medical School, on a study of health beliefs and practices of Cantonese-speaking residents of Boston's Chinatown. We interviewed, in Cantonese and English, 30 non-patient informants concerning their general attitudes and beliefs about health and sickness. The bilingual questionnaire and structured interview schedule we developed for this study formed the basis for those later revised for use with Mandarin-speaking and Hokkien-speaking subjects in Taiwan. I also had the opportunity, between 1972 and 1975, to interview (in English and Chinese) 49 Chinese patients with a variety of psychological and physical disorders both at the Massachusetts General Hospital and in Boston's Chinatown. For each patient I collected information on the present sickness episode, including: ethnomedical beliefs, coping strategies, health care seeking choices and behavior, experiences with Western-style medical and psychiatric services, and treatment outcome at time of three-month follow-up interview. I performed physical and mental status examinations, and I collected all available laboratory, radiologic, and psychometric findings. Thirty of these patients I interviewed for more than 10 hours each, and five patients I interviewed for more than 20 hours each. I draw upon these cases later in the book when I present evidence in support of a model of how Chinese culture patterns depression and other psychological disorders. I make use of both these case analyses and the Chinatown survey when I compare Chinese-American responses to sickness with those collected for Taiwanese informants and patients.

In 1973 and 1974, I carried out ethnomedical studies among non-Chinese patients at the Massachusetts General Hospital and among non-Chinese informants in the Boston area, the results of which I refer to when I compare Chinese and American (mainstream and ethnic) responses to sickness. One study had to do with the elicitation of conflicts between patient and health professional views of sickness and treatment goals in a coronary care unit and the impact of these conflicts on clinical communication, patient compliance with the medical regimen, and patient and family satisfaction with the quality of care. Another study duplicated the health beliefs and health care-seeking behavior survey among fifty Caucasian families in the Boston area.

When I returned to Taiwan in 1975 to conduct the field studies described in the book, I had sufficient facility in Chinese (Mandarin) to conduct structured interviews with informants and to carry out psychiatric evaluations, again following a structured format. I possessed only minimal knowledge of Taiwanese, however; therefore, when interviews could not be conducted in Chinese or English (about one third of the interviews), I worked through my trilingual research assistants, who were native Taiwanese speakers.

From January, 1975, through Spring, 1976, five separate research studies were carried out in Taiwan:

1. One hundred and fifty families were interviewed both with lengthy questionnaires and structured interview sessions that elicited their beliefs about sickness and responses to specific sickness episodes (Kleinman 1975b, 1975c). The interviews systematically collected data on sicknesses occurring within 1- and 6-month periods prior to the interview and also about general beliefs and responses to a list of specific disorders. Data were obtained about health-seeking behavior for each episode of sickness recorded and about attitudes toward utilization of indigenous and professional care. An additional thirty families, who had members suffering from mental illness treated at the two large local psychiatric hospitals, were interviewed with respect to their beliefs about mental illness and their decisions about and evaluations of the psychiatric care given their family members. One hundred and twenty-five families in the first group were selected from registration lists in the local health stations of the three Taipei districts I have mentioned. All but ten were ethnic Taiwanese; roughly half were lower-class, one

quarter lower middle-class, and one-quarter middle or upper middle-class. The ten non-Taiwanese families were lower-class and lower middle-class mainland families, predominantly with military affiliations. This mix was selected because it was felt to be broadly representative of the demographic profile in the study area. The remaining twenty-five families in the first group represented Hokkien- and Hakka-speaking families from four separate rice-farming and fishing villages in north and central Taiwan. Most interviews were conducted by my research assistants, who were trained in nursing or anthropology and in the same ethnomedical interviewing technique. I participated in or conducted myself 20 percent of the interviews. Findings from this study are reported in Chapter 6.

2. Practitioner-patient communication was studied among the following groups of practitioners and patients: Chinese-style doctors (5)—patients (25); private Western-style doctors (5)—patients (25); public hospital outpatient clinic Western-style doctors (5)—patients (25); and shamans (_tâng-ki_) (5)—patients (25). This study made use of a quantitative methodology for comparing patient and practitioner explanatory models of the same sickness episode that I briefly describe in Chapter 3. By comparing the initial discrepancies between patient and practitioner explanatory models with subsequent discrepancies determined after practitioner-patient communication, it is possible to analyze statistically the effect such discrepancies exert on outcome measurements, including: patient compliance, satisfaction, subsequent use of health facilities, and the prevalence of clinical management problems. Although statistical analysis has not been completed, the early findings support the general comments about explanatory models discussed in Chapter 3 and illustrated with case vignettes in Chapters 7 and 8.

3. Twenty-five consecutive Taiwanese patients with the depressive syndrome who attended the National Taiwan University Psychiatric Clinic were compared with a group of matched non-Chinese patients assembled at the Massachusetts General Hospital in Boston in order to compare the phenomenology of depression in the two settings and to examine cul-

tural patterning of depression. This study is referred to in Chapters 4 and 5 (see also Kleinman 1977a).

4. One hundred patients, from the three Taipei districts, who were treated by folk healers (especially shamans) were observed during treatment, as were another 500 patients treated by Chinese-style and Western-style doctors. Follow-up was made with a subsample of patients from the folk healer group in order to study treatment response to and evaluations of indigenous healing. This study is presented in detail in Chapter 9.

5. Approximately twenty-five Western-style doctors, twenty-five Chinese-style doctors, twenty-five _tâng-ki_, and fifteen folk practitioners of other kinds were observed during their clinical practice. Most came from the three areas of Taipei where the study was centered, but some came from other areas of Taipei as well as from three large market towns and several villages in north and central Taiwan. Out of this group, fifteen Western-style doctors, fifteen Chinese-style doctors, ten _tâng-ki_, and five practitioners of other kinds of folk healing traditions were systematically interviewed by my research assistants and me. We used structured interviews that included—besides ethnomedical elicitation of explanatory models concerning specific cases—life history, family history, mental status examination, history of medical training and apprenticeship, reasons for becoming a healer, information about type and style of practice, and systematic assessment of their attitudes about practice (their own and others') and patients (see Kleinman 1975b and c). Multiple interviews were carried out with a sub-group of five Western-style doctors, five Chinese-style doctors, and five shamans. These informants were interviewed from 5 to 25 hours each by one of my research assistants and myself; most interviews were tape-recorded. In addition, I consulted with most of these practitioners about specific cases that I examined with them. The interviews and systematic observations provided the data discussed in Chapters 7 and 8.

The reader will readily recognize that these five field studies were designed to test certain of the questions provoked by my initial experience in Taiwan. They also comport with my un-

derstanding of the chief issues in clinically applied medical anthropological research (see Kleinman 1977d). In the two introductory chapters that follow, I will set out the theoretical
framework that forms the backdrop to these studies and that
also is illuminated by their findings. The body of the book examines many of these findings and explores their implications.

I do not wish to give the erroneous impression that *Patients
and Healers in the Context of Culture* is a final report. As the
reader will soon see, many important questions remain un-
answered and none that I have examined receives an exhaustive analysis. I think of this book as an interim report of work-
in-progress that will continue at least another decade. Future
field studies will take as their point of departure certain issues
discussed in the ensuing chapters, chapters that I hope raise
as many questions for readers as they answer and thereby provide an accurate reflection of the "state of the art" in this nas-
cent field.

2

Orientations 2:
Culture, Health Care Systems,
and Clinical Reality

The single most important concept for cross-cultural studies of medicine is a radical appreciation that in all societies health care activities are more or less interrelated. Therefore, they need to be studied in a holistic manner as socially organized responses to disease that constitute a special cultural system: the *health care system*.[1] In the same sense in which we speak of religion or language or kinship as cultural systems, we can view medicine as a cultural system, a system of symbolic meanings anchored in particular arrangements of social institutions and patterns of interpersonal interactions. In every culture, illness, the responses to it, individuals experiencing it and treating it, and the social institutions relating to it are all systematically interconnected. The totality of these interrelationships is the health care system. Put somewhat differently, the health care system, like other cultural systems, integrates the health-related components of society. These include patterns of belief about the causes of illness; norms governing choice and evaluation of treatment; socially-legitimated statuses, roles, power relationships, interaction settings, and institutions.

Patients and healers are basic components of such systems and thus are embedded in specific configurations of cultural

1. This subject is covered in Kleinman (1973a, 1974a, 1976). For other models of health care systems, see Alland (1970); Colson (1971); Dunn (1976); Fabrega (1976); Field (1976); Freidson (1970); Janzen (1977); Kunstadter (1976b); Leslie (1976a); Litman and Robins (1971); and Montgomery (1976).

meanings and social relationships. They cannot be understood apart from this context. Illness and healing also are part of the system of health care. Within that system, they are articulated as culturally constituted experiences and activities, respectively. In the context of culture, the study of patients and healers, and illness and healing, must, therefore, start with an analysis of health care systems.

The rest of this chapter elaborates this still not well-appreciated notion, and explores its implications for cross-cultural studies of health care as well as for a general anthropological understanding of patients and healers in society. This topic is indispensable for understanding the rest of our theoretical framework and our analysis of the empirical evidence, for the perspective it entails alters in a fundamental way our habitual orientation to patients, healers, illness, and healing. It dissolves old questions and creates new ones, introducing several analytic concepts for making comparisons across social, cultural, and historical boundaries. And it will bring our inquiry closer than hitherto possible to a phenomenological description of clinical processes in different settings and a hermeneutic interpretation of the beliefs and behaviors constituting and expressed in those processes.

Although this definition of health care systems is implicit in contemporary medical anthropological thinking, few formal models, such as the one I outline here, have been explicitly stated, and there has been no attempt to explore its clinical implications. For scholars from the health sciences, this is an "alien" concept that imposes a way of looking upon health-related phenomena that runs counter to the ethnocentric and reductionist view of the biomedical model, in which biological processes alone constitute the "real world" and are the central focus of research interpretation and therapeutic manipulation. Medical anthropologists have repeatedly criticized the biomedical model, but with a few exceptions (Fabrega 1974) they have refrained from openly challenging it by articulating the model of medicine as a cultural system as an alternative explanation of clinical phenomena. I see this as my task: to make this alternative theoretical framework transparent, directly relevant to clinical issues, and, I hope, compelling.

The health care system is a concept, not an entity; it is a conceptual model held by the researcher. The researcher derives this model in part by coming to understand how the actors in a particular social setting *think* about health care. Their beliefs about sickness, their decisions about how to respond to specific episodes of sickness, and their expectations and evaluations of particular kinds of care help the investigator put together a model of their system of health care. What I am describing is the process of medical ethnography through which local health care systems are reconstructed. In order to conduct such an ethnography, the investigator usually needs to step outside of the cultural rules governing his beliefs and behaviors, including his own health care involvements. Otherwise he risks contaminating his analytic model of the health care system with his largely tacit actor's model of his own health care system. Here is a reason for doing cross-cultural research or for studying a different sub-culture or social group within one's own society. If he chooses to study his own culture, however, the researcher must systematically alienate himself from his inner model of the system within which he is an actor, a most difficult task.

The model of the health care system also is derived from studying the way people *act* in it and *use* its components. It is both the result of and the condition for the way people react to sickness in local social and cultural settings, for how they perceive, label, explain, and treat sickness. The health care system, then, includes people's beliefs (largely tacit and unaware of the system as a whole) and patterns of behavior. Those beliefs and behaviors are governed by cultural rules. Hence, the health care system meets Geertz's (1973:3–30) definition of a cultural system: it is both a map "for" and "of" a special area of human behavior. Like other cultural systems, it needs to be understood in terms of its instrumental and symbolic activities. The beliefs and behaviors that constitute those activities are influenced by particular social institutions (e.g., clinics, hospitals, professional associations, health bureaucracies), social roles (e.g., sick role, healing role), interpersonal relationships (e.g., doctor-patient relationship, patient-family relationship, social network relationships), interaction settings (e.g., home, doctor's office), economic and political constraints, and many other factors, including, most notably, available treatment interventions and type of health problem. The health care system is organized as a special portion of the social world through the interaction of these variables. It is the nexus of adaptive responses to the human problems created by sickness, and, as such, the issue of "efficacy" is central to it.

As we shall see, the model of the health care system developed in this book can be used across cultural, historical, and social boundaries to describe considerable variation in specific content along with recurrent structural and functional features. The model is not the only one that can make sense of the social and cultural context of health care. It is derived from my field research and clinical experiences. It is based upon the materials I have elicited and analyzed from informants, patients, families, and practitioners (Kleinman 1975a, b, c). But it is based as well on my reading of the cross-cultural literature (Kleinman 1973a, 1974a, 1976). Although I initially present this particular model at a high level of abstraction, it will be used to explain the inner workings of clinical care: illness behavior, practitioner-patient transactions, and healing mechanisms (see Figures 1, 2, and 3). Thus, it differs from models of health care systems that aim to explain the macro-social and bio-environmental aspects of health care in terms of large-scale social structural, economic, political, and epidemiological factors. I am primarily interested in a microscopic, internal, clinical view, but the model I employ does not ignore the large-scale external factors that other models emphasize.

The next sections of this chapter discuss the social construction of health care systems and examine their external determinants, their internal structure, and certain of their functions. They also discuss the development of this concept. These sections, together with a sketch of Chinese health care systems, define systems of health care and indicate what is to be gained from studying them.

ON THE ORIGIN AND DEVELOPMENT
OF THE CONCEPT OF HEALTH CARE SYSTEMS

When cross-cultural studies focus on disease, patients, practitioners, or healing without locating them in particular health care systems, they seriously distort social reality. This flaw is found in many studies in cross-cultural medicine and psychiatry and in research in our own society. Studies of our own society, and comparative research, must start with an appreciation of health care as a *system* that is social and cultural in origin, structure, function, and significance.

Figure 1
Types of Reality

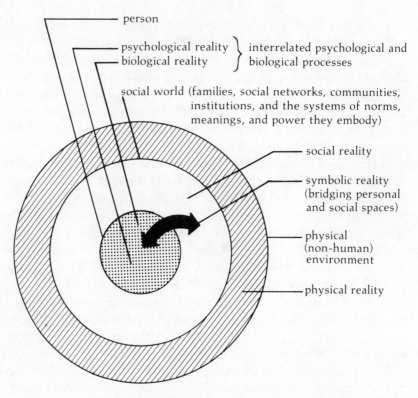

person

psychological reality ⎫ interrelated psychological and
biological reality ⎭ biological processes

social world (families, social networks, communities,
institutions, and the systems of norms,
meanings, and power they embody)

social reality

symbolic reality
(bridging personal
and social spaces)

physical
(non-human)
environment

physical reality

One might well ask why this concept is still not fully appreciated. Both Rivers (1924) and Sigerist (1951), two pioneers in the social scientific exploration of the relationship between culture and medicine, advocated holistic conceptions of that relationship and attempted to organize the findings available to them within unified theoretical frameworks. Neither one successfully unified the empirical evidence, much of which was either inadequate or inaccurate. But the idea of cultural systems of health care was held by these founders of cross-cultural medicine. After their efforts, the holistic approach to medicine in society fragmented into narrower views. Because much of the early interest in this subject grew out of the ethnographic study of religion in "primitive" societies, it is not surprising that anthropologists restricted their interest to the sacred forms of healing found in small-scale, preliterate societies and virtually disregarded the non-sacred aspects of healing and the overarching relationship of culture and medicine (see Seijas 1973).

Clements (1932) and Ackerknecht (see Walser and Koelbing 1971), for example, not only advanced a misleading dichotomy between "primitive" and "modern" medicine, but limited their comparative research to traditional forms of medicine and traditional societies. Ackerknecht, who has had an enormous impact on studies in this field, viewed non-Western cultures from an ethnocentric perspective based on the organizational structure professional medicine had evolved in the West. Thus, Ackerknecht wrote articles on "primitive surgery," "primitive psychotherapy," and "primitive prevention," in which he searched the ethnographic literature for cultural practices that he fit into these Procrustean categories. Clements worked in the same manner to compile a list of five fundamental beliefs about the cause of illness that he claimed exhausted the ideas about illness held by all traditional societies. The most far-fetched of these early cross-cultural medical studies was Benveniste's (1945) argument that all Indo-European societies have the same three basic illnesses, treatments, and types of healers. Most ethnographers, however, simply ignored medicine or studied exotic folk healers and healing rituals for their symbolic and religious, rather than their medical, interest. The legacy of this type of cross-cultural work frustrated the development of a holistic perspective on disease and health care in society. It had little or nothing to do with the basic issues of medical and psychiatric practice (indigenous or Western): the experience of illness on personal and social levels, health seeking behavior, patient-practitioner relationships, and the healing process. Such core issues only recently have received the systematic attention of investigators, after the "clinical" aspects of illness and health care were recognized as a key research focus by anthropologists and other cross-cultural researchers (cf. Adair and Deuschle 1970; Erasmus 1952; Gonzalez 1966; Gould 1965; Hallowell 1963; Harwood 1971; Hughes 1968; Janzen 1977; Kennedy 1973; Pouillon 1972; Press 1969; Rubel 1964; Saunders 1954; Snow 1974; Wallace 1959), and after cross-cultural research attracted the interest of medical and psychiatric investigators concerned with the social and cultural determinants of problems in clinical care (cf. Caudill and Lin 1969; Eisenberg

1976; Lambo 1969; Leighton et al. 1968; McDermott et al. 1972; Yap 1974).

The fact that some anthropologists are themselves clinicians and, as a result, have studied clinical questions in the field undoubtedly helped to advance the new perspective in cross-cultural research (see Fabrega 1974; Kleinman 1977d; Lewis 1975; Levy 1973; Loudon 1976). This clinical interest pushed researchers to formulate general principles to make sense of ethnographic variation and thereby contributed to the recognition that medicine is a cultural system (see references cited in Kleinman 1973a, 1977b). The contributing factors leading to the development of this concept included: the emergence of studies in the new field of medical anthropology concerned with health-seeking behavior and other clinically relevant issues (cf. Fabrega and Manning 1973; Good 1977; Harwood 1971, 1977; Schwartz 1969); sociological studies of patterns of utilization of health care facilities and particularly patterns of popular (lay) health behavior (cf. Chrisman 1977; Freidson 1961; McKinlay 1973; Zola 1972a); interest in the health care and public health aspects of modernization (cf. Leslie 1976a; Paul 1955; Polgar 1962); the tendency of ethnoscientific research to focus on medical taxonomies (cf. Berlin et al. 1973; Frake 1961; Fabrega and Silver 1973); the propagation of a new generation of transcultural psychiatric research, much of which concerned itself with comparisons of healing traditions (cf. Kiev 1964; Wittkower and Prince 1974; Kleinman 1977a, 1977e); the theoretical models constructed by anthropologists working on the health aspects of cultural ecology (cf. Alland 1971; Dunn 1976; Kunstadter 1976b); the influence of systems theory on the models developed in ethnomedicine (Fabrega 1972); and comparative studies of medicine in large-scale, non-Western societies (cf. Kleinman et al. 1976; Leslie 1976b). Certainly, the macrological approaches to medical care developed by political scientists, economists, and public health planners contributed as well (cf. Field 1973), although these were far removed from clinical issues.

One development played a crucial role in the recognition of the health care system: medicine, like religion, turned out to be an appropriate subject for linguistic and symbolic analyses. The work of Frake (1961), and especially of Victor Turner (1967), is famous for this kind of analysis. Both showed that medical beliefs in small-scale, preliterate societies were part of well-developed cultural systems. Turner also demonstrated that Ndembu beliefs linked symbolic referents to diseases with psychophysiological reactions and culture-specific tensions in social relationships, on the one side, with treatment practices aimed at instrumental and symbolic efficacy, on the other (1967: 299–358). The result was a tightly integrated symbolic system.

This important research epitomizes a line of symbolic studies in which medicine is frequently the subject matter, though rarely the principle source of interest (cf. Beidelman 1966; Currier 1966; Glick 1967; Ingham 1970; Nash 1967; Rosaldo 1972; Tambiah 1968, 1975; Topley 1970; Yalman 1964). Nonetheless, these studies helped establish the concept of medicine as a cultural system. The fact that they were carried out by ethnographers who were not interested in health care itself, and who therefore did not write for an audience of medical and psychiatric researchers, may have contributed to the slowness with which this concept has been taken up in medicine, psychiatry, and public health. Such analyses have been recently carried out by medical ethnographers who are oriented to clinical issues. For example, Byron Good (1977), a student of Victor Turner, has made a semantic network analysis of illness terms in Iran in which he shows how popular illness categories make available particular health care options and set out criteria for evaluating the quality of patient-practitioner interactions and treatment outcomes—a line of analysis developed further in the chapters that follow. In works such as this, the relevance of the cultural analysis approach and the health care system model for health professionals has been unmistakable.[2]

Forces operating among professional specialists in the health

2. Certain medical sociology and social psychology studies also added to the health care system perspective. These studies, moreover, tended to widen that perspective to include family-based care, the modern medical profession, the United States, and other technologically advanced societies, as well as clinically relevant issues. Freidson (1970) developed perhaps the most inclusive theoretical framework for studying health care in society, one directed primarily at our own. The work of Suchman (1965) was an important early attempt to conceptualize health care systems and to provide a typology of the social organization of care. The ideas of Mechanic (1962), Zola (1966, 1972a), and especially Freidson figure importantly in the model of health care systems presented in this book.

sciences are responsible for their neglect of a holistic view of the health care system. Three of them are worth noting:

1. The ingrained ethnocentrism and scientism that dominates the modern medical and psychiatric professions (both in developed and in developing societies) follows the paradigm of biomedical science to emphasize in research only those variables compatible with biological reductionism and technological solutions, even if the problems are social ones. This disastrous bias has diminished the significance of all social science inputs into medicine and psychiatry, especially at the clinical level. It has strongly discouraged views of medicine in which health care is seen to include anything more than the modern medical profession and biomedical science or in which medicine is studied as a social institution from a "systems" perspective. Cultural and sociopolitical analyses of the determinants of health care delivery, for example, have not been considered appropriate venues for medical research, and the description and analysis of the total environmental context that ethnography provides has not yet been accepted as an appropriate scientific approach for medical research.

2. The bias of many health professionals in developing societies is to restructure health care delivery in their countries by copying an idealized model of *professional* care in technologically advanced societies. This fictive view of health care does not correspond to the actual situation in developed societies, where 70 to 90 percent of all illness episodes are treated solely in the family context (Hulka et al. 1972; White et al. 1961), and is even a greater distortion of the more desperate situation of health care in developing societies. This interest (frequently no more than professional self-interest) militates against using the health care system model, with its crucial sociopolitical, economic, and cultural concerns, to deal with health problems in developing societies. For example, it has delayed informed evaluations of self-care and treatment by indigenous practitioners, along with research on how these ubiquitous therapeutic approaches might be used in state planning for health care services.

3. The longstanding tendency of clinicians is to treat *healing*

as if it were a totally independent, timeless, culture-free process to be understood either as an isolated special case or by comparisons with clinical practices in psychoanalytic therapy, hypnosis, biofeedback, and the like. Medical researchers seem embarrassed by this archaic relic in their midst and have devoted little attention to healing, the most basic of all health care processes. They do not regard healing as a core function of health care systems to be studied in its own terms within specific social and cultural contexts. Instead, they make simplistic reductions or superficial comparisons to fads such as brain washing, occult forces, etc., which obscure more than they reveal. This bias can be found even in important works, such as Frank's otherwise excellent account of *Persuasion and Healing* (1974a). It is more commonly found in the misuse of cross-cultural comparisons, such as purposefully naive raids into ethnography to debunk psychiatrists by equating them with a vulgar, tendentious view of priests, shamans, and witch-doctors (e.g., Torrey 1972).

Contrary to these trends, the model that I advocate calls for the analysis of health care systems in the same way that political systems, religious systems, kinship systems, language, and other symbolic systems are analyzed. First, it is necessary to study the relationship of a health care system to its context. Cultural settings provide much of the specific content that characterize health care systems and, therefore, are major determinants of the peculiar profiles of given systems. For example, Chinese culture is the chief determinant, though certainly not the only one (local political, historical, and economic factors are others [cf. Unschuld 1976]), shaping the components of the local Taiwanese system limned at the beginning of the preceding chapter. In the past decade, anthropological studies have analyzed in detail how cultural rules and meanings shape health care systems, or at least certain of their key components. [3]

3. Among a substantial, though still growing body of such studies, those by Fabrega (1974), Fabrega and Silver (1973), Glick (1967), Hallowell (1963), Ingham (1970), Kunstadter (1976a), Leslie (1974), Lewis (1975), Messing (1968), Nash (1967), Obeyesekere (1976a, 1976b), Press (1969), Rosaldo (1972), Spiro (1967), and contributors to a recent volume edited by Lebra (1976) are notable. This approach has been carried over to the study of the health care systems of ethnic minority groups in the United States, for example, in re-

Although many ethnographies and comparative studies now begin with a holistic conception of medicine in society and examine the impact of culture on medicine, most anthropological, psychiatric, and public health researchers still isolate individual components of health care systems for study without exploring their linkages with the system as a whole or with its other components. Folk healers are the most popular subject for cross-cultural research, but studies of them fail to show: how they are related to other kinds of practitioners in the same system; how their relationships to patients and their style of practice compare with those of other practitioners in the same society; how their beliefs and "interests" contrast with those of patients and other healers; and how patients decide to consult them. Ethnoscientists who study ethnomedical systems elicit taxonomies of illness terms, but they do not demonstrate how these taxonomies are *used* in different clinical relationships and health care institutions to *treat* illnesses. Since beliefs about illness are always closely linked to specific therapeutic interventions and thus are systems of knowledge *and* action, they cannot be understood apart from their use. Freidson (1970) has argued that to understand any single component in health care, one must locate it structurally within its social context and show how it functions within that setting. The interrelationships between component parts form the *system* and guide the activities of its components.

Janzen (1977) has reviewed various models of "medical systems." He notes that some are too complex to use in field research or for cross-cultural comparisons, while others fail to confront the ways that systems respond to change. Janzen

search by Harwood (1971), Saunders (1954), and Snow (1974). It also has been used to study psychiatric disorders and psychiatric care (Kaplan and Johnson 1964; Reynolds 1976). There even have been efforts to write the history of medicine from the standpoint of the historical reconstruction of medicine and psychiatry as cultural systems, though the largely institutional quality of available evidence, plus the absence of evidence from the oral traditions of folk healing, make such efforts difficult (Foucault 1965; Lain-Entralgo 1970; Shryock 1969; Thomas 1971). Nor have studies in Chinese culture lagged behind. Ahern (1976), Gould-Martin (1976), and Kleinman (1977c) have performed similar studies in Taiwan, and the Andersons (1968), Potter (1970), and Topley (1970, 1976a, 1976b) have done much the same for Hong Kong. Recent volumes edited by Kleinman et al. (1976) and Leslie (1976b) analyze and compare various Asian medical systems as cultural systems.

maintains that comparative schemes for analyzing medical systems are vague and superficial when they stress universals rather than differences. He argues that models of medical systems must deal with *both* micro- and macro-analysis. Thus, they should examine specific episodes of sickness and treatment, showing how small-scale events within healing systems relate to large-scale social structures and processes of change.

Kunstadter (1976a, 1976b) sums up comparisons of medical systems in Asian societies with the view that perhaps all medical systems are pluralistic, that they contain multiple choice points for deciding among often quite different treatment options, and consequently that it is wrong to speak of *the medical system* of any society as if it were single and unchanging. Instead, Kunstadter, like Dunn (1976) and Leslie (1976a), reasons that medical systems are best examined as *local* social systems, which can be related to a potentially large number of variables impinging on a specific setting and which may differ from one locality to another.

We will return to this question about how medical systems are best conceptualized in later sections of this chapter. Now that I have sketched the background for the concept of medicine as a social and cultural system, I will focus on one particular conceptualization of the health care system. Before I specify the dimensions of this model, we need to examine the perspective on social reality within which it is embedded.

HEALTH CARE SYSTEMS AS FORMS OF SOCIAL AND SYMBOLIC REALITY: THE CULTURAL CONSTRUCTION OF CLINICAL REALITY

Health care systems are socially and culturally constructed. They are forms of social reality.[4] Social reality signifies the world of human interactions existing outside the individual and between individuals. It is the transactional world in which

4. This subject is treated slightly differently in several of the author's publications, see Kleinman (1973a, 1973b, 1976). My approach is based on the by now classical statement by Berger and Luckmann (1967), which itself is based on the seminal work of Alfred Schutz (1970). Another statement of this position is found in Burkart Holzner (1968). Translation of the concept of social reality to the medical field is principally the result of writings by Eliot Freidson (1970). A sociological cameo of the social reality forming the context of gynecological examinations is provided by Emerson (1970). Certain writings by Michel Foucault (1965, 1973) come close to being historical reconstructions of clinical reality.

everyday life is enacted, in which social roles are defined and performed, and in which people negotiate with each other in established status relationships under a system of cultural rules. Social reality is constituted from and in turn constitutes meanings, institutions, and relationships sanctioned by society. Social reality is constructed or created in the sense that certain meanings, social structural configurations, and behaviors are sanctioned (or legitimated) while others are not. The individual absorbs (internalizes) social reality—as a system of symbolic meanings and norms governing his behavior, his perception of the world, his communication with others, and his understanding of both the external, interpersonal environment he is situated in and his own internal, intrapsychic space—during the process of socialization (or enculturation). Socialization takes place in the family, but also in other social groupings via education, occupation, rituals, play, and the general process of internalizing norms from the world we live in. As Berger (1973) notes, the individual not only fashions his own sense of personal identity with the aid of this internalized view of the "real," but also externalizes (objectivizes) it and by so doing affirms or discovers this same social reality out there in the "real" world, like a self-fulfilling prophecy. The tremendous power of social reality is in large part due to this fit between inner (personal) and outer (social) beliefs, values, and interests. It fashions a world we accept as the only "real" one, commit ourselves to, often passionately, and react to so as to shape our own life-trajectories. In Chapter 4, I sketch some salient features of the social reality surrounding individuals in Chinese culture and suggest ways by which it influences the personal management of dysphoric affects and the presentation of symptoms of affective disorders in that culture. This brief outline of the concept of social reality is elaborated in the rest of this section for the special form of social reality that is established, learned, and expressed in clinical settings.

Quite obviously, social realities differ. They differ between different societies, different social groups, different professions, and even at times different families and individuals. Certain small-scale preliterate, traditional societies seem to some anthropologists to contain more or less homogeneous social realities shared by all individual members of those societies. On the other hand, sociologists describe the social reality of developed societies like the United States as fragmented into many distinct social worlds—the coexisting, small cognitive and behavioral fields that Schutz (1970) called plural life-worlds. Developing societies are often viewed in an overly simplistic schema, as moving from the putative unified social realities (often called symbolic universes) of the traditional world to the plural life-worlds of modern states. Where such societies contain both indigenous literate and oral traditions, they are usually thought of as containing two quite distinct (classical, high-order/folk, low-order) kinds of social reality. Developing societies are said to be of special interest from this viewpoint since in them one can observe the change from old to new social forms, e.g., as expressed in their systems of beliefs, behavioral modes, and institutional structures.

The change from old to new social forms holds the same profound implications for health care systems as for other cultural systems. In such modernizing societies, one finds social realities that are a strange amalgam of modern and traditional beliefs, values, and institutions, held together in varying patterns of assimilation, complementarity, conflict, and contradiction. Since modern medical ideas and practices are often at the tip of the wedge of technology introduced during the modernization process, it is not surprising that health care systems provide some of the sharpest reflections of the tensions and problems of social development.

Social reality frequently varies as one moves from one locality to another. It may vary owing to family differences in past experience, differences in socioeconomic class, education, occupation, religious affiliation, ethnicity, and so on. These differences will be expressed by individuals who do not share the same perception of and response to their social environment, whose tacit knowledge and value-orientations may differ considerably. Furthermore, some may be incompletely or inadequately socialized or for other reasons may be deviant from the norms of their social world. Of course, for all individuals there is a distance between the ideal and the actual, between group beliefs and interests and individual ideas and motives. This gap represents an aspect of sociological and anthropolological theory that is still poorly formulated, but one that holds considerable significance for our purposes, since it underscores the fact that individuals differ, often greatly, even in supposedly homogeneous social worlds. They differ in their conscious understanding and acceptance of social norms and in the degree to which they follow those norms in actual practice. All of this affects the way individuals think about and react to sickness and choose among and evaluate the effectiveness of the health care practices available to them.

With this theoretical orientation, I assert that clinical practice (traditional and modern) occurs in and creates particular social worlds. Beliefs about sickness, the behaviors exhibited by sick persons, including their treatment expectations, and the ways in which sick persons are responded to by family and practitioners are all aspects of social reality. They, like the health care system itself, are cultural constructions, shaped distinctly in different societies and in different social structural settings within those societies. These health-related aspects of social reality—especially attitudes and norms concerning sickness, clinical relationships, and healing activities—I shall call *clinical reality*. By this expression I mean to evoke a mixed image: namely, that clinical phenomena are socially constituted and that the social world can be clinically constructed.

Health care systems and the clinical reality such systems create and express can be studied at different levels. Most research takes a macro-social view aimed at whole societies or regions (Field 1976). In this book, health care systems are principally discussed in terms of a model based on localities: communities, neighborhoods, groups of families (cf. Kleinman 1977b; Dunn 1976). But occasionally our orientation will change when we consider particular social groups independent of locality. This model will allow us to narrow our focus progressively from the community to social institutions and roles and then on to families and individuals. Because health care systems exist and function by right of socially legitimated norms governing how the social group and the individual in the group react to sickness, as well as through social perception and use of available health care resources at the local level, views of health care systems may vary as much as views of social reality may vary from family to family and even from individual to individual.

Rather than refer to health care systems as they are differentially construed by individuals, however, I shall present a model of more or less integrated local systems composed of separate sectors, clinical relationships, and roles. According to this model "clinical reality" is differentially construed in these different sectors, roles, and relationships.

In other words, the health care system is created by a collective view and shared pattern of usage operating on a local level, but seen and used somewhat differently by different social groups, families, and individuals. Social factors such as class, education, religious affiliation, ethnicity, occupation, and social network all influence the perception and use of health resources in the same locality and thereby influence the construction of distinctive clinical realities within the same health care system.

Health care systems may be both socially and culturally unified on the local level (e.g., small village in preliterate society), heterogeneous but still integrated (e.g., the illustration from Taipei given at the beginning of this chapter), or multiple and unintegrated in the same locality (e.g., Hispanic-American and Hasidic Jewish groups living in the same urban neighborhood in New York City or middle-class Westerners and lower-class Chinese living in the same neighborhood in Taipei). In the last situation, separate groups may even attend some of the same health facilities. Yet, from the standpoint of how they view and use health care resources, their health care systems would appear to be almost entirely distinct. In developing societies, like Taiwan, rural/urban and social class differences may create multiple and divergent health care systems.

Greater variation tends to occur between localities than within the same locality, but a locality may contain diverse belief systems, clinical roles, and healing traditions. The analytic power of our model of health care systems comes from its association with local environments. It is preferable to think of one health care system in one locality, even when it contains considerably different configurations of social reality.

Systems of health care may differ with respect to many variables, including what falls within their boundaries. Co-existing systems within a society may illustrate the ways that cultural, historical, socioeconomic, and political factors shape the *content* of health care systems. For example, in the United States, drug abuse and alcoholism only recently have become problems more appropriately managed within health care systems than within legal and ethical systems, where they previously were located. Foucault (1965) has shown how a similar redefinition happened to mental illness over a much longer historical period in the West.

Irving Zola (1972b), a medical sociologist, has argued that modernization carries with it a strong and potentially dangerous tendency to include within the health care system more and more problems traditionally located in other cultural systems. He has referred to this process of redefining social reality and enlarging the social space of health care systems as the progressive medicalization of modern society (see also Illich 1975). This process, he argues, also results in the increasing use of medicine and psychiatry for purposes of social control. This argument asserts that health care systems occupy a larger social space in modern societies than in traditional societies, and that they now perform functions formerly performed by other cultural systems. This hypothesis has not been systematically documented, but it could be validated or falsified by comparative social historical and cross-cultural empirical studies.

This is an instance of the value of the concept of the health care system for comparative research. The chief questions are: How do health care systems differ? How are they alike? Related questions concern: the factors determining those differences and similarities; the nature of the relationship within given systems of illness experiences, practitioner-patient transactions, and healing; and the reciprocal influence of health care systems on their particular social and cultural settings. One interesting question is whether the relative size and salience of health care systems is a function of culture alone. For example, it is my strong impression that health care systems in Chinese culture, independent of particular historical period or contemporary social setting, occupy a relatively much larger space and hold much great salience among their populations than do health care systems in the United States and other Western societies (see Kleinman 1976). Chinese people seem to be much more concerned about questions of health, illness, and health care than Americans; and health care systems in Chinese societies seem to possess many more elements and take up more time in the lives of people than do those in our own society. This impression might be treated as a hypothesis to be tested by systematic cross-cultural comparisons. If it was confirmed, Zola's hypothesis would need to be recast in a more complex manner. While the territory under medical control may be increased in contemporary Western societies, that territory may have been reduced in a preceding period with respect to functions that health care systems frequently carry out in traditional societies. In traditional societies, for instance, health care systems may be *the major* mechanism for social control (Cawte 1974).

To return to the main argument, it is worthwhile for analytic purposes to distinguish social reality from: (1) *psychological reality*, the inner-world of the individual; (2) *biological reality*, the infra-structure of organisms, including man; and (3) *physical reality*, the material structures and spaces making up the non-human environment. For the purposes of our study, I also will distinguish between two aspects of social reality: (1) the social and cultural world that we have been describing and that I shall refer to as *social reality* per se; and (2) a bridging reality that links the social and cultural world with psychological and biological reality, to which I shall apply the term *symbolic reality*[5] (see Figure 1, p. 28). I have coined a new term, *clinical reality*, to designate the socially constituted contexts that influence illness and clinical care, which I shall describe as consisting principally of social and symbolic reality, but relating as well to psychobiological and physical realities (see Figure 2, p. 42).

Symbolic reality is formed by the individual's acquisition of language and systems of meaning. We know socialization, via the acquisition of language and other symbolic systems, plays a major role in the individual's response to his behavioral field of interpersonal relationships and social situations. But there is much evidence to support the additional thesis that the internalization of symbolic reality, as Mead (1934) long ago suggested, also plays an essential role in the individual's orientation to his own inner-world (Berger 1973; Church 1961;

5. See Kleinman 1973b for a formal philosophical presentation of the concept of symbolic reality in medicine and psychiatry.

Figure 2
Clinical Reality

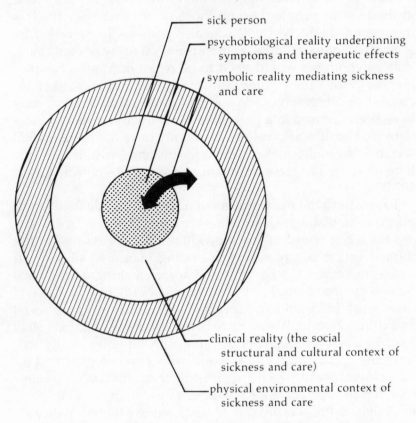

sick person

psychobiological reality underpinning
symptoms and therapeutic effects

symbolic reality mediating sickness
and care

clinical reality (the social
structural and cultural context of
sickness and care)

physical environmental context of
sickness and care

"Clinical Reality" = The beliefs, expectations, norms, behaviors, and communicative transactions associated with sickness, health care seeking,
practitioner-patient relationships, therapeutic activities, and evaluation
of outcomes. The *social reality* that expresses and constitutes clinical
phenomena and which itself is clinically constructed.

Cicourel 1973). That is, symbolic reality enables individuals to
make sense out of their inner experience. It helps shape personal identity in accordance with social and cultural norms. In
this view, symbolic meanings influence basic psychological
processes, such as attention, state of consciousness, perception, cognition, affect, memory, and motivation. What is much
less certain is by what mechanisms symbolic reality, either directly or via its effect on psychological reality, connects the social environment with physiological processes. Much evidence

is now available to suggest that this occurs, but how this happens remains unclear (cf. Kagan and Levi 1974; Mauss 1950; Kiritz and Moos 1974; Teichner 1968; Weiss 1972).[6] Recent evidence further suggests that symbolic reality may also link the physical environment to psychobiological processes (cf. Kiritz and Moos 1974).

In Chapters 4 and 8, I will use the concept of symbolic reality to analyze illness and healing. Here it is enough to underscore the fact that the clinical reality of health care systems is mediated by symbolic reality. Neither health care systems nor their clinical reality can be fully appreciated without examining how this biosocial bridge relates culture, as a system of symbolic meanings, norms, and power, to illness and treatment. An analogy may make this clearer: much as language can be thought of as a cultural system linking thought and action, health care systems can be considered cultural systems linking

6. Various models have been advanced to explain the symbolic connections between social environment and psychophysical processes, including operant conditioning, social learning, information theory, and others (Werner and Kaplan 1967; Platonov 1959; Schmale et al. 1970; Lipowski 1973). However this is accomplished, symbolic reality seems to be able to mediate changes in the social environment affecting the biological substratum of the individual (Kiritz and Moos 1974). Holmes and Rahe (1967) demonstrate this in the way stressful life-events lead to the onset of physical or psychological disorders. Lipowski (1973) indicates that the analysis of the mechanisms involved in the symbolic bridge between psychophysiological processes and environmental stimuli, which lead to psychosomatic and sociosomatic pathology, is one of the chief research quests in the new psychosomatic medicine. Mason's research (1976) already points to the critical involvement of neuroendocrine responses in psychophysiological disorders. Ader and Cohen (1975) have demonstrated that immunological reactions can be behaviorally conditioned. And Fabrega (1973, 1974) has suggested ways by which cultural beliefs may affect these mediating processes. Most recently, discovery of enkephalins and endorphins suggests that endogenous opiates in the brain may function as naturally occurring analgesics with a potentially important role in perception and reaction to pain and in placebo response. It is likely that these factors, triggered by the context of "meaning" established in therapeutic relationships and perhaps also by core symbols in healing rituals, mediate the effects of psychotherapy and other symbolic therapies on psychophysiological pathology (cf. Adler and Hammett 1973; Brody 1977; Frank 1975). Recent research on physiological correlates of biofeedback, meditation, hypnosis, and placebo effects is beginning to tell us more about the mechanisms by which symbolic reality acts as a biosocial bridge linking social and cultural contexts with the sick person and his treatment.

illness and treatment. Both of these cultural systems are forms of symbolic reality. Both are anchored in cultural beliefs and social roles and relationships, as well as in individual behavior and experience. Just as we divide language into distinct structural units—e.g., phonemes, morphemes—which convey meaning and create sanctioned behavioral options (Halliday 1976), so too, health care systems can be divided into interlaced structural components that establish a context of meaning and legitimation within which sickness is labeled and health care-seeking behavior is initiated. In the chapters that follow I will analyze Taiwanese health care systems precisely in these terms.

One aspect of social and symbolic reality requires further attention. Cultural systems are grounded in concepts and sources of legitimated power in society. Glick (1967) hypothesized that knowing a culture's chief sources of power (social, political, mythological, religious, technological, etc.) allows one to predict its beliefs about the causes of illness and how it treats illness. In a metaphorical sense, we can speak of socially legitimated power as the active principle fueling health care systems and of social reality determining what that power is (witchcraft, fortune-telling, science) and how it is to be applied (rituals, injections, psychotherapy), while symbolic reality lays down the pathways by which the application of that power may be effective. In turn, political, socioeconomic, and cultural power will determine which of a number of alternative perspectives on social reality (or alternative social realities) is legitimated (cf. Cohen 1976). For example, when differing views of clinical reality are in conflict, the sources of legitimation and power impinging on the health care system will eventually determine which view prevails, which clinical reality is sanctioned. Hence, such power is responsible for a certain clinical construction of reality. That type of clinical reality, which is culturally fashioned, in turn will have a major effect on the course of illness and treatment, as well as on the behavior of patients and health "professionals." The marginal status given to shamanistic healing in the People's Republic of China and the efforts there to integrate professional Chinese medical and Western medical therapies, the emergence of the peyote cult in Navaho healing as a new source of therapeutic efficacy related to changes in traditional Navaho values, the conflicting public health approaches in many African societies vis-à-vis indigenous healing systems, the excessive application of hysterectomy and coronary artery bypass surgery in the United States, and the steep rise of consumer dissatisfaction with professional clinical practice in the West and concomitant increase in both demands for changes in the nature of that practice and use of alternative therapeutic systems all reflect the legitimation in those societies of quite different kinds of clinical reality established in quite different socio-political, economic, and cultural contexts. As Giddens (1976) demonstrates, a cultural analysis of any concrete aspect of the social world should attend to the effects produced by the interplay of three types of forces: systems of meaning, norms, *and* power. Surely this also holds for analyzing concrete episodes of sickness and therapy, in which, for example, power differentials in social status are built into the sick role and therapeutic relationships.

Describing the "powers" bearing on health care systems requires an analysis of a number of different *external* factors affecting those systems and the clinical realities they create. Therefore, before we relate social and symbolic reality to the internal structure and core clinical tasks of health care systems, it is necessary to review the external factors that function as important determinants of change. This review should provide a glimpse of the ecology of health care systems.

EXTERNAL INFLUENCES ACTING ON HEALTH CARE SYSTEMS: AN ECOLOGICAL MODEL

Besides culture, other factors shape the configuration of the health care system. These factors can be separated into those that are part of the internal structure of the system (to be discussed in the next section) and those external to it. The external factors include political, economic, social structural, historical, and environmental determinants. They act on or in the local setting of the health care system. Most research on health care has emphasized these factors, but since our orientation is principally concerned with the inner workings of health care systems, I shall only list them. Though they have received a great deal of attention, they are usually not studied in relation to health care as a cultural system or to the inner workings of clinical care.

The environmental determinants include: geography; climate; demography; environmental problems, such as famine, flood, population excess, pollution; agricultural and industrial development; and so forth. In addition, there are local epidemiological patterns of disease (prevalence, attack rates, and virulence of specific disorders) that combine with genetic endowment and susceptibility of the population and specific stressors to influence not only health, but also health beliefs and healing practices. Conversely, as Dunn (1976) argues, health care systems have an effect on these environmental factors. Historians and public health specialists claim that health care has a relatively small impact on populations when compared to major social, economic, nutritional, and other external changes (McKeown 1965). They are probably correct, but we know far too little about what health care systems (especially traditional ones) have accomplished with respect to specific disorders and health maintenance. We do not know whether traditional health practices have had positive effects on public health, since only their negative influences have been documented. For example, health care systems in China in the pre-1949 period were overwhelmed by epidemic diseases, but part of the problem was the general social dislocation of the period that promoted and spread these disorders and disrupted indigenous health care responses. In earlier periods these systems seemed to function more adaptively, though it is doubtful that they ever had much influence on epidemics (see Kleinman 1973c; Kleinman et al. 1976). The reciprocal effect of health care systems on external factors and vice versa is an important one, but it falls outside the scope of this book.

Dunn (1976), a physician-epidemiologist and anthropologist, and Alland (1970), an anthropologist who has written on medical anthropology from an evolutionary perspective, have suggested that medical systems should be evaluated and compared to each other with respect to their ecological success in coping with a variety of external stressors, such as epidemic and endemic diseases. They have argued that such comparisons of the "efficacy" of medical systems should lead to an appreciation of the evolutionary significance of these systems in biological and cultural adaptation. Adair and Deuschle (1970) and McDermott et al. (1972) have described health care systems

46

of American Indians in the Southwestern United States with respect to the major health problems they have had to respond to, the resources they have had access to, and their success in applying these resources to those problems. These studies also report experiments in changing local health care systems and evaluate the significance of those changes. Here, then, are exercises in the practical ecology of health care systems that differentiate between external and internal factors and demonstrate the differential effect of both on health care practices and outcomes. The complex and disappointing results, especially of McDermott's introduction of technologically advanced Western medical practices into an impoverished Amerindian society, indicate how extremely difficult it is to change these factors systematically and predict the result of those changes. One consequence of this research seems straightforward: just introducing biomedical technology without making needed social, economic, and cultural changes has little, if any, effect on most serious health problems. This highlights the crucial impact that external factors exert on the solution of health problems. Such studies suggest that technological changes alone can improve individual case management without having a major effect on the health of a population and also without improving (and possibly even worsening) the non-technological quality of clinical care. Although these lessons have been repeated throughout the world, they do not seem to have changed the habitual orientation of health planners.

The Chinese case offers numerous examples of the influence of historical (Croizier 1968), political (Oksenberg 1974), and socioeconomic (Wegman, Lin, Purcell 1973) factors, not only on health problems, but also on health care systems. That is, they have been demonstrated to contribute to the distribution of diseases in Chinese populations as well as to the particular beliefs, practices, and institutional arrangements that Chinese communities have elaborated to cope with disease. These influences extend right down to the level of primary care, as will be documented in the chapters that follow. I will attempt to show that the health care systems model enables us to determine how external factors bring about these effects (see also Kleinman 1974b, 1976).

Barefoot doctors; the use of acupuncture anesthesia on a

47

mass scale; the reported elimination of venereal disease, drug addiction, and starvation; the subordination of professional demands to political control and public interest; and the integration of traditional Chinese-style and modern Western-style doctors' services in local health facilities, which the public apparently can choose to use separately or together, are pertinent examples from the People's Republic of China. We have much to learn about health care systems in the People's Republic, especially what changes have taken place at the level of the inner workings of clinical care, about which we know virtually nothing at present. They may teach us about mechanisms through which small-scale changes in the structure and content of health care systems occur in response to major changes in external factors.

Obviously, external influences on health care systems can be demonstrated in all societies, albeit less dramatically than in the Chinese case or in the infamous instance of the use of psychiatry to control political dissidents in the Soviet Union. In the United States, for example, sociological essays in books edited by Dreitzel (1971), Freidson and Lorber (1972), and Kosa et al. (1969) summarize major social, economic, and historical-political influences on almost all aspects of health care, from professional practices and organizational structures to consumer interests and behaviors. For example, Brenner (1974) has demonstrated convincingly that mental illness is strongly influenced in our society by major socioeconomic changes, as evidenced by the fact that increases in admissions to mental hospitals in the United States have historically correlated most closely with periods of severe economic decline. Navarro (1975, 1976) shows that a Marxist analysis can be applied to medical systems because of the enormous impact these "external" factors exert so as to define better, for example, the way power relationships in capitalist societies simultaneously contribute to inequality in access to and allocation of limited health care resources and to grave socioeconomic and political constraints on the nature and growth of those resources. Whether or not one accepts this line of analysis, awareness of the enormous effect societal-wide forces exert on health care systems is essential if one is to avoid the mistake made by Illich (1975), among others, in attributing the failures of health care systems solely to the machinations of the medical profession, as if it were able to operate entirely independent of its social and political context. While an ecological perspective on health care systems prevents this type of solecism, it does not resolve the question of how much of their efficacy or failure is constrained from "outside" and how much reflects the autonomy of the system and its components. That conundrum cannot be settled until we examine specific health care systems in concrete situations.

Health care systems are particularly affected by the level of technological and social development, including the status of therapeutic institutions, biomedical technologies, treatment interventions, and professional personnel. These aspects of the modernization of health care systems make them a locus of the tensions accompanying modernization (cf. relevant chapters in Leslie 1976b) and turn our attention from the outside of the system to its interior. Here we part company with most research on health care, since it has tended to stay outside the system itself and to disregard how external factors relate to the inner workings of clinical care, either to facilitate or impede clinical practice. In order to accomplish this shift in orientation, we first must examine the inner structure and core functions of health care systems: What are they? What do they do?

THE INNER STRUCTURE OF HEALTH CARE SYSTEMS

Health care systems are composed of generic as well as particular, "culture-laden" components. The internal structures are roughly the same across cultural boundaries, while the content varies with the social, cultural, and environmental circumstances of each system. The structural model I shall describe can be altered to analyze different cultural and other external conditions. Owing to these conditions, the structure may encompass and even generate distinctive content. The model can be applied to research in developed and developing societies and, especially, to study post-traditional societies that contain both high-order, literate (or classical) and low-order, oral (or folk) indigenous healing traditions. In our model, health care

49

is described as a *local cultural system composed of three overlapping parts: the popular, professional, and folk sectors* (see Figure 3).

1. Popular Sector of Health Care

Although the popular sphere of health care is the largest part of any system, it is the least studied and most poorly understood. It can be thought of as a matrix containing several levels: individual, family, social network, and community beliefs and activities. It is the lay, non-professional, non-specialist, popular culture arena in which illness is first defined and health care activities initiated. In the United States and Taiwan, roughly 70 to 90 percent of all illness episodes are managed within the popular sector (Hulka et al. 1972; Kleinman 1975a, 1975b; White et al. 1961; Zola 1972b, 1973). When people resort to folk or professional practitioners, their choices are anchored in the cognitive and value orientations of the popular culture.

Figure 3
Local Health Care System: Internal Structure

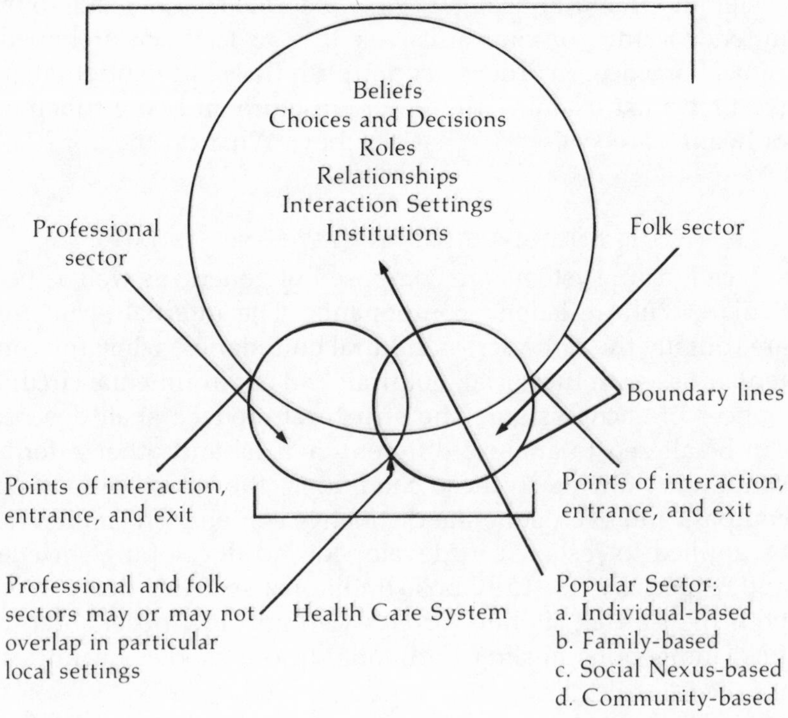

Beliefs
Choices and Decisions
Roles
Relationships
Interaction Settings
Institutions

Professional sector

Folk sector

Boundary lines

Points of interaction, entrance, and exit

Points of interaction, entrance, and exit

Professional and folk sectors may or may not overlap in particular local settings

Health Care System

Popular Sector:
a. Individual-based
b. Family-based
c. Social Nexus-based
d. Community-based

After patients receive treatment, they return to the popular sector to evaluate it and decide what to do next. The popular sector is the nexus of the boundaries between the different sectors; it contains the points of entrance into, exit from, and interaction between the different sectors. The popular sector interacts with each of the other sectors, whereas they frequently are isolated from each other. The customary view is that professionals organize health care for lay people. But typically lay people activate their health care by deciding when and whom to consult, whether or not to comply, when to switch between treatment alternatives, whether care is effective, and whether they are satisfied with its quality. In this sense, the popular sector functions as the chief source and most immediate determinant of care.

Anthropological and cross-cultural studies in medicine and psychiatry have been slow to examine this central part of the health care system (Chrisman 1977). Medical sociology has just begun to conduct sophisticated analyses of family-based health care, but these are limited largely to research on families in the United States and Western Europe (Litman 1974; Mauksch 1974). In cross-cultural studies, the popular sector has received far less attention than the usually more dramatic and exotic, but less important, folk healing traditions. The popular sector is excluded from most studies dealing with "indigenous" healing traditions, yet ironically it is for almost all societies *the* most active and widely used indigenous healing tradition. Self-treatment by the individual and family is the first therapeutic intervention resorted to by most people across a wide range of cultures. This is only one of the essential activities taking place in the popular sector (and especially within the family). The relative inattention given to this sector is responsible in part for the fact that so much past work in medical anthropology and cross-cultural medicine and psychiatry has been irrelevant to practical issues in health care.

In the popular sector, individuals first encounter disease in the family. We can think of the following steps occuring, at least initially: perceiving and experiencing symptoms; labeling and valuating the disease; sanctioning a particular kind of sick role (acute, chronic, impaired, medical, or psychiatric, etc.); deciding what to do and engaging in specific health care-seeking behavior; applying treatment; and evaluating the effect of self-treatment and therapy obtained from other sectors of the health care system. The sick person and his family utilize beliefs and values about illness that are part of the cognitive structure of the popular culture. The decisions they make cover a range of possible alternatives. The family can disregard signs of illness by considering them to be ordinary or "natural," or they can validate the sick person's sick role. They can institute therapy with treatment modalities known to them, or they can consult with friends, neighbors, relatives, and lay experts about what to do. Should they decide to move outside the popular sector, which frequently means going beyond the physical as well as the health care boundaries of the family, other alternatives must be considered. They can enter professional or folk sectors and within each can choose among a range of treatment alternatives (cf. McKinlay 1973; Zola 1972a, 1972c, 1973).

Once people decide to enter either the professional or folk sector, they encounter different sets of beliefs and values in the cognitive structures of professional or folk practitioners. They make these encounters in the process of entering and exiting from healing agencies. The clinical realities of the different sectors and their components differ considerably. Popular, professional, and folk cultures and their subcultural components shape the illness and therapeutic experiences in distinct ways. But the power to create illness and treatment as social phenomena, to legitimate a certain construction of reality as the *only* clinical reality, is not equally distributed. The professional sector is paramount because social power is in large part a function of institutionalization, and the professional sector is heavily institutionalized (cf. Lee 1976) whereas the popular sector is diffused.

An individual is a "sick family member" in one setting, a "patient" in another, and a "client" in yet another context (cf. Fox 1968; Siegler and Osmond 1973; Twaddle 1972). In each setting, his illness is perceived, labeled, and interpreted, and a special form of care is applied. Each arena has entrance and exit roles and rules. For example, the sick person enters the modern professional medical sector by establishing his patienthood in a clinic or hospital. Similarly, in the family or folk arenas, he must receive sanction from others for a particular type of sick role. He may claim and be given an acute, chronic, or impaired role, or he and those around him may disagree about the character of his sick role. He also will exit from the modern professional medical sector in a particular manner, as one who has been cured, remains ill, or is dying.

The sick person encounters different medical languages as he moves between the health care system's sectors (cf. Cassell 1976; Quesada 1976). He must translate from one language to another. Much of this book focuses on that process of translation, since it is crucial in the interaction between patients and practitioners, in the process of healing, and in the creation and resolution of communication problems that are "endemic" to clinical care. In the next chapter, I shall describe and illustrate a framework for conceptualizing the cognitive and communicative structures found in the symbolic space of patient-practitioner relationships, but already we see the outline of a central hermeneutic problem in clinical transactions: there are different interpretations of clinical reality reflecting different systems of meanings, norms, and power. In this sense, each of the health care system's sectors can be supposed a separate "culture."

Before turning from the popular sector, it is important to emphasize that most of it is not preoccupied with sickness and care but with "health" and "health maintenance." Just as the popular sector has not received its due from medical anthropologists, so too its preventive and health maintenance functions have been neglected. For instance, in Chinese culture we know much less about beliefs regarding health (*chien-k'ang*) and health maintenance (*wei-sheng*) practices than we know about sickness beliefs and treatment practices, yet most observers would concur the former take up more of the time and expenditure of families than do the latter. The increasing concern among social scientists and public health experts with self-care and the family context of prevention should remedy this oversight (cf. Dunn 1976; Zola 1972a).

2. Professional Sector of Health Care

A second sector of local health care systems is the professional sector, comprising the organized healing professions. In most societies, this is simply modern scientific medicine.

But in certain societies, e.g., Chinese and Indian societies, there are also professionalized indigenous medical systems: traditional Chinese medicine and Ayurvedic medicine, respectively (Croizier 1968; Leslie 1976a). In both of these societies, as well as in certain Muslim countries possessing Galenic-Arabic medicine (see Verma and Keswani 1975), the classical indigenous healing traditions have professionalized along lines similar to those of the modern medical profession.

In the United States, Freidson (1970) has succinctly described how the modern medical profession (allopathic medicine), using legal and political means, gained professional dominance in the health care field by forcing all other healing traditions to disband, submit to its professional control, or retreat into the quasi-legal folk fringe. Professional organization became a source of social power. For example, homeopathy and certain other non-professional healing traditions, which competed for patients with the modern medical profession well into the twentieth century, were eventually driven from the field, especially after the Flexner Report in 1910. Osteopathy at first was treated in this way but later gained a professional foothold, owing to its popular appeal in certain sections of the United States and its success in creating a professional organization. Recently, it has largely been absorbed into professional medicine. Chiropractic has remained a marginal practice but with too many adherents to be abolished. Naturopathy maintains an even more precarious existence. Pharmacy and nursing, severely restricted in practice, received professional status only by submitting to the authority of the medical profession. Indeed, Freidson claims they are virtually the only examples of professions that lack full autonomy.

In recent years technological advances and prolific medical subspecialization have combined to create many other health professions in the United States, all licensed as subsidiary, para-professional organizations functioning under medical hegemony and severely restricted in scope of practice. As recent studies show, however, the battle for professional independence is still going on: chiropractic (Kane et al. 1974) and certain of the non-medical ocular specialties (Shaver 1974) even seem to be making something of a comeback. In certain instances they have been shown to be as effective as and more popular with health consumers than physicians treating the same problems. Increasing clinical responsibilities assumed by nursing practitioners and medical assistants give additional evidence of the changing character of the professional sector in the United States. Such changes are the result, not simply of pressures from within this particular sector itself, but also from the lay sector (health consumers) and from external political and economic forces in American society (White 1973).

Just as each sector of the health care system creates its own clinical reality, so too do the different healing professions (professional subsectors). These can vary greatly, as in the Chinese or Indian cases, or only minimally, as with certain paraprofessional and alternative professional medical organizations in technologically advanced societies. Within the professional sector, furthermore, institutional structure helps determine clinical reality. In America, chiropractic's clinical reality matched the beliefs, values, and life-style of mid-Western farm life and flourished in that particular environment (McCorkle 1961). Likewise, psychoanalysis flourished in the United States within a special social group attracted to the ideas and therapeutic approach of Freud and his followers: urban middle-class intellectuals (Roazen 1971).

Although studies comparing the modern medical profession in different societies are now common, one rarely sees studies that specifically look at differences in their clinical realities. This is equally true of research on the modern medical profession in our own society. Little attention has been devoted to differences in the cognitive and communicative processes, texture of relationships, and treatment styles of modern professional health services in urban or rural, inner city or suburban, public clinic or private office, fee-for-service or health-insurance medical settings. Yet these clinical aspects of social reality are significant criteria for judging differences that really matter in clinical care, differences that reflect social structural and economic contingencies of practice in home, market-place, and bureaucracy. I will have a good deal more to say on this question.

One of the more important insights into the professional sector of health care illuminated by cross-cultural research is the process of "indigenization." By this term is meant changes that modern professional medicine and psychiatry undergo after they are introduced into non-Western societies. These changes involve the system of knowledge, health care institutions, and all the factors encompassed by the term "clinical reality." The result is the cultural re-patterning of professional clinical care to a greater or lesser degree. When I discuss Western-style medicine in Chinese culture in Chapter 8, I shall give examples of this process, which is a concomitant of modernization and Westernization. The health care systems developed over the past several decades in the People's Republic of China represent a unique form of medicine, which in part involves the indigenization of the professional sector. From the standpoint of clinical reality, indigenization transforms an essentially Western orientation into one more appropriate (even if frequently not appropriate enough) to the particular social conditions of non-Western cultures.[7] Many more problems for clinical care seem to result from insufficient indigenization than from too much of it. A related process is "popularization," by which certain aspects of professional care, such as scientific health concepts, are altered and diffused after they enter the popular health sector. This process will concern us later in this chapter and in the next.

So dominant has the modern medical profession become in the health care systems of most societies (developing and developed) that studies of health care often equate modern medicine with the entire system of health care; such studies become mere accounts of professional medical organizational structures and services, leaving out the rest of the health care system (Dreitzel 1971). Research by physicians and public health personnel, in most instances, is systematically limited to problem-frames defined by biomedicine; the solutions offered fit professionally sanctioned solution-frames and are evaluated only from that standpoint. Such researchers are unaware of their bias, since they are trained to see all of health care through the cognitive framework of their profession. Professional socialization of modern health professionals causes them

7. In a recent book, edited by Charles Leslie (1976b), containing essays on the varied experiences of Asian nations in the health field, examples of indigenization are frequent, sometimes amusing, but almost always important. Morita therapy represents indigenization of modern psychotherapy in Japan (see Reynolds 1976).

to regard their own notions as rational and to consider those of patients, the lay public, and other professional and folk practitioners as irrational and "unscientific." As Polanyi and Prosch (1975) argue, implicit concepts determine what will be considered "data," the analysis of which, not too surprisingly, supports the professional orientation like a self-fulfilling prophecy.

It is amazing to see how intensely this professional ideology is held by otherwise sensitive and responsible health professionals. It is maintained with blind conviction even in the face of evidence to the contrary. Other components of this professional ideology are such commonly encountered dogmas as: Any health-related activities undertaken by patients themselves or by members of the other sectors of the system are dangerous and should not be tolerated. The biological aspects of medical problems are the "real" ones, while the psychosocial and cultural aspects are second order phenomena and are thus less "real" and important. The encounter between doctors and patients (and families) is one between experts and those who are ignorant, so that the doctor's role is to "tell" or give orders to patients, and the patient's role is to listen passively and comply. Closely related is the professional bias that the doctor (or other health professional) is most responsible for the patient's care. Lack of compliance with the medical regimen is frequently regarded from the professionals' perspective as a moral offense (Stimson 1974). This view is not only found in those areas of the world where the medical profession does in fact control the health care system. It also is espoused by doctors in societies where most health care outside of the family in fact is in the hands of alternative professional and folk healers.

In the People's Republic of China, several decades of political indoctrination against the primacy of expert knowledge (and interests) over popular knowledge (and interests) apparently was insufficient to break the dominance of this professional ideology among health workers, since the public health establishment and the modern medical profession were criticized repeatedly for precisely this during the Cultural Revolution (Oksenberg 1974). Only very recently in the West have consumers spoken out against the loss of their autonomy in primary health care decisions to the modern professional medical leviathan. In technologically advanced societies especially, there has been a general shrinking of popular autonomy, as more and more of its traditional functions have been usurped. Indeed, progressive medicalization has enlarged primarily the professional health sector of modern society.

One of the major contributions anthropologists and sociologists have made is to demonstrate repeatedly that the health care system is a great deal wider than the boundaries of the modern medical profession, even in technologically advanced societies. They also have shown how the locus of responsibility for health care decisions is beginning to shift from patients and families to health professionals (Zola 1972a, 1972b). These studies support the conclusion that the professional sector requires that its form of clinical reality be accepted as the only legitimate clinical reality. Health professionals usually are insensitive to the views of clinical reality held by other healers, and to the expectations and beliefs of their patients. This insensitivity is systematically fostered in both undergraduate and postgraduate medical education. The increasingly strident polemics of social scientists against the medical and psychiatric professions are one result of the conspicuous inattention of those professions to the lay public's viewpoint. When such arguments surface in the medical profession itself, they are met with considerable resistance. The most difficult aspect of clinical practice to teach to medical students, interns, and residents is how to elicit and evaluate objectively patient beliefs and values with respect to their illnesses and treatments and to negotiate with (or translate between) these differing perspectives in the same way an advisor gives expert advice to an advisee, who retains the right to accept, alter, or reject that advice. It is difficult to challenge the clinical reality imposed on patients by medical professionals or to get them to view it as not the "only" or "true" one, but as one among a range of clinical realities operating in the greater health care system. Especially difficult for medical and psychiatric professionals is juxtaposing their diagnostic and treatment formulations with those of their patients. Thus, one of the most significant contributions of the cross-cultural perspective is to foster a broadly based view of the entire health care system. It makes the researcher increasingly skeptical about the normative perspective on health care entailed by the socially constructed biomedical professional ideology. It highlights terms like "compliance" and "denial" as value judgments dictated by the medical profession. Knowledge about the extent of self-treatment, the impact of the family on care, the role of the individual's values in determining satisfaction, and the activities of alternative professional and folk practitioners, taken together with knowledge of the impact of external factors on health care systems and their variation across societal boundaries, can be sobering. Cross-cultural studies can play an essential role in opening the eyes of health professionals and the public to these other sides of medicine.

3. *Folk Sector of Health Care*

The folk (non-professional, non-bureaucratic, specialist) sector shades into the other two sectors of the local health care system. Folk medicine is a mixture of many different components; some are closely related to the professional sector, but most are related to the popular sector. In those societies lacking professionalization, the folk sector and the popular sector constitute the entire health care system. Folk medicine is frequently classified into sacred and secular parts, but this division is often blurred in practice, and the two usually overlap. Early students of medicine in different cultures stressed sacred healing, since their interest emerged from studies of folk religion. Shamanism and ritual curing have continued to hold the attention of anthropologists up to the present. Far less attention has been given to the mundane secular forms of healing: herbalism, traditional surgical and manipulative treatments, special systems of exercise, and symbolic non-sacred healing. Recent ethnographies have begun to turn to these other traditions, but the ethnographic literature still remains heavily weighted toward sacred healing. Within medical anthropology more attention is being given to folk medicine as part of a broader health care system, but ethnographic descriptions based on this wider perspective are only now being written.

The efficacy of folk healing presents a serious question for cross-cultural clinical research. Virtually no systematic follow-up studies of patients treated by folk healers exist, with careful evaluation of their status before and after treatment. Similarly, almost no empirical work has been done on the mechanisms of folk healing although this subject has attracted considerable speculation. In Chapter 9 I shall present field research findings that go beyond anecdote and speculation to throw new light on this problem. That data includes a prospective study with follow-up of patients treated by shamans in Taipei, as well as individual case studies and follow-up of patients treated by other folk healers in Taiwan. I will use this material to compare folk healing with other forms of healing and to discuss the healing process generally.

The many new forms of folk psychotherapies in the contemporary Western world, linked to the popular culture and to a recrudescence of traditional healing in these societies, and the persistence or even increase of folk healers in some developing societies indicate the significant function of folk medicine in many parts of the world. This phenomenon creates a difficult question for professionals and for society generally: what to do about folk practitioners in planning for health care. This question will be dealt with when we discuss the concrete situation of folk practitioners in contemporary Taiwan.

The structural components of health care systems—the three sectors introduced above—primarily interact because patients pass between them. The popular sector forms an undifferentiated matrix linking the more highly differentiated professional and folk sectors. The boundary lines between sectors function as points of entrance and exit for patients who follow the trajectories of their illnesses through the intricacies of the health care system. Before examining the distinct social worlds created by these differing sectors, I shall illustrate the model by analyzing the Taiwanese health care system described at the beginning of the first chapter.

HEALTH CARE SYSTEMS IN A CONTEMPORARY CHINESE SOCIETY:
TAIWAN, AN OVERVIEW

The phenomenological fragment presented in the Prologue is part of a local system in urban Taiwan. But it is a quite special instance, for it records a tremendous concentration of health care components in a small geographical space. In other sections of Taipei and in other cities in Taiwan, the same components (and many others besides) are dispersed in a much larger area.

Instead of viewing the various health-related phenomena

described in the Prologue atomistically, our model helps us recognize an integral system.[8] It pictures elements of the professional, folk, and popular sectors. The professional sector is represented by the Chinese-style and Western-style practitioners, along with the Chinese and Western pharmacies. Here we have, side-by-side and intermingled, the elements of two completely different professional systems. Western-style and Chinese-style doctors have separate licensing procedures, practitioner associations, and bureaucratic organizational structures. They have their own clinics, hospitals, and pharmacies. These two professional subsectors maintain a competitive relationship, with little or no referral and other connections between them; in the People's Republic, they are said to be integrated by active referral, professional consultation, combined treatment, and even an attempt at sharing (to some degree) knowledge and skills.

PAPER

The *Western medical profession* in Taiwan controls most of the power. It alone receives financial support from the state and is represented in the national and local government. The National Health Service, Provincial Department of Health, and municipal health departments are composed entirely of Western-style doctors (*hsi-i-sheng*) and other modern health professionals and have a structure indistinguishable from parallel organizations in the West. But there are distinct levels within the profession. At the top is the National Taiwan University School of Medicine and Hospital in Taipei. This institution is comparable to university medical centers in the United States. Although the clinical reality created there resembles that found in academic medical settings in the West, there are still some major differences: Families can and usually do stay with hospitalized patients in order to cook, nurse, and sleep near them at night. There are no appointment times in public or private clinics, including psychiatry clinics. Payment is made primarily for treatment received and hardly at all for the time the doctor spends taking a history or doing an examination.

8. A recent volume I edited (Kleinman et al. 1976) examines in detail the various aspects of health care systems in Taiwan and other contemporary Chinese societies. The interested reader is referred to the relevant chapters in that source for a fuller picture of health care systems in Chinese societies, since covering the same ground here is not feasible.

These and other practices make expectations and valuations of clinical care quite different from those in university hospitals in the United States.

The private practice of Western medicine in Taiwan varies enormously. Some practitioners function on the same level as the university hospital medical staff. Other physicians were inadequately trained in China prior to 1949 at third-rate (in some cases bogus) schools, or have received minimal training in the military or under the Japanese occupation. In addition to doctors, nurses and biomedical technicians have been trained as they are in the United States. Pharmacists form an especially important professional group, since they often provide primary care. Also, many unlicensed doctors practice illegally and, until quite recently, were tolerated by the authorities.

Chinese-style doctors (*chung-i-sheng*) vary even more in background and quality. Some have graduated from schools of Chinese medicine on the mainland before 1949 or from the China Medical College in Taichung, Taiwan. The latter is an unusual institution that teaches both Chinese and Western medicine; its graduates can be licensed in either one or both but usually practice only Western medicine. Most Chinese-style doctors study in a master-disciple relationship, which is the way Chinese medicine was taught over the centuries in China. They may, and often do, study very different books and are exposed to idiosyncratic teachings or different "schools" via the oral tradition. Their educational, social, and economic backgrounds are quite dissimilar. Some practice entirely along traditional lines, while others have self-consciously modernized their ideas and practices. Within this profession, acupuncture is frequently practiced as a separate specialty; its status is greatly enhanced by its new popularity in China and the West. There are also many part-time, unlicensed practitioners of Chinese medicine. Every educated Chinese in the past is said to have read some of the classical texts in order to treat certain illnesses for family members, neighbors, and friends. In present day Taiwan, education is in modern subjects rather than classical Chinese subjects, and educated people tend to know more about Western than Chinese medicine. But older people often possess some knowledge and skills to diagnose and to prescribe Chinese medicaments. Such knowledge, usually kept secret (i.e., not shared outside the family or social network), is considered to be an important family heritage. Skills of this sort are part of the family-based popular culture, separate from the practice of Chinese medicine as a profession.

The Chinese medical profession in Taiwan has benefited from unprecedented development in the past five years, owing to the worldwide interest in Chinese medicine. The number of candidates studying for and taking the licensing examinations in Chinese medicine is said to have increased considerably.[9] The fees for drugs and acupuncture have climbed steeply. Foreigners visit Taiwan to receive instruction or treatment in Chinese medicine, and well-known Chinese-style doctors have traveled to the United States and Europe to teach and practice. Chinese herbal medicines are now widely distributed throughout Asia and the West, though they still trail acupuncture in popularity. Chinese medicine, furthermore, is receiving much more attention in the mass media in response to public interest. Chinese-style doctors are pushing for government financial support, which they have never had in Taiwan, and, in general, have become much more active in asserting their professional status. As in the past (Croizier 1968), they claim a special cultural and national identity as the only indigenous medical profession in Chinese society.

Bone-setters (*chieh-ku shih-fu*) represent a case that illumines the boundaries of professional medicine and its relation to the other sectors of the health care system. They are not considered to be Chinese-style doctors by lay people or by Chinese-style practitioners. They are regulated by the government as if they were an entirely separate licensed profession, even though they maintain virtually no professional organizational structure. Except for a few who are also Chinese-style doctors, bone-setters do not enjoy the social standing of Chinese-style doctors. The situation is confused by the fact that some bone-setters practice folk healing, including fortune-telling and shamanism. This reflects the competitive, commercial nature of healing in Taiwan and the overlap between the sectors of the health care system. Bone-setters are so specialized and nu-

9. Personal communication from the President, Chinese Doctors' Association, Taipei, April, 1975.

merous that, while their skill is highly valued and the public makes routine use of it, each one tends to attract only limited numbers of patients. To increase their earnings, many do other things besides bone-setting. Some run businesses or function in other capacities that have nothing whatsoever to do with medicine; others practice other forms of healing to attract a larger clientele. Most bone-setters I interviewed regarded themselves as part of the professional health care sector, separate from and admittedly less prestigious than Chinese-style doctors. On the other hand, many Chinese-style doctors looked "down" upon this specialty as part of the folk system of care. Bone-setters need not take qualifying examinations and frequently have had limited training from books. Here is a peculiarity of health care in Taiwan, since bone-setting in traditional China was one of the techniques used by physicians, along with herbalism and acupuncture, within the same theoretical framework. Yet, even in traditional China, bone-setting seems to have been practiced occasionally as an independent specialty, along with other specialities in the unmarked borderland between folk and professional medicine.

In contrast to Taiwan, bone-setters in Hong Kong have a higher status than physicians who employ herbs or acupuncture (Lee 1976), and in the People's Republic of China the techniques for setting fractures are said to be a major contribution of traditional medicine to health care. In Taiwan, although bone-setters are not licensed to practice as physicians, many of them also treat arthritis, low back pain, and skin disorders. Thus, their practice overlaps that of physicians.

Bone-setting and the specialized treatment of hemorrhoids, other proctological problems, and skin disorders belong to the "external" branch of Chinese medicine (*wai-k'e*), which traditionally classified health problems and therapeutic practices into "external" and "internal" (*nei-k'e*) branches. The "external" specialities (whose name in Chinese is used to designate modern surgery) have a marginal professional status, though some Chinese-style doctors still practice them. In the poorer areas of Taipei bone-setters outnumber Chinese-style physicians, and in education, income, and life-style, they are more like their lower-class clients than the wealthier, better educated physicians.

Herbalists provide another borderline case between the professional and folk sectors of health care. Unlike bone-setters, they are not licensed and are, therefore, illegal practitioners. Until 1975 they were tolerated by the health officials, but since then the government has begun to arrest some unlicensed practitioners. Such actions have occurred before without affecting this category of practitioners, so that it is unclear what will result from the current policy. Government officials and modern medical professionals call all non-Western practitioners "herbalists," which they use pejoratively.

Herbalists diagnose and prescribe as well as sell herbs, unlike Chinese pharmacists who are licensed solely to prepare and dispense Chinese medicine, although they, too, often prescribe. Few herbalists have formally studied traditional Chinese medicine; many are illiterate or barely literate and unable to read the texts; almost all have learned their occupation as a family trade or as apprentices in the shops of other herbalists. In this last respect, they are not unlike Chinese-style doctors. Both possess "secret knowledge," reputed to be passed from generation to generation and jealously guarded from outsiders. Medicine was a hereditary profession in ancient China, and most traditional practitioners today claim family practitioners in at least three preceding generations. But lay people and health professionals frequently regard herbalists merely as proprietors of small shops rather than practitioners. They have no occupational associations and do not belong to the sacred tradition of folk medicine. They are part of the secular folk tradition but reject classification with other folk practitioners.

Both cases—herbalists and bone-setters—illustrate the importance of the boundary between professional and nonprofessional practice. On the professional side of the boundary, practitioners generally are of higher social status, earn higher incomes, have their interests represented by associations, and possess some kind of professional organization. They are licensed by the government and are concerned about controlling the entrance of practitioners into their sector. These two examples, however, demonstrate that the essential differences are government recognition of professional organization or the general social recognition of a kind of practice as "professional." This is further evidenced by the fact that unlicensed

Chinese-style and Western-style practitioners enjoy a "professional" image in the eyes of lay people and many fellow practitioners, even though their practice is illegal and they do not belong to professional associations.

The *folk* sector of medical practice is more heterogeneous than professional medicine. Herbalists belong to the secular tradition, while Taoist priests, shamans, ritual specialists in "calling back the soul," and temple-based interpreters of *ch'ien* belong to the sacred tradition. But the division is not clear-cut. For example, *tâng-ki*s (shamans) while in a state of possession commonly prescribe Chinese medicine or local herbs. Fortune-tellers, astrologers, physiognomists, and geomancers are more difficult to characterize. They are non-professional specialists who participate in healing and whose systems of beliefs involve some of the oldest and most classical Chinese theories. Not uncommonly, they practice just outside the doors of temples. Although it is usual to classify them as secular healers, some make use of religious beliefs and paraphernalia. Those who divine by means of the eight characters (*pa tzu*) designating a person's time of birth and the related *pa kua* (Eight Diagrams or Trigrams from the *I Ching*) often work closely with nearby temples, telling clients which ceremonies they should have performed. The ideas they work with, while not usually including gods and ghosts, nonetheless belong to the Chinese religious tradition. But the popular culture differentiates between them and temple-based practitioners as if they were secular. Geomancers in fact are regarded as akin to "scientists," and geomancy is frequently referred to as "Chinese science." Since one of the key uses of divination is to help patients choose a particular treatment and practitioner, diviners play an important part in determining the hierarchy of resort in local health care systems.

The folk tradition also contains an assortment of other practitioners, many of whom are itinerant or part-time and some of whom are commonly found in market towns or traveling between festivals in rural areas. These include itinerant drug peddlers who also prescribe herbs and patent medicine, unlicensed specialists in particular diseases such as skin and eye disorders, teachers and practitioners of a variety of minor therapeutic techniques—massage, breathing exercises, systems of calisthenics (e.g., *t'ai chi ch'uan*). These individuals sometimes combine healing functions with circus-like performances and with business practices. In some towns, one sees them lined up at night along market streets, healing, selling, and entertaining. Moreover, some folk practitioners, such as local or family experts, traditional midwives, and the like, function largely in the popular sector and shade into popular health care. Indeed, these examples illustrate that a too simple classificatory use of the distinction between folk and popular sectors is not useful.

In addition to these folk practitioners, a wide range of businesses also claim a therapeutic function. These include the tea shops and food and drink vendors pictured in the Prologue, as well as snake shops where live snakes (poisonous and non-poisonous) are kept and used to treat skin and eye disorders, sexual problems (especially impotence), and other sicknesses. In these shops, the healing function is only one of a number of money-making activities. For example, in snake shops wines containing pickled snakes are sold to treat illness or for their reputed cosmetic effects; purses and wallets made of snake skin are sold at another counter; snake food is sold as both a medicinal agent and a culinary delicacy. In tea stores, the healing power attributed to some teas accounts for a very small part of their business. This is not at all to say that the business activities of these stores distinguish them from the rest of the health care system. It is obvious that all components of the professional and folk sectors (including the religious sector) are competing in a special field of commercial life, and financial matters, as we shall see, also play an important role in the popular sector.

The unclear and overlapping relationships between various activities subsumed under the title "folk healing practice in Taiwan" are illustrated by a middle-aged owner of a small store in a traditional Taiwanese section of Taipei (Yen-Ping District). The store sells both Western and Chinese patent medicine along with local herbs, but it is not a Chinese or a Western pharmacy, nor is it an herbalist's shop. It is licensed as a drug store in which no prescription medicines can be sold. The owner is himself a Taoist priest and a shaman (*tâng-ki*). His shrine takes up more than half of his store. His calling card states that he treats problems relating to bad fate and ghosts, geomantic questions, mental illness, and other illnesses that are "not cured by doctors." He also has a special office behind his shop and shrine where he and his wife practice bone-setting.

The *popular sector* of our Taipei health care system is represented by the people in the market street seeking to buy tonics, herbs, and foods believed to be symbolically "hot" or "cold." Self-treatment by individuals and families with foods and Western and Chinese medicines is by far the most common treatment in Taiwan. In a survey of illness episodes suffered during a one-month period by members of 115 Taiwanese families in Taipei, for example, 93 percent of these episodes were first treated at home, and 73 percent received their only treatment there (see Chapter 6 for a report of this survey). Lee (1976) similarly has found extensive resort to self-treatment in Hong Kong.

The sick individual or his family decide which type of practitioner to go to. Family, neighbors, or friends frequently accompany the sick person to consult a practitioner. Most families we interviewed saw themselves, rather than the government, the practitioners consulted, or the sick person himself, as most responsible for making decisions about health care and for assuring that the patient was adequately treated. This is a view supported by most indigenous practitioners I interviewed and even by many public health workers. Families develop criteria for when to use certain types of practitioners, and when to seek help from others. Since individuals can purchase from pharmacies virtually any Western or Chinese medicine they desire, they can prescribe and treat themselves with a wide variety of agents. This makes lay people considerably more autonomous in controlling their health care in Taiwan than in societies like the United States, Great Britain and the Soviet Union, where there is stricter enforcement of the laws that regulate medical practice and drug sales.

Many Chinese families claim to possess some "secret knowledge" or special herbs for treating particular illnesses. This knowledge frequently is quite different from that of the classical medical texts, although it is derived from that source. Nowadays, the health beliefs of families and communities in

Taiwan contain many notions from modern scientific medicine as well. What I am describing is a separate domain of medical knowledge belonging to the popular sector of health care systems and derived from the classical Chinese medical tradition, Chinese folk healing traditions, and more and more from Western medicine, psychiatry, and public health. This popular cognitive domain is the focus of discussion in the next chapter.

In studies conducted in fishing and rice-farming villages in Taiwan, I found that the popular sector frequently could be equated with the extended family, lineage, or even the entire village community. In urban areas, sick individuals, who often lived in nuclear families, turned to friends and co-workers much more often than to the extended family or community for advice and referral. Therefore, in talking about the popular sector it is essential to define the level: individual, family, social network, or community. Ethnicity, social class, and education also exert important influences on popular care.

Just as our structural model can be applied to the Chinese health care system, it also can be applied to studies of health care in other societies.[10] For example, Boston not only has easily identified institutions and practitioners of modern professional medicine, but also possesses chiropractors, podiatrists, and various licensed eye specialists who are not part of the medical profession but form alternative health professions. Christian Science healers, scientology practitioners, and a myriad of practitioners of popular forms of psychotherapy, so conspicuous in the area around Harvard Square in Cambridge, including non-licensed practitioners of various forms of meditation and occult religious practices, form a well-advertised folk healing sector. But this sector also includes people who specialize in healing herbs, massage, sexual therapies, and many other therapeutic practices. Indeed, folk healing in urban America is undergoing something of a renaissance. Furthermore, the popular sector of health care in Boston is still central

10. For example, the model of the health care system seems applicable to the following ethnographic reports of medical systems: Adair and Deuschle (1970), Fabrega and Manning (1973), Good (1976), Gould (1965), Ingham (1970), Kunstadter (1976), Leslie (1976), Obeyesekere (1976), Press (1969), Spiro (1967), and Wolf (1965). The model seems to hold for the United States as well (cf. Freidson 1970; Harwood 1971; Saunders 1954; Snow 1974).

in determining when and where a patient seeks care, and how he complies with and evaluates that care (Kleinman 1975a), despite the fact this is no more accorded "official" recognition by most medical professionals and public health planners in the United States than in Taiwan. The chief differences between this American example and the Chinese case are that the choices open to Americans have been greatly narrowed and the boundaries between the sectors of American health care systems are more sharply defined, largely owing to the laws regulating health care in the United States. Thus, Chinese residents of Boston's Chinatown, though they hold many traditional views about illness (Gaw 1976), do not have recourse to shamans or other sacred Chinese folk practitioners, who are not available in the United States, nor can they make as full use of drugs because of stricter laws covering prescription of medicinal agents. But their health care system can be readily described in terms of our model, where the popular cultural sector shows a fascinating mixture of both Chinese and American components.

Thus far I have described and drawn upon the Taiwanese example to illustrate the morphology of health care systems. Now I will turn to their clinical activities.

3

Orientations 3:
Core Clinical Functions
and Explanatory Models

Review of the cross-cultural literature on local health care systems discloses universal clinical activities (see Kleinman 1973a, 1974b, 1976, 1977b). Each of the health care system's sectors contributes to a greater or lesser extent to these core clinical tasks. Therefore, they are best regarded as functions of the system as a whole, even though certain of them may be primarily performed by a particular sector. When I use the term "clinical," then, I am not referring to a specific activity of professional medical care, but instead to these general health care functions. For analysis and comparison, five core clinical functions can be distinguished. These are:

1. The cultural construction of *illness* as psychosocial experience.

2. The establishment of *general* criteria to guide the health care seeking process and to evaluate treatment approaches that exist prior to and independent of individual episodes of sickness.

3. The management of *particular* illness episodes through communicative operations such as labeling and explaining.

4. Healing activities per se, which include all types of therapeutic interventions, from drugs and surgery to psychotherapy, supportive care, and healing rituals.

71

5. The management of therapeutic outcomes, including cure, treatment failure, recurrence, chronic illness, impairment, and death.

Great variation occurs in the mechanisms that perform these functions in different systems. But the core clinical functions are performed by all health care systems. Health care, in the broadest sense, may be thought of as the summation of these activities. Thus, the system as a whole, not just the healer, heals. Each of the chapters that follows will examine a different core clinical function.

• *The construction of the illness experience, Function 1,* is itself a health care function and, indeed, the earliest one. Sickness as a "natural" phenomenon is cast into a particular cultural form through the categories that are used to perceive, express, and valuate symptoms. The cultural construction of illness experiences, as we shall see in the next chapter, is frequently a personally and socially adaptive response.

A key axiom in medical anthropology is the dichotomy between two aspects of sickness: disease and illness. *Disease* refers to a malfunctioning of biological and/or psychological processes, while the term *illness* refers to the psychosocial experience and meaning of perceived disease. Illness includes secondary personal and social responses to a primary malfunctioning (disease) in the individual's physiological or psychological status (or both). Illness involves processes of attention, perception, affective response, cognition, and valuation directed at the disease and its manifestations (i.e., symptoms, role impairment, etc.). But also included in the idea of illness are communication and interpersonal interaction, particularly within the context of the family and social network. Viewed from this perspective, illness is the shaping of disease into behavior and experience. It is created by personal, social, and cultural reactions to disease. Constructing illness from disease is a central function of health care systems (a coping function) and the first stage of healing. That is, illness contains responses to disease which attempt to provide it with a meaningful form and explanation as well as control. Paradoxical as it may sound, illness is part of care. It is both a psychosocial and cultural adaptive response. In some instances it may provide virtually all there is of therapeutic efficacy; in others it may cause more problems for clinical care than disease does, but in all cultures it is considerably more important than has heretofore been realized (cf. Eisenberg 1976; Fabrega 1974; Kleinman, Eisenberg, Good 1978).

Disease affects single individuals, even when it attacks a population; but illness most often affects others as well (e.g., family, social network, even at times an entire community). In some cultures, the illness is believed to be constituted by both the affected person and his family: both are labeled ill.

As was noted of our model of health care systems, disease and illness are explanatory concepts, not entities. Engelhardt (1974) properly views them as representing relationships. Their components (*disturbed* biochemical processes, anatomical structures, physiological reactions, patterns of behavior and communication), though features of the "real" world, can only be understood as part of pictures assembled by our explanatory models, in which these elements form coherent patterns. Our explanatory models (see the next sections) enable us to see disease/illness as ideal-type relationships, and it is in terms of those models that we identify, assemble, and interpret the clinical evidence that confirms these relationships. Disease and illness exist, then, as constructs in particular configurations of social reality. They can be understood only within defined contexts of meaning and social relationships. As we shall see, they are explanatory models anchored in the different explanatory systems and social structural arrangements comprising the separate sectors (and subsectors) of local health care systems. Disease/illness can be thought of as expressing different interpretations of a single clinical reality, or representing different aspects of a plural clinical reality, or creating different clinical realities.

Though, generally speaking, the explanatory models of professional practitioners are oriented toward disease while those of the laity are oriented toward illness, this is not always the case. Biomedical models are of course disease oriented, but when applied by clinicians they may reflect concern for illness factors as well (Engel 1977). Indigenous professions of medicine, such as the Chinese and Ayurvedic traditions, tend to be disease oriented, but their explanatory frames take into account illness issues to a greater degree than does the biomedical perspective. In the United States and other technologically advanced Western societies, lay accounts of sickness (especially those of the educated, secularized middle class) not infrequently are heavily influenced by the biomedical paradigm, and consequently more and more a disease orientation is incorporated into illness models in the popular sector of their health care systems.

In chronic disorders (e.g., diabetes, ischemic heart disease, asthma, or schizophrenia), it may be difficult to distinguish the disease from the illness. In such disorders, illness may exist when the disease is in remission, and recurrence of the disease itself may be due to the illness. Conversely, disease may be present with minimal or no illness. More usually, however, these two aspects of sickness undergo reciprocal changes such that they either worsen or improve together. In fulminant acute disorders, like massive trauma, acute intoxication, or overwhelming acute infection, there often is little or no time for the disease to be shaped into illness experience. On the other hand, illness can occur in the absence of disease, for example, in hypochondriasis, chronic "functional" complaints, and various other abuses of the medical sick role, including malingering. Minor (non-psychotic) psychiatric disorders, such as hysteria and personality disorders, and life problems and psychosocial crises requiring psychiatric intervention may be examples of illness in the absence of disease. In that sense, illness is a reaction to an imagined, perceived, or even desired disease; we also can think of illness behavior as if it were mimicked consciously or unconsciously. Clearly, this comes down to a question of the conceptual models used to label those problems. Homosexuality, alcoholism, and drug abuse can be thought of in the same way. Interpreted from the standpoint of a psychiatric explanatory system, these are illnesses which may or may not be diseases depending upon whether the explanation used is derived from a psychoanalytic, biological, behavioral, or social orientation (see Lazare 1973; Siegler and Osmond 1966). Interpreted from the sociological standpoint of the labeling theory of deviance explanatory system, these are instances of social deviance that are labeled medical deviance or disease/illness solely for external cultural, social, political, and economic reasons having nothing whatsoever to do with the "real" attributes of disease or illness.

If we examine symptomatology, we see just how terribly complex is the interrelationship between disease and illness. Here we also have an occasion to review some mechanisms by which culture influences disease/illness. Although it would be analytically desirable to distinguish between the symptoms of disease and those of illness (e.g., calling them "primary" and "secondary" symptomatic manifestations respectively), this distinction is not easily sustained. Since illness behavior includes the perception, affective response to, cognizing, and valuation of the symptoms of disease, along with their communication (verbal and non-verbal), *all* symptoms are molded by the illness experience. Illness usually begins with the sick person's attention to and perception of the early manifestations of disease.[1] Personal and family beliefs and experiences, and through them culture and social systems, are powerful influences on these processes (see, for example, Mechanic 1972; Zborowski 1969; Zola 1966). For instance, an individual, for entirely personal or sociocultural reasons, may evaluate early symptoms as not worth worrying about, minimal, natural, or not part of sickness but representing some other state, or he may deny their potential significance (Lipowski 1969). On the other hand, he may become frightened and view them as a threat or loss that must be immediately responded to. And his attitude will be different depending on his affective state and interpersonal situation at a particular time. It also will be influenced by the way he has come to regard his body generally and particular normal bodily processes, again based on idiosyncratic, family, and cultural predilections (cf. Blacking 1977).

1. Of course, illness also may begin with a person being labeled ill by others when he himself has no subjective complaints. But this is a great deal less common than self-labeling owing to subjective complaints. This is a difficult problem for the labeling viewpoint, unless a distinction is made between primary (patient labels himself) and secondary (patient is labeled by others) deviance. Even then a corrective is needed, since the overwhelming tendency of deviance research is to disregard the former, which is by far the most common occurrence in medicine and psychiatry (see Gove 1975). Of course, illness can commence with the sick person's desire to achieve a socially legitimated sick role for reasons unrelated to disease, and can occur—and, as we have already noted, often does—in the absence of disease.

The label he applies to subjective feelings or objective signs will in itself exert a powerful influence, and that label is *always* a cultural category. Suppose a person feels dull, lacks his usual energy, becomes disinterested in work, recreation, and family, and is unhappy. If he (or his family) begins calling this state "sickness," he will start to feel sick, whereas these nonspecific complaints need not be regarded at all as symptoms of sickness but could be labeled "misfortune" or some other nebulous, general term, or they could be given a specific but non-medical label, such as a moral, religious, or economic problem. In that case, it is highly probable the individual would not feel ill, even if these complaints were indeed manifestations of a particular sickness. (Here would be an example of disease without illness.) On the other hand, over the course of recent history in the West, it has become usual for individuals with the complaints described to label themselves ill—indeed to label themselves, and be labeled by others, with a psychiatric term, "depression." That in turn helps shape the problem. (The symptoms I have listed could represent the insidious onset of a number of discrete diseases other than depression or might be associated with no disease at all.) The individual and his family use that label to interpret other experiences and behaviors, some of which may have nothing to do with his problem. In applying the label, the afflicted person and his family make use of the explanatory accounts available to them in a particular cultural, historical, and health care sector context. For example, as we shall see in the next chapter, Chinese popular sickness categories label depression as a somatic problem, while American popular categories label it as a psychological problem. Those labels shape the quality of the experience of depression in Chinese culture into a bodily or vegetative experience and in American culture into an intrapsychic and existential experience. Similarly, Hispanic-American patients who apply the illness category *susto* to depressive or anxiety symptoms do not merely construe these symptoms differently than do members of other groups in American society but actually construct distinctive illness experiences that resemble their expectations of how patients with this culture-specific disorder are supposed to feel and behave. Thomas (1971) has cited examples of how individuals in sixteenth-century England who suffered similar

symptoms or those due to hysterical conversion came to display possession behavior when accused of witchcraft. Further
examples could be given for virtually every ethnic group and
historical period for which we possess adequate ethnomedical
descriptions.

Thus, through labeling and the other cognitive processes,
symptoms are socially constructed. Throughout this book I
present detailed case illustrations of this critical activity—the
shaping of symptoms—by which sickness is saturated with
specific meaning and cast as a particular configuration of human action and thereby made into a special cultural form. That
cultural form is illness. The cultural shaping of symptoms may
be minimal and may produce illnesses that look roughly the
same cross-culturally. Much more often, this core clinical process produces illnesses that differ significantly in meaning and
in which the quality of the experience may be different. And
sometimes the patterning of symptoms produces "culture-
bound disorders," which I interpret to be illnesses associated
with culturally unique patterns of meaning superimposed on
diseases that are universal. Disease commonly has a typical
course and characteristic features that are independent of setting. Illness is always more or less unique. At times we can talk
securely about disease *qua* disease, but illness cannot be understood in that way: it can only be understood in a specific context of norms, symbolic meanings, and social interaction.

Psychophysiological interactions and disorders disclose more
about the complex interrelationships between disease and illness. Indeed, the very complexity and ambiguity involved in
applying our analytical dichotomy to these cases should free
us from the dangerous temptation to treat disease and illness
as if they are entities rather than explanations. For example,
a somatic disease giving rise to a somatic illness, in which the
behavioral component by definition is dominant, can also at
times give rise to a psychological disease/illness, as in the case
of depression caused by diabetes, or schizophrenia caused by
temporal lobe epilepsy, or acute anxiety reaction caused by a
tumor secreting epinephrine. These somatopsychic disorders
are less common than psychosomatic disorders (here used in
the sense of general psychophysiological problems, not as a
specific disease category based on psychoanalytic concepts). In

77

each we find interlaced together psychological disease and illness and somatic disease and illness. Moreover, Holmes and Rahe (1967) have demonstrated that psychosocial stress can produce either psychological or physiological disease, or both. Their work is eloquent testimony to the fact that both disease and illness are bound up in psychological-physiological-social interrelationships.

The usefulness of this distinction is its emphasis on the fact that, no matter what the nature of the disease and its causes, the disease involves a psychological, social, and cultural reaction, the illness. Though both disease and illness may involve psychosocial and cultural factors, they are of a different order: in physical disease they may cause, maintain the course of, or determine the outcome of the disease; in psychological disease, they are the stuff of the disease itself. But in illness, they are the behavioral and societal *response* to the disease that provide it with meaning and constitute it as a symbolic form. Without illness, there is no signification attached to the disorder. That is why illness is always a cultural construction. Without setting disease in a context of meaning, there is no basis for behavioral options, no guide for health-seeking behavior and the application of specific therapy. Hence, the major mechanism by which culture affects the patient and his disorder is via the cultural construction of illness categories and experiences.

In psychophysiological disorders there is a constant feedback between disease and illness. In an acute anxiety reaction occurring in the course of a chronic anxiety neurosis, the acute anxiety (the disease process) is manifested in part by rapid heart rate. Perception of the rapid heart rate is part of the illness experience. It assigns a special subjective meaning to this physiological activity. Since all of this is happening to a patient with a chronic anxiety disorder, we might expect the rapid heart rate to represent a serious threat to the patient, suggesting to him that he is suffering a recurrence of his sickness. As a result, we would expect the rapid heart rate to exert a positive feedback on the anxiety, significantly worsening it. Here the illness plays an important role in determining what happens to the disease. In a person without an anxiety disorder, acute anxiety might produce a rapid heart rate, but, unless some other factors are at work, that will not be interpreted as threatening and should not have a positive feedback on the anxiety.

For similar reasons a disease in which the symptoms generated are not perceived as a threat but are thought to have no significant consequences will not develop this positive feedback between disease and illness and should be easier to treat than disorders that do have such positive feedback. The vicious cycle of escalating disease and illness set off in the case of chronic anxiety is not an infrequent complication in chronic disorders, such as asthma, diabetes, low back pain, etc. Personal experience, social setting, and cultural beliefs may or may not be instrumental in precipitating acute exacerbations of these chronic problems, but they almost certainly will be essential in interpreting them and thereby will affect (exacerbate or meliorate) the disease via the illness. Here again I would point out that we must not think of disease and illness as two separate entities, but as a way of talking about (and hopefully simplifying) a complex set of interrelationships. As the example just cited demonstrates, these interrelationships need not always have adaptive consequences. Core clinical functions, such as the one described here, sometimes may disclose a maladaptive cultural effect in which the illness creates worse problems for health care.

Two quite different mechanisms exist by which culture can pattern disease/illness: one involves subjective interpretation, while the other suggests a direct effect upon the physiological substrate. I have emphasized the former, i.e., a mechanism involving cognitive appraisal. Culture influences the cognitive appraisal of external stimuli; it helps determine whether they will be evaluated as stressful or not. It also influences the cognitive appraisal of bodily and emotional states, determining if they are to be labeled as illness or not. It is at work in the labels themselves and the logic of their application. Lipowski (1969, 1973) summarizes the cognitive appraisal of illness quite neatly as involving the assessment of sickness as threat, loss, gain, or of no significance. And for him this is the pathway from context to person and physiology, from symbolic stimulus to psychobiological response. We can regard these assessments as the core determinations made in each case of illness. But culture also can *directly* affect the psychological and physiological processes in disease/illness. This pathway bypasses cog-

79

nitive appraisal, affecting the body and the mind via symbolic systems and relationships established in early experience (Werner and Kaplan 1967) and, therefore, outside of conscious awareness. This pathway may be responsible for the fact that much of illness experience also falls outside of patients' awareness. The possibility that we are observing what I have previously termed "symbolic reality" mediating socio-somatic effects should be kept in mind when we examine specific cases, but it is not clear when and to what extent this direct pathway from environment to illness operates.

I have described the first core clinical function in detail because the following sections of this chapter require an understanding of how illness is culturally constituted. Chapters 4 and 5 illustrate this process extensively with materials from Chinese culture. I discuss and illustrate the other core clinical functions elsewhere in this book, and I do not elaborate in the same detail now.

• *Core Clinical Function 2, the establishment of general strategies and criteria for choosing and evaluating health care alternatives*, signifies what Schutz (1968) has called structures of relevance and what Schwartz (1969) has referred to as hierarchies of resort— the health ideology and values that guide the health seeking process, the rules that govern individual and group decisions, independent of specific episodes of sickness. This activity begins with the values embedded in generic illness labels. For instance, leprosy, tuberculosis, and mental illness all have carried strong and usually quite negative valuations in Western culture (see Dubos 1952; Foucault 1965; Gussow and Tracy 1970)—valuations that exist prior to and independent of specific instances of these disorders. But these are extreme examples of what occurs routinely for even the most common sicknesses. Medical anthropologists have shown that the application of values to types of illness has an important influence upon the decisions people make in responding to particular episodes of sickness (Chrisman 1977). Following Schutz (1968), we can view these values as functioning to order illnesses within frameworks of relevance. Those frameworks define which health problems are most important, most feared, and require most immediate action. In turn, therapeutic responses are similarly typed. The fit between categories of illness and types of care represents the applied structure of relevance within a sector of a local health care system. Quite obviously, these often differ between sectors. They also may differ for individuals and families. The same structure of relevance is used to decide how long to continue one type of care and when to change to another. In this case it contributes to the health care ideology of the popular culture. For example, in Taiwan lay people often expect a Western-style doctor to remove major symptoms in two or at the most, three visits, or else they try another Western-style doctor or even move on to another type of practitioner. Value structures play a crucial role in evaluations of therapeutic efficacy, with frequent conflicts between the evaluations of practitioners and patients. Such conflicts often lead to major problems in clinical care. For example, researchers in one study in Great Britain have shown that many patients treated with gastric surgery for peptic ulcer disease evaluated their surgery as unsuccessful, whereas their surgeons maintained an opposite assessment, because the former relied on behavioral criteria (how they felt and functioned after surgery) to assess outcome, while the latter used technical criteria (whether the surgical wound healed properly and complications were avoided) (Cay et al. 1975). In another study, patients with low back pain who were randomly sorted into two groups, one of which was sent to orthopedic surgeons for treatment while the other was sent to chiropractors, disclosed no objective evidence of difference in outcome; but those who received treatment from chiropractors reported greater subjective satisfaction with their treatment than those who were managed by orthopedists, largely because the former responded positively to the chiropractors' evident interest in the psychosocial management of their *illness problems*, while the latter responded negatively to the orthopedists' disinterest in this aspect of care and sole concern for the technical management of *disease problems* (Kane et al. 1974). Cross-societal variations in these evaluative criteria also are striking. Navaho patients, for example, treated for tuberculosis at modern hospitals, when released after being evaluated as cured by modern physicians, return to native healers to have healing ceremonies performed to "complete the cure" and remove the negative effects of Western-style medicine (Adair and Deuschle 1970).

81

Ndembu healers and communities may view the efficacy of treatment primarily as successful resolution of social tensions associated with sickness and only secondarily as successful removal of the patient's symptoms (Turner 1967:299–391).

• *Function 2 and Function 3, the communicative operations and interactions required to manage particular illness episodes*, will be examined in the next sections, which set out a framework for their analysis and comparison.

• *Healing activities and the management of therapeutic outcomes, Functions 4 and 5,* are the most familiar aspects of health care and consequently should not require additional definition at this point. It is worth noting, however, that cross-cultural studies reveal that healing refers to two related but distinguishable clinical tasks: the establishment of effective control of disordered biological and psychological processes, which I shall refer to as the "curing of disease," and the provision of personal and social meaning for the life problems created by sickness, which I shall refer to as the "healing of illness." These activities constitute the chief goal of health care systems.

"Cultural healing" may occur when healing rites reassert threatened values and arbitrate social tensions. Thus, therapeutic procedures may heal social stress independent of the effects they have on the sick person who provides the occasion for their use (Douglas 1970). Similarly, problems affecting the clinical process are "systematically" built into health care systems ("cultural iatrogenesis") as a result of social and cultural organization. Such problems include: the shaping of maladaptive illness behavior (as was described above); conflicts in the "medical" labeling of social deviance; and, most importantly, conflicting interpretations of clinical reality based upon discrepancies between the health beliefs and values held by members of the different sectors of health care systems. These may eventuate in patient non-compliance and dissatisfaction with the quality of care, misuse of available health care resources and culturally inappropriate care, as well as ineffective or noxious professional care.

Function 5 suggests that health care includes more than simply cure. The management of therapeutic outcomes, besides cure, ranging from treatment failure and recurrent sickness problems to chronic illness, impairment, and dying, clearly

takes up the largest portion of professional health care in technologically advanced societies (Rogers 1977; McDermott 1977).
But it is an equally important activity in the popular and folk
sectors, and it is by no means a minor clinical task in developing and traditional societies.

Dunn (1976) has argued that health maintenance is also an
essential function of "medical systems" and that it and disease
prevention should be added as another core function of health
care systems. I do not list it here because what I am describing
are "clinical" functions concerned with the management of
sickness. Since my approach to "medical systems" is largely
limited to their health care activities, I refer to them as "health
care systems." Conversely, Dunn's orientation leads him to
describe medical systems as "health systems," which implies
a much broader view of their functions. Health care systems
also perform non-medical functions, such as social control,
which overlap and merge with clinical tasks. Mitchell (1977)
rightly draws attention to the bias that may be introduced
through use of biomedical concepts to describe "therapeutic
systems" and suggests that such modern "clinical" terms may
superimpose a medicocentric suprastructure upon cultural
phenomena that are articulated in different ways. But neither
he nor anyone else has proposed a suitable alternative for analyzing indigenous "therapeutic systems" in terms that are less
influenced by Western models.

The argument of this book is that the core clinical functions
are universal aspects of medicine in society that are fully appreciated only when clinical issues are the primary concern of
the ethnographer. "Clinical," in the sense that I have discussed
it, is not a Western category, but a category intrinsic to all societies. The problem with most ethnomedical studies is not that
they impose an alien clinical category on indigenous materials,
but rather that they fail to apprehend a profound cross-cultural
similarity in clinical interest and praxis.

EXPLANATORY MODELS IN ILLNESS AND CLINICAL CARE

In this and the next section, I present a conceptual model for
studying the cognitive and communicative features of health
care (core clinical functions 2 and 3). First, I shall report field
notes of clinical ethnography to illustrate the phenomena that

need to be understood.[2] This demands that I discuss a variety of issues that relate to the health ideologies of the different sectors and to the communicative exchanges between actors from those sectors that are central to the management of almost all episodes of sickness—issues that are exemplified by the ethnographic descriptions from Taiwan. In this manner, I will review the many relevant questions that any interpretive framework aimed at analyzing and comparing the cognitive and communicative aspects of health care needs to address. The model itself is presented at the end of this wide-ranging discussion to demonstrate how it aids in resolving certain problems examined in the preceding commentary. This line of argument allows the reader to recapitulate the author's personal experience in working out the explanatory model framework in response to specific questions posed by ethnographic findings from Taiwan and by the work of others studying conceptualizations of sickness and care in Chinese and other cultures. Thus, I am in part describing the process whereby I discovered that the biomedical perspective I had acquired in my professional training was inadequate and at the same time came to recognize the virtues of an ethnomedical approach that overcomes the limitations of the biomedical model precisely because it studies medicine as an inherently semantic subject inseparable from the conceptualizations of it held by patients, communities, and practitioners. In other words, the inadequacies of the biomedical perspective and the strengths of the ethnomedical approach were revealed to me by a cluster of ethnographic fragments that called for an interpretive method to mediate between different systems of "medical" knowledge— a method that the former could not provide, but the latter could.

Example 1

Not infrequently one hears a term for illness, <u>*ut siong*</u>, used in Hokkien by Taiwanese in the popular culture. There is no equivalent expression in Mandarin (the national language of

2. All examples and cases cited in this book come from field research and clinical studies in Taiwan or Boston. I have given patients and informants pseudonyms and have slightly altered case histories in order to render them anonymous and protect the identity of the individuals involved.

Taiwan), in which the separate characters compounded into this term, *yu shang*, convey no meaning together. Individually, they mean anxious, grieved, and depressed (*yu, ut*), and to injure, to wound, to grieve, and to be distressed (*shang, siong*) (Mathews 1963: 778, 1151; Barclay 1923: 27, 203). *Shang* (*siong*) is used in combinations to denote both physical and psychological wounding. Some Chinese-style doctors, especially ones from mainland China, either do not know *ut siong*'s meaning or state flatly that it is not part of the classical (and professional) body of Chinese medical concepts, but is rather a popular belief. Other Chinese-style doctors, especially older Taiwanese ones, do know this expression. Though some of them pass it off as a popular corruption, others say it is a legitimate traditional Chinese medical concept. In fact, patients only use this expression with Chinese-style doctors of Taiwanese ethnicity and not with those from the China mainland. The former almost always, in my experience, respond to their patients' inquiries as if this were a "real" illness, even if they are skeptical about it. Folk practitioners, especially herbalists and *tâng-kis*, use this concept frequently, as do older Taiwanese family members who are supposed to possess special knowledge about illness.

Both can remember when *siong* was used in combination with other characters in the period of the Japanese occupation of Taiwan to refer to tuberculosis, a dreaded and quite prevalent disease that often had a fatal outcome before the introduction of effective chemotherapy and modern public health measures after World War II. The present-day popular notion of *ut siong* is not easily defined and varies somewhat from informant to informant. For some it conveys the idea of a disorder with physical and psychological aspects, whereas for others it signifies only a physical disorder. The expression was much more commonly used in a rural rice farming village in central Taiwan than in areas in Taipei where we conducted family interviews, though it was generally known and used there as well. A typical lay informant definition is: "It is sometimes a physical illness, sometimes a psychological illness. It can be caused by not enough exercise. Dress makers and students catch it for that reason. . . . Anxiety produces bad circulation of blood in the chest, and it can be caused by that . . . you feel pressure in the chest. There is a tendency to breathe too quickly. Sometimes there are sighs. Worrying too much can be a cause. Sitting too long in one position also can be a cause."

Older lay informants report this term was often used in the

past to refer to scholars and students who, it was believed, spent too much time sitting in one place over their books and who people felt were likely to injure their health and, especially, to contract tuberculosis. Some informants add the idea of a scholar or student who sits alone and may be sad or lonely. Those Chinese-style doctors who know and use the term, on the other hand, tend to define it as a physical disease and less frequently as one with both physical and psychological causes. They attribute it to working too hard, too many worries, and frustrated ambition. But these psychosocial stresses they view as engendering a physical disorder with physical pathology and primarily or only physical symptoms. They associate it with a range of symptoms, beginning with a sense of pressure on the chest, rapid and strong heart beat, difficulty breathing, particularly a sense of something caught in the throat and interfering with breathing, and moving on to cough, weight loss, insomnia, difficulty with mental concentration, and in the most severe cases, bloody sputum. Some attribute this disorder especially to adolescents. They argue it is frequently brought on by rapid change from immoderate exertion to inactivity, when adolescents become chilled by an accompanying change in body temperature or due to drinking very cold water, both of which also predispose adolescents to being affected by "wind." These same Chinese-style doctors claim adolescents eventually grow out of this problem when they become adults. They also associate this disorder in other age groups with symptoms of fatigue and low back pain, and nonspecific bodily complaints. Of particular interest, most Chinese-style doctors whom I interviewed, although emphasizing the traditional therapeutic dictum that the underlying disorder must be treated if this illness is to improve, nonetheless refrained from placing this illness in any of the classical diagnostic and pathophysiological categories (*cheng*) essential to identify the underlying disorder and prescribe medicines. All diseases held to be part of the classical Chinese medical corpus are classified in terms of these classical categories or "manifestations types" (Agren 1976), whereas disease concepts taken over by Chinese medicine from Western medicine are much less frequently handled in that way. Thus *ut siong* is treated by Chinese-style doctors as if it were foreign to their conceptual system. A Western-style doctor of my acquaintance, himself Taiwanese, dismissed *ut siong*, as Western-style doctors in Taiwan usually do, by labeling it "nonsense." He suggested that it probably had something to do with tuberculosis but made no mention of any psychological components being involved.

Example 2

A 70-year-old retired Chinese government employee from a mainland family famous for its traditional-style scholars, who possesses a Ph.D. in one of the physical sciences from a prestigious American university, has held various high-level posts in the education system of pre-1949 China and Taiwan, and refers to himself as a modernizer with some traditional values, explains what he thinks are the differences between Chinese and Western medicines (drugs). In reporting these ideas, he gives expression to notions commonly heard in Taiwan, from Taiwanese and mainlanders alike who possess very different social and educational backgrounds:

"Chinese medicines have fewer side effects than Western medicines. Western medicine works much quicker, but it only removes symptoms. It does not, like Chinese medicine, remove the underlying cause of the illness. (The term he uses is *tuan-ken,* literally to "cut down the root," denoting radical cure or cure of the underlying problem.) Chinese medicine may not help you sometimes, but it won't hurt you. Western medicine may remove your symptoms or illness, but sometimes the treatment is worse than the illness. There are many ways of treating an illness, not just one. Different ways must be used depending on the specific illness and the person. But as for your talking therapy (said with a laugh), I don't think it is of any use at all. You can't treat anyone with that alone."

Example 3

In the course of a home visit to a 20-year-old Taiwanese mother and her two-year-old son, who is recovering from measles complicated by a bout of pneumonia, both of whom we had met in the small shrine of a nearby *tâng-ki,* where they had gone for treatment and advice about the child's sickness, the illiterate, middle-aged mother-in-law in this lower-class family tells us her views about measles:

"All children must catch it. For most this is no problem, but for certain children it is a big problem. Those children have measles crisis! In order to pass this crisis they must go to the god (the *tâng-ki* when possessed is believed to be the god speaking through the shaman) and have a special ritual performed. But you must be careful to give all children with measles proper foods. Don't give them fruit or they will have a problem with diarrhea. Also it is dangerous for a child with measles to catch cold. If a child catches a cold at that time it can lead to asthma when the child is older."

This mother-in-law went on to say that if the child with measles developed a high fever it was dangerous, and then it was important to treat the child with Western medicines to prevent the child from getting "brain fever" (encephalitis). She recommended the use of "Ilosone" (erythromycin, a potent antibiotic) for such a complication. Soon after mentioning this she stated that gods could protect a child from getting "measles crisis" and from other complications. (Her grandchild wore a red packet (hû-á) around his neck containing a shaman's charm to protect him.) The mother-in-law added:

"We in Taiwan give children who have measles an herb tea to drink. That makes the poison (tu, tók), which gives you measles, come out. Once the poison comes out, you get better. Once you get over measles, you never get it again."

She goes on to tell us Western medicine can "cure" the symptoms of measles, but keeps the poison in, preventing it from coming out. This she says is "unnatural and could be dangerous." She is against vaccination for measles, saying that everyone must get measles once in their lifetime. Vaccination, like Western medicine, might suppress the poison of measles, preventing it from coming out and so might lead to something bad later on in the child's life. It is worth noting her grandson was treated with Western medicine as well as by the shaman, "but only after the child refused the herb tea and had a high fever." This woman's daughter-in-law, who has a primary school education, states she is not sure what has been responsible for her son's cure—charms from the tâng-ki, Western medicine, or the natural course of the illness (which she considered only after we asked her about it)—but she believes that for any illness one needs the power of both "god (tâng-ki) and man (doctor)."

Example 4

In a small shrine in a lower-class area of a Taipei suburb, a middle-aged female tâng-ki, who has just entered into a trance in which she is possessed by one of the shrine's gods, is treating an elderly Taiwanese grandmother, who is suffering from a chronic illness and looks both quite ill and frightened. This elderly client has come to Taipei from her home in a small village in the south of Taiwan in order to be treated by this *tâng-ki*. Her daughter is a devotee of the shrine and of its female healer. The possessed healer's god, speaking through her, after the shaman has carefully taken the client's pulse, tells the client that she has "liver fire" and also a problem with "fire of the nerves." The client is told that she is suffering from an excess of internal hot energy or "fire" (*huo-ch'i ta*), "rising up from the intestines." That is the cause of her stomach and intestines being "blocked up," and it is also "blocking up" and generally interfering with the circulation of her "air and blood." This is the chief cause of the client's symptoms. The *tâng-ki* tells the patient her problem is serious, and to rid herself of it she must have a ritual performed to drive away "ghosts" and "bad things" that have caused this problem.

After hearing this diagnosis and explanation with her hands clasped in prayer, the client bows to the *tâng-ki*. She talks about her complaints, especially her gastro-intestinal symptoms. The *tâng-ki* listens carefully and acknowledges she has heard and understood the client's problems. She then begins to palpate the client's abdomen and finally massages the client's arms, chest, abdomen, and back. She also performs a short ritual, during which she makes passing movements with a writing brush over the client's body as if she were writing a charm on her, the significance of which is that the power of the charm is transferred directly to the client's body, and ends by giving this woman paper charms and an herb. After that she tells the client and her daughter that they need not pay money but should tell other people about this shrine and advise them to come for treatment. The *tâng-ki*'s female assistant adds a whispered aside: "Don't worry about your illness so much . . . worrying will make it worse, cause a bigger problem." The elderly client walks away from the altar table looking quite confused. Later on we learn that she has not really understood all that the *tâng-ki* explained to her, but nonetheless she is hopeful the *tâng-ki*'s god will be able to cure her.

Example 5

I am talking with a 65-year-old Chinese-style doctor and his 30-year-old son, who is a Western-style doctor specializing in ophthalmology, in their middle-class home in a large market town in central Taiwan. We are talking about the causes of certain disorders. The father, whose grandfather and father I was informed were also Chinese-style doctors, tells me imbalances in the body's *yin/yang* or in a single organ cause disruption in the internal organs and their interrelated functions (*wu-tsang*). He feels it is not necessary to take a history from the patient, since the cause of a disorder usually can be ascertained directly from examination of the pulse in most cases. He admits he uses several Western medical terms for which there are no Chinese medical equivalents (such as hysteria and problems relating to the use of modern birth control agents), but he feels Chinese medical theory is sufficient for understanding and treating most disorders. If he suspects pregnancy, he sends the patient to a laboratory for a urine test. He does not feel talking to patients in itself has any efficacy, but he states it is essential to inform patients which foods they may and may not eat when they take particular Chinese medicines. He does not discuss cause or pathophysiology with patients because "they would not understand." He does not inquire about patients' own views of their disorders or what they wish to receive as treatment, nor does he expect his patients to tell him these things. He values Western medicine for certain things, especially treatments such as surgery and antibiotics and accurate, detailed diagnoses. But, though he refers patients to Western-style doctors for these procedures, he thinks Chinese medicine is better for treating most chronic sicknesses.

Afterward his son tells me that he could not follow this discussion. He points out the concepts of traditional Chinese medicine are utterly foreign to him, even though his family has had three generations of Chinese-style doctors. He thinks his father's understanding of modern scientific medicine is also limited.

"We never discuss our cases or talk about medicine generally for that matter. I don't follow his ideas, and he doesn't understand mine. Since he is my father, it is best to be silent. A lot of his patients seem to have minor problems or something chronic with minimal pathology. Do you think there is anything to these theories? Some traditional medicines may be useful, but the theories . . . they seem so unscientific."

The selections from field notes illustrate different aspects of the cognitive and communicative processes operating in health care systems generally and in Taiwan's health care systems specifically. Beliefs about illness, the central cognitive structure of every health care system, are closely tied to beliefs about treatment (cf. D'Andrade 1976, for an illustration from American culture). Thus, ideas about the cause of illness (as well as its pathophysiology and course) are linked to ideas about practical treatment interventions. Part of medicine's therapeutic mandate is that sickness beliefs organize health care seeking choices and treatment interventions. Such beliefs differ across health care systems and between the different sectors of any given health care system. For example, Porkert (1976) attributes differences between Chinese and modern scientific medical notions to a conceptual system in modern medicine, concerned with material substance and its division into component parts, and a Chinese conceptual system, concerned with the functional attributes of an organic whole. Thus, classical Chinese medicine regards most diseases to be caused by disharmony in the system of correspondences that extends from the cosmos to man, while Western medicine regards most diseases in terms of the organ-specific lesions they produce. Classical Chinese medicine speaks in a "functional" language of imbalances in the body's *yin/yang,* of disharmony in the systematic correspondences of the Five Evolutive Phases (*wu-hsing,* also rendered Five Elements—wood, fire, earth, metal, water), including the integrated functioning of the five interrelated internal organ systems (*wu-tsang,* Five body Spheres),[3] and of blockage of the balanced circulation of *ch'i* (vital essence). Western medicine speaks in a "structural" language of pathology in a particular organ. These two cognitive structures yield distinctive disease categories and lead to very different therapeutic actions.

In my field notes the medical concepts of a Chinese-style doctor were meaningless to his son, trained in Western medicine. The son claimed to be unable to discuss cases with his father because of the differences in their knowledge and logic. He judged his father's theories to be unscientific. On the other hand, the father regarded modern medical science as an alternative theoretical framework, not the only one, and no more

3. While the classical Chinese medical texts tended to categorize phenomena into groups of *six* (e.g., Six *Yin* Organs; Six *Yang* Organs; Six Etiological Factors of Disease—*liu-ch'i*), Chinese-style medical beliefs in contemporary Taiwan, both among laity and practitioners, tend to be articulated into groups of *five* (e.g., *wu-hsing; wu-tsang*), a characteristic feature of traditional Taoist thought. Because of this tendency, I refer throughout the book only to the latter.

"true" than his own theory. He, like many other Chinese-style doctors, claimed that the two systems of ideas were complementary and should be used together, insofar as this was possible. His son had no use for Chinese medical ideas or for traditional Chinese-style practitioners other than his father. He conceded, however, that some Chinese medicines were probably efficacious and should be analyzed in the theoretical framework of modern scientific medicine, but their use should be limited to modern health professionals. It is not uncommon in these matters for traditional physicians to act with more tolerance than their Western-style counterparts. But the main point is the huge gap between the medical cognitive systems employed by father and son.

The popular sectors of health care systems largely possess orally transmitted beliefs derived from the professional and folk sectors. But they are "popularizations" of those formally articulated ideas, and as such they show much distortion, condensation, and syncretization. In Example 1, we have an illness category (*ut siong*) which appears to have developed as an indigenous local concept in Taiwan, though it is unquestionably modeled on professional ideas from both Chinese and Western medicine. It is of particular interest because it shows an amalgamation of the Western disease category tuberculosis with psychological and psychophysiological symptoms that might be labeled depression, anxiety neurosis, or hysteria in Western psychiatry, but that are labeled by Chinese culture to emphasize physical symptoms and provide a psychosomatic sick role. This is an illness category that makes little sense to Chinese-style or Western-style practitioners, since it is a cultural construction of the *popular sector* of health care systems in Taiwan. However, not all individuals and families in those health care systems understand and use this illness concept. Even where people use it, there is a wide range of beliefs about cause, pathophysiology, symptomatology, and course attached to it. Indeed, it almost seems that two quite different problems are brought together here: a psychophysiological disorder resulting from stress and tuberculosis and other chronic pulmonary diseases.

Although professional practitioners look upon popular medical beliefs as debased transforms of their ideas contaminated by folk ideas that they label "superstitions," physicians who practice Chinese medicine usually respond to questions about cause, pathophysiology, and course, even though few of them think that lay people know much about their theories. Also, they do not offer theoretical explanations unless queried by their patients. Western-style doctors in Taiwan frequently behave like the one described in the first excerpt from my field notes. They are contemptuous of the homely, non-scientific ideas of the public and unwilling to explain much about cause and course of illness, even when directly asked to do so by patients (see Ahern 1976; Gould-Martin 1976).

Example 3 from my field notes illustrates the union of Chinese and modern ideas in a hybrid popular construction of measles that is widespread among rural and lower-class city people. The belief that measles involves a poison that must come out of the body belongs to the popular system of categories of "hot/ cold," "wet," "poisonous," and others. However, the grandmother's reasoning included the modern observation that measles can be complicated by encephalitis. From the point of view of the modern health profession, the bias against vaccination for measles illustrates a maladaptive aspect of popular medical beliefs. The young mother's uncertainty about what actually caused her child's improvement, along with her belief in the combined efficacy of religious and scientific healing, shows the practical empiricism of the popular culture (cf. Obeyesekere 1976b). The syncretic blend of ideas may seem bizarre and untenable to a physician trained in Western medicine, but laymen are not concerned with their theoretical rigor so much as the treatment options they give rise to. The use of all available treatment interventions is pragmatic. Topley (1970) has shown that indigenous beliefs about measles in Chinese culture include both treatment for the disease and rites of passage for the sick child, who is thought to be passing through a necessary developmental crisis. Once we understand the grandmother's beliefs that measles crisis is inherently dangerous and must receive sacred treatment, that it becomes even more dangerous if there is an intercurrent infection, and that if the latter leads to a high fever, it must be treated with antibiotics to prevent encephalitis, we can appreciate the "logic" of the family's treatment choices, which include both traditional remedies for the developmental crisis and Western medicine for the inter-current infection and its feared consequence. This popular logic is different from scientific medical reasoning in that it integrates modern medical and traditional premises and does not distinguish between their truth value or the treatment options they lead to. Whereas modern medical logic discriminates among differential diagnoses and treatment alternatives so as to yield a single diagnosis with a single treatment, the popular medical logic enumerates all the problems that are most feared and matches each with a specific remedy. Clearly, these are very different ways of reasoning about sickness. As this case illustrates, scientific and popular medical logics not only rationalize distinct treatment approaches, but set out different criteria for evaluating treatment outcome and attributing efficacy to a particular source. For example, whereas natural course of self-limited disease is often viewed by Western health professionals as the reason for loss of symptoms, the popular health care ideology in Taiwan assumes that sicknesses only resolve when treated. The Chinese popular culture's concept of measles makes it likely that *both* shamanistic and modern medical treatments will be viewed as the source of effective treatment and that "natural course of the disorder" will not be considered. The modern medical conception of measles makes the opposite evaluation appear more reasonable.

Example 2 from my field notes illustrates a popular ideological comparison of Chinese and Western medicines. This ideology is widespread in Taiwan among all social classes and ethnic groups. It influences the initial choice of treatment, subsequent change to other treatment, and evaluations of "efficacy." For example, I witnessed several instances in which patients experienced side effects at the time they were taking Chinese medicines but did not complain as they would have done had they been taking Western medicines because the popular ideology asserts that Chinese medicines have no side effects. On the other hand, merely a bad taste from Western medicines often leads Chinese to believe they are experiencing side effects because of the expectations generated by popular ideology. (Conversely, many traditional Chinese medicines have a bad taste, but people do not worry about side effects because of that.) Finally, Example 2 includes a quite negative evaluation of talk therapy (or psychotherapy, when people understood that term) widespread in Chinese society. To be effective any therapy must involve physical ingredients (especially herbs or foods) or active interventions (such as a healing ritual), not simply talking to the patient. This holds for indigenous as well as modern treatment. Chanting Buddhist sutras is viewed as no more effective than psychotherapy, unless accompanied by somatic, interpersonal or ritual interventions. This popular belief runs counter to that found in many cultures where spoken words per se are thought to possess magical efficacy (Tambiah 1968). It stands in striking contrast to the magical powers attributed to written words (charms) in Chinese culture (see Topley 1953). This view has had a major influence on the direction taken by psychiatric care in Taiwan, inasmuch as it devalues psychotherapy and demands that when practiced it must be accompanied by somatic therapies. As a result, psychiatrists in Taiwan have not established psychotherapy as a routinely available treatment option.

Unlike the widely shared beliefs that form a public ideology, idiosyncratic sets of beliefs are also held by individuals and families. Berger et al. (1973) describe them as individual packages of ideas, no two of which are exactly alike, made by assembling components from various systems of belief. These cognitive packages contribute to the pluralism of meaning systems associated with diverse life styles in both industrial and developing societies. Because they are the result of oral tradition, as Goody and Watt (1963) note, they do not receive the kind of critical analysis they would receive if they were formally articulated in written form. Therefore, they frequently contain contradictions, illogicalities, and even mistaken ideas from the popular viewpoint. Nor do these family-based sets of beliefs reflect the complete range of beliefs of the popular health sector; instead, they tend to be highly focused, restricted in range, and particularistic. Thus, to record the full range of beliefs in the popular sector, many informants must be consulted. For example, when I studied conceptions of mental illness among families in Taipei, some of them listed as possible causes ghosts, sorcery, hot/cold imbalance, and *feng-shui* (geomancy), but maintained that other traditional agents such as imbalances of *yin/yang,* bad fate, and sinful behavior did not cause mental illness. Members of these families also might attribute mental illness to heredity, contagion, or psychological and social stress. Families varied greatly and unpredictably in the ways they combined professional, folk, and popular beliefs (similar findings are reported by Lamson 1936; Yap 1967). Surprisingly, 90 percent of the members of 150 families interviewed did not know the medical meaning of *ch'i* (vital essence), one of the most widely used concepts in the traditional Chinese medical classics. As was expected, most families had only the most rudimentary conception of modern psychiatric etiology, yet some knew a great deal about this subject. A metaphor for this situation is the Chinese smorgasboard-like meal (*tien hsin*) where families pick and choose from a very large assortment of individual dishes carried by waiters who circulate among their tables. No two families may end up with exactly the same selection of dishes, and individual family members may differ in the assorted foods on their plates. These patterns are probably more heterogenous in urban than in rural families, but even rural families do not exhibit unified systems of belief. I say this despite the picture of "integrated systems" of beliefs presented by some anthropologists and contrary to the usual Sinological view that belief systems in Chinese culture are organized into a theoretical whole.

This lack of integrated ideas reflects in part variation between localities in Chinese society. It is less powerful a factor today than in the past, when communication between local areas in China was quite difficult and limited. As a result, beliefs and customs remained isolated as a living tradition for people residing in one area, whereas other local beliefs and customs characterized other areas.

Because of the relative isolation of local areas in China, this may have been more true of that society than others. But it cannot be unique. Vestiges of such localism still are found in Taiwan. Even more impressive are the differences between Chinese culture in Taiwan and Hong Kong, differences relating directly to local healing traditions. Thus Hokkien-speaking people from Fukien province in Taiwan have a much more elaborately developed tradition of spirit possession by gods and shamanistic healing practices (which in earlier periods of Chinese history was apparently widely disseminated throughout China) than Cantonese-speaking people in Hong Kong from neighboring Kwangtung province, who hold stronger and more widespread beliefs in *feng-shui* (geomancy) (e.g., compare Potter 1970 and Jordan 1972). In this fashion, classical Chinese medical beliefs must have undergone local transformations, while local popular beliefs may have had some influence on the classical tradition. This process of "localization" (or "particularization," the term used by anthropologists working in India) almost certainly is responsible for peculiar regional integrations of high-order (classical) and folk traditions that affect indigenous healing in many societies (see, for example, Tambiah 1975). This phenomenon is lessened by the mass communication that accompanies modernization.

The beliefs of the Chinese folk healing sector, like those of the popular sector, are heterogeneous and contain what amount to separate disciplines with special systems of belief. Historically, many of these beliefs developed within the Taoist tradition. At present in Taiwan, they function as a congeries of separate beliefs and practices, without an overarching integration. Folk practitioners, like lay people, employ individual (often family-based) integrations including certain beliefs and practices but leaving out others. This mirrors the syncretic folk religious tradition, which, despite a general belief in gods, ghosts, and ancestors (see Jordan 1972), varies by locality, by temple, and by family as to which Taoist, Buddhist, and Confucian elements are united and most salient.

Sivin (1972) cites a medical concept found in both classical and folk belief systems but in greatly altered form. This concept has been transformed in passing from classical Chinese medical texts to the folk religious healing tradition. *Hsieh-ch'i* denotes an invading pathological tendency or agency in abstract, general terms in the Chinese medical classics, while in the sacred folk healing tradition it has come specifically to denote possessing demons that cause sickness. This same process of transformation must have been at work in creating the popular cultural system of medical beliefs out of concepts borrowed and transformed from the folk and professional (Chinese and Western) health sectors.

This pattern of transfer and transformation between the interconnected sectors of health care systems is a special instance of the more general phenomenon of interchange between high-order (classical) and low-order (folk) components of post-traditional cultures. The distinction between high-order and low-order cultural traditions is derided by some anthropologists. As I have already noted, it greatly oversimplifies and distorts the structural organization of healing traditions in Taiwan. Nonetheless, a pluralistic model that discriminates between various interrelated literate and oral traditions and that conceptualizes their separate and integrated uses (both pragmatic and symbolic) in the popular culture is essential for comparative studies of health care systems. In technologically advanced societies, science may have been socially legitimated as the most powerful component in the high-order tradition, but it, as well as other components of that tradition (religious, philosophical, etc.), interacts with a wide array of folk traditions giving rise to a bewilderingly complex popular culture.

Just as in the Chinese example, health care systems in the United States and in the West generally possess the same tripartite division of beliefs. Those beliefs and the cognitive structures undergirding them must be viewed as operating in the tripartite contexts of meaning and social structural arrangements that constitute the social and symbolic reality of health care. It is essential to think of these beliefs as belonging to the sectors and not merely to the individuals occupying them. When the doctor leaves his office and returns home to his family, or when he becomes ill and is a patient rather than a healer, he shifts from a professional to a popular cognitive orientation. At such times, he resorts to the commonsense rationality of the popular sector (albeit with a strong dose of professional opinions) instead of the scientific cognitive structure of the professional sector. That reflects something about his work as a clinician as well: when he talks with his patients, he may leave behind abstract, scientific rationality and make use of his participation in the popular culture in order to apply a functional clinical reasoning to the patient's *illness* and to communicate with him and his family. This functional clinical reasoning also attaches to a social role rather than a person: the healer's mode of reasoning and communicating. As such, it aids him in mediating between the divergent clinical realities socially constructed in the professional and popular sectors.

From what has been said about health care systems in Taiwan and the United States, we can see that individuals are in contact with different belief and normative systems as they move from sector to sector. As they move between distinct clinical realities of health care, they carry with them their own cognitive and value orientations and encounter other cognitive and value frameworks. Contact with another system of meanings and norms may mean simply a shift between conceptual frameworks and behavioral styles the patient himself possesses or has had experience with and can negotiate with. Such would be the situation for the doctor returning from the clinic to his home or becoming the patient of one of his colleagues. Quite commonly, this contact is a more demanding and difficult experience, because it entails conflict between markedly divergent orientations. What is more, it occurs in situations (social interactions involving power differentials) that press upon the patient a particular view of social reality as the one he must accept: the clinical reality socially constructed by the professional or folk sectors of health care. Furthermore, a patient at times may be exposed to different explanations and value statements about his illness at home, among friends, and at work—all in the popular health sector—and again when he encounters the more formal explanations tended him by professional and folk practitioners.

Major discrepancies occur among the explanations patients, families, and practitioners use to understand health problems. Such discrepancies may not be consciously perceived by the participants, since the sectors we act in have provided us with the cognitive and normative rules we use to interpret illness experiences. We are so deeply immersed in these rules that we accept them without conscious reflection. That is why it is so difficult to see clinical reality the way others see it. Such a change requires a major shift in cognitive frameworks, which in turn entails changes in basic values and behavior. As part of our cognitive orientations, beliefs about illness and care are deeply embedded in our tacit systems of "personal knowledge," to which we are strongly committed (cf. Polanyi and Prosch 1976). Because these cognitive frameworks are tacit, problems in care in professional Western medicine arising from discrepancies in cognitive orientations (and their consequently discrepant interpretations of clinical reality) are usually hidden. The negative results—lack of compliance, misuse and abuse of health facilities, and incomplete or inadequate treatment—have great significance for contemporary health care. Because these issues are masked from awareness, they are not dealt with in the course of professional allopathic treatment. These problems, among the most common and difficult in clinical care, are part of the cultural response to sickness mediated by the health care system, like the core clinical tasks. There is nothing paradoxical here. If healing and the construction of adaptive illness experiences are the positive effects of the workings of health care systems, the clinical problems we are talking about represent the negative effects of the structural organization of those same health care systems.

Horton (1967) has suggested, based upon his research in Nigeria, that explanations of sickness in the popular and folk sectors nearly always convey personal and social meaning for the illness experience and treatment. Contrariwise, he argues that explanations given by biomedical practitioners are usually delivered in an impersonal, objective, scientific idiom; they provide technical information but lack personal and social significance. Horton draws attention to a characteristic of Western medicine in an African setting that sets it off entirely from indigenous African healing traditions. He argues that the cognitive and communicative structures of modern professional health care are not comparable with those of folk and popular health care. Horton questions whether modern scientific medicine, so structured as to be oriented toward and effective against biological problems of "disease," for the same structural reasons, is systematically unable to treat the human problems of "illness." Horton's analysis goes to the heart of the controversy surrounding modern clinical care: it has split apart traditionally holistic healing practices, separating social meaning from biological efficacy; it has produced physicians much better than their predecessors in responding to biological problems but worse at psychosocial or cultural ones, physicians distant from and unresponsive to the human problems posed by illness. Modern Western medical care is unprecedented, inasmuch as it has failed to develop a clinical rationality that performs certain of the basic functions of health care systems and that meets needs well handled by traditional patterns of care (Kleinman 1974a).

This is a deeply disturbing thesis. Example 4 is the only example presented thus far that describes the cognitive and communicative interchanges at the core of practitioner-patient relationships; in Chapters 7 and 8 many such illustrations are given. Ironically, Example 4 provides a one-sided explanatory interaction characteristic of modern Western medicine, but in it the practitioner is a sacred folk healer. Studies of these clinical interactions demonstrate that folk healers, too, may fail to convey personal or social meaning to their clients, though this usually does not happen. Professional Chinese-style doctors tend to perform this clinical task much less well than folk healers; perhaps all elite health professionals are socialized to provide technical information rather than meaningful explanations. Indeed, modern psychotherapy comes closer to the latter traditional clinical function than do the clinical practices of a variety of indigenous Chinese practitioners.

In sum, then, the various issues raised by an analysis of the five ethnographic vignettes from the standpoint of the health care system model point to an interpretive problem at the heart of clinical care. This problem appears in two guises, both as a problem *in* actual clinical practice and as a problem *for* the cross-cultural analysis of core clinical activities. Let us examine it at each of these levels.

A short case illustration should make the interpretive problem in day-to-day clinical communication apparent:

Case 1

Mr. Hsu is a 40-year-old, first-generation Chinese-American cook with a history of "spells" consisting of palpitations, dizziness, and sweating of several years duration, worsening over the previous three months. He visited the internal medicine clinic at a large urban hospital, where repeated physical examinations, electrocardiographic studies, treadmill tests, and analyses of blood chemistry disclosed no abnormalities. Mr. Hsu was told by the clinic's doctors that he had no "medical disease" and that his problems were "all in the head." He was referred to that hospital's psychiatry clinic for psychotherapy but did not follow through and dropped out of care. He complained bitterly about undergoing an expensive work-up but not receiving any treatment. He denied having psychological problems and angrily rejected the notion that it was "all in the head." Mr. Hsu reported an alternative belief about his sickness. He thought that he was suffering from a "cold" disorder owing to loss of *yang* (male principle and therefore "hot") from too frequent intercourse with his wife, whom he had married five months earlier and who was 14 years younger than him. He disclosed the fear that either he would not be able to fulfill his wife's sexual needs or his sickness would worsen because of continued diminution of *yang* through loss of *ching* (semen). He had not disclosed this belief to his doctors because he felt they would not understand it and might ridicule him for holding it.

Although the clash occurring in this case between indigenous Chinese and biomedical views of sickness is perhaps starker than more routine conflicts in clinical communication in the West, it is essential to appreciate that such conflicts are ubiquitous in professional health care. Mr. Hsu and his doctors not only held different views of his sickness, but they held conflicting treatment expectations as well. From a psychiatric perspective, Mr. Hsu was suffering from acute bouts of anxiety neurosis precipitated by his recent marriage; from his perspective, his problem was a culturally specific disorder based on indigenous Chinese categories that he knew were not shared by Americans. To the doctors in the internal medicine clinic, he did not have a "real" disorder since they could not demonstrate organic pathology. Their biomedical perspective reified a "mind/body" dichotomy that has been characteristic of Western thought since Descartes but that runs counter to both the psychosomatic perspective of contemporary psychiatry and the somato-psychic viewpoint of traditional Chinese medical thought. Here we find conflicts between different clinical constructions of social reality that negatively influenced treatment, chiefly because they remained tacit.

This illustration demonstrates the need for translating or interpreting different "languages of medicine," i.e., the divergent, and in this case conflicting, lexical and semantic systems operating in the different health care sectors and subsectors. These medical languages constitute and express separate clinical realities, and conflicts between them, as this case reveals, create substantial difficulties for clinical practice. Miscommunication or lack of communication is a frequent obstacle to adequate professional health care, as is further demonstrated by the following case vignette.

Case 2

Mrs. Smith is a 45-year-old Caucasian American housewife with chronic low back pain who has sought out the help of a noted orthopedic surgeon at a university hospital. Her conceptualization of her sickness is that it has a definite relationship to psychological and social stress as well as to physical exertion. She believes it important to understand what is wrong and to participate in planning her course of treatment. She places considerable value on the quality and time spent communicating with her doctors. She was disappointed with the care she received from this orthopedic surgeon, primarily because he spent little time with her, did not offer her a detailed explanation of what was wrong, and told her that all she had to concern herself with was taking the medicines and carrying out the program of rest and graduated exercises he prescribed. Interviews with this doctor revealed that he did not recognize explaining to patients as essential and played down the role of psychosocial stress, which he believed fell outside the purview of surgical treatment.

Mrs. Smith failed to comply with her regimen and soon discontinued care completely. She later consulted a chiropractor, whom she characterized in positive terms as meeting the expectations she had of a care-giver. She reported symptom improvement under his care, whereas she had experienced no such improvement while undergoing treatment from the orthopedist.

In this case, lay and surgical perspectives created divergent clinical expectations, expectations that led to failure to comply and poor care. Again we discover a tacit discrepancy between patient and practitioner that requires, but has not received, *translation* and *interpretation*.

The clinical vignettes suggest that the biomedical model is inadequate as a practical guide to clinical care because it does not conceptualize these common interpretive conflicts in clinical communication and indeed because it is largely responsible for creating them. What obviously is needed on the level of day-to-day patient care is a model that recognizes this central hermeneutic question and that offers a feasible strategy that can be routinely applied in the clinical encounter.

In sketching the applied interpretive problem embedded in clinical communication, its theoretical counterpart in cross-cultural studies of the core clinical functions of health care systems also is illuminated. Here the chief question is *how to compare the systems of medical knowledge and praxis constituted by and expressed in the different sectors of health care systems.*

Resolution of this problem requires a framework that allows the investigator to place various cognitive systems side by side. Juxtaposition permits comparative study of a variety of systems of medical beliefs, from the concepts of scientific medicine through those of other professional medical forms to folk beliefs and "commonsense" popular ideas. For local health care systems in Taiwan, such a framework would compare the categories of Western medicine and traditional Chinese medicine with the functioning systems of beliefs of popular health care and sacred and secular folk medicine. For the United States, we would compare the clinical rationalities of scientific medicine, popular health care, and alternative professional and folk medical traditions, including osteopathy, chiropractic, Christian Science, and the like. In order to get at clinical praxis, however, such a framework would need to go beyond meaning systems, inasmuch as systems of norms and sociopolitical power also constitute and are expressed in clinical communication and other core clinical tasks.

In the next section, I shall describe a model I believe meets these requirements. This approach does not pretend to be a definitive framework for conducting cross-cultural and cross-sector comparisons, but it does address the central hermeneutic problem on both practical and theoretical levels.

EXPLANATORY MODEL FRAMEWORK

I have found it useful to distinguish explicitly the *explanatory models* (EMs) held by individual patients and practitioners and anchored in the separate sectors and subsectors of health care systems (see Kleinman 1975a, 1976, 1977b). Explanatory models are the notions about an episode of sickness and its treatment that are employed by all those engaged in the clinical process. The interaction between the EMs of patients and practitioners is a central component of health care. The study of practitioner EMs tells us something about how practitioners understand and treat sickness. The study of patient and family EMs tells us how they make sense of given episodes of illness, and how they choose and evaluate particular treatments. The study of the interaction between practitioner EMs and patient EMs offers a more precise analysis of problems in clinical communication. Most importantly, investigating EMs in relation to the sectors and subsectors of health care systems discloses one of the chief mechanisms by which cultural and social structural context affects patient-practitioner and other health care relationships.

The field notes at the beginning of this chapter contain observations relevant to differences between explanatory models. They differ in analytic power, level of abstraction, logical articulation, metaphor, and idiom. They are embedded in larger cognitive systems, which in turn are anchored in particular cultural and social structural arrangements, i.e., the health care system's sectors and subsectors. They lead to therapeutic options that are dissimilar (sometimes markedly so) in technological sophistication and actual therapeutic efficacy.

Explanatory models are held by patients and practitioners in all health care systems. They offer explanations of sickness and treatment to guide choices among available therapies and therapists and to cast personal and social meaning on the experience of sickness.

Structurally, we can distinguish five major questions that EMs seek to explain for illness episodes. These are: (1) etiology; (2) time and mode of onset of symptoms; (3) pathophysiology; (4) course of sickness (including both degree of severity and type of sick role—acute, chronic, impaired, etc.); and (5) treatment. EMs differ in the extent to which they attempt to answer some or all of these concerns. Practitioner models (even if they are not transmitted to patients—and frequently they are not) answer most or all of these questions, whereas patient and family models address what are regarded as the most salient concerns. Lay explanatory models disclose the significance of a given health problem for the patient and his family, along with their treatment goals.

Explanatory models need to be distinguished from *general* beliefs about sickness and health care. As we have seen, such general beliefs belong to the health ideology of the different health care sectors and exist independent of and prior to given episodes of sickness. EMs, even though they draw upon these belief systems, are marshalled in response to *particular* illness episodes. They are formed and employed to cope with a specific health problem, and consequently they need to be analyzed in that concrete setting. In practice, laymen either do not volunteer their EMs to health professionals or, when they do, report them as short, single-phrase explanations because they are embarrassed about revealing their beliefs while in formal health care settings. They fear being ridiculed, criticized, or intimidated because their beliefs appear mistaken or nonsensical from the professional medical viewpoint.[4] Patient and family EMs often do not possess single referents but represent se-

---

4. As a result, EMs are much more easily elicited in patient's homes by a researcher who is not involved in the delivery of medical care to the patient and who expresses a genuine, non-judgmental interest in the patient's perspective. Ethnoscientific elicitation procedures are useful to avoid contaminating informant EMs with the researcher's own beliefs (for example, Fabrega 1971; Fabrega and Silver 1973; Metzger and Williams 1963). Not infrequently, patient EMs differ when elicited in clinical setting and at home. The latter usually represent a more accurate and full disclosure of the patient's model. Nonetheless, EMs can be elicited in clinical settings if health professionals are persistent and demonstrate a genuine, non-judgmental interest in patients' beliefs and, what is more, express the conviction to patients that knowledge of their EMs is important to plan an appropriate treatment regimen. In clinical settings, I have found it useful to ask general, open-ended questions about patients' EMs first. If these prove unrevealing, the following questions are helpful in eliciting the details of patient explanatory models:
1. What do you call your problem? What name does it have?
2. What do you think has caused your problem?
3. Why do you think it started when it did?
4. What does your sickness do to you? How does it work?
5. How severe is it? Will it have a short or long course?
6. What do you fear most about your sickness?
7. What are the chief problems your sickness has caused for you?
8. What kind of treatment do you think you should receive? What are the most important results you hope to receive from the treatment?

mantic networks that loosely link a variety of concepts and experiences (Good 1977). For example, in Chapter 4 we discuss
illness terms that are part of popular EMs in Chinese culture
that connect expectations about the symptoms and psychological processes typically associated with particular illness categories, along with beliefs about their cause and significance,
with specific kinds of interpersonal problems and social tensions also held to be typical concomitants or precipitants of
these illnesses. These semantic sickness networks draw upon
beliefs about causality and significance to make available particular treatment options; they enable instrumental and symbolic therapies to be used together without concern about mixing or confusing concepts from very different sources. Within
the semantic networks of the popular health care sector, EMs
interrelate illness beliefs, norms, and experiences and function
as the clinical guides to decisions that we have called "hierarchies of resort" and "structures of relevance" (see Figure 4).
Thus, from the ethnomedical perspective, it is the EM and the
semantic sickness network it constitutes and expresses for a
given sickness episode that socially produce the *natural history
of illness* and assure that it, unlike the *natural history of disease*,
will differ for different health care systems.

To analyze popular EMs into the five categories enumerated
above is to attribute more formal organization and specificity
to them than they usually possess. Vagueness, multiplicity of
meanings, frequent changes, and lack of sharp boundaries between ideas and experiences are characteristic of lay EMs. The
idioms, metaphors, and logics they employ are substantially
different from those of scientific medicine. For example, rather
than the single causal trains of scientific logic, popular EMs
may involve symbolic connections like those of traditional
Chinese medical thought: a logic of symbolic balance and res-
onant harmonies. Even the logical principles of "identity" and
"contradiction," so fundamental to formal reasoning, may be
contravened in popular EMs. Obviously, ethnicity, social class,
and education influence choice of metaphor and idiom (cf.
Apple 1960; Campbell 1975; Elder 1973; Mabry 1964).

The metaphors used to articulate both patient and practitioner EMs disclose substantial cultural patterning. Popular
and professional EMs in the West, for example, are saturated

107

Figure 4
Popular EMs, Semantic Networks, and Health Care Seeking

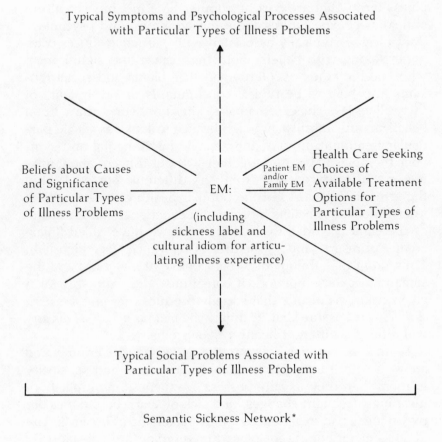

Typical Symptoms and Psychological Processes Associated
with Particular Types of Illness Problems

Beliefs about Causes
and Significance
of Particular Types
of Illness Problems

EM:
(including
sickness label and
cultural idiom for articulating illness experience)

Patient EM
and/or
Family EM

Health Care Seeking
Choices of
Available Treatment
Options for
Particular Types of
Illness Problems

Typical Social Problems Associated with
Particular Types of Illness Problems

Semantic Sickness Network*

*Also referred to in the text as semantic illness networks.

with the metaphors of war: "fighting" infection, "vanquish-
ing" disease, "invaded" by pathogens, immunological "defenses," and so forth. Battle metaphors appear in the Hippocratic
Corpus and can be traced through the Gallenic tradition to the
present. They are by no means universal, however. The imagery of the body as a machine and the related mechanistic
version of sickness also are indigenous to the West, at least
since the Enlightenment. Taiwanese popular EMs frequently

employ the metaphor of persons being "hit" (*ch'ung, chhiong-tioh*) by ghosts, either purposefully or inadvertently, and thereby becoming ill.

Practitioners present their EMs to investigators more freely than do laymen. The ease with which they are elicited reflects the practitioner's role as the purveyor of expert knowledge, as well as his tendency to dominate clinical interactions with laymen. Models elicited by researchers from practitioners, in my experience, tend to be considerably different from those actually transmitted to patients or used to make day-to-day clinical judgments. Thus we can divide practitioner EMs into theoretical and clinical types. The latter must be inferred from observing practitioners in practice and by systematically recording what they communicate to patients. This point requires emphasis: most anthropological research on practitioners has relied on what the practitioner *tells* the researcher about a type of illness or a particular patient's disorder. This is not an adequate determination of functioning clinical rationality. Much that has been written about practitioners, especially folk practitioners, is distorted by this error or because investigators who observed practitioners at work inferred their reasoning without systematic inquiry. Even less research of this kind has been carried out with practitioners in the West than is available in the cross-cultural literature.

An explanatory model is partly conscious and partly outside of awareness. It is based on a cognitive system that directs reasoning along certain lines. Since EMs involve tacit knowledge, they are not coherent and unambiguous. In responding to an illness episode, individuals strain to integrate views in part idiosyncratic and in part acquired from the health ideology of the popular culture. Hence, it is characteristic of EMs that they undergo change fairly frequently. Popular EMs often use symbols whose referents the individual may not be aware of and whose treatment options he may not fully understand. The "diffused" nature of popular medical knowledge contrasts to the "institutionalized" nature of professional and specialized folk medical knowledge. For this reason popular EMs are rarely invalidated by experience. They are plastic enough to cover a wide range of experiences and imprecise enough not to be refuted by specific happenings (cf. the discussion of Zande divination in Evans-Pritchard 1937). Finally, the degree of commitment to EMs varies among individuals.

Practitioner EMs and popular EMs are alike in many ways. For instance, practitioner EMs are largely tacit. They are not likely to be formulated as testable hypotheses, as official teaching would have us believe. Rather they may be the product of circumstances, impressionistic assessments to which practitioners become committed even in the face of contrary evidence. They are bound up with the practitioner's therapeutic imperative to act and his compelling need to rationalize his actions. The choice of an EM may be no more than ad hoc justification for use of one of a limited number of treatment alternatives or post hoc explanation of why the others were not tried. Consequently, the "clinical EMs" applied by practitioners need to be distinguished from "scientific EMs," which, in particular instances, they may closely approximate or diverge from greatly and might be regarded as a special type of the "commonsense" rationality found in the popular culture. In Chapters 7, 8, and 9, I will contend that the fact that practitioner EMs and patient EMs draw on the same popular rationality contributes importantly to the therapeutic process, and I will present data to illustrate how the EMs employed by clinicians frequently must diverge considerably from biomedical and other "professional" theories if they are to be practically effective. Intuitively, of course, this could also be regarded as a potential source of untoward effects and iatrogenic problems.

Explanatory models determine what is considered relevant clinical evidence and how that evidence is organized and interpreted to rationalize specific treatment approaches. Hence explanatory models are the main vehicle for the clinical construction of reality; they reveal the cultural specificity and historicity of socially produced clinical reality, regardless of whether it is based upon scientific medical knowledge. Rosen (1975) has shown, for example, how "nostalgia," which was one of the most common "psychiatric" diagnoses during the American Civil War, disappeared by the beginning of the twentieth century, when it was replaced by newer concepts (e.g., "neurocirculatory asthenia," "shell shock," "battle fatigue," etc.) to describe similar problems in the two world wars, problems in part altered in clinical presentation as well as interpretation by the norms and meanings these sickness categories expressed. Wartofsky (1974) has demonstrated how biomedicine's understanding of diabetes changed over the past few decades and may have constituted clinical data in keeping with the theories prevailing at a given time. The now well-known story of how Charcot's patients with "la grande hystérie" imitated the "classical" signs and symptoms of that disorder, which he had come to expect of them and which he regularly "elicited" from them, further indicates how EMs may come to create the behaviors they seek to explain (Eisenberg 1977).

Taking as our starting point the special form health care relationships have taken in the West and in modern professional medicine elsewhere, we can conceptualize the patient-doctor relationship as a transaction between EM_p (patient explanatory model) and EM_d (doctor's or practitioner's model) (see Figure 5). Pilot studies document that follow-up of such clinical transactions yields four types of *outcomes*: $EM_p + EM_d$, both the original patient model and the medical model together are held by the patient; $EM_p > EM_d$, there is systematic distortion, usually in favor of the patient's original model; EM_p or EM_d, either the original patient model or the medical model is held alone by the patient; and EM_n, a totally new model is reported by the patient, usually based on a new source of information (Kleinman 1975a). Patient explanations not infrequently can be distinguished from family explanations (EM_f), with which they may be divergent and even in conflict. The "dyadic relationship" is decidedly a special case in cross-cultural perspective, as we shall see in Chapters 7 and 8. But analysis of clinical dyads will provide us with a self-conscious instrument for looking at the ways that other health care relationships vary.

The explanatory model outcomes are the result of a transactional process that in theory might be likened to Nida's (1974) paradigm for translation between two languages, though in practice, as we have seen, actual translation rarely takes place. There is in principle a process of elicitation, followed by processes of analysis, transfer, restructuring (in the new language or EM), and feedback. Elicitation is the process by which patient or practitioner may obtain the other's EM through questioning. In clinical transactions, practitioners commonly do not elicit the patient EM but spontaneously transmit at least part

Figure 5

Dynamics of Interactions between Explanatory Models
in Practitioner-Patient Relationships

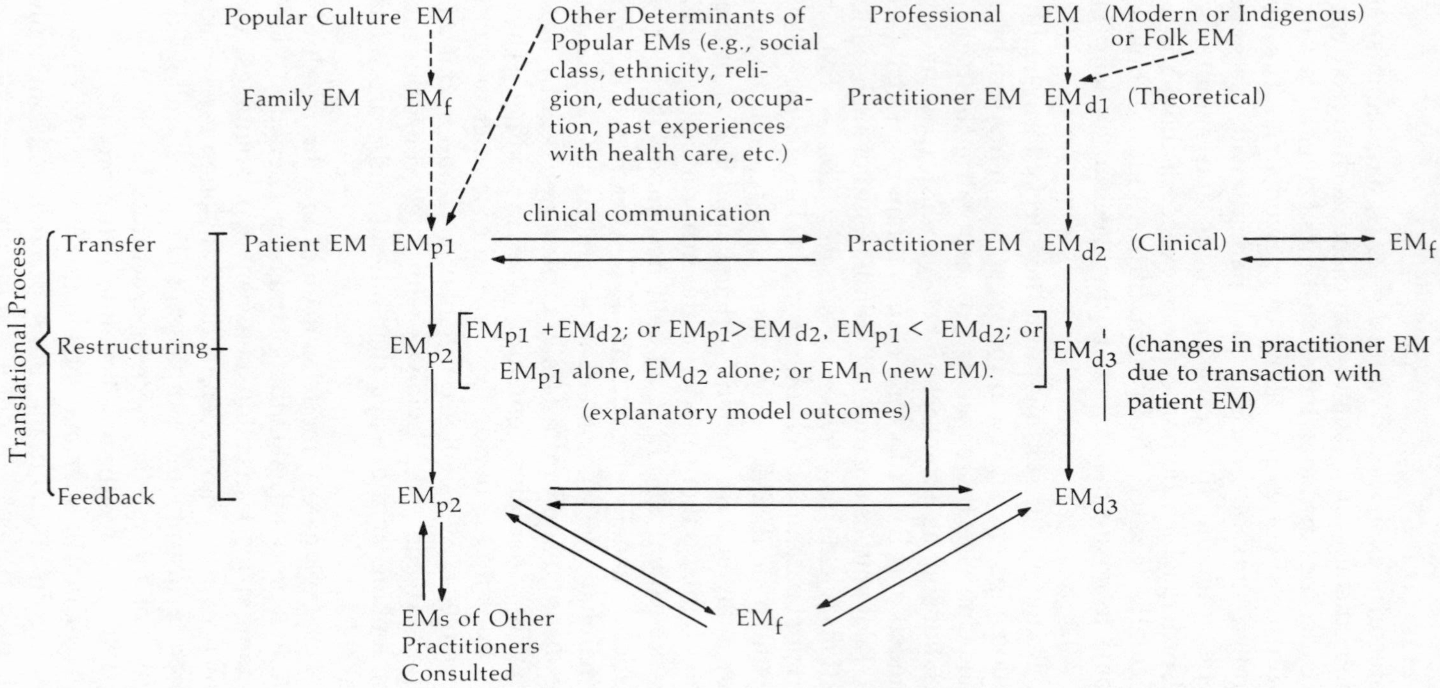

of their EM. While patients frequently do not spontaneously disclose their own EMs, they may elicit the practitioner EM. Analysis is the process by which one EM is analyzed in terms of the other. Transfer means that the analyzed EM is transferred into the other EM, which as a consequence is restructured. The restructured EM feeds back potentially to influence the EMs of other actors. Unquestionably, in our own and in other societies, practitioner EMs also change in response to patient EMs, but we know virtually nothing about that process.

By eliciting the patient EM before the doctor and patient interact with each other and then comparing that EM (EM_{p1}) with the EM the doctor transmits to the patient (EM_{d2}) for the five major questions they may concern, we can estimate the initial cognitive distance between them (Distance A = $|EM_{p1} - EM_{d2}|$) (see Figure 5). Similarly, the cognitive distance following patient-doctor interactions can be calculated by comparing the model the doctor communicates to the patient (EM_{d2}) with the model the patient holds subsequent to the interaction (EM_{p2}) (Distance B = $|EM_{d2} - EM_{p2}|$). Distance B is a rough measure of the communication between practitioner and patient. Distance A compared to Distance B will reveal the "efficacy" of clinical communication insofar as the degree to which the discrepancies are reduced or enhanced is a function of clinical communication.[5] Another measure is Distance C between the practitioner's theoretical model (EM_{d1}) and the model (EM_{d2})

5. If for each of the five major issues they cover, EM_p and EM_d are scored "0" if they agree, "1" if they reveal a minor discrepancy, and "2" if they show a major discrepancy, a range of scores can be worked out for each comparison in which models that are maximally alike are scored "0," while those that are maximally discrepant are scored "10." For example, if the patient's EM holds that being "hit" (ch'ung) by a ghost is the etiology of his problem, while his internist's EM holds that an infection has caused his problem, these EMs are maximally discordant for etiology and would be scored "2." Whereas if EM_p implicates a viral etiology, while EM_d articulates a bacterial etiology, then these EMs disclose only a minor discrepancy for etiology and would be scored "1." The remaining four items would be scored in the same fashion, and the sum of the scores for all five items would yield a total score for the distance separating the EMs. Using this system, we can apply a rough quantitation to the analysis of EM interactions. A 5-point scale would yield a more discriminating analysis, as would the "semantic differential" if it were applied to measure cognitive distances between EMs.

actually transmitted to patients in the clinical encounter. This distance is an indicator of the clinician's ability to translate from an esoteric theoretical idiom to an idiom accessible to laymen. Change in EM_{d2} subsequent to the clinical transaction in principle also could be measured.

Distances A, B, and C are potentially important variables that deserve to be examined in future research. For example, they might be examined as predictor variables to see if they correlate with such outcome variables as patient compliance, satisfaction, subsequent use of health facilities, treatment response, and reporting of medication side-effects or other untoward effects of treatment. The kinds of hypotheses one might test using these measures are:

1. Health care outcomes (compliance, satisfaction, etc.) are directly related to the degree of cognitive disparity between patient and practitioner EMs and to the effectiveness of clinical communication. That is, where Distance A is large (and Distance B remains large), we predict poorer health care outcomes than where either Distance A is small or Distance A is large but Distance B is significantly smaller.

2. Folk practice in any given society, as compared with professional practice, involves fewer social and cultural differences between the healer and the patient, so that Distances A and B also are smaller and health care outcomes are better. Similarly, greater degrees of cultural heterogeneity will increase Distances A and B, and, therefore, worse health care outcomes should occur between matched patients from societies with high compared to low degrees of heterogeneity.

3. Where Distance C is large but Distance A is small (i.e., where the clinical explanation given the patient is not isomorphic with the practitioner's theoretical EM but is closer to popular explanations), the measures of explanatory effectiveness and health care outcomes will be better. The results of our tests for this and the other hypotheses are not yet in, but there is encouraging early evidence that simply attending to clinical communication and eliciting the patient perspective leads to

improved outcome in professional health care (cf. Inui et al. 1976; Lazare et al. 1975).

Walsh McDermott (1977) has recently argued that we do not yet possess adequate measures of either the supportive or the technological aspects of the physician's work. The EM framework suggests that there are now ways to evaluate the quality and success of at least one clinical task: communication with patients. It may prove interesting to apply this framework or some variant of it to analyze clinical communication and to compare it for different categories of practitioners and patients. Would this approach help to evaluate clinical skills acquired in medical school and postgraduate training? Might it even prove of use in assessing the clinical skills of practicing physicians and in assuring quality of care along this axis? These questions suggest that the EM framework needs to be studied in field trials.

Some illustrations drawing upon the ethnographic examples presented earlier in the chapter may clarify what explanatory models are and the functions they serve.

EMs for *ut siong* are assembled from translations and transformations of disease concepts from both Western and Chinese medicine to form, as we have seen, an illness category specific to Taiwan's popular culture. As in the case with popular health sector EMs generally, they may show considerable variation. For example, one patient who labels himself as suffering from *ut siong* might include in his explanatory model the psychophysiological complaints attributed to this disorder. A second patient might leave these out so that his EM would be limited to respiratory symptoms. As a result, these EMs for the same illness category would differ significantly with respect to pathophysiology, course of sickness, and treatment expectations. The differences could lead to different patterns of utilizing available services. The first patient might consult a sacred folk healer for treatment of the psychophysiological problems, even if he visited a Chinese-style physician for definitive therapy for *ut siong*. The second patient might consult a Western-style doctor for control of the respiratory problems, regardless of whether he, too, visited a Chinese-style physician. Similarly, the EMs

115

would almost certainly yield divergent criteria for evaluating treatment outcome. For the first patient, effective treatment would mean control of both psychophysiological and respiratory problems, whereas for the second patient, effective treatment would mean simply control of respiratory problems. Neither patient might claim to experience all the problems he associated with *ut siong*, even though he was committed to the belief that they *should* be present.

Both of these patients would be likely to receive legitimation of a sick role for *ut siong* from their family and friends. If they used a label (e.g., asthma or psychophysiological reaction) from modern psychiatry, they might not be granted an appropriate sick role. Moreover, family and patient EMs might attribute different etiologies to *ut siong*. The patient might attribute the cause to working too hard or insufficient exercise (secular etiologies), whereas the family might contend the cause was bad fate or a ghost (sacred etiologies). These attributions could result in conflict over choice of treatment. The patient would favor physical exercise and a decrease in or change of work. The family would call for recourse to a folk practitioner to change the sick person's fate or to drive away the ghost. Both models would also use different criteria for evaluating the treatment.

When a Taiwanese patient holding an EM of *ut siong* consults a Western-style doctor, it is unlikely the doctor will be aware of the patient's EM. The doctor will label the problem depression, or asthma, or adolescent adjustment reaction, or "functional complaints," or tuberculosis. The medical EM will lead the doctor to interpret the patient's symptoms and history in a different way, and it will suggest a particular treatment regimen, e.g., antibiotics, antidepressants, or supportive psychotherapy. These treatments will not make sense from the perspective of the patient though he might accept them, at least initially. If the doctor transmits part of his EM to the patient (most probably he will not explain anything), he may help the patient understand the treatment regimen. But the doctor's EM may be so different from the patient's that the patient will misinterpret it. The doctor almost certainly will fail to treat problems that are part of the patient's EM, but not the medical EM. For example, the patient might believe that there was an imbalance of "hot/cold" constituents of the body with a pathological excess of "cold" that required "hot" remedies. This would be nonsense from the perspective of the doctor's model. But failure of the doctor to recognize and treat his problem would lead the patient to seek treatment from another source or reject the doctor's treatment. The latter would be especially likely if the doctor suggested the medicine he prescribed be taken with "cold" fluids, a recommendation that would appear dangerous from the patient's standpoint.

Lack of understanding of popular EMs renders Western-style doctors in Taiwan unable to recognize and respond therapeutically to typical social tensions that are associated with culture-specific sickness categories. Thus, the family's EM in the case of measles that we reviewed earlier included the notion that the patient was experiencing a special crisis which required a particular psychosocial intervention in addition to the biomedical intervention. This knowledge was not available to the Western-style doctor they consulted, and if it had been available, it is likely it would have been considered irrelevant from the perspective of his biomedical model. Thus, the family was pressed to rationalize the patient's treatment by drawing upon different treatment systems (Western medicine and sacred Taiwanese folk healing) to fulfill the requirements of their composite EM. Alternatively, it could be argued that a doctor with culturally relevant knowledge could integrate psychosocial and technological treatments—an issue we will explore further in later chapters. Figure 4 outlines how popular EMs link psychosocial and technological treatments to sickness beliefs, to culture-specific symptom patterns, and to social tensions that cannot be adequately conceptualized and treated by doctors operating with biomedical EMs.

What we have said about EMs suggests that it is reasonable to apply to them Shapin's (1977) caveat about the function of natural knowledge:

> But people are not trapped by the natural knowledge of their society. They adopt it, shape it, modify it as suits their interests. They use natural knowledge as a tool, and one of the most important tools, in processes of social suasion. In so far as that special species of natural knowledge called 'science' is concerned, it will, in general terms, be accorded credibility to the

extent that it furthers both technical and social interests. But the two interests always bear upon all bodies of natural knowledge.

Summing up, the EM model describes the dynamics of cognitive and communicative transactions in health care (see Figure 5). Also, it provides a means of comparing these transactions in traditional and modern medical settings, and of evaluating their efficacy. I will draw upon this model of the clinical process throughout the book.

4

The Cultural Construction of Illness Experience and Behavior, 1:
Affects and Symptoms in Chinese Culture

The purpose of this chapter, and of the next, is to analyze several common pathways down which cultural beliefs and norms channel illness experiences and patient roles. We will examine cultural influences on cognition, affect, psychophysiological processes, behavior, and social role, and we will study the psychocultural mechanisms that mediate these influences. To accomplish this end, I will discuss a particular instance of culturally constituted illness experience and sick role in Taiwan: the somatization of dysphoric affects and affective disorders. Our concern is to derive an appreciation of the cultural construction of illness in Chinese culture that can be extrapolated to other illnesses and cultures.

The reader is cautioned that after presenting the case material we will make a brief detour through several psychocultural themes in Chinese culture that are prerequisites for our discussion of the cultural patterning of depression and other dysphoric affective conditions. By restricting this analysis I will not consider other ways in which culture affects sickness, such as its frequently important influence on epidemiological determinants of disease.

I present the following case to illustrate somatization and through it introduce the cultural construction of illness experience discussed in this chapter and the next and recapitulate the cultural organization of clinical transactions conceptualized in the preceding chapter. Somatization demonstrates the vital semantic links between illness and treatment aspects of cultural therapeutic systems. The analysis of the case reveals the utility of the concepts I have introduced to interpret health care systems, their plural clinical reality, and core clinical tasks. It also shows that explanatory models are as central to our appreciation of how illness is culturally constituted as they are to our understanding of the workings of health care. Thus, we can observe the same cultural mechanism at work in the somatizing of psychological distress as illness behavior and in the way it is clinically explained and managed. Analyzing this dynamic activity of cultural construction enables us to build upon our discussion of semantic illness networks and health care systems. Explanatory model transactions point up the cognitive basis of illness experiences just as their analysis discloses the cognitive operations at the heart of clinical practice. It is this cognitive structure that demonstrates most clearly the relationships between patients and healers, illness and healing, and their cultural context.

Our model forces us: (1) to juxtapose the healers' perspectives with those of the patient and family, (2) to relate these divergent perspectives to their concrete cultural and interactional settings, and (3) to assess the sickness episode and the treatment from the various actors' viewpoints. Because I wish to emphasize the interpretive·problem created by these divergent perspectives, I have organized the case presentation almost entirely around the different explanations, leaving out data about other aspects of the illness and its treatment. Ideally, this case should be presented as a congeries of the different perspectives of the patient, his family, and the practitioners who were consulted, in which we present the actual words of each actor and describe the therapeutic interactions as they really happened. Unfortunately, I was not able to interview the Chinese-style and Western-style doctors whom this patient initially consulted. Although this account falls short of the ideal, it gives a sense of how a case can be discussed from a broad health care system viewpoint. The upshot is that we see that the ethnomedical researcher needs to apply an "emic" analysis to both indigenous and biomedical EMs, since both are cultural constructs. The concepts we have discussed provide him with an "etic" framework in which EMs can be compared so that universal and culture-specific aspects of the clinical process can be discerned.

Case 3

Setting and Tâng-ki's EM

We are in the dark, hot, almost airless shrine of a middle-aged Taoist adept, who also is a *tâng-ki* of some fame in Lukang, a large market town on the west coast of Taiwan that was one of Taiwan's largest towns in the Ch'ing Dynasty and that is popularly regarded as a center of traditional Taiwanese culture. The shrine's chief god is Ong-ia-kong, the plague god (see Gould-Martin 1976).

An elderly lady enters and is greeted by the *tâng-ki*, who tells us that she has come several times before with her son for treatment. The son remains outside the shrine, forcing the mother to go out and order him to enter, which he does with obvious embarrassment. The son, who is 22 years old, is thin, well-groomed, fine-featured, shy, and very anxious.

Quickly and without much ado, the *tâng-ki* enters a trance (he is reputedly possessed by the chief god of the shrine). In an undramatic manner he begins chanting in a falsetto, mimicking the formal delivery of characters in Taiwanese folk opera. He directs his remarks (believed to be the words of the god within him) entirely to the mother, paying no attention whatsoever to the son. He tells the mother that he knows the cause of her son's illness. Her son is being attacked by the ghost of a girl who died unmarried and who is pursuing her son and causing his problem. The *tâng-ki* does not name the problem. He advises the mother to make use of some charms he has given her and to burn a large amount of spirit money. He performs no rituals but does listen to the mother's account of the most recent aspects of her son's case and answers a few questions she asks. Then he rapidly comes out of his trance; he gets up and leaves the shrine saying that he has some business to attend to elsewhere. The mother looks quite disappointed (she apparently had other questions to ask), but the son, who stared at the floor in an embarrassed fashion for most of the séance, smiles and looks relieved.

Mother's EM

The entire transaction took approximately ten minutes, of which the *tâng-ki*'s explanation made up less than two minutes.

121

The mother, speaking to people in the shrine in general, recounts her son's problems in a deeply troubled voice. She says his illness began at age seven, after he was hit on the head with a hammer by an older brother. Since then he has complained of poor memory and difficulty concentrating. He did badly in school and dropped out of middle school before graduation. In more recent years, he has suffered from recurrent bleeding gastric ulcers and other problems: dreaming too much and frequent nocturnal emissions. The last she blames as the real cause of his present condition, since the semen loss causes him to lose *yang* (male principle) and thus produces weakness, fatigue, and lack of energy. The mother reveals her annoyance at: (1) other practitioners of various types whom she and her son have consulted, none of whom has effected a cure; (2) her son, who seems never to get better, but rather goes from one health problem to another; and (3) the *tâng-ki*. She accuses that practitioner (who has already departed, but whose family members remain to hear her complaints) of not recommending the obvious solution if indeed the problem is what he says it is: a "spirit marriage" between her son and the girl's ghost haunting him. She angrily suggests perhaps the *tâng-ki*'s desire is to make as much money as he can by having them return for frequent consultations without completing the treatment.

Patient's EM

The patient tells us that recently he has suffered from stiffness and tenseness in his neck along with insomnia and inability to concentrate at work. He feels weak and remains quite troubled by his chronic ulcer problem. He admits to feeling anxious. He tells us under my direct questioning, he is under great pressure at work, where he is a foreman and has the responsibility both to perform and supervise complicated technical work. He adds that he has few friends, no girl friends, feels very shy, and has neither hobbies nor other interests which give him enjoyment. (When he mentions girl friends he blushes and looks away from us, staring at the floor, much as he did when his mother reported his nocturnal emissions and during most of the *tâng-ki*'s séance.) He also states there are other things bothering him, but he cannot tell us about them at present. The patient reports contact with numerous Western-style doctors and one Chinese-style doctor for his health problems. The former have treated him with many different kinds of medication, including "pep" pills. None of these have worked. Nor did the Chinese-style doctor's medications cure his symptoms. And the patent med-

122

icine, herbs, and tonics his family has given him have been similarly ineffective. He and his mother show considerable interest in my being a psychiatrist. They ask me what I think is wrong and what I would advise them to do.

Practitioner EMs

The Western-style doctors the patient and his mother consulted told them he was suffering from "neurasthenia" (*shen-ching shuai-jo*), which they understood to signify a physical illness, but otherwise did not know much about. The Chinese-style doctor told them the problem was a "broken kidney" (they seem to mean "kidney weakness" or "kidney deficiency" since those are the terms used by Chinese-style doctors and found in the classical medical texts). They also took that to mean a physical disorder, one producing weakness as well as the other complaints the patient suffered from. Since no medicine had helped him, the patient remained uncertain about these diagnoses, as did his mother. But he let us know he felt even more uncertain about the *tâng-ki*'s explanation, which he came to hear because his mother demanded he come and also because he had failed to get well and remained quite concerned about whether he ever would improve. Therefore, he was willing to try anything.

I was able to carry out a limited mental status examination. It revealed normal orientation, attention, memory, and cognition; no delusions or hallucinations or other signs of psychosis; and considerable anxiety. The patient denied depressive feelings and also denied loss of appetite, weight loss, or any other of the biological concomitants of depression, other than the insomnia he had reported. The patient noted his symptoms were much worse when he was under stress at work. He refused to talk about what else troubled him, but he let me know he would talk about other problems if we could meet privately at a later time. (All the above had occurred in "public" in the *tâng-ki*'s shrine, just as most clinical care in Taiwan takes place in more or less "public" settings, lacking the privacy basic to professional care in the West (see Chapter 7). Because of this, I referred him to a Taiwanese psychiatrist for a full psychiatric evaluation.

My own psychiatric formulation of this case ran as follows: a late adolescent, unmarried male with a chronic anxiety neurosis associated with both acute anxiety reactions provoked by psychosocial stress and a variety of psychophysiological symptoms (somatization and psychosomatic peptic ulcer disease). The latter worsened whenever he suffered an acute exacerbation

of his primary psychological problem. However, I felt this evaluation to be inadequate because of the limited information I had
been able to elicit; I expected the evaluation of the Taiwanese
psychiatrist to produce considerably more information, especially since the patient appeared to want to talk privately about
his problems.

That psychiatrist learned from the patient that he engaged in
frequent masturbation, which troubled him greatly because of
his fear that he was losing seminal essence (*ching*) representing
irreplaceable *ch'i* (vital essence) and *yang*. He believed that the
masturbation was dangerous to his health and was the cause of
his problems. This made him feel guilty and frustrated because
he felt himself unable to stop masturbating and consequently
felt condemned to suffer the various symptoms he had, which
he was in fact "causing." This psychiatrist diagnosed a sexual
neurosis, a problem that in his experience is common among
young males in Taiwan. He explained this to the patient along
with informing him about normal psychosexual development
and also told him that his problem was a psychological one that
only secondarily produced somatic complaints; those would
disappear after the psychological problem was cured. He recommended tranquilizers and psychotherapy. Although the patient filled the prescription for tranquilizers, he did not return
to see the psychiatrist.

Here, then, are different perspectives on the same case. They
are not the only ones. Fortune-tellers and *ch'ien* interpreters and
a physiognomist all had been consulted, as had several pharmacists, but I did not obtain the details of their explanations.

When he returned to his shrine, the *tâng-ki* was not pleased
to find me interviewing his client and was patently disturbed
by the referral to a psychiatric colleague. Before we departed
and after the patient and his mother had left, he told us that
even if the patient suffered from neurasthenia he would not get
well until the ghost (*kuei*) was properly taken care of, since that
supernatural influence would neutralize any medicine the patient took and counteract the effect of the doctors who treated
him by exerting a negative influence on their fates.

DISCUSSION OF CASE 3

The first question to be considered is the nature of this patient's disorder. Everyone agreed that a disorder was present
and that it was a physical sickness, but their explanatory models

differed. The patient had no difficulty obtaining consent to take a sick role, but until I consulted him, his psychological symptoms were not considered a separate entity, and no one had suggested an illness that required psychiatric care. The patient and his mother were willing to consider psychiatric treatment because they had failed to secure effective therapy by other means and because I was a prestigious and possibly powerful foreigner.

In Chinese culture, tremendous stigma attaches to mental illness. The concept is employed only to cover psychotic behavior and mental retardation. Minor psychiatric problems frequently are given a medical sick role by the popular culture and by the other health care sectors, including Western and indigenous health professionals. The patient received support and active care, much of it indisputably psychotherapeutic, though directed toward his physical complaints. He obtained release from the obligation to work, the right to stay at home, to be passive, and to seek help from family members, and the legitimation of failure in examinations, work, and interpersonal transactions. As in the Parsonian sick role, he was expected to seek treatment, but not necessarily by professionals. In Taiwan, it is unusual for others to question the patient's right to occupy the sick role.[1] The role frequently is a legitimated mechanism for managing personal and interpersonal problems.

The sick role was redefined as the patient moved out of the family and into the other sectors of the health care system. He moved to a patient role in professional Chinese and Western medical settings, then to a client role in the _tâng-ki_'s shrine, and eventually to a psychiatric sick role, which he quickly jettisoned. Each of these roles involved different expectations and behaviors. As a psychiatric patient, he talked about psychosexual concerns that he would not talk about in his family or in any other patient role. As a client in the shaman's shrine, he engaged in rituals and expected to take part in other healing ceremonies, perhaps including exorcism and a spirit marriage. As the patient of a Chinese-style doctor, he expected and re-

1. My impression is that among Chinese generally the sick role is much more quickly and easily sanctioned than among Americans (cf. Twaddle 1974). Such an impression could be tested in comparative cross-cultural research; I am not aware of any studies to date on this subject.

ceived a physical diagnosis that led to treatment for "kidney weakness," which included herbal medicine and regulation of his diet to treat the "cold" imbalance by eating "hot" foods, avoiding "cold" foods, and taking tonics. He was expected to manage this treatment with the help of his family. In the offices of Western-style doctors he was told that he suffered from neurasthenia. He had expected and received Western medicines, especially by injection. He and his mother still considered themselves to be principally responsible for his care, but they also anticipated that Western-style doctors would be more assertive than their Chinese-style colleagues.

The sick role is not the disorder, but until it is described, we cannot analyze the sickness in terms of disease/illness. This case illuminates the distance between ideal and actual roles. The patient's mother was angered and embarrassed by her son's performance in the shrine. She also was critical of the shaman's performance. And both she and her son exhibited varying degrees of commitment to the different EMs attached to the roles they occupied. In the shrine the mother occupied the prime client role and received the chief attention of the shaman. In the Chinese-style doctor's office and in the Western-style doctors' practices, this situation was reversed. In the psychiatric clinic the mother did not appear at all. That is, in the shaman's shrine the sickness was treated to include the mother, whereas in the psychiatrist's office it was narrowed to exclude all but the patient himself.

Within the boundaries of an agreed-to physical sickness, the patient, his mother, and the practitioners they consulted took different positions on the nature of the disorder. The patient's mother held that semen loss, owing to frequent nocturnal emissions, was the cause of her son's complaints. She felt that loss of *yang* upset the balance between *yin/yang*. But she related this *proximal* cause to two *distal* causes: (1) a supernatural cause, the ghost disturbing her son and (2) a childhood cause (he was hit on the head with a hammer at age seven by his older brother). She combined both causes in her EM, conforming to the tendency of Chinese to see "gods, ghosts, and ancestors" as part of the "natural" world. Included in her concept of the sickness were her son's poor memory, difficulty in concentrating, and poor school performance in childhood; gastric ulcers; frequent dreams and nocturnal emissions; semen loss and loss of *yang*; and his current symptoms of weakness, fatigue, and lack of energy, as well as inability to get better even with recourse to a number of different practitioners. This woman presented the whole as if all the parts fit together logically. The mother's ideas about cause related directly to specific treatment interventions. That is, her EM functioned to open up behavioral options. She helped her son obtain access to virtually all of the available interventions. This series of actions was an entirely pragmatic hunt for a treatment implicated by her model that would remove her son's complaints. Frustrated by repeated failure, she was even willing to entertain psychiatric treatment, with the stigma surrounding it.

The childhood event in her EM supported her claim that this son differed from his siblings, and explained why he had suffered repeated problems in school and social relationships. Like the supernatural element, it attributed responsibility for the problem to something other than herself or her son.

Her son did not express his ideas fully in the presence of his mother. He did not hold to either the childhood or supernatural causal notions but utilized other components in his explanatory model. He believed he had a physical disorder, neurasthenia, caused by masturbation. He lumped his anxiety together with these other problems. He viewed himself as the cause of his illness, since he found himself unable to cease masturbating, and regarded that as the shameful and real cause of his physical sickness. While noting stress at work, recurrent anxiety, and interpersonal problems, at no time did he suggest these were evidence of mental illness. His failure to return to see the psychiatrist strongly suggested that he rejected a psychiatric illness label. He included psychosexual factors and interpersonal stress in his explanatory model, however, so that it was psychologically more sophisticated than his mother's model.

The Chinese-style doctor applied a classical Chinese medical notion of kidney insufficiency (*shen-k'uei*). This concept often subsumes hormonal and sexual problems (including impotence) as well as weakness and neurasthenia in contemporary clinical usage. But it was reported as "broken kidney," which either was a transform applied by the clinician or, more likely, a distortion on the part of the patient and his mother. Here a functional metaphor in the classical Chinese medical texts (insufficient strength of the kidney in terms of the putative functional interrelationships of the kidney and other internal organs) has become a structural metaphor: the kidney as an independent organ is "broken." (The patient said this pointing to his right flank.) This concept further denotes a symbolically "cold" disorder. But the concept's assocations were not fully appreciated by the patient or his mother.

Under kidney weakness, cold disorders, neurasthenia, and other related terms, Chinese-style doctors label a large variety of sicknesses. Some of these overlap with what Western-style doctors and psychiatrists label as hysteria, anxiety neurosis, depression, psychophysiological problems, hypochondriacal personality, etc. Most of these problems are accompanied by somatic complaints. It is the somatic rather than the psychological complaint that is the focus of diagnostic and therapeutic interest in Chinese-style and in Western-style medical practice in Taiwan. This is the case as well in the popular sector. The Chinese-style doctor may refer to psychological complaints, but does so in terms of a physical disorder with a reputed organic pathophysiology.

Western-style doctors do much the same thing, making use of a concept such as neurasthenia as if it were a physical disorder. Among themselves, Western-style doctors will use terms like depression, anxiety neurosis, hysteria, and mental illness and will describe neurasthenia most frequently as a psychological disorder; but with their patients, neurasthenia generally is used to convey the idea of a physical disorder and the other terms are avoided. Neurasthenia is the single most commonly used label for sanctioning a medical sick role for minor psychiatric and interpersonal problems in Taiwan.

Chin and Chin (1969) point out that this term was picked up with great interest in China before 1949, where it was frequently used as a label of sickness. With the Communist victory in 1949 this label quickly went into disuse. The Communists held that it was a disorder produced by capitalism and a problem characteristic of middle-class intellectuals. This disorder, they further held, was incompatible with socialism, where socially productive labor would prevent intellectuals from succumbing to it. Whatever its vicissitudes were in China over the past several decades, neurasthenia now again is in very wide use and appears to function in the People's Republic in precisely the same way as it does in Taiwan.

Neurasthenia has passed out of the diagnostic manuals of the medical profession in the West. Sir George Pickering, an eminent English physician, notes this term was used in the 1920s when he was a medical student and was defined in Osler's textbook, which he used, in the following way: "A condition of weakness or exhaustion of the nervous system, giving rise to various forms of mental and bodily inefficiency. The term covers an ill-defined, motley group of symptoms, which may be either general and the expression of derangement of the entire system, or local, limited to certain organs; hence the terms cerebral, spinal, cardiac, and gastric neurasthenia." (Pickering 1974: 166.)

Pickering goes on that neurasthenia is now recognized as the manifestations of psychoneurosis. There is much to suggest that early in the century and during the First World War this term was used in England and the United States as it currently is used in Taiwan and the People's Republic of China: to cover minor psychiatric disorders under the more respectable mantle of physical disorder. This usage was probably introduced by Western medical men and medical missionaries in the late nineteenth and early twentieth centuries.[2] The Western-style doctors consulted by our patient and his mother seem to have applied the term in just that sense.

The Chinese term for neurasthenia, *shen-ching shuai-jo,* conveys the same vague idea of organic pathology that the term connotes in English. *Shen-ching* means neurological and *shuai-jo* means weakness (in the classical Chinese medical senses of physical weakness and weakness of the body's processes leading to sickness). The picture is of an ailment involving non-

2. An interesting question for cross-cultural comparisons would be how neurasthenia has been used in other cultural settings and under what circumstances it has played a similar role to that I have described for Chinese culture. The larger issue implicit in that question is how mental illness is evaluated (i.e., whether it is stigmatized or not) in different cultures. A simple comparative analysis of this issue based on recorded ethnographic findings should be feasible for many cultures.

specific signs and symptoms associated with a "weakness" of the nerves and a general "weakness" of the body produced by the weakness of the nerves. In Taiwan, it is common to hear practitioners classify neurasthenia into two chief types: neurasthenia primarily involving the "nerves" or "brain," and "sexual" neurasthenia. The latter includes a wide variety of sexual problems, including impotence, hysteria, and excessive masturbation. Besides these major types of neurasthenia, one less commonly hears about neurasthenia involving the heart.

As Pickering notes, neurasthenia is no longer used as a diagnostic category by physicians and psychiatrists in the West. Instead they use the labels I have used for the diseases most frequently subsumed under neurasthenia. Hence, I and the Taiwanese psychiatrist characterized this case respectively as anxiety neurosis with somatization and sexual neurosis with somatization. I formulated the patient's *disease* as a psychological disorder with physiological manifestations that included peptic ulcer. The *illness* was his experience over the years in trying to cope with this disease. The onset of the disease was probably insidious, beginning in late childhood. The ulcer symptoms were a direct physiological correlate of his disease, and the substitution of nonspecific physical complaints for psychological complaints, i.e., the somatization of the mental disease, expressed the cultural patterning of his illness.

Masturbation was a component of his anxiety neurosis that carried particular cultural significance. The Taiwanese psychiatrist, who obtained more information than I did, thought that the anxiety was secondary to another constellation of psychosexual problems: (1) excessive masturbation associated with feelings of guilt *and* shame; (2) misinformation about normal sexual development, which contributed to the guilt and shame and which in large part resulted from the peculiar way issues concerning sexuality are handled (or more precisely, avoided) in Chinese culture;[3] and (3) a specific "culture-bound" illness (*shen-k'uei*, "kidney deficiency") characterized by the belief

3. The question of how sexuality is handled in Chinese folk culture falls well outside the scope of our concern, but it is directly relevant to understanding Case 3. Hsu's brief analysis (1949, 1971a) of this question relates the discrepancy between utter suppression of public and parent-child talk about sexuality and the presence of (and frequent resort to) brothels, concubinage,

that masturbation produces an irreplaceable loss of *yang* that leads inexorably to a disorder with physical complaints similar to those he was experiencing. The Taiwanese psychiatrist held that this problem occurred fairly frequently among adolescent and young adult males in Taiwan, whom he considered to be suffering from a culturally specific form of sexual neurosis. This is not a diagnostic term in most psychiatric nosologies employed in the West, although symptoms related to masturbation in adolescents are also quite common but labeled in other ways. The term represented this psychiatrist's attempt to place our case with others that exhibited the same features and that seemed to originate in an interplay of biologically based behavioral problems and Chinese cultural problems concerning psychosexual development.

No single, unified modern psychiatric explanation can be applied to this case. Modern psychiatry contains multiple (and at times conflicting) explanatory models (cf. Lazare 1973). A psychoanalytic model will stress the patient's early childhood development as it relates to his unconscious conflicts. A behavioral model will stress the current environmental and psychological contingencies reinforcing the patient's deviant behavior. A social model will place emphasis on the role of stress in this patient's work and family. A psychobiological perspective will underscore neurobiological processes. Each explanation selects different clinical evidence to build an argument, just as I constructed an argument from the various EMs. And each, in turn, will lead to a specific treatment approach, just as the differing patient, family, and practitioner EMs led to

---

and a highly developed erotic tradition in traditional Chinese culture to the situation-oriented structure of that culture. The child learns nothing about psychosexual development in his home or at school and is taught to suppress all outward signs and questions concerning that topic. On the other hand, in adult life with his peers and in married life, sexuality will be handled directly in appropriate settings. Adolescence, then, presents a tremendous problem, as certain of our case illustrations reveal, since masturbation, sexual relationships, and general sexual interest, stimulated in part by hormonally dependent psychosexual development, are faced with total suppression in the context of the family, where such feelings and activities are held to be shameful and are said to lead to loss of vital essence and, potentially, to illness.

different treatments in this case. These explanations will be much more psychologically oriented than those applied by the patient, his mother, and the various non-Western practitioners they consulted. They show the psychological orientation of Western society. That culturally patterned orientation has been transferred in the modernization process to Taiwan, and to the professional sectors of other non-Western societies, where it is usually in striking contrast with indigenous beliefs and values.

The health care system orientation leads me to place different perspectives side by side, my own included. By so doing, I am able to piece together a total picture of this patient's system of care. This approach compels me to move outside of the ethnocentric and medicocentric confines of my role as a psychiatrist. Of course the patient and his mother were quite conscious that they were actors among an array of differing forms of medical knowledge and action; a social scientist may find little that is surprising here. But this perspective creates real problems for practitioners trained to see illness and care only from their professional point of view. One of the chief virtues of ethnomedical and cross-cultural research is that the medical, psychiatric, or public health practitioner finds himself lifted out of his narrow professional orientation and exposed to all the aspects of health care that are frequently hidden from him by the role and social space he occupies in his own culture. That alienation offers him a much needed sensitivity to the larger health care system, as well as to the impact of culture on that system. He sees distinctive semantic illness networks as well as alternative clinical realities with quite different directions for treatment. It remains unclear, however, how the clinician will go about comparing and mediating these different perspectives, though we have set out one method by which the ethnomedical researcher can do this. Indeed, in the case just presented, I remain uncertain how I, as a clinician, can relate the differing points of view to my own professional orientation to derive an appropriate basis for intervening. Nonetheless, the broader framework seems to me to be of potential clinical use; perhaps it provides the only method for unifying treatment, even if it was not applied here in that way.

If we turn back to the Prologue's description of a local health care system in Taipei, we should now find ourselves prepared to see that the separate components described there are related to each other in a unique cultural system. The description in the Prologue did not reveal a "clinical system," since no specific case of illness was described whose trajectory through the system demonstrated the clinical reality composed by the separate parts, but our case shows how a particular illness experience brings various elements of the health care system into an integral structure.

The case also suggests how this cultural system shapes illness both through the categories we employ to label and explain disease and through the influence of those categories on the way we perceive and experience symptoms. I will now examine this meaning-mediated relationship between culture and illness in more depth as it is revealed in the cultural shaping of affects and affective disorders in Taiwan.

CHINESE CULTURAL PATTERNING OF
AFFECTIVE EXPERIENCE AND BEHAVIOR

1. Expression of Affect

I shall describe in this section only those background themes bearing directly on our subject. The review is highly focused, yet I feel that it is also a tentative and incomplete account of Chinese cultural categories and values that affect disease and illness.

During their primary socialization, individuals in Taiwan learn that their own personal affects, especially strong and negative ones, should not be openly expressed (see Hsu 1949, 1971b; Solomon 1971; Tseng and Hsu 1969). They learn that doing so will endanger close interpersonal relationships whose harmonious arrangement is more important to them than their own psychological status. Their well-being, in fact, depends on these finely balanced relationships. Revealing their own feelings might result in shame for themselves and their families. Concomitantly, close interpersonal relationships, not intrapsychic experience, are of primary interest and importance (Hsu 1971b). The family is an entity that existed before one was born and will exist after one is dead. Through the family and ancestor worship, the core of Chinese religion (A. Wolf 1974), people are part of an immortal vehicle. Their place in that vehicle assures their link with past and future, offering them personal and cultural meaning transcending death. Their tenure in the family places upon them privileges and obligations, the chief of which is to improve the family's fortune, while not bringing shame on it. Related to this obligation is another, requiring them to treat their own person and body as if they are as inviolable as the family.

Since neither fully belongs to them alone, injury to the person is in part injury to the family. The family is frequently thought of in Taiwan as a circle whose perfect roundness symbolizes the ideal of harmonious integration of all individual members (Jordan 1972). Children learn that within that circle are the most significant meanings and transactions in their lives, and that how others come to regard and value them determines and is determined by how they regard their families. Achievement is not only for them, but also for the family. Shame falls on them and on their families together. Misfortune, including sickness, affects both.

As Hsu points out (1971b), the chief model for the individual's interactions in society is the father-son dyad. The ancient Confucian relationship is still thriving in Taiwan. That relation is the template for relationships with teachers, supervisors, those older and socially superior as well as those younger and socially inferior. It acts as a model for practitioner-patient relationships. As a cultural metaphor it holds significance for almost all other relationships. It constrains the individual, among other things, from revealing his personal emotions openly. Even more strikingly, it invests intimate relationships with more affective significance than one's own thoughts, fantasies, desires, and emotions. Family and other close interpersonal relations become a person's paramount interest; coping with them becomes a sign of adult competence, and problems with them are more important to him than other personal problems. The worst problems are family problems. Emotions are expected to be appropriate to situation and family setting, and they should be managed in reaction to external events. There should be ongoing reflexive monitoring of how others perceive how one feels and acts, and this information should be used to interpret and modulate one's behavior to respond appropriately to others.

These things are constantly reinforced in the family. As a

young child, for example, the individual must observe *hsiao* (filial piety), *pao* (reciprocity in social relationships), and other virtues. "Face" is as much due to success in maintaining these relationships as success in the larger world (Hsu 1971a, 1971b; Hu 1944; Yang 1957). When personally upset, one is to "endure" disturbed feelings, and not to value them over those of parents and sibs. Excessive expression of emotion, the Chinese child is taught, will upset the harmonious functioning of the body and cause disease. When physical complaints accompany psychological complaints, family members attend only to the former. Indeed, in such situations, the individual learns a much more sophisticated set of terms and beliefs for somatic distress than for psychological distress. And one learns to talk about the latter in terms of the former, just as care for the latter results indirectly from care given to the former. Family members, friends, and teachers do not apply negative terms to physical complaints, as they do to psychological complaints. Physical sickness, not emotional distress, is an excuse for failure in school, sports, work, personal transactions, and sexual relations. Children learn that others will rarely challenge the legitimacy of their physical sicknesses and medical sick roles. But psychological excuses lack social efficacy and at times suggest the stigmatized domain of mental illness.

The Taiwanese individual speaks Hokkien and Chinese, languages rich in terms for bodily states and their dysfunctions, and for interpersonal transactions and their problems, but relatively impoverished in psychological terminology. People learn not to attend to their feelings, and acquire little skill in identifying emotional states. Non-specific names lump together emotions that contemporary Westerners readily differentiate. Moreover, many terms for emotional states (e.g., *mên*, depressed or troubled; *fan-tsao*, anxious or troubled; *kan-huo*, angry; *hsin-ching pu-hao*, generalized, non-specific emotional upset, bad spirits; etc.) express emotion in terms of bodily organs (*mên* and *fan-tsao* contain the heart radical; *hsin* is the word for heart; *kan* is the word for liver). In classical Chinese thought, and even today in Taiwanese popular thought, the heart is regarded as the seat of the emotions and the liver as the bodily agency associated with anger. When people use these terms, they not infrequently point to the chest and to the right upper abdomen. The terms link feeling states and physical symptoms with interpersonal relations and their problems (see Figure 4 in Chapter 3). This semantic network expresses emotion in bodily imagery and constitutes it in bodily experience (cf. Leff 1977, for similar examples from other cultures including traditional Western society).

In interviews and psychotherapy with Taiwanese, I found ideas and feelings were frequently divided into those held to be superficial and public and those held to be deep and private. The former were available upon questioning, and from a contemporary Western perspective, they were shallow, unreflective, unsophisticated, and conventional. The latter, on the other hand, were never shared with anybody, except on special occasions with intimate friends. They were held to be utterly personal and were protected from others. Many informants asserted that these deeply held ideas and feelings were virtually the only privacy they possessed. To ask about or freely talk about such matters was "embarrassing" and "shameful." The cultural norms governing interpersonal transactions protect one from ever having to communicate one's most private inner world, and tend to keep the door to this inner sanctum closed, even to the individual himself. Most patients and informants I pressed about this subject used denial and displacement to block or divert my inquiry. Even after relationships of trust were established, and even in the course of short-term psychotherapy, I found it extremely difficult to elicit personal ideas and feelings—in part because the orientation of most people was outward rather than inward and individuals had remarkably little past experience with self-scrutiny to draw upon. These findings, quite obviously, contrast strikingly with those to be found among most middle-class Caucasian Americans.

Socialization into Chinese culture leads individuals to be preoccupied with the concrete situational context of personal problems, rather than with their experiential effects (Hsu 1949, 1971b). When enmeshed in family, business, or school problems, individuals are oriented to external causes and practical remedies. This fundamental attribute of Chinese cognitive style (Nakamura 1960) conveys personal ideas, values, and feelings *indirectly* through descriptions of situations. Personal comments are added as one observes the listener's response. This is a method for saying what the other agrees with and withholding what the other responds to negatively. Since the listener is also skilled in this process, interpersonal transactions with significant others are characterized by a mandate for mediation, harmony, and consensual agreement. They are not characterized by the direct and full expression of individual points of view. (The commonly observed verbal aggression between strangers in the street or marketplace that marks relationships that are not culturally significant simply discloses the reverse side of the behavioral paradigm.) At times, traditionally oriented Chinese seem to hold personal views completely anchored in the concrete situation at hand, so that each situation gives rise to a "new" view produced by a cautious, indirect disclosure of mutually shared opinion. But at the same time, there is little doubt that quite divergent views are held. In master-disciple relationships, the beliefs of the dominant person are treated as authoritative, and in relations with peers separate opinions that contradict a conventional viewpoint are simply withheld or understated. These traits of Chinese culture are well known to students of that subject. [4]

4. Most, if not all, of what I have discussed in general terms has been recognized and more precisely described by students of Chinese culture and behavior, including those whom I have previously referred to in this and other sections: C.C. Chen, personal communication; Chiang 1952; C.C. Hsu, personal communication; Hwu 1975; Y.H. Ko 1973, and personal communication; Lin 1953; Rin et al. 1966; M. Wolf 1970; Yap 1974. What I have said here holds, I believe, for Chinese generally in Taiwan and other traditional Chinese cultural settings, but it almost certainly requires major modification for Chinese in the People's Republic of China, although I am not sure what kind of modification, and perhaps also for women in Chinese society (M. Wolf 1972; Wolf and Witke 1975). Our description also needs to be modified before it can be applied to Chinese-Americans (cf. Kingston 1977; Sue and Wagner 1973). Even though modernization in Taiwan and other Chinese cultural areas clearly has changed traditional behavioral paradigms, I do not believe those changes have been radical enough to challenge the validity of the general framework. Listing such a series of concise generalizations is bound to make a complex behavioral field appear superficial and one-dimensional. But, at the possible expense of turning an ideal-type characterization into a caricature, these few paragraphs do set out in a very short space what I take to be the abiding symbolic meanings and norms guiding individual behavior in "traditional" Chinese culture.

The pattern I have described is one in which the family inhibits the expression of dysphoric or strong affects; people examine and express only superficial and usually shared ideas and feelings and tie their feelings to concrete interpersonal transactions and situations; individuals are more interested in managing close interpersonal (mostly family) relationships than in delving deeply into their own interior psychological states; people gain more facility in describing interpersonal than psychological problems; and they substitute physical for psychological complaints.

2. Cultural Patterning of Symptoms: the Somatization of Dysphoric Affect

In Taiwan and in other Chinese societies patients rarely complain of anxiety, depression, and other psychological problems. Seventy percent of patients with documented psychological disorders who visited the Psychiatry Clinic at the National Taiwan University Hospital initially complained of physical symptoms (Tseng 1975). The overall incidence of major psychiatric problems in Taiwan, with possible exception for psychoneurotic disorders, seems to be roughly the same as in the United States (Lin 1953; Lin et al. 1969). While Singer (1975) claims that the prevalence of depression amongst Chinese is probably not significantly different than in the West, this impression has not been established with any certainty. What has been determined is that in Taiwan patients with depression do not complain of feeling depressed to psychiatrists, but instead go to internists or general practitioners for treatment of the biological concomitants of depression (insomnia, weight loss, dry mouth, constipation, loss of energy, etc.). In the United States such patients are frequently found in psychiatric clinics complaining of feeling depressed, though some, particularly members of ethnic minorities from lower-class backgrounds with limited education, still are to be found complaining of somatic symptoms in medical clinics. This major discrepancy in the phenomenology of depression in American and Chinese populations (Kleinman 1977a; Tseng 1975; Yap 1965), must be explained by the cultural patterning of this illness. The *illness* is markedly different, but the *disease* would be the same in both populations.

Let us again consider the sickness of the young male Taiwanese patient in the *tâng-ki's* shrine. The disease is a chronic
anxiety neurosis, with actue exacerbations that are stress-
related and associated with psychological and somatic symptoms. American patients would report both the psychological
and the somatic manifestations to the doctor. However, they
would focus on anxiety as the main complaint. Along with this
complaint, they would report other psychological difficulties.
In Taiwan this does not happen very often. Our patient, like
the great majority of Chinese patients, reports physiological
symptoms generated by the high level of anxiety affecting the
autonomic nervous system and the structures it innervates.
The focus is on anxiety-induced symptoms, such as the Taiwanese patient's gastric complaints, as well as insomnia and
fatigue. Other complaints associated with autonomic nervous
system hyperactivity caused by intense anxiety are rapid heart
rate, often with accompanying chest discomfort, hyperventi-
lation, sweating, tremors, diarrhea, and abdominal discomfort,
and a wide variety of other complaints, including amenorrhea
and impotence. Any of these might be reported, and frequently
a number occur together. Non-specific complaints such as
weakness, malaise, loss of appetite and other interests, frequent dreams, and hypo- or hyper-sexual behavior also occur,
as in the case of our Taiwanese patient. When the anxiety state
becomes chronic, for personal and social reasons, a specific
configuration of complaints is patterned (the illness). Personal
experience and physiological status play an important role in
determining which organ system will be affected (Lipowski
1973, 1977). Cultural, along with personal, meanings influence
which kinds of stimuli are perceived as stressful, and those
perceptions in turn provoke anxiety and the somatic symptoms
associated with it. Cultural beliefs and experience help determine which symptoms are most threatening and bothersome.
This is exemplified by the cases we have described involving
Chinese-American and Taiwanese patients who believed they
were suffering from sicknesses due to loss of *yang*. Such psychophysiological syndromes mimic other diseases and often
are not readily diagnosed.

In Taiwan and the United States many patients in general
medical practice suffer from somatic complaints that are due

to psychological problems. Estimates are that up to 50 percent of all patients in general medical practice may fall into this category both in the United States (Stoeckle et al. 1964) and Taiwan (Kleinman 1975b and c). All of the patient's symptoms in Case 3 can be attributed to anxiety and its various physiological manifestations. I have also described Chinese-American patients at the Massachusetts General Hospital who suffered from physical symptoms (insomnia, loss of weight, weakness, dizziness, fatigue, non-specific and chronic pains), all of which could be attributed to the autonomic nervous system correlates of depression (Kleinman 1977a). These patients' illnesses represent the patterning of the underlying disease by cultural determinants that yield characteristic types of somatization.

For example, in other cases of anxiety neurosis in Taiwan, the illnesses are frequently characterized by chest and heart discomfort. In Chinese the term *fan-tsao* (anxiety, trouble, worry) includes, as we noted, the radical for heart. This radical is used in many Chinese characters related to emotional states, since the heart was the seat of the emotions. Similarly, emotional upsets are referred to by expressions that use the heart as a metaphor. The linguistic association of heart and affect, heart disturbance and disorders of affect[5] supports the tendency to locate tension or angry or despondent feelings in the chest and the heart. Many patients I interviewed associated a psychological state with the heart. In one patient chest discomfort may have been related to anxiety-induced tachycardia or dyspepsia with esophageal irritation. In such cases, the secondary physical symptom is verbalized and responded to, rather than the primary problem. Chinese culture defines the somatic complaint as *the* primary illness problem.

Another example is the term *mên* (depressed). The character for this term includes the heart radical enclosed within a doorway radical. Patients and informants told me they picture this

5. Although semantic sickness networks involving somatization via psychosomatic metaphors for the "heart" are found in Western and other non-Western cultures (cf. Good 1977; Leff 1977), the particular configuration they take on in Chinese culture is unique, as I demonstrate in this and the following chapter. Hence, somatization is a coping strategy found in a number of different cultures, but it varies among cultures both in the degree to which it is employed and in the specific symptom and behavioral patterns it presents.

character when they used the term. Their hearts were "locked in," "closed off," or "suffocating behind a door." They pointed to their chests to locate the feeling there. To them *mên* meant this physical sensation and its associated psychological state. The metaphors communicate how they feel in physical imagery in which the affect is inferred. The physical imagery rather than the affect is most real. The idiom makes the experience primarily somatic. Chinese patients who are psychologically depressed sometimes complain that they feel something "depressing" into their chests or "pressing down" on their heads. Thus, quite commonly, physical complaints serve to describe psychological as well as physiological states and are so understood by adults. The term for "depression" as a symptom in the psychiatric lexicon in Taiwan, *yu-yü,* is rarely used by patients because it lacks the psychophysiological meanings of *mên* and cannot function as a somatic metaphor.

I often have felt exasperated and quite helpless trying to get Chinese patients to talk about a specific dysphoric affect. Patients who have told me they are feeling depressed or anxious or frightened, for example, seemingly cannot go beyond naming the feeling. Unlike middle-class Caucasian-American patients with similar disorders, who will often describe the dysphoric affect in considerable detail and relate it to many different aspects of their lives, Chinese patients commonly move directly from naming the affect to the situation they believed caused it or to its somatic and interpersonal concomitants. They will not elaborate upon its intrapsychic characteristics and state that they do not themselves think about it in such terms. They appear to lack more refined terminology for what they are feeling. This is not merely a function of suppression or denial, since they were willing to talk about emotions and personal problems and were frustrated by our mutual difficulties in exploring their disturbed feelings. Indeed, an important aspect of psychotherapy with such patients is teaching them a language to communicate their intrapsychic experiences, especially disvalued ones. I saw such patients in the Department of Psychiatry, National Taiwan University Hospital in short-term (4 to 15 sessions) psychotherapy. I interviewed ten of them in Chinese and eight in English. I interviewed 15 additional patients in Taiwanese with the help of native Taiwanese speaking assistants. Moreover, my experience is confirmed by psychotherapists who are native Chinese speakers (cf. Tseng and Hsu 1969; Hsu and Tseng 1972; Gaw 1976). I have had similar results in psychotherapeutic interviews with 35 Chinese patients in the United States, many of whom were fluent in English. Hence, I do not believe my experience is a result of errors in translating or inadequate command of language.

Let us examine other examples of the cultural patterning of symptoms in Chinese culture. *Huo-ch'i ta* is a common expression used by patients to refer to a set of complaints, and by Chinese-style doctors to indicate a pathophysiological phenomenon believed to underlie those symptoms. The meaning this term possesses among Chinese-style clinicians is restricted. They refer to an excess of hot energy or "fire" rising in the body as a pathological excess of the energies or "fires" of the five internal organs (*wu-tsang*): liver, heart, spleen, lung, kidney. Following Porkert's (1973) terminology for translating classical Chinese medical concepts, it is an "orbisiconographic" idea symbolizing the disordered interrelated functions of the internal organs. But as presently applied by Chinese-style doctors in Taiwan, it often glosses simply as inflammation. Chinese-style doctors and patients associate it with too much heat "rising up" from the lower abdomen toward the head. The metaphoric range of meaning this term holds for patients is much wider than its technical meaning in the indigenous profession of medicine. Some patients regard it as actual fire rising up within them. One patient complained to me of fire burning the nerves of his chest, just as a real fire burns wood or an electrical appliance. Whereas for Chinese-style doctors the subject of *huo-ch'i* is *ch'i* (vital energy), for patients the subject is *huo* (fire). A burning sensation caused by gastric irritation or hypersecretion of gastric acid with esophageal reflux is a commonly reported sensation in the United States and Taiwan. In the United States metaphors like "burning acid," "trapped gas," and "open sore" are used to describe this complaint, whereas in Taiwan *huo-ch'i ta* is applied to this sensation. The label exerts some influence on the symptom for *huo-ch'i ta* is not limited to abdomen and chest but "rises up" into the mouth, where it produces a sense of the gums swelling, bad taste, bad odor, and throat irritation. For many people the essence of *huo-ch'i ta* is in the mouth, but a range of meanings are attached to the term. In the popular sector it covers what I take to be acute viral disorders with gastrointestinal and upper respiratory manifestations, but it also includes symptoms associated with chronic disorders. People routinely employ the term to label the symptoms of different disorders. Once the label is applied it remains unclear to what extent the expectations alter the very nature of the symptoms, but something of this kind might well happen. Patients describe feeling out of sorts, in bad spirits, dull, easily angered, unhappy, and having difficulty concentrating and lacking energy. Many whom I have interviewed suffer insomnia, loss of appetite, and headache along with *huo-ch'i ta*, and they associate it with problems I would diagnose as depression or psychophysiological syndromes. Thus, *huo-ch'i ta* may at times generate somatization.

Symptom terms may be unique to a specific cultural context. For example, Chinese patients not infrequently refer to a somatic complaint of *suan* (literally sourness) in limbs, joints, and other bodily locations. Sometimes they complain of this feeling throughout the entire body. When I questioned patients, they denied it meant "ache," "pain" or "soreness," and stressed the quality of "sourness" as the essential characteristic. Sourness in the classical Chinese medical system of correspondences relates to the phase Wood and the hepatic functional system of the body (Sivin 1975), but most patients had little or no understanding of this system. When I explained it to them, they made it clear that they meant only the flavor, yet I still wonder whether the classical symbolic associations persist in the popular culture. I have not come across this symptom among non-Chinese patients, nor am I aware of it being reported in the clinical literature. In a few cases of arthritic joint pain and low back pain, as well as in several cases of generalized malaise associated with viral infections, I have asked Caucasian patients in the United States if they could identify "sourness" in their limbs or joints and they have not recognized such a sensation. Yet these are disorders in which Chinese patients complain of *suan*. Several Chinese patients have complained of *suan* affecting their hearts. Each was recovering from the death of a parent and appeared to be actively grieving, yet this physical complaint was presented instead of the feelings of loss and sadness.

Suan is not the only instance among Chinese of a culturally unique symptom; another example is *t'ou-yün*. Western-style doctors frequently translate this to mean dizziness, but it is a more specific sensation than that. Patients and informants report the sense that a film has been placed before the eyes so that images appear hazy. Associated with this core symptom are complaints that things outside the body are moving and that you feel like you will fall down. Thus, this term can incorporate at once both dizziness and vertigo, which modern scientific medicine distinguishes as two separate symptoms. Patients differentiate *t'ou-yün* from *t'ou-t'ung* (literally head pain, the most common general term for headache) and *t'ou-chung* (a sensation of fullness or heaviness in the head). All three symptoms are aspects of headache. There is general agreement on the meaning of *t'ou-yün*; like *huo-ch'i ta* it is associated with both physiological and psychological (insomnia, bad spirits, fatigue, irritability) features. Use of the term dizziness has passed from the United States to Taiwan in the textbooks and has distorted the perception of clinicians in Taiwan, who often miss the popular meaning conveyed by *t'ou-yün*.

Patients in Taiwan employ these and other terms to refer to problems affecting the brain more commonly than they employ terms to refer to psychological complaints. Thus, they often refer to *sensations* of damage affecting "brain nerves" (*nao-chin*). Expressions of primary symptoms related to the brain are rare in the contemporary West. Clinicians may diagnose brain damage, but Western patients usually complain of such problems in psychological terms. When we examine complaints of "brain nerve" damage among patients in Taiwan, we do not find neurological pathology but depression, anxiety neurosis, hysteria, psychophysiological reactions, and so on.

Here again we have examples of the cultural patterning of symptom perception and communication. I could adduce other Chinese symptom and affect terms to further substantiate this thesis, but I think the point has been made well enough. Similar examples could be cited for other cultures, including our own. "Colds," "hyper-tension," "lumbago" or "backache," "nerves," "lump in the breast," "upset stomach" are terms that need to be situated in the semantic illness networks particular to contemporary American popular culture before they can be adequately explicated. They, too, convey both cultural and personal meaning. It is this meaning-centered aspect of affects and symptoms that requires detailed ethnographic and clinical description. Biomedical and psychological reductionism strips away what is most unique to these terms and the experiences they constitute and express. To correct this distortion ethnomedical and ethnopsychiatric research must provide phenomenological accounts of common symptoms and affects for different cultural systems. Such accounts, which are not abundant, are needed to establish the grounds for delivering psychologically and culturally appropriate clinical care; hence, they are a key desideratum for anthropologically oriented medicine and psychiatry.

5

The Cultural Construction of Illness Experience and Behavior, 2:
A Model of Somatization of Dysphoric Affects and Affective Disorders

In the preceding chapter I analyzed selected Chinese terms for affects and symptoms to disclose the cultural loads they bear. We now ask whether cultures always create unique symptoms or fundamentally alter the features of common emotions. Does somatization function systematically in Chinese culture? How is it brought about? How does it relate to other coping strategies by which Chinese patients manage troublesome affects and affective disorders? And what can such a highly focused analysis teach us more generally about routine psychocultural processes mediating the cultural transformation of disease symptoms to illness experiences and behaviors?

A MODEL OF SOMATIZATION AND THE MANAGEMENT OF DYSPHORIC
AFFECT AMONG CHINESE

To conceptualize somatization as a basic feature of the construction of illness in Chinese culture and answer the questions raised in the preceding paragraph, I propose a model to explain how dysphoric affect and affective disorders are shaped and managed among Chinese. I shall relate it to several cases where it seems to offer a plausible mechanism of action by which universal diseases are turned into culturally specific illnesses. I hope to demonstrate how social and cultural context influence the biological and psychological process underpinning the presentation of symptoms, which should lead to a more discriminating assessment of the cultural construction of illness.

In the model, affects are fundamental psychological phenomena engendered in an individual by external (e.g., interpersonal) and internal (e.g., intrapsychic or somatic) stimuli. Stimuli giving rise to intense or dysphoric affects are stressors (environmental, social, psychological, physiological). Culture determines the evaluation of stimuli as stressors (Kagan and Levi 1974; Levi 1971; Spradley and Phillips 1972). What is perceived as a stressor in one culture may not be so perceived in another, or there may be a difference in the relative weight attached to each stressor. Hsu (1971b), for example, argues that the Chinese usually regard interpersonal problems (especially family problems) and financial difficulties as the most serious sources of stress, and they usually regard intrapsychic problems as relatively less stressful. This same hierarchy of perceived stress was found by my research assistants in interviews with families in Taipei. On the other hand, Hsu suggests that Americans perceive intrapsychic problems as relatively more stressful than family or financial problems.

The affects engendered by these stimuli, such as anger, anxiety, depression, guilt, etc., are known to the person in whom they are evoked only via cognitive processes: perception, labeling, classifying, explaining, valuating. Thus affects exist as such for the individual only after they are cognized. *Prior to cognition*, affective states are an essential psychobiological phenomenon, with physiological correlates, and as such are universal. Stated simply, there is no difference in quality or intensity of the primary (uncognized) affects felt by Americans and similar affects felt by Chinese or individuals from any other culture, leaving aside, of course, individual psychological differences found in all cultures. There is a cultural difference in quality or intensity of secondary (cognized) affects, however; that is to say, once labeled "anger," "sadness," or *huo-ch'i ta*, affects differ.

Social and cultural factors shape affects principally through cognitive processes. Such shaping most commonly is not extreme, so that most affects are identifiable cross-culturally, but it may be so extensive that it appears as if certain affective states are culturally unique. *Amae* among the Japanese, a positively valued feeling of dependency, has been described by Takeo Doi (1962) as just such an affect. Like illness, then, affects are socially constructed through the effect of cultural categories and interpersonal transactions on universal psychophysiological processes.

Differences in quality of secondary (cognized) affects result from their cognitive processing, not from their psychobiological substrate. For example, the somatic idiom for cognizing and expressing depressive feelings among Chinese constitutes that affect as a vegetative experience profoundly different from its intensely personal, existential quality among middle-class Americans. Similarly, Marsella (1977) shows that among Japanese the same affect is cognized and communicated in an external, naturalistic metaphor—clouds, rain, mist—that again appears to produce a distinct difference in the quality of the experience of depressive affect.

I propose the following schema for the Chinese management of dysphoric affective states. These affects are initially recognized by using the non-specific term *hsin-ching pu-hao,* which connotes general emotional upset. This label is used with family and close friends and by the subject to identify and think about his inner state Usually he does not further define the emotion, but uses the vagueness of this general term to cope with various distressing affects. That is, Chinese reduce the intensity of anxiety, depressive feelings, fears, and the like by keeping them undifferentiated, which helps both to distance them and to focus concern elsewhere. Other related coping strategies are (1) *minimization* or *denial,* (2) *dissociation,* and (3) *somatization.*

1. *Minimization* is an active process of suppressing the intensity and sequelae of dysphoric affects by minimizing their significance. This can extend to *denial,* in which the presence of troubling emotions is simply not acknowledged. I have frequently found denial among Chinese patients with depression, and it usually involves conscious suppression, which operates until trust has been established. Sometimes the denial appears to be unconscious, when a patient seems honestly unaware of the dysphoric affect, though he is usually quite aware of its somatic concomitants.

2. *Dissociation* includes a whole range of coping practices by which affect is separated from consciousness, cognition, be-

havior, or the specific stimuli provoking it. The dissociated dysphoric affect is expressed in isolation (if at all), most usually in a culturally sanctioned way. For example, in Taiwan I have seen angry, sad, and anxious feelings expressed via outbursts of hysterical behavior indigenously labeled as illness, in trance states in the shrines of shamans, and displaced to other objects, such as socially legitimated anger at children, strangers, and deviants. In Buddhist and Taoist states of meditation and in the guise of Confucian intellectual and aesthetic refinement, one finds active attempts to isolate (and thereby master) grief, fear, hostility, and so on, and thereby block such dysphoric affects from overt expression. Dissociation also is frequently associated with denial.

3. *Somatization* is the substitution of somatic preoccupation for dysphoric affect in the form of complaints of physical symptoms and even illness. We can at times isolate the specific cognitive coping mechanisms involved in somatic substitution for psychological problems (see below). The Chinese sometimes claim to be able to differentiate those physical complaints that are a somatic language for expressing other kinds of distress, and they seem to be remarkably tolerant of these forms of somatic masquerade. On the borderline between somatization and dissociation is the group of hysterical behaviors, which run from hysteria (a chronic disorder characterized by recurrent episodes of usually vague, alternating physical symptoms of many bodily systems in the absence of organic pathology and closely related to hypochrondriasis), to hysterical personality disorder, conversion reactions, and hysterical psychosis. The last is a quickly self-limiting psychosis with full return to the normal pre-morbid state that seems to arise in response to severe psychosocial stress. One striking variant is a hysterical psychosis in which the chief delusion is somatic. I shall give examples of several of these hysterical syndromes.

A peculiar type of displacement of dysphoric affect among the Chinese is the tendency to shift concern from the affect itself to the concrete situation that generated or is maintaining the affect. Many Chinese patients are unable to delineate the dysphoric affect they are experiencing and move directly from superficial and vague appreciation of the dysphoric affect to detailed analysis of the external situation that provoked and sustains it. They lavish most of their concern on the latter while avoiding the former and thus escape from the disturbing affect itself. Patients with depression and other disorders of affect have told me it is better to forget about bad feelings without trying to probe into their depth.

The socially legitimated and usually un-self-conscious cognitive mechanisms for coping with disordered or difficult emotions discussed above all function to reduce or entirely block introspection as well as direct expression. They place dysphoric affects in a nonpsychological idiom, the idiom with which Chinese apprehend and express emotional distress. Unlike the "internal," psychologically-minded idiom used by Westerners, it is an "external" idiom. It communicates affects indirectly (if they are expressed at all) as referents of somatic, situational, or dissociated behavioral metaphors. The result is a peculiar cultural configuration taken on by affective disease in Chinese culture, disclosed not only in illness behavior but also in the type of clinical reality fashioned in practitioner-patient interactions to treat these illnesses. The culturally constituted illness behavior in some instances can be shown to have personally and socially adaptive consequences, but frequently the impact is demonstrably maladaptive.

I have now shown at least three ways cultural categories and norms may shape affects and affective disorders. Each works through the medium of cognitive coping mechanisms. (1) The effects of these universal structural processes are differentially expressed owing to their culturally constituted content (e.g., Chinese behavioral models for displaying somatization or dissociation result in distinctive types of somatization and dissociation). (2) Cultures possess different profiles of the particular cognitive mechanisms most frequently employed by their individual members, as well as differing hierarchies of resort to these strategies and differences in the intensity with which they are expressed. For example, somatizers are found in American culture (particularly among lower-class ethnic groups) as well as in Chinese culture, but they are much less prevalent in the former, commonly express less intensity of denial and substitution, and present different constellations of associated coping strategies. (3) Certain cognitive coping processes may be unique to a culture or group of related cultures. The expression "culturally constituted coping strategies" (or "defenses" as Spiro [1977] labels them) suggests this possibility, yet we have hardly any firm data on this subject, or even speculation on how such processes differ from the universal psychological coping strategies that we have examined.

Because I am interested in somatization as the most frequently resorted-to mechanism for coping with dysphoric affect in Chinese culture—one that illumines the psychocultural process of illness construction generally, while creating in particular one of the most common problems health care systems face—I will give a few clinical illustrations that suggest how somatization operates among Chinese patients suffering from depression. In each instance, I shall describe particular mechanisms of action that I believe also function in other cultures.

Case 4

Mr. Wang is a 26-year-old unmarried Taiwanese male, a government telegraph operator and night student in a junior college, who complains of dryness of his throat of more than one year's duration. He has been to Western-style and Chinese-style doctors for his complaint without any relief. Recently he was referred by the Ear, Nose and Throat Clinic at National Taiwan University Hospital to that hospital's Psychiatry Clinic because his physical examination, x-rays, and blood tests have disclosed no abnormalities. Mr. Wang notes his chief symptom either begins or worsens when he is psychologically upset. But it is his physical symptom, not his psychological problems, that worries him. He is preoccupied by this complaint. He blames it for difficulty studying, poor school performance, lack of close friends, and family problems. It embarrasses him. He does not like to socialize with peers, date girls, or talk with others because of this problem. It makes him feel inferior to others and also leads him to fear losing face.

Besides this symptom, he reports insomnia with early morning wakening, weight loss, and periodic bouts of dizziness, rapid heart rate, sweating, and tremor of hands when he is under stress. In addition to these physical complaints, he reports some psychological complaints, which he feels are unrelated to the physical problems, including: low self-esteem, feelings of shame and guilt, frustration with his job and schooling, chronic tension, and periodic feelings of sadness, hopelessness, and helplessness.

The third of six sibs, he is the only one who has not done

well in school and who is neither in a profession nor studying to enter one. His academic performance has been so poor that he knows he cannot get his college degree, but he keeps attending classes because he fears his family will be ashamed of him and reject him if he cannot complete his studies successfully. He feels constantly frustrated, faced by an untenable situation that he declares "cannot change." He already believes his parents and sibs look down on him, and he fears they don't really care about him. But he does not relate his personal and family problems to his physical complaints. Even though he recognizes that as the former worsen, the latter also become more severe, he rejects a psychophysiological explanation. When the dryness in his throat is most severe he thinks of nothing else but this "physical" problem. At such times, he worries continually about whether or not he can be cured.

On examination Mr. Wang is a thin Chinese male, appearing quite anxious. His speech reveals a partial impediment: he frequently uses the sound "ong," which he describes as a meaningless habit and which increases in frequency and loudness as he becomes anxious and feels under stress. Whenever he is asked to define or express his feelings or to talk about his school and family problems, he hesitates for long periods of time, looking off in space with tears in his eyes and repeating this same sound. The rest of his mental status exam is remarkable only for the feelings of sadness, hopelessness, and helplessness he reports. There are no delusions, hallucinations, evidence of thought disorder, phobias, or paranoid ideas. He has little insight into his problem and is able to characterize his feelings only with great difficulty and after receiving considerable help from the psychiatrist, who has to constantly prevent him from jumping directly from labeling his feelings "upset," in vague terms like *hsin-ching pu-hao*, to talking about his physical symptoms or social problems.

Psychiatric evaluation led to a diagnosis of mixed anxiety-depression syndrome with somatization and serious family and school problems. The patient rejected this diagnosis, refused to return to the Psychiatry Clinic, and discontinued his medication (a minor tranquilizer and an anti-depressant) after several days (an inadequate course of therapy) because of no symptomatic relief.

Mr. Wang's physical symptoms were physiological concomitants of his mixed anxiety-depression syndrome; most could be attributed to involvement of his autonomic nervous system.

The dryness of the throat (affecting only speaking and not swallowing) could also be explained on that basis. But we might posit another related mechanism. The adventitious sound the patient uttered when he was anxious *"ong,"* was made in the back of his throat. The more he made this sound, the drier his throat became, a finding he himself had noticed. Whenever he became anxious or depressed he made the sound repeatedly and produced his chief symptom. It substituted for thinking about those feelings and also kept him from talking about them. Though meaningless as used, this sound was the same one as the Taiwanese word for his family name, Ong (Chinese, Wang; English, King). We might speculate on the possible unconscious significance of this term as a symbol of his ambivalent relationship with and feelings toward his family as the central component of the social conflict he was in and the chief source of his personal stress. By producing this physical symptom, Mr. Wang substituted an external somatic preoccupation for his deeply upsetting psychological and family problems. Furthermore, he could communicate about this symptom to family and friends and to himself, which he could not do with his other problems. The physical symptom provided him with an excuse for his academic and interpersonal difficulties, one that was culturally sanctioned even though it was beginning to wear thin with his family and friends. Whereas the organic diagnosis was acceptable to him (and them), the psychiatric diagnosis was not. From his standpoint and his family's, if he was not physically sick, then he was morally culpable for his failure, a source of shame for himself and for them. The physical symptom also generated a caring response, which indirectly may have mollified (but not removed) his psychosocial troubles. Indeed, only that symptom enabled him to receive "care."

Case 5

Miss Liu is a 32-year-old unmarried Taiwanese accountant who came to the Psychiatry Clinic at the National Taiwan University Hospital with headaches of several months duration. Besides headaches, she suffered from insomnia with early morning wakening, easy fatigue, and loss of energy. She had been to Western- and Chinese-style doctors and had used self- and family-treatment without success. Her symptoms had begun shortly after the collapse of a love affair, one of several which her family had forced her to end over the years because the prospective husband and his family were held to be unsuitable for her in one way or another. (In this instance, the man was thought to be too old for her, and it was learned that his father had treated his mother very harshly. Miss Liu's father made her abruptly end the budding relationship, one which he had initially encouraged her to take an active part in, in spite of her own initial feelings to the contrary. He did so feeling he was doing the best thing for her, whereas she blamed him for upsetting her plans and manipulating her at will.) Following that loss, Miss Liu became despondent. She now believed, apparently for the first time, that she would never marry, owing to a combination of her age and basic disagreement with her family over who constituted a suitable husband.

During her first visit to the Psychiatry Clinic, Miss Liu denied repeatedly any deep or significant psychological problems. Slowly, over a number of sessions, she admitted feeling depressed and frustrated and entertaining suicidal thoughts. Whenever queried in detail about her "bad feelings" (the general label she used to refer to them), she would quickly change the subject to her physical complaints or social problems. Beyond defining her feelings as depressed (mên) she claimed she was unable to be more specific about them, but she admitted that they were intense and quite disturbing. Thinking about them made her feel much worse. She noted that talking about them in a vague way made them seem less severe, more distant, and less overwhelming. Minimizing or denying their existence made her feel better, as did talking about her family and somatic problems. She could see no value in talking about her feelings to a doctor, though she reported feeling better on those occasions when her feelings were most intense when she spoke to close girlfriends about them.

Miss Liu pointed out to us that the most effective method she had found for dealing with her "bad feelings" was to occupy herself completely with her work and, after she returned home, to eat immediately and then go to sleep. That kept her from being preoccupied with her depressed mood. Falling asleep so early, however, resulted in her being unable to sleep throughout the entire night; instead she would wake up quite early in the morning and then find herself unable to go back to sleep. "I was no longer tired," she explained. But as soon as she awoke she found herself preoccupied with her dysphoric affect. At such times she noted she felt better if she could distract her mind by reading, working, or performing physical activity. Not infrequently, headaches would occur at this time. When they were present, she felt totally preoccupied with them and was unable to think about anything else, including her depressed feelings. Because of her unusual sleep cycle, Miss Liu often felt tired and sleepy in the late afternoon, so that by the time she returned home she was ready to eat and then immediately go to bed, thus perpetuating this behavioral cycle.

Miss Liu's physical symptoms either related to the behavioral mechanisms she employed to cope with her depressive affect or were themselves biological concomitants of the depressive syndrome. In the first instance, they were symptoms of her illness; in the second, of her disease. Probably both could be implicated. Fortunately, Miss Liu's psychological and physiological symptoms remitted after a full course of anti-depressant medication without any other form of therapy. Unlike most depressed Chinese patients I have studied or treated, Miss Liu was quite willing to entertain a psychophysiological explanation of her disorder. Even more impressive, she was able to share her depressed feelings with me, albeit on a superficial level. Like most Chinese patients in my experience, however, Miss Liu did not analyze her own feelings, and she did not try to integrate her depressed feelings into the explanatory model she applied to her family problems and her spinsterhood, but she did include her physical symptoms in that explanation. She talked about her depressed feelings as if they were an entirely separate and not quite relevant concern, isolated from the rest of her personal and social life. This represented dissociation (of affect from cognition), though of a much less striking form than in hysterical conversion symptoms or trance.

Case 6

Mr. Hung is a 60-year-old retired Navy captain from the China mainland, a widower living alone in Taipei. He has suffered from the following constellation of symptoms over the past two years: weakness in all extremities; tremor of hands; unsteadiness of gait; heart palpitations; easily fatigued; profound weight loss; and insomnia. Full medical and neurological work-ups revealed no organic pathology on several occasions.

Medical doctors told him he had neurasthenia. Since tranquilizers did not help and since Western-style medical doctors spent very little time talking to him about his problem and led him to believe there was nothing further they could do for his condition, Mr. Hung began visiting the clinic of a noted acupuncturist, a friend who had retired from the Navy. There, over the last six months, he has begun to feel much better with return of strength and appetite, increase in weight, improvement in gait, and greatly improved sleep pattern. He spends three full mornings each week in this Chinese-style doctor's clinic. He receives a half hour of acupuncture therapy and some herb teas each visit and spends the remainder of the morning sitting in the clinic talking with his friend and the patients who come there. He feels that his friend's acupuncture has benefited him, but admits also that his friend has inspired confidence in him, helped him relax, and encouraged him to socialize—things that have been problems for him since the onset of his disorder.

Mr. Hung was in good health upon retiring from the Navy three years ago. However, over the next year, he experienced severe financial reverses in his business ventures that left him without any income other than his small government pension. These reverses destroyed both his savings and the plans for retirement he had made. He found himself deeply disturbed and ashamed. He felt that he had failed in life and had brought shame on himself and his family. He feared his friends would ridicule him if they knew his plight. He felt unable to express his sadness to anyone. And he began to avoid his friends and his grown children. He experienced his depressive affect as a "pressure" on his head and chest. Whenever he felt sad or wished to cry, he associated his despondent feelings with the somatic sensations. His depression came to mean not the psychological symptoms but the physical ones:

"First the bad financial problem caused my depression on the heart and brain. (He demonstrates this with his hands as a physical pressure, a pressing on heart and brain.) Then that depression pressed further on me causing my nerves to become weak and also my heart to become weak . . . Now I take tonic and get acupuncture to make my heart and brain stronger."

Mr. Hung would tell me he was depressed, but he described that in somatic terms. If I asked him about his personal feelings, he would not tell me anything other than that he was getting better. He mentioned repeatedly that his financial problems caused his sickness (which he believed to be a physical disorder), but if I asked him how this made him feel, tears would come to his eyes, which his facial muscles would strain to hold back, and he would look away for minutes at a time. He told me that these were things that were better not talked about, that he never talked about them with anyone, *even with himself,* that after all they were getting better; then he would politely but firmly introduce another topic. Even after four months, when his depression had largely subsided, Mr. Hung refused to talk about what his feelings had been like. In fact, on one occasion he told me that he himself did not know what they were like since when they came to mind he felt his somatic symptoms greatly worsen and became preoccupied with the latter. He also admitted that he spent most of the time watching television, reading, collecting stamps, or playing card games in order to keep his "mind blank." Keeping his mind blank seemed to him important because he felt his physical symptoms less at such times. Even at the time of my last visit, he could talk about his financial reverses in detail but could not say how they affected him beyond stating they depressed his heart and brain, thereby hurting his nerves and bringing on all of his physical complaints.

Mr. Hung clearly suffered from a severe depressive syndrome. He recovered, probably owing either to natural remission of his disease or the non-specific, placebo effect of treatment at his friend's clinic. A specific response to the acupuncture, herbal therapy, or the supportive psychotherapy he received also may have been responsible for his improvement. It is not possible to tell which of these was effective. Certainly, he did not receive appropriate medical management from the Western-style doctors he consulted, who did not diagnose his masked depression and thus failed to treat it. He denied he had a mental illness and told me there was nothing I or my psychiatric colleagues could do for him. Most strikingly, Mr. Hung used an idiom in which psychological feelings were not only expressed by but actually experienced as somatic affects. That is, his illness behavior was entirely organized around physical symptoms. Even though those symptoms manifested a psychological disease (depression), Mr. Hung perceived and experienced them as a physical illness. I could describe many other cases similar to Mr. Hung's.

Somatization may involve several family members or an entire family. For example, one lower middle-class Taiwanese family I studied in Taipei complained of backache affecting all the family members when they visited a shaman. This was perceived by each individual as something attached to their backs and experienced by them as a heavy weight or "burden." One month before a daughter-in-law had died in a motorcycle accident which the family feared might have been a suicide. The family members held deeply ambivalent feelings about the dead woman. She had been discovered stealing money from the family business, which she sent to her father and brothers, and subsequently had quarrelled repeatedly with her in-laws demanding that her husband leave and take with him his share of the business. On several occasions she had threatened suicide, saying that if she and her husband were thwarted her ghost would haunt the family in revenge. After her death the family became terrified that her ghost would "attack" them. They also feared the retribution of the dead woman's father who was believed to possess knowledge of sorcery. During the period of mourning, the symptom of backache was experienced by each member of the family. They did not complain of the terror they experienced, their ambivalent feelings, or their acute grief. The backache substituted for these problems. It isolated the family's distress, strengthened family bonds, and sanctioned their desire for help. The shaman treated them in part with exorcistic rituals to drive away the ghost, but also reassured them about their fears. On the negative side, the somatization delayed the family's grief reaction, perhaps making it more difficult for the family to come to terms with their conflicted feelings. This could lead in future to depression associated with pathological grieving. The point I wish to emphasize, however, is that the shared somatization experience— which some might view as an instance of group hysteria— served as a culturally constituted coping mechanism for the family as a whole, providing a legitimated medium for communicating and handling extremely distressing emotions.

Somatized illness behavior is an important adaptive mechanism in Taiwan, where mental illness is heavily stigmatized and psychotherapy is both unsanctioned and unavailable for the general population. It also seems for many to be personally adaptive as well. For some patients, the culturally constituted illness experience may play a dominant therapeutic role. On the negative side, in the case of depression it masks a disease for which we now have specific biological and psychological treatments, and consequently it is responsible for many patients being treated unsuccessfully for physical problems that will remit only when the underlying psychological disease is effectively treated. Furthermore, for some patients the illness behavior is quite clearly maladaptive.

Since psychological disorders among Chinese, such as the cases of depression described above, fit better into the somatic treatment orientation of Western-style and Chinese-style medical practice than into the psychotherapeutic orientation of psychiatry, it is not surprising that we find psychiatric practice with Chinese patients frequently following a medical rather than a psychotherapeutic treatment approach. Nonetheless, psychotherapy increasingly appeals to the younger and better educated in Taiwan, who have assimilated Western values and are quite "modern" in most regards, notwithstanding that psychotherapeutic treatment services are still not widely available there (Ko 1974; Tseng 1976). Yet even among this elite group, psychotherapy must be practiced in a special manner that makes sense within the Chinese cultural context. It needs to be more directed and supportive and less insight-oriented. It cannot be separated from general medical questions and procedures. And it must be extremely sensitive to the culturally shaped coping mechanisms for managing dysphoric affect and the behavioral norms we have discussed (see Gaw 1976; Hsu and Tseng 1972; Kleinman 1975b). Of all the coping mechanisms, somatization is perhaps the most difficult problem to manage in psychotherapy with Chinese patients. Most patients with somatization, such as those described in the preceding case presentations, often remain unconvinced that their problems are psychological rather than medical (and indeed their illness is "medical"). They see little reason to talk about issues that are personal. Many are simply unable to define or articulate personal problems in psychological terms, and they do not believe that talk therapy without medication can be effective or worth paying for. Because these illness beliefs and behaviors are sanctioned by Chinese culture, they are especially hard to deal with effectively in psychotherapy. Morita therapy was developed by a Japanese psychiatrist to provide a culturally appropriate psychological treatment, oriented away from intrapsychic analysis and self-preoccupation and toward the control of external behavior, for a neurotic disorder among Japanese, *shinkeishitsu* (neurasthenia), which involves somatization (Reynolds 1976). Unfortunately, in Chinese culture there is no analogy to date of this "indigenization" of psychotherapy, which constructs a modern cultural fit between illness and its treatment—unless work "therapy" and self-criticism in the People's Republic of China can be viewed in this way.[1]

That is why indigenous healers and general medical doctors tend to do better in treating patients experiencing somatization than do psychiatrists, though they too may encounter difficulties. If the depression underlying cases of somatization responds to anti-depressant medication, then the psychiatrist has an opportunity to cure the disease and remove the somatization (the illness). But to do so, these patients must come to him and remain in treatment until they have had a full therapeutic course of medication. This frequently does not happen, as in the case of Mr. Wang. Cultural values function to push patients away from agencies that can cure their disease and toward those that can treat their illness. Ideally, both should be treated. In the folk-healing sector of developing societies,

1. It would be intriguing to learn if being sent to the countryside to engage in "socially productive labor" and public self-criticism in the People's Republic of China is used not just to enforce political control, but also to manage deviance, including alienation and neurotic problems (e.g., hysteria and hypochondriasis) that interfere with work performance, in place of sacred folk healing, which has been suppressed, and modern psychotherapy, which has not been legitimated. If this is indeed so, in a sense these modern techniques elaborated during the Communist Revolution in China build upon traditional cultural norms by defining personal problems in extra-individual rather than intra-individual terms and by "treating" these problems with interpersonal and physically oriented "therapies." While this surely does not represent "indigenization" of psychotherapy, it may exemplify "indigenization" of modern forms of social control. Rather than "medicalizing" and "psychologizing" personal problems as in the contemporary West, this approach might be regarded as "moralizing" and "politicizing" them. Self-criticism, for example, in certain cases might be viewed as transforming dysphoric affect into cognitive errors and moral delicts in understanding and applying the sanctioned political ideology, which draws on institutionalized Confucian strategies for managing behavioral deviance through social suasion and moral rectification under the guidance of paradigmatic behavioral exemplars.

and in the popular health care domain of virtually all societies, illness experience is almost always treated, while disease is treated only haphazardly. This can be tragic when the disease is lethal but curable by practitioners of modern scientific medicine. On the other hand, practitioners of modern scientific medicine often do little or nothing to treat the illness behaviors and experiences that account for most of the patient-management problems in their clinical practice. In the popular culture of technologically advanced societies, increasing acceptance of the biomedical perspective means that over-concern with biological disease problems may weaken traditional cultural processes for treating psychosocial illness problems.

It is intriguing to consider the adaptive and maladaptive consequences of the cultural patterning of depressive illness in the United States and in the contemporary West generally. The psychological-existential pattern that depressive illness usually assumes in those societies and the large number of mental health professionals certainly makes it more likely that the disease (depressive syndrome) will receive adequate diagnosis and effective treatment. But somatically masked depressions in general medical practice in the West are not always properly diagnosed because of the great stress given to depressive affect. Is something lost if we no longer possess a sanctioned somatic idiom for expressing depression and other psychological problems among certain groups of patients in the West? For example, patients with limited psychological insight and patients with marked denial, including patients from minority groups that have traditionally handled such disorders in somatic or other non-psychological terms, arguably might do better experiencing depression somatically, since they would receive appropriate family and social support for somatization but perhaps not for "psychologization." Again, psychiatric treatment, which would include anti-depressant drugs, could focus on the somatic difficulties and could avoid intrapsychic issues. My own experience in Boston treating lower-class Italian-American and Irish-American patients with depression supports this conjecture. In this instance, then, the overly psychological preoccupation of American society might be a hindrance to appropriate treatment for such patients.

Because of their clinical strangeness, it is worth discussing the most extreme forms of somatization I encountered among Chinese: cases of somatic delusion unassociated with any other psychiatric disorder or evidence of significant psychopathology. For example, on two separate occasions I interviewed male college students in Taipei who had initially complained of headache and visual problems that both attributed to putative lesions in their brains. Both had undergone extensive medical and neurological examinations with no evidence of organic pathology. Both refused to accept the findings. They persisted in believing their brains were damaged. They then underwent full psychiatric evaluations, which in each case revealed no other major psychopathology. Both patients, in spite of the negative evaluations, were diagnosed as suffering from an early form of schizophrenia, principally because of these "somatic delusions." There were no family histories of mental illness, and both students performed satisfactorily in school.

In both these cases belief and perception so intermingled that the patients reported distorted (delusional) perceptions: in one instance, pain in a specific location in the brain associated with a conception that brain nerves were dying in that spot; in the other, a sensation that the right half of the brain was unable to function and that cognitive operations therefore had to be carried out in the left half of the brain. From a neurological standpoint, these perceptions were absurd. From a psychiatric standpoint, they were not just autistic but frankly delusional, since they occurred systematically and were firmly believed in by the patients even in the face of evidence to the contrary; i.e., they were systematic misperceptions of reality, which is the definition of delusion. Unlike mistaken EMs, these explanations were fixed and unshakable. It was impossible to alter them or to reason with the patients. But these patients were not suffering from schizophrenia. Over months of observation they lacked any other evidence of disturbed thought processes, suffered no other delusions or hallucinations, and generally acted effectively and appropriately. The single loculated abnormality in each case was a somatic delusion. Although neither case involved manic-depressive disorder or psychotic depression, both patients experienced strong dysphoric affects, which they admitted only with great difficulty after many interviews. Both were anxious about the possibility of academic failure, with associated loss of face and shame. These are common fears among students at all academic levels in Taiwan and are a major source of stress and a cause of adolescent suicide. Since academic success is often the only vehicle for economic advancement and upward social mobility, there is tremendous pressure from families placed on students to succeed.

After disclosing their anxiety, both students went on to deny that it played a role in their sicknesses. But in each case, the somatic delusion seemed to function as an extreme means for mastering anxiety by masking this unacceptable affect from others and from the patient himself. In one case, this symptom had occurred several times, always around major examinations. Both patients had built an autistic EM out of a culturally sanctioned EM, the popular concept of "brain nerve weakness." Their autistic EMs allowed them to substitute a physical symptom for a psychological symptom (displacement), involved a dissociation of affect from cognition so that they both seemed entirely unaware of this process, and resulted in total preoccupation with the somatic symptom (isolation).

It is not uncommon to find patients, lay people, and even practitioners who are not initially persuaded by evidence contradicting their EMs, yet in almost all cases when they are directly and repeatedly confronted with such evidence, they will alter or reject those EMs. In these two cases, culturally sanctioned beliefs and the psychological adaptation provided by the autistic EMs made it extremely difficult to treat the somatic delusions. In fact, it became apparent that these loculated delusions did little harm, once doctors knew about them, so that they did not perform dangerous tests or treatment procedures, and obviously they were quite helpful to the patients in the management of their extreme anxiety. Thus, in both cases it seemed preferable to give up further investigations and to leave the "illness behavior" untreated. Indeed, both patients enjoyed spontaneous improvement over a period of several months.

Certain culture-bound disorders seem to be constructed in the same way: they represent loculated somatic delusions involving culturally specific EMs that shape a universal disease into a culturally specific illness. For example, on the psychiatric ward at National Taiwan University Hospital is a long-term patient suffering from "frigophobia" (name applied by Professor Hsien Rin, see Chang, Rin, Chen 1975). As I understand this patient, he is not psychotic but has developed a culturally specific fear of being cold, *p'a leng* (here a mixture of symbolic coldness and cold temperature), which correlates with a belief that he is losing *yang* and is thus in a state of weakness and susceptibility to illness. He treats himself by keeping warm, avoiding potential chill, taking tonics, and eating "hot" food. He wears several layers of clothing at all times and in all seasons, keeps many blankets on his bed, and has his windows shut tightly even in hot weather. This patient is totally preoccupied by his fear, and we could label him as suffering from an isolated phobic delusion, but otherwise exhibiting relatively normal cognition. His passionate and single-minded absorption in this EM is autistic, since he employs it to explain all that has happened to him in life and refuses to give it up despite evidence that it is inappropriate and unhelpful. The case history indicated that his EM was used to cope with a series of catastrophic losses suffered soon after he came to Taiwan in the late 1940's. We can posit that these events engendered a depressed affect for which the frigophobia was a dysfunctional coping mechanism. The coping mechanism over years became petrified because the disease went untreated and the illness was both psychologically adaptive and socially rewarding. He has his own room and a way of life in the hospital that is quite congenial to him, so much so that he has resisted all efforts to discharge him over many years. Here psychopathological behavior is reinforced by social gain and may be inseparable from chronic abuse of the sick role.

We can interpret other so-called culture-bound disorders among the Chinese (e.g., *koro*, pathological fear that one's penis will retract into the abdomen causing death, Yap 1974:98) in a similar way: as cases of depression, anxiety neurosis, and other ubiquitous psychiatric diseases or non-psychiatric behavioral deviances whose cultural patterning is so marked, owing to the fact that these disorders symbolize the society's core meanings and behavioral norms, that the illness appears unique to one culture or a group of related cultures (cf. Carr 1978). *Ut siong*, the sickness category in Taiwanese popular culture that lumps together pulmonary disease and psychological problems which I described in Chapter 3, is an illustration of this cultural mechanism at work constructing a culture-bound illness out of an organic or psychophysiological disease. In that instance, it is not autistic commitment to the cultural EM that is responsible for the c. ction of a culture-specific disorder. Instead, the cultural EM itself constructs a unique category of illness behavior and, through that behavioral paradigm, affects the perception of symptoms and the labeling of the patient. If we take _ut siong_ to be a culture-bound disorder, it significantly widens that category to include any culturally distinct categorization of illness behavior, regardless of whether or not that behavior symbolizes meanings and norms central to the society. All illnesses, as we have seen, are culturally constructed, but the "culture-bound disorders" of current literature are those illnesses that particularly strike outside observers as odd (cf. Neutra et al. 1977). That is to say, the cognitive categories that constitute and express illness (and non-medical deviances as well), which are always culture-specific, appear unique from an extra-societal comparative perspective in the culture-bound disorders.

Our model of the cultural patterning of affective disorders in Chinese culture through the influence of beliefs and values on the cognitive coping mechanisms that manage affects[2] also is applicable to other questions concerning illness. Closely related to the nature of culture-bound disorders are questions

2. Our model of the cultural processing of dysphoric affect and affective disorders among Chinese gains support from several sources: Yap's (1965) work on the phenomenology of depression among Chinese and his work on Chinese culture-bound syndromes (1974), the work of Rin et al. (1966) on psychophysiological disorders in Taiwan as well as his work on _koro_ (1965), and the ground-breaking epidemiological findings of Lin and his co-workers (1953, 1969), including their demonstration of the high prevalence of the somatic presentation of psychiatric disorders in Taiwan. The model is further supported by the clinical experience of a number of psychiatrists who have carried out clinical work in Chinese cultural areas (cf. Gaw 1976; Tseng and Hsu 1969; Tseng 1974; Yap 1974), including psychiatrists in Taiwan with whom I have discussed this model. Moreover, it seems to fit with anthropological accounts of presumed culture-bound disorders from other cultures (cf. Geertz 1968; Newman 1964; relevant chapters in Lebra 1976; and Yap 1974, who reviews the relevant anthropological and clinical literatures) and with a recent cross-cultural model of depression (Marsella 1977).

concerning hysterical psychosis and culturally specific delusions in psychotic diseases. For instance, schizophrenic patients in Taiwan incorporate Chinese popular culture EMs into their delusional systems, so that their paranoid ideas are conveyed by metaphors like fear of Chinese Communist spies (modern concern) or angry shamans carrying out sorcery (traditional concern). Similarly, hallucinations and delusions in schizophrenia, in which the patient hears voices inside his head and experiences such total estrangement of self that he comes to think he is carrying within himself others' ideas, feelings, and even personalities, are often interpreted through popular and folk EMs that define (for the patient, the family, and traditional practitioners) these abnormal intrapsychic states as possession. Possession behavior due to psychosis thereafter follows the same pattern as non-psychopathological shamanistic possession. Paranoid and pathological possession states are examples of severely disordered cognitive processes in psychoses—delusions, hallucinations, and so forth—providing the universal structure of the disease, while the popular cultural beliefs that are associated with usually less substantial changes in those processes provide the culture-specific structure of the illness.

Hysterical psychosis is a more complex question with additional implications. Let us review a Chinese case:

Case 7

Mrs. Li is a 34-year-old married Taiwanese female who was admitted to the Psychiatry Ward of the National Taiwan University Hospital for several weeks with her second episode of an acute recurrent psychosis. Both episodes occurred in response to severe psychosocial stress and were limited to several months of abnormal behavior followed by complete return to normal function without significant sequelae. In the periods prior to her first attack, between attacks, and following her last attack, her behavior has been unremarkable, and she has performed effectively as a housewife and mother of three small children. There is no family history of mental illness.

The patient, who was the second youngest in a family with eight children living in dire poverty in a small market town in central Taiwan, experienced the death of her mother when she was eight years of age. The following year her father, an odd job man, remarried. The stepmother apparently abused the patient with frequent beatings, gave her an inadequate diet, and failed to comfort her or show her real affection. Mrs. Li remembers having been terrified of her stepmother and having developed other strong fears, especially of rats. At 15 years of age, she went to work as a house maid. She was raped by the son of her employer, who threatened her with a knife and told her he would kill her if she disclosed what had happened. At the time, she felt terribly frightened. She entered what she now describes as a state of panic, characterized by agitation, profound immobilizing fear, and inability to carry out her work, which lasted for several days and then spontaneously subsided. She had experienced less intense episodes of "panic" at the time of the death of her biological mother and on another occasion, when she was seriously abused by her stepmother.

In 1971, following the birth of her third child, she exhibited abnormal behavior diagnosed at National Taiwan University Hospital as an acute psychosis. During that pregnancy she had become frightened by periodic bleeding. On one occasion she had experienced a transient illusion that a ghost was at her window threatening her. Her child was delivered by a Cesarean section, during which the patient claims she briefly awoke, owing to inadequate anesthesia. She remembers having been terrified by the specter of the surgeon gowned with a knife in his hand. It is unclear if this actually happened or was a fantasy later reified. Shortly after leaving the hospital, Mrs. Li entered a panic state similar to the one described above. But over a period of weeks she became increasingly agitated, experienced delusions of persecution and reference, and developed violent behavior. Following several months of hospitalization, her symptoms entirely disappeared. She apparently never developed a thought disorder characteristic of schizophrenia. Up until 1975 her behavior was entirely normal. During this period, and throughout her life, this patient frequently attended _tâng-kis'_ shrines. In the last few years she began to trance regularly at one shrine. She asked that shrine's _tâng-ki_ if she could become a shaman, but he told her no (an unusual response), because it was "too early" and she was "not yet ready." This rejection apparently occurred because the patient was unable to control her trance behavior and acted inappropriately during her trances.

The present episode began several weeks prior to hospitalization, when an eight-year-old girl fell from the roof of Mrs. Li's apartment house and died. The patient became terrified that the same thing would happen to one of her own children. She locked up her apartment and then locked the door to the roof, which angered her neighbors, who dried their wash there. She became increasingly fearful and thereafter quarrelled frequently with her neighbors. Then she suffered prolonged periods of crying, when she would talk aloud to herself; that was followed by the development of possession-like behavior. During that time, Mrs. Li acted as if she were possessed in rapid alternation by a god and a ghost. She hallucinated their voices inside her head and also experienced paranoid fears. On no occasion, however, did she exhibit the definitive signs of schizophrenic thought disorder. When possessed, Mrs. Li acted like a *tâng-ki*. Her usually diffident personality was replaced by either a demanding, angry god or an actively grieving and frightened ghost. The latter would weep and fearfully recall Mrs. Li's bitter past life and present terror, while the former would accuse her family and neighbors of causing her distress and would angrily demand that they, and the hospital staff, apologize and repent. After several weeks of hospitalization, all of Mrs. Li's symptoms and behavioral abnormalities subsided. She returned home to her ordinary pre-ictal life. Although she took antipsychotic drugs during her hospitalization, she did not take them after discharge, nor does she take medication at present. During this most recent hospitalization, she left the hospital for one day in order to undergo a brief shamanistic treatment at the shrine she had regularly attended, aimed at exorcising the spirits possessing her. Following that healing ritual, she showed no signs of any significant therapeutic response over the next few days.

In summary, here is a case of acute, recurrent psychosis associated with normal inter-ictal behavior and provoked by acute stress producing extreme fear. The patient has a past history of panic states associated with psychosocial crises. The phenomenology and course of her psychosis are unlike schizophrenia or manic-depressive disorder. What disease/illness is this?

Following Langness (1967), I will call it hysterical psychosis. Briefly, hysterical psychosis appears to be a short-lived acute psychosis, without significant sequelae, in which the patient thinks and acts normally between attacks and in which symptomatology during an attack shows marked cultural patterning, e.g., stereotyped behavior, possession behavior, etc. Unlike other psychoses, it does not become chronic and may never recur or will recur only on a few occasions, over a lifetime, characterized by marked stress. The cross-cultural evidence suggests that this kind of psychotic disorder is not uncommon in non-Western societies but is uncommon in the West, where it tends to affect individuals from certain socioeconomically and educationally deprived ethnic minorities, such as rural blacks and Puerto Ricans in the United States.

In terms of our model, hysterical psychosis represents a potential (if dysfunctional) mechanism for coping with intense and deeply disturbing affect. The mechanism is a marked form of dissociation. Dissociated psychotic behavior can give expression to dysphoric affects: for Mrs. Li, fear, deep sadness, and anger. These affects cannot be expressed otherwise in a socially sanctioned manner. It is not uncommon in Taiwan to observe clients (without major psychopathology) at shamans' shrines who exhibit strong affect only during trance, when they are believed to be possessed by gods. Such possession behavior in the setting of a shaman's shrine acts as a form of affective release in Chinese culture, where few other opportunities exist for such release. Affective release may be thought of as an individual coping mechanism that also may have secondary interpersonal significance: it transmits a message concerning otherwise unexpressed (and inexpressible) desires and problems that may influence the behavior of others and thereby change stressful situations. Something of this sort may be happening as the result of one of Mrs. Li's attacks of panic. An episodic psychotic behavioral disorder may be a coping mechanism (albeit an extreme, frequently disastrous, and unconscious one) for extricating persons who have few other culturally sanctioned and personally available resources from untenable life situations. Individuals suffering severe borderline personality problems (Gunderson and Singer 1975), or other severe neurotic conditions, who characteristically lack such resources, might be particularly prone to such behavior if a culture's behavioral norms make this a possible form of behavioral deviance. Hysterical psychosis, from this perspective, might be thought of as an illness that is culturally constructed via extreme dissociation in reaction to an acute, overwhelming affective state (e.g., phobic anxiety) generated by severe psychosocial stress.

Other forms of hysterical behavior (non-psychotic), from

conversion reactions to hysterical outbursts, are fairly frequent in Taiwan and appear at times to play a similar role. They seem to be attempts to master or release strong, unacceptable, and deeply disturbing affects—affects that cannot be simply suppressed or displaced. These behaviors may receive cultural sanctioning, given the appropriate setting, whereas alternative coping responses may not be so sanctioned or may not be part of the individual's behavioral repertoire.

Another example may make this point clearer. I investigated a shaman's shrine in Taipei (for details see Chapters 7 and 9) where an enterprising, charismatic _tâng-ki_ had established a large cult, many of whose members experienced trance states every night. I had the opportunity to interview ten young and middle-aged women in this cult. All of them gave histories compatible with hysteria (Briquet's Syndrome) with frequent resort to medical care prior to entering the cult. A few had apparently suffered periodic hysterical behavioral eruptions, and one or more may have experienced several episodes of hysterical psychosis, though that remains uncertain. In the cult, they exhibited various strong and dysphoric affects while in trance: shouting angrily, wailing, passionately jumping around, occasionally acting as if they were in a sexual frenzy. They no longer complained of somatic problems or attended the clinics of Chinese-style or Western-style doctors for chronic, recurring, non-specific, functional complaints, nor did they experience hysterical behavioral eruptions at home. In each case, culturally sanctioned trance behavior substituted for somatization and/or hysterical behavior as a mechanism for managing dysphoric affect. Since most of these cult members came from quite poor families and had histories of severe marital and other family problems, we can infer that sources of stress were still active and that the intensity of their present affective responses were generally comparable to those which they experienced prior to entering the cult. Consequently, their culturally sanctioned trance behavior would seem to be both socially adaptive and personally therapeutic.

In passing, another implication of our model for the relation of affect to cognition argues for a more fundamental and far-reaching effect of culture on affects. Beck (1971) has suggested that affective pathology is determined by conditions of the cognitive processes related to affect rather than of the affects themselves, which only become dysphoric or pathological affects after they are cognized. That is, affective disorders are really disorders of cognition. This hypothesis, in turn, suggests that the social and cultural context of the individual plays a role in the primary development of affect and affective disease, as well as in the secondary cultural elaboration of affective behavior and affective illness. By molding how we perceive, interpret, and react to external and internal stimuli, culture contributes to the genesis of affective disease like anxiety neurosis, depressive syndrome, and affective psychosis, as well as to normal affective experience. For example, a hypervigilant cognitive orientation that scans the environment for potential threat predisposes the individual to anxiety, while a cognitive orientation that tends to appraise external stimuli as frustrating, to deprecate the self, and to attribute efficacy to external forces beyond the control of the individual underlies depressive affect. This implicates a much more fundamental impact of culture on individual behavior than is presently acknowledged. In China, for instance, it would suggest that dysphoric affects are not merely handled differently by culturally constituted cognitive coping processes than among Americans, but that such processes engender affects whose very nature differs significantly from those experienced by Americans. Depressive feelings, then, are not simply suppressed by Chinese and expressed by Americans, but rather are different feelings. Seen in this way, for example, *pao* (reciprocity) and *jen* (human heartedness) may have distinct emotional correlates in Chinese (see Hsu 1971a, 1971b). Similarly, masked depression with somatization in Chinese patients may not represent substitution or displacement of a universal dysphoric affect, but a different type of depressive feeling (i.e., vegetative rather than psychological or even a special type of vegetative state). This is a fascinating question for cross-cultural psychology and psychiatry, but one not answerable at present (see Marsella 1977 for further consideration of this question).

In summary, our model states that affects occur as universal psychobiological states, but that they are *cognized before* they take on the form of perceived, felt, labeled, and valuated experiences recognized as emotions (see Figure 6 and Table 2).

171

The individual learns to employ culturally constituted cognitive coping mechanisms for managing affective experience. Culture has its major influence on affects, therefore, through the influence of beliefs and norms on cognition. The cognitive coping strategies may vary in type and in pattern of use across cultures. In Chinese culture, suppression, lack of differentiation, minimization, displacement, and somatic substitution are the dominant mechanisms employed by individuals. In the United States, expression, differentiation, and vigilant focusing are the dominant cognitive coping strategies for managing affects, at least among middle-class Caucasians. Other mechanisms are also used in the United States, including those described for Chinese, but these are minor strategies in contemporary mainstream American culture, though they are to be found as major strategies among Chinese-Americans and other ethnic groups.[3] Individual and group behavioral responses accord with the established pattern of cognitive coping mechanisms, as do indigenous therapies.

Culturally constituted cognitive strategies influence affective disorders in the same way. Our data demonstrate this influence on the phenomenology of depression and other affective disorders (see also Kleinman 1977a). Only further research will determine if there is also a significant influence on incidence and course of these disorders. Awareness of these mechanisms and their effects should help clinicians respond more appropriately to affective disorders in different social and cultural contexts; it may also prove to be useful to public health planners concerned with the delivery of culturally appropriate mental health services.

The cognitive coping strategies are a powerful reflection

3. Cognitive coping strategies also are influenced by social class, education, and life-style. For instance, somatization is more common in the United States among members of the lower-class who are blue-collar workers with a high school education or less and who have a more "traditional" life style, whereas "psychologization" is more common among upper middle-class professionals and executives with a college or graduate school education and a more "modish" life-style. But for Chinese and other ethnic groups, it is commonplace to find ethnic features of cognitive coping style override social class and educational influences. Thus, well-educated Chinese professionals and executives (and their families) routinely present with somatization.

Figure 6
Model of Cultural Impact on Affects and Affective Disorders

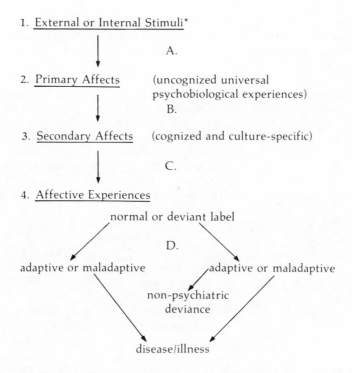

A. Cultural beliefs and values will in part determine if a stimulus is perceived as a stressor and how it is ranked in a hierarchy of potential stressors.

B. Cognitive processes through which an affect is perceived, labeled, and valuated. Culture will exert an impact here via the cultural construction of affective categories and the ways such categories are applied and interpreted.

C. Culturally constituted cognitive coping mechanisms come into play to manage secondary affects, especially strong or dysphoric affects.

D. A, B and C give rise to affective experiences that are either socially sanctioned as normal or labeled as deviant. Either social category may include personally adaptive or maladaptive experiences. Maladaptive normal or deviant affective experiences may be further classified as disease/illness. Adaptive deviant experiences fall into a class of non-psychiatric deviance.

---

*Only stressful stimuli, or those perceived as stressful, will generate disease/illness.

Table 2

Cognitive Coping Processes in Chinese and American Cultures

Cultural influences on:	Chinese	Americans*
1. Perception of stimuli as stressors, and relative ranking of stressors	Primary concern with interpersonal stimuli	Primary concern with intrapersonal stimuli
2. Perception, labeling and valuation of affects	Recognition and expression of strong or dysphoric affects are disvalued. As a result, there is lack of experience in precisely defining, labeling, and communicating about affects.	Recognition and expression of strong or dysphoric affects are valued. As a result, there is greater experience and skill in precisely defining, labeling, and communicating about affects.
3. Chief cognitive coping strategies used to manage affective experiences	Suppression Somatization Undifferentiation Minimization Externalization, situation-orientation	Expression Psychologization Differentiation Overemphasis Internalization, focusing on intra-psychic self
4. Pattern of affective experience and of experience of affective disorders	Vegetative idiom	Psychological-existential idiom
5. Lay and indigenous folk treatment approaches	Family-based Externally oriented clinical reality (somatic and inter-personal)	Individual Internally oriented clinical reality (psychological)
6. Evaluation of therapeutic efficacy	Interpersonal and somatic criteria	Personal-existential criteria

*Middle-class, college-educated Caucasians.
Note: This model of cognitive coping processes is presented as a bicultural dichotomy between Chinese and Americans. It should not be mistaken, however, for dichotomiz-

ing individual cognitive coping strategies in Western and non-Western societies generally. It is intuitively plausible to suppose that careful analysis of the cognitive coping mechanisms exhibited by individuals in a range of Western and non-Western cultures would reveal substantial differences for each culture. Moreover, these mechanisms obviously will be somewhat different for individuals in the same culture who possess distinctive social class, ethnic, and educational backgrounds, personality styles, and traditional versus modern orientations. Just as it is apparent that "psychologization" of affects in the contemporary West represents an historically grounded psychocultural change that has not proceeded at the same pace or to the same extent among all members of Western culture, it would seem reasonable to suppose that "somatization" of affects in non-Western societies (or in the West for that matter) may differ considerably among different groups of individuals in quality, degree, and the psychological processes responsible for it. That is to say, it is to be expected that as we obtain more discriminating phenomenological accounts of somatization among Chinese and other groups, we will develop a typology of basic attributes of such experiences that will distinguish between somatization in different cultures and perhaps also in different individuals in the same culture. These differences are likely to be small and not readily detected by the rough criteria (sleep disturbance, appetite, libido, etc.) presently employed to differentiate between somatized illness experience. The chief danger to be avoided in psychocultural studies is elaborating grand schemes for cross-cultural comparisons that fail to do justice to these important, if often subtle differences and that end up dichotomizing experience and behavior into crude polar opposites. This tendency has a long history in anthropology and psychiatry, as in the case of distinctions between "primitive" and "modern" thinking.

Marsella (in press), for example, suggests that "psychologization" in the contemporary West and "somatization" in the traditional non-Western world are brought about by a series of psychocultural dichotomies, including: diffused versus individuated self-structures, metaphorical versus abstract languages, imagistic versus lexical mediations of reality, subjective versus objective definitions of reality boundaries, externally perceived loss of control versus internally perceived locus of control, and use of linear versus non-linear causal thinking. While Marsella's oppositions are interesting, each is simply too superficial and artificially uniform to account for the major differences in thought, feelings, and behavior described among individuals in non-Western and Western societies. (Nonetheless, Marsella's work should be credited as a major advance beyond the ethnocentrism and psychologistic reductionism characteristic of most cross-cultural psychology; he also deserves high praise for demonstrating the importance of examining cultural differences affecting several major cognitive and behavioral variables at the same time.)

The model of cognitive coping processes that I describe, however, suggests that universal psychological processes may be organized and applied very differently among groups of individuals to produce more or less unique patterns of culturally constituted experiences of emotions. Carr (1978), drawing on ethnographies and psychological studies among Malays, has reasoned that much the same may occur in the way universally occurring cognitive processes that mediate social learning of behavior constitute culturally specific behavioral responses. The point to be underlined is that only models of experience and behavior that lend themselves to fine discriminations among both specific individuals in groups and specific groups of individuals are likely to be crossculturally valid for building a comparative understanding of normal and deviant behavior. Put differently, we need to grasp semantic networks of emotions just as we apprehend semantic networks of illness, if we are to determine the concrete details of universal and culture-specific aspects of emotional experience. Somatization and psychologization, furthermore, represent only two of the cultural codes within which such experience is organized. We also need to study morally, sociologically, and cosmologically articulated emotions. A related point is the disturbing recognition that theory and research in the psychocultural field may be one of the few remaining areas to which the term "primitive" still can be appropriately applied.

175

of how cultures define the self and its behavioral field. They also give insight into cultural hierarchies for ranking various stimuli as stressors. The analysis and comparison of these processes lead to an appreciation of how cultural beliefs and values act upon normal and deviant sides of human experience (Hallowell 1955; Spiro 1976).

Certain hypotheses emerge from this model that could be examined in future ethnographic and comparative cross-cultural research:

1. Cultures should fall into a typology of beliefs and values concerning the self and its behavioral field that should, in turn, link to typologies of cognitive coping strategies and affective experience (normal and deviant).

2. Through these cognitive and behavioral typologies, cultures may vary systematically in making individuals more or less susceptible to depressive affect and the depressive syndrome. They may also vary systematically in the relative success of the coping strategies they impart to individuals for managing affective experiences. This cultural variation may exert a definable influence on rates and course of affective sickness,[4] and also on the nature and relative efficacy of indigenous healing approaches to affective disorders. Determination of these

4. We need comparative epidemiological studies of affective disorders equivalent to the WHO International Pilot Study of Schizophrenia (*Schizophrenia Bulletin:* 11, 1974), which compares schizophrenia in a number of Western and non-Western societies and thereby provides baseline data on the prevalence and course of that disorder (Sartorius 1976). The problem with that particular study is it enforces a definition of schizophrenic symptomatology that cannot fail to act as a "cultural category," patterning the behavior observed by the investigators and systematically filtering out local cultural influences in order to preserve a homogeneous cross-cultural sample. Such a study can tell us little about the influence of culture on schizophrenia. What is even more needed is a comparative cross-cultural phenomenology of schizophrenia and affective disorders that emerges from naturalistic descriptions of behavior unbiased by a unified definition, but from which such a definition later can be established. Such a study would compare illness behavior as well as prevalence and course of disease; it also would compare emic and etic categories. It might test one or more of the hypotheses I have listed at the end of this chapter. The upshot would be an ethnomedical epidemiology, one that might provide the kind of mesh between ethnographic

potential effects will require epidemiological and outcome studies that consider illness as well as disease.

3. Somatic, interpersonal, and naturalistic idioms for articulating dysphoric affects should give rise to affective illness experiences that are clearly distinguishable from that entailed by a psychological idiom.[5] Similarly, treatments that fit specific cultural idioms should demonstrate relatively greater efficacy and relatively fewer management problems.

4. Westernization will have a predictable impact on the cultural idiom of affective experience and typologies of cognitive coping strategies, changing them toward those characteristic of the contemporary West. This change may be associated with changes in incidence, course, and outcome of affective sickness.

5. In contemporary Chinese societies, it is to be expected that women and the elderly, because they are more culturally conservative, will demonstrate the most characteristic traditional patterns of affective experience and disorders. This should hold for other non-Western societies as well.

---

and epidemiological findings which is presently lacking in both anthropological and cross-cultural psychiatric studies and without which comparative studies are not likely to advance very far our understanding of the relation of cultural context to deviance.

5. Metzger (1978) suggests that another cultural idiom for communicating emotion among Chinese is "morally articulated affect." He believes the Neo-Confucian tradition developed a sense of individual emotion as a moral ideal that provided a normative framework for personally assessing and expressing affect. The result was that Chinese intellectuals described affect not as an experiential psychological state (as in the contemporary West) nor as a vegetative state (as among Chinese generally), but as a moral percept. From the perspective advanced in this chapter, "morally articulated affect" would serve a coping function similar to somatization and dissociation. It would enable traditionally oriented Chinese intellectuals to manage dysphoric feelings by distancing, substituting, and minimizing them and by splitting them off from inner experience. Following Metzger, we might think of other cultural idioms for communicating emotion that might operate among other classes of Chinese: e.g., a combined cosmological and sociological channel among lower-class participants in ritual healing activities. Such an idiom would have the same coping effect as somatization and moral articulation of dysphoric affect. Each idiom also would shape the illness response to affective disease into a distinctive type of illness behavior.

6. Differences in how specific stressors are ranked in distinct cultures may be registered in comparable differences in rates and patterns of stress-related disorders.

7. The key distinctions between differing cultural patterns of affective experience and affective sickness will be better characterized only by more precise studies of different patterns of cognitive processes and illness behavior. Conversely, studies which attempt to measure affects per se will be less productive.

Finally, I want to emphasize that what we have been saying about psychiatric and psychophysiological disorders also holds for physical sickness. Culture affects the way we perceive, label, and cope with somatic symptoms as well as psychological ones (see, for example, Helman 1978; Mechanic 1972; Zborowski 1952; and Zola 1966). The impact may be (and probably is) greater when the focus is behavior rather than physiology, but there still is an important impact on the latter. There may be a sharper distinction, furthermore, between physical disease and physical illness, since the latter always involves behavior while the former sometimes does not. But the main points are that all *illness* is normative (i.e., socially learned and guided by cultural norms) and that culture shapes illness behavior principally through its effect on cognitive processes.

6

Family-Based Popular Health Care

Thus far, we have looked at patients largely in terms of disease/illness, but now we shall view them from a wider perspective. This change in orientation is essential if we are to appreciate fully what patienthood entails and how it relates to social and cultural context.

To paint this fuller picture, I draw upon interviews that my research assistants and I conducted with lower-class and middle-class families in Taipei's two oldest and most culturally traditional districts—Lung-Shan and Yen-Ping—concerning their responses to actual episodes of sickness as well as their general beliefs about different kinds of health problems. Families were selected from the registration lists of two local health stations because they were representative of demographic and health patterns in those communities. It is not my intention to review all the findings; instead, I shall present those data that illustrate what being sick in Taiwan entails and how beliefs about sickness affect individual and family decisions in the health seeking process (see also Kleinman 1975b and c, and Chapters 7 and 8 in this volume).

In addition to 125 family interviews conducted in Taipei, we also interviewed 25 families from rural rice-farming and fishing areas in Taiwan. With a few exceptions, the rural interviews gave similar results to the urban interviews. Except for ten mainland Chinese families interviewed in Taipei and five Hakka families interviewed in the rural areas, the families we studied were Hokkien-speaking Taiwanese. There are some differences in the health beliefs and practices of Taiwan's mainland Chinese (2,000,000) and Taiwanese (14,000,000) populations, but for the most part these populations share similar ideas and values with

179

respect to illness and care. The mainland population tends to be somewhat more oriented to Western-style medicine, especially since many Mainlanders are associated with the Chinese military, where only Western-style medicine is practiced. But many of the Mainlanders retained a strong attachment to Chinese medicine and held popular health ideas similar to those held by Taiwanese. One large difference is that Mainlanders rarely consult shamans (all of whom are Taiwanese), whereas Taiwanese frequently select this healing approach to treat sickness. But Mainlanders do use other kinds of sacred folk healers, especially fortune-tellers, *ch'ien* interpreters, and geomancers. Mainlanders tended to have greater belief in the value of acupuncture, and, while both groups believed in the efficacy of Chinese medicine, Taiwanese valued local herbs more than Mainlanders did. Our field studies did not detect any significant differences in the health beliefs and practices of Hokkien and Hakka, but our sample of the latter was too small to support any firm conclusions.

Each interview occupied 2 to 3 hours. For each family, the mother and/or grandmother were interviewed together with various other family members who were present at the time the interview took place.[1] Each interview covered the same set of questions about family health beliefs and health care. Answers were recorded on questionnaires administered by one

1. All interviews were conducted in the homes of the families in the study. The interviewers emphasized that the interviews were confidential and would not be available to medical or public health authorities; that the interviewers did not belong to the government's public health or health care organizations; that information given in the interviews would have no effect on the family's health care either at present or in future; that it was essential the interviewers learn about *all* health care decisions and choices, regardless of whether they involved professional or folk forms of care; and that the interviewers were interested in learning about any and every type of family treatment practice. I believe such an approach is essential if informants are to provide an accurate picture of their health care seeking beliefs and activities. Conversely, when such studies are performed in medical settings by personnel identified as part of the informant's system of care, it is my impression that they fail to elicit the full extent of family-based health care (and also utilization of folk and alternative professional treatment resources), which informants are hesitant to reveal in such settings. Many studies by health services' researchers can be faulted in this respect, and this is also a problem in some medical anthropological investigations.

of three research assistants or myself. Interviews were conducted in Chinese or Hokkien. I participated in or conducted 20 percent of the interviews. Each interview was conducted in a standard format, which the research assistants had been trained to use. We asked each family about all sickness episodes that had occurred to family members in the *preceding month*. We asked them to: (1) enumerate and describe each sickness episode; (2) name the sick person; (3) describe the treatment decisions that had been made and give reasons for those decisions; (4) list all treatments that had been given and practitioners who had been consulted in the sequence they were chosen; and (5) assess the outcome. Tables 3 through 8 summarize the findings. In addition to the quantitative data, the interviews provided a considerable body of qualitative ethnomedical description of health beliefs and practices that I will draw upon in this discussion as well.

There were 411 sickness episodes suffered by 724 family members in the 115 Taiwanese families interviewed in Taipei during the one-month period covered by the study[2] (see Tables 3 and 4). Two hundred twenty-three (31 percent) of the family members in our sample were children; they accounted for almost half (49 percent) of all sickness episodes. Pediatric problems were the single most common type of health problem. One hundred thirty-nine (19 percent) of the family members were elderly (over 60 years of age). They accounted for 27 percent of all sickness episodes, which demonstrates the well-known cross-cultural fact that the elderly, like children, are at a much higher risk than other adults for developing sickness. These differences are represented in Table 4 by the different rates of sicknesses per person per month for the different age

2. Although it is a routine methodological practice in health services research to study utilization of health facilities in relation to all illness episodes reported by subjects in the two-week or one-month periods preceding the interview, it is clear that this introduces a particular bias into the research. Depending upon the time of year when the sample is surveyed, for example, either winter respiratory disease or summer febrile disorders, or both, may be missed. Notwithstanding this limitation, a two-week or one-month period is preferable to longer time frames, because the former appear to represent periods for which subjects retain reasonably accurate recall, whereas this does not seem to be the case when longer periods of time are surveyed.

Patients and Healers in the Context of Culture

categories. While the rate per child was .91 and per elderly person was .81, it was strikingly lower (.27) per adult (aged 16 to 60). Moreover, about two-thirds of the chronic sicknesses in our sample were experienced by the group of elderly patients. Also of note is the fact that 20 percent of family members were responsible for 39 percent of the sickness episodes, a finding that has been observed repeatedly in the United States. Eighteen of the 23 families with the highest number of sickness episodes per family member were from the lower-class, yet lower-class families made up less than half (48 percent) of the sample population.

This study confirms the enormous extent of family treatment worldwide. Ninety-three percent of all sickness episodes were *first* treated in the family, and 73 percent of all sickness epi-

Table 3
Sickness Episodes in Month Preceding Interview

	Number	Percentage	Rate*	
Total Sickness Episodes of Family Members	411	100%	.57	
Sickness Episodes in Children	203	49.4%	.91	(85,95)†
Sickness Episodes in Elderly	112	27.2%	.81	(72,88)
Sickness Episodes in Other Adults	96	23.4%	.27	(18,37)

*Sickness episodes per person per month.
†95 percent confidence interval.

Table 4
Analysis of 115 Taiwanese Families Interviewed in Taipei in 1975

	Number	Percentage
1. *Composition of the population surveyed*		
Family members reported on	724	100%
Children (under 16 years of age)	223	31%
Elderly (over 60 years of age)	139	19%
Other adults	362	50%
2. *Families' socioeconomic status**		
Lower-class	55	48%
Lower middle-class	30	26%
Middle middle-class	20	17%
Upper middle-class	12	10%

*Assignment to socioeconomic group was based upon a formula that took into account: size and location of home; number, type and age of electrical appliances; number, type and age of motor vehicles; and educational and occupational status of family members.

182

sodes received their *only* treatment from the family (see Table 5). As was expected, this was less true of children's sicknesses than of adult sicknesses. Forty-two percent of sickness episodes in children received treatment from professional or folk practitioners, while only 14 percent of sickness episodes in the elderly and 9 percent of sickness episodes affecting other adults received such treatment. Also, a smaller, if still very high, percentage of children (88 percent) were first treated at home than adults (98 percent) or the elderly (100 percent). I will discuss the reasons for these differences later.

The only significant findings relating to social class, besides the fact already mentioned that most families accounting for the greatest number of sickness episodes came from the lower-class, were that only families in the upper middle-class treated *all* sickness episodes by resort to Western-style doctors, while only families who belonged to the lower-class treated *all* sickness episodes at home without resorting to professional or folk healers. When care was received outside the family, almost three-quarters of upper middle-class families resorted to more than three practitioners, while only one-fifth of lower-class families resorted to more than three practitioners. These differences fit with well-documented cross-cultural patterns in

Table 5
Sickness Episodes Only *or* First *Receiving Treatment from Family*

	Number	Percentage
Total sickness episodes *only* receiving family treatment	300	73%
Total sickness episodes *first* receiving family treatment	383	93%
Sickness episodes in children *only* receiving family treatment	117	58%
Sickness episodes in children *first* receiving family treatment	178	88%
Sickness episodes in elderly *only* receiving family treatment	96	86%
Sickness episodes in elderly *first* receiving family treatment	112	100%
Sickness episodes in other adults *only* receiving family treatment	87	91%
Sickness episodes in other adults *first* receiving family treatment	94	98%

which greater utilization of health care services correlates with higher socioeconomic status when such services operate on a fee-for-service basis.

Table 6 lists the various determinants of health care seeking behavior. Perceived severity of sickness by family members appears to dominate. *All* sickness episodes labeled by families as "severe" received treatment from professional or folk practitioners, but fewer than one-fourth of those labeled as "minor" were so treated. Of the 56 sickness episodes evaluated by the research team as severe acute medical problems, all received treatment from Western-style doctors either at the outset or following family treatment. Forty-seven sickness episodes were labeled by the research team as serious chronic medical or psychiatric sicknesses. Of these, 45 received treatment from at least one practitioner outside the family, but only 29 were treated by Western-style doctors, as compared with 45 who received treatment from Chinese-style doctors and 40 from sacred folk healers. These findings demonstrate the influence of popular beliefs on health care seeking behavior: Western-style practitioners are selected more frequently for the treatment of acute sickness and indigenous practitioners are selected more frequently for the treatment of chronic sickness, which follows the popular culture's ideology concerning the relative efficacy of these therapeutic systems.

Choice of practitioners varied in at least one significant respect across the age groups. Of sicknesses affecting children that were treated outside the family (n = 86), 80 percent were treated by Western-style doctors, 79 percent by sacred folk practitioners, but only 12 percent by Chinese-style physicians (see Table 7). In contrast, of the 16 sickness episodes affecting the elderly treated by practitioners, 12 (75 percent) were treated by Chinese-style physicians, the same percentage by Western-style doctors, and 10 sickness episodes (63 percent) by sacred folk practitioners. Of the nine adults with sicknesses treated by practitioners, five were treated by Western-style doctors, three by sacred folk practitioners and six by Chinese-style physicians. Thus, children were much less frequently treated by Chinese-style doctors than were adults. This was because most sicknesses they suffered were labeled acute medical problems (e.g., diarrheal or respiratory disorders) that were believed to require Western medicine (i.e., antibiotics) or folk illnesses

Family-Based Popular Health Care

Table 6
Determinants of Health Care Seeking Behavior

Type and severity of symptoms
Course of sickness
Type of sick role
Specific sickness labels and the etiologies they implicate
Evaluation of specific therapeutic interventions
Age, sex, family role, occupation, and educational level of patient
Family's socioeconomic status, ethnic background, orientation to Western or
    traditional values, and past experiences with health care
Urban or rural setting
Proximity to particular treatment resources
Nature of patient's social network and lay referral system

Table 7
*Sickness Episodes Receiving Treatment from Western-style,
Chinese-style, and Sacred Folk Practitioners*

	Number	Percentage
Total sickness episodes in children treated		
by practitioners	86	100%
Treated by Western-style doctors	69	80%
Treated by Chinese-style physicians	10	12%
Treated by sacred folk healers	68	79%
Total sickness episodes in elderly treated		
by practitioners	16	100%
Treated by Western-style doctors	12	75%
Treated by Chinese-style physicians	12	75%
Treated by sacred folk healers	10	63%
Total sickness episodes in other adults treated		
by practitioners	9	100%
Treated by Western-style doctors	5	56%
Treated by Chinese-style physicians	6	67%
Treated by sacred folk healers	3	33%

(e.g., "fright") that were believed to require sacred folk healing. Following family care, adult and elderly women were
twice as likely to turn next to sacred folk practitioners as were
men, which was the only salient difference between men and
women that we determined.

Table 8 lists the frequency of the most commonly applied
home remedies. Obviously, diet (e.g., balancing "hot" and

"cold" constituents or eating foods held to be easy to digest, like rice congee) and special foods (e.g., coconut milk to lower *"huo ch'i"*; hot and sour soup for nasal congestion and cough; bird's nest for respiratory diseases; snake meat for eczema; etc.) were the mainstays of family treatment. But significantly, prescription and non-prescription medicines (both Chinese and Western) and herbs were used without consulting practitioners. In the rest of this chapter, I will describe salient qualitative findings and provide representative examples of the different patterns of health care seeking that we encountered.

The features of the sick role and illness behavior varied with age, sex, family role, social class, education, and occupation. In the families of the urban poor, for example, one is told that children and adults must "endure" sickness. Unless adults suffer from severe sickness, the cost of visiting doctors or even buying medicine directly from a pharmacy may be prohibitive. Consequently, adults have to make do with inexpensive herbs and patent medicine, rice congee, soups made with ginger, black sugar, garlic, or other "special" but relatively cheap ingredients, other inexpensive food therapy or tonics. But even in the poorest families, if children are significantly ill and do not immediately respond to home remedies or medicines purchased from pharmacists, as our data show, they are straightaway taken to Western-style doctors, where their parents expect treatment by injection, which is believed to be the most efficacious form of Western medical treatment.

Table 8
List of Most Common Treatments Used by Families

Type	Frequency of Use
Diet	93% of all sickness episodes
Special foods	85% of all sickness episodes
Patent medicines	83% of all sickness episodes
Prescribed medicines obtained directly from Chinese or Western pharmacies	71% of all sickness episodes
Minor first-aid materials (bandages, antiseptics, etc.)	30% of all sickness episodes
Tonic	27% of all sickness episodes
Local herbs	23% of all sickness episodes
Exercise	20% of all sickness episodes
Massage	9% of all sickness episodes

For adults and children there is a rough hierarchy of resort providing a logic to family-based health care choices and practices. As noted, in 98 percent of all episodes of adult sicknesses and 100 percent of all episodes in the elderly, recourse was made initially to self-treatment. If this did not produce symptomatic relief or if the sickness did not remit spontaneously within several days, recourse was made to family members, neighbors, local lay experts, pharmacists, or professional or folk practitioners. The various patterns of health care seeking are diagramed in Figure 7. Our study disclosed three major patterns: simultaneous resort; hierarchical resort, exclusive type; and hierarchical resort, mixed type. Each of these was associated with a very different type of sickness problem. Future comparative studies should be able to determine to what extent these three patterns are universals in the health care seeking process and to what extent they are specific to Taiwanese health care systems. Decisions regarding whom to consult are based on illness beliefs, course and type of sickness, past family experiences with health care, and other factors, such as local health care ideology, as is outlined in Table 6. Figure 8 diagrams three quite different instances of health care seeking behavior. In these, the various determinants we have enumerated are illustrated and the actual steps involved in the health care seeking process are shown in the sequence they followed. The diagrams show how the sickness labels applied by particular labelers implicated etiological agents, which in turn provided the logic for choice of treatment and evaluation of outcome. They thus furnish further examples of the semantic illness networks that were discussed in Chapter 3. The sickness problems they present—somatization, an acute infectious disease in a young child, and a chronic incapacitating disorder in an elderly person—are important because they were common problems in our survey of family health care and because the responses to them exemplify different aspects of the distinctive patterns of popular health care seeking behavior outlined in Figure 3.

Other patients turn to Western-style doctors only after they have tried and received no relief from self-treatment and medicines obtained at pharmacies. But patients will change rapidly from one Western-style practitioner to another, or from Western-style practitioner to Chinese-style practitioner, based

Patients and Healers in the Context of Culture

Figure 7
Patterns of Health Seeking Behavior

Type A: Simultaneous Resort

Usually a serious childhood sickness

Popular treatment with diet, tonics, patent medicines, herbs, and perhaps Chinese and Western medicines	Western-style practitioner (doctor or pharmacist)	Chinese-style doctor or Chinese pharmacy	*Tâng-ki* or other sacred healers

Type B: Hierarchical Resort, Exclusive Type

Usually acute but non-life-threatening sickness in adult

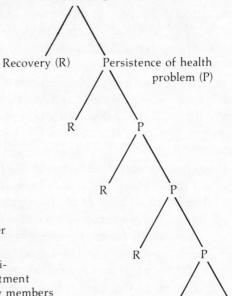

Self-labeling and self-treatment

Labeling and treatment by family and by social network   Recovery (R)   Persistence of health problem (P)

Resort to Western-style or Chinese-style practitioner based upon lay referral system

Change to another practitioner of same type or another type of practitioner

Resort to sacred folk practitioner for referral *and* treatment (may involve female family members without the patient)

If no cure, resort to any of the above.

188

Family-Based Popular Health Care

Type C: Hierarchical Resort, Mixed Type

Usually a chronic or recurrent sickness in an adult

Self-treatment, family treatment, and labeling and treatment by social network

Continuation of popular care. Resort to Western-style doctor or pharmicist

Continuation of popular and Western-style treatment and resort to Chinese-style doctor or pharmacy

All or some of the above as well as resort to secular and sacred folk practitioners. (The latter may involve female members without the patient.)

Change to other practitioners of same type or to other types of practitioners

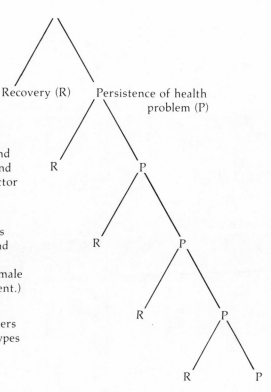

Recovery (R)   Persistence of health problem (P)

Figure 8

Diagram of Health Seeking Behavior of Three Taiwanese Patients

1. Somatization

<u>Health Problem</u>: 30-year-old mother of five small children from a lower-class Taiwanese family in Taipei with non-specific abdominal complaints, malaise, lack of energy, and sleep disturbance of several months' duration.

Labeler	Label	Etiologies Implicated	Choice of Treatment	Evaluation of Treatment Outcome
Patient →	"weakness" →	hot/cold imbalance →	self-treatment with diet and tonic →	unsuccessful, no change in symptoms
Family →	"weakness" →	several non-specific secular causes implicated →	family treatment with diet, tonics, special foods, massage, patent medicines →	unsuccessful, no change in symptoms
Family →	"weakness" →	hot/cold imbalance →	herbalist, who prescribed a special local herb and continuation of family-treatment →	unsuccessful, family decided to take patient to Western-style doctor
Western-style doctor →	enteritis →	bacterial →	injection of antibiotics →	unsuccessful, after two visits family took patient to another Western-style doctor
Another Western-style doctor →	neurasthenia →	non-specific somatic cause →	injections of vitamins and hematinics and prescription of sedative to be taken by mouth →	unsuccessful, patient developed rash that family attributed to injections; family decided to go to a Chinese-style doctor

Chinese-style doctor → neurasthenia → imbalance of *yin* and *yang* and inharmony in the functioning of the *wu-tsang* → Chinese medicines → unsuccessful, after one month of weekly or twice-weekly treatments, no change in complaints; family took patient to a fortune-teller

Fortune-teller → bad fate → due to sins committed by ancestors in a past life → *táng-ki* for ritual to treat bad fate → after three visits family felt not effective for this problem, though perhaps effective in improving family's fate. On my suggestion, patient went to a psychiatric clinic

Psychiatrist → depression with somatization → marital and family stress as well as genetic basis owing to history of depression in patient's family → antidepressant medication and marital counselling with a social worker → successful, symptoms disappeared and patient reported feeling "much better."

Figure 8 (cont'd.)

Diagram of Health Seeking Behavior of Three Taiwanese Patients

2. Acute Infectious Disease

<u>Health Problem</u>: 18-month-old female infant with diarrhea and fever of one day's duration who comes from a lower-class Taiwanese family in Taipei.

Labeler	Label	Etiologies Implicated	Choice of Treatment	Evaluation of Treatment Outcome
Mother and grandmother	→ "diarrhea"	→ ingesting "irritating" foods	→ rice congee, local herb tea, restricted diet	→ unsuccessful, no improvement over 24 hours
Mother	→ "enteritis," based on experience with similar problem in her two older children	→ infection	→ antidiarrheal tablets from a Western-style pharmacy	→ unsuccessful, no improvement over 24 hours
Mother	→ "enteritis"	→ infection	→ Western-style pediatrician to whom she had taken her other children in past and this child for injection of antibiotics	→ successful, patient brought child daily to clinic for three consecutive days. By fourth day all symptoms had disappeared. On the second day in this type of care, grandmother took patient to a *táng-ki*'s shrine for treatment
Táng-ki	→ "child's sickness from inside the body"	→ perhaps "infection," bad fate may make it difficult for Western-style doctor to treat	→ ritual to treat bad fate. Grandmother advised to return with patient to pediatrician	→ Grandmother said treatment of bad fate helped doctor cure patient; mother felt doctor and god had been effective

3. Chronic Disease/Illness

Health Problem: 60-year-old Taiwanese grandmother from a lower-class family in Taipei with hypertension and mild left-sided hemiparesis from a cerebrovascular accident she experienced one year before.

Labeler	Label	Etiologies Implicated	Choice of Treatment	Evaluation of Treatment Outcome
Patient →	"stroke" →	"high blood pressure," hot/cold imbalance, bad fate	→ local health station for treatment of high blood pressure; diet, herbs, and tonic for treatment of high blood pressure and hot/cold imbalance; *tâng-ki* and Taoist priest for treatment of bad fate	→ partially successful, patient states her hemiparesis cannot be cured, but she can prevent another stroke

*Choice of treatment in this case and the preceding two cases that I diagrammed should not be taken to suggest that Western-style medical practice is the final or most successful solution to health problems in Taiwan. In fact, we came across many instances where this simply was not true (see Chapters 7 and 8).

on how long it takes to obtain symptom relief and on beliefs about the cause and severity of the problem. In difficult-to-treat, chronic, and severe acute disorders, patients commonly use several forms of therapy simultaneously until relief is obtained. This is especially true of the family response to children's sicknesses that they perceive to be "serious." Recourse to sacred and secular folk practitioners may occur at any stage of illness, but it is increasingly more likely to occur when a sickness persists. As already noted, expectations vary considerably when patients are treated by Western-style and Chinese-style doctors. The former are expected to relieve symptoms in several days, two to three visits at the maximum. If they do not, then patients will change doctors. On the other hand, Chinese medicine is reputed to act slowly. Because it is believed to treat the "underlying cause" rather than symptoms, patients usually are willing to wait for considerable periods, even in the face of persistent symptoms, before deciding that a Chinese medicine has failed to work. Our data show that recourse is more frequently made to Western-style doctors for severe acute disorders and to Chinese-style physicians and sacred folk healers for chronic sickness. Some people hold that Chinese medicines can refine the activities of Western medicines, which are thought to be powerful but crude in action. Accordingly, Chinese medicines not infrequently are taken along with Western drugs. Patient and family expectations include much more than the beliefs about side-effects reported in Chapter 3. Such expectations extend to the behaviors patients expect doctors to show, the treatments they expect them to give, and the explanations they expect to receive. It is commonly assumed that Western-style doctors will be quick, matter-of-fact, and have little to say. Chinese-style doctors are expected to act more fatherly and more slowly, to give detailed answers to questions, and to show somewhat more concern for their patients. Undoubtedly, these explanations shape clinical reality.

Sick roles and associated patterns of health seeking behavior vary by age, sex, and family role. Children with sickness will be put to bed; husbands, much less often, since they usually cannot stay home from work unless the sickness is quite severe; wives, least of all, since even when quite ill they must perform the housework and cooking. People do not expect most sickness to lead to social withdrawal. Indeed, the common expectation is that withdrawal is an indicator of serious sickness, especially among the elderly and the very young. For severe illnesses, family members claim they worry more about the family head and his wife than anyone else, since the family's livelihood and routine functions depend on them. But considerable concern also is shown young children and the elderly when they are ill, since they are believed less resistant to serious sickness and death. This notion reflects both empirical observation and popular medical theory, which holds that children and the elderly are more susceptible to sickness because they are "weaker" and have less *yang* and less tightly attached souls. For the same reason, infants, the elderly, and women following delivery, who are believed to be in a state of weakness and heightened susceptibility to disease, are the chief targets for health maintenance practices. For example, they are given special diets and tonics to "supplement" or strengthen their constitutions. Even more attention is focused on health maintenance than on the treatment of disease, and one could describe different perceptions of "health roles" or "health status" to complement the different views of the sick role I am describing.

Perhaps an example will make these points clearer. When an infant takes ill (especially a male infant), parents and grandparents show considerable concern because of the feared susceptibility of infants to serious illness and death, a worry supported by extremely high infant mortality rates in urban and rural areas of China (and Taiwan) for much of this century (see Worth 1963). If an infant begins to cry at night, seems disturbed, and cannot be mollified, a decision is made almost immediately about what to do. If the infant is febrile, he may be given an antipyretic and then taken to a Western-style doctor or pharmacist for an injection (usually containing an antibiotic). But if he is not febrile and instead seems to be colicky without good reason, recourse is made to special ritual practitioners—usually old women in the neighborhood (*sien-si^n-má*), *tâng-ki*s, or other temple-based ritual experts—for performance of a particular ritual by which the soul of the patient (believed to have departed the body) is called back. At the same time, the infant also may be taken to a modern medical clinic, so that several different but potentially effective remedies may be tried simultaneously.

Children with this problem are believed to be suffering from "fright" (*ching*) that has scared away (or "dispersed") their souls. This sickness category in our survey was the commonest label assigned by families to the sickness episodes of children (37 percent of all children's sickness episodes were so labeled).[3] Treatment for "fright" is a ritual that calls the lost soul back to the body. Even if a small child is treated successfully by a Western-style doctor for his sickness, he still may be taken by female members of his family to a shrine for "calling back the soul" (*chao hun*), and he may not be considered cured until he has had this ritual performed. Here we have an example of the interplay of pragmatic and "theoretical" thinking and of concern for both instrumental and symbolic efficacy that typifies popular health beliefs and decisions (cf. Erasmus 1952; Kleinman 1975a, 1976; Obeyesekere 1976). This problem also demonstrates the importance attached by Chinese to non-verbalized behavioral indicators of physical sickness. Children are routinely scanned for such cues, and behavioral deviances of many kinds are often first interpreted as signs of physical sickness.

This particular example illustrates discrepancies concerning the evaluation of care: for the doctor who treated the child, the medicine is a sufficient treatment; but for the family concerned that their child may have lost its soul, it is insufficient until the soul has been called back. Such discrepant beliefs and values not infrequently are found in the same family. Female members of Taiwanese families tend to be culturally more traditional and, therefore, are more commonly involved with sacred folk medicine. They may at times have healing rituals performed in secret, because they fear other members of the family (usu-

3: Although roughly 90 percent of children labeled as suffering from "fright" whom we studied were afflicted with an acute sickness, the remainder were children who had chronic listlessness, irritability, unexplained bouts of crying, and developmental problems of one sort or another, which parents often expressed as "isn't growing well." Hence, this indigenous illness category relates to two quite different kinds of problems, though the vast majority are acute sicknesses.

ally males) would otherwise prevent them from employing such practices. Frequently male family members are unaware of the range of treatments applied to sick children. In my experience, it is not uncommon to find families where one adult family member favors one treatment approach, while others favor other approaches. Indeed, sometimes different family members have expertise in different kinds of treatment. Obviously, these discrepancies can cause real problems when decisions must be made about how to respond to sickness. In our sample, in one-third of cases we were able to unearth several different EMs and related treatment alternatives in the same family for the same illness episode. Decisions often came down to the choice made by a key family member, usually the mother or grandmother if a child was ill. But, in the case of children, lay expertise would be sought from the wife's family, too, and from local experts. The older family members and neighbors with special experience form a "lay referral system" that plays a major role in what type of health care is sought and how the health care received is evaluated. Eighty-five percent of the patients we studied who were treated by practitioners had selected these practitioners (or, in the case of children, had the selection made for them by parents) on the advice of family members, friends, and other members of their social networks. Practitioners themselves are aware that the lay referral system is the chief determinant of choice of practitioner. Unlike children, adults are expected to make their own treatment decisions, but they also are expected to accept (and act on) family advice. In fact, the major role assigned to the family, even over the individual, in the health seeking process is one of the chief differences in illness behavior and the sick role between Taiwan and the United States. Although this societal arrangement for making popular health decisions generally seems to work effectively, it is not at all uncommon to discover divergent family beliefs that lead to major conflicts in deciding which of the different treatment alternatives should be followed. We could easily imagine this happening in the example of "fright" just presented and in the example of measles discussed in Chapter 3 (see Figure 8 for other examples). But as Kunstadter (1976a) suggests, such points of conflict, and the system of multiple choice points for selecting alternative forms of treatment upon which they are based, instead of creating cognitive dissonance and intrafamily strife, may serve an important set of adaptive functions in forcing families to scan an entire range of therapeutic alternatives, one of which may be effective, and in providing families with a sense of stability since they are not locked into a single choice that may fail. My impression is that this also commonly happened among the families we studied.

Another example of the fact that popular health beliefs hold direct implications for choosing between treatment alternatives comes from popular conceptions of mental illness.[4] Most Taiwanese appear to distinguish two chief types of mental illness: violent psychotic behavior and mental retardation. Minor psychiatric disorders may be added as a third group, which is further subdivided into those regarded as part of the sickness category and those held to be psychological "problems," not medical or psychiatric "disease." The popular explanation frequently runs along the following line. Both categories of major mental disorders are essentially incurable. If an attempt is to be made to control patients with these problems, however, one should choose Western-style doctors who specialize in these problems and who use electroconvulsive therapy (ECT) or drugs or hospitalization, instead of Chinese-style doctors or folk practitioners. Western-style doctors can use somatic ther-

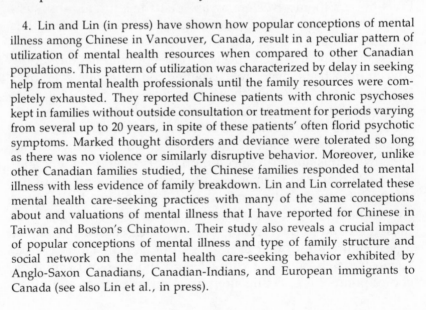

4. Lin and Lin (in press) have shown how popular conceptions of mental illness among Chinese in Vancouver, Canada, result in a peculiar pattern of utilization of mental health resources when compared to other Canadian populations. This pattern of utilization was characterized by delay in seeking help from mental health professionals until the family resources were completely exhausted. They reported Chinese patients with chronic psychoses kept in families without outside consultation or treatment for periods varying from several up to 20 years, in spite of these patients' often florid psychotic symptoms. Marked thought disorders and deviance were tolerated so long as there was no violence or similarly disruptive behavior. Moreover, unlike other Canadian families studied, the Chinese families responded to mental illness with less evidence of family breakdown. Lin and Lin correlated these mental health care-seeking practices with many of the same conceptions about and valuations of mental illness that I have reported for Chinese in Taiwan and Boston's Chinatown. Their study also reveals a crucial impact of popular conceptions of mental illness and type of family structure and social network on the mental health care-seeking behavior exhibited by Anglo-Saxon Canadians, Canadian-Indians, and European immigrants to Canada (see also Lin et al., in press).

apies to calm patients, even though they cannot cure them. Chinese-style doctors and folk practitioners are thought to be unable to control such patients. Patients with minor mental illness, on the other hand, are thought to derive benefit from Chinese-style medical management or temple-based healing, not Western medical therapies. Such popular beliefs not only determine what choices will be made but also influence the way practitioners view these health problems. Thus, Chinese-style doctors and folk healers are usually unwilling to treat major psychiatric problems because they are aware of their own limited efficacy as well as popular recognition of that limitation.

Beliefs lead to valuations of sicknesses. This is an essential aspect of the cultural construction of illness behavior. Popular explanations in Taiwan mark leprosy, mental illness, and tuberculosis as very dangerous and the most shameful of disorders. Venereal disease is considered much less shameful than tuberculosis, a reversal of the contemporary popular valuation of those disorders in the West. Popular beliefs have changed in response to epidemiological realities and the status of biomedical technologies, so that today in Taiwan no longer are infectious diseases most feared in the popular sector. Instead cancer and stroke, which have in fact become the major causes of mortality, are the most feared disorders. The marked stigma attached to mental illness is further revealed in the euphemisms, "eccentricity" and "psychological problem," used by family members to label a kinsman referred to as "mentally ill" or "crazy" by people outside the family. Indeed, the former terms mark one as a kinsman or close friend, while the latter designate an outsider or a neighbor not in a close association with the sick person's family.

Within the web of beliefs and values, the patient and his family manage illness and its consequences. The logic they employ indicates several key polar opposites. We have already had much to say about the hot/cold dichotomy. Poison/clean, wet/dry, yin/yang, and other polar oppositions are also important. Another dichotomy almost as widespread in the popular sector, especially in rural areas, is a distinction between disorders whose causes are "within the body" and those that are "outside the body." The former includes disorders thought to have a physiological etiology, for which one goes to Chinese-style or Western-style doctors for a technological intervention (herbs or injections, respectively). The latter includes super-naturally caused disorders, for which one goes to shamans and other folk practitioners for sacred healing. This schema is used to help make choices about which kind of care to receive and also to evaluate the care that is applied. For example, with this schema in mind, patients would not expect personally and so-cially meaningful explanations from Western-style doctors any more than they would expect injections from shamans. In fact, however, folk practitioners often provide both technical treat-ment and meaningful explanations, and their patients expect to receive both (see Chapter 7). With some exceptions—such as the fact there are no sacred Chinese folk healers in Boston and, thus, people don't employ beliefs related to them—what we have been saying about the popular health care sector in Taiwan holds as well for the popular sector in Boston's Chinatown.

The family response to sick persons in Taiwan attempts to contain the person, his sickness, and the social problems it generates within the circle of the family. As we have seen, fam-ilies there have much more autonomy in treating sickness than do families in the West. From the standpoint of modern health care, family responses may facilitate or impede clinical care. But from the much broader viewpoint of the health care sys-tem, family responses provide most of the health care. Not only is care of most adult episodes of sickness in Taiwan lim-ited to the family circle, but even in those illness episodes where care is sought outside the family, decisions about whom to consult, when to consult, and when to comply or change practitioners are made within the context of the family or social network. Patients rarely go to practitioners unaccompanied by family members; indeed, as I report in Chapter 7, family mem-bers sometimes consult folk healers on their own, without the patient being present. When there is severe sickness, it is to the family member rather than the patient that the practitioner will talk about the problem. And patients expect this to hap-pen; for it is the family, not the practitioner or the patient, that in Taiwan is seen as most responsible for the sick person and his care.

Family-Based Popular Health Care

Once having said this, it is striking how little we still know about this most important component of Taiwanese health care systems. In the final section of Chapter 8, I will examine the family as a "practitioner" in terms of the health care relationships and activities that occur in the family and how they compare to the clinical reality fashioned in the professional and folk arenas of health care.

Modernization has made some inroads into the family locus of care. Public health authorities claim additional responsibilities for health problems. Western-style doctors tend to take a more activist view of their role in the patient's care. But the family is still viewed as most responsible for the patient. A tragic anecdote illustrates the point. On one occasion I visited a small private mental hospital outside Taipei with public health workers from the Taipei City Health Department. They were checking the status of patients with mental illness who were public patients from Taipei sent to these small private mental hospitals by the Taipei City Government because there simply are not enough public beds in Taipei. Most cases suffer from chronic psychoses and either have no families or have been rejected by their families. They are supported by the Taipei City Health Department, which pays the proprietors of these hospitals a sum approximately equal to one U.S. dollar per patient per day. Even by Taiwan standards this is insufficient to cover all the costs. In return, these small hospitals operate more like warehouses or prisons than hospitals, since patients often are incarcerated for life with minimal treatment.

In one such institution, I entered a small, dirty, poorly ventilated room where I was struck by the sight of an attractive young female patient surrounded by five or six others who were middle-aged women with chronic psychoses, several of whom were chained to their beds, rocking back and forth, exhibiting total asocial behavior. The young girl was weeping, because, though she suffered from a mild manic psychosis, she could visualize herself condemned to this room for life like her neighbors. By psychiatric standards, she had a disease which could normally be well-controlled in outpatient care with modern psychotropic agents. She received none of those, however, because the hospital did not have the money to pay for them and the Taipei Health Department would not provide addi-

201

tional funds. I was shocked by this case and expressed my dismay to the public health workers I was with. They understood my reasons for being concerned but did not understand the intensity of my concern or why I insisted they had to do something about this problem. "But," I was told, "her family has rejected her . . . it is her family's responsibility . . . if her family will not care for her then there is nothing we can do." This case is a sad illustration of the adverse therapeutic effect that occasionally results from the dominant role of the family in the care of the patient in Taiwan and doubtless in China before 1949. It also documents a social evil: There are many levels of care in Taiwan's pluralistic health enterprise and, as our data suggest, differential access to those levels reflects discrepancies in socioeconomic status. Financial resources are the ultimate determinant of the quality and the availability of care, so that care in Taiwan, just as in the United States, suffers from inequalities based on the socioeconomic inequalities that are a basic feature of that society's social system.

7

Patients and Healers:
Transactions Between
Explanatory Models
and Clinical Realities
*Part 1: Sacred Folk Healer-Client
Relationships*

PROLOGUE

So, Oliver . . . soon fell into a gentle doze, from which he was awakened by the light of a candle: which being brought near the bed, showed him a gentleman with a very large and loud ticking gold watch in his hand, who felt his pulse, and said he was a great deal better.

"You are a great deal better, are you not, my dear?" said the gentleman.

"Yes, Thank you sir," replied Oliver.

"Yes, I know you are," said the gentleman.

"You're hungry too, ain't you?"

"No, sir," answered Oliver.

"Hem!" said the gentleman. "No, I know you're not. He is not hungry, Mrs. Bedwin," said the gentleman: looking very wise.

The old lady made a respectful inclination of the head, which seemed to say that she thought the doctor was a very clever man. The doctor appeared much of the same opinion himself.

"You feel sleepy, don't you, my dear?" said the doctor.

"No, sir," replied Oliver.

"No," said the doctor, with a very shrewd and satisfied look. "You're not sleepy. Nor thirsty. Are you?"

"Yes, sir, rather thirsty," answered Oliver.

"Just as I expected, Mrs. Bedwin," said the doctor. "It's very natural that he should be thirsty. You may give him a little tea, ma'am,

and some dry toast without any butter. Don't keep him too warm, ma'am; but be careful that you don't let him be too cold; will you have the goodness?"

Charles Dickens, Oliver Twist
(New York: Pocket Library Series, Pocket Books, 1957), pp. 86–87

The latter proposed to tell the physician of his wife's symptoms, but the physician said, "I should like to feel her pulse first and see for myself the cause of the illness. . . ."

"This is what I found," the physician answered. "The pulse on her left hand is deep and agitated under my forefinger; it is deep and faint under the second finger. On her right hand it is vague and lacks vitality under the forefinger. The first indicates a febrile state arising from a weak action of the heart; the second, a sluggishness of the liver. The vague and spiritless forefinger pulse of the right hand suggests a disturbance in the lung humors, while the vague second finger pulse bespeaks a wood element in the liver too strong for the earth element in the spleen. The symptoms of the first disturbance should be pain in the ribs, tardy menses, and a burning sensation around the heart. Disturbance of the lung humors generally leads to giddiness and perspiration in the early morning hours during sleep. The prevalence of the wood element in the liver over the earth element in the spleen should lead to lack of appetite, general fatigue, and soreness of the limbs. If I am correct in reading the action of the pulse, these symptoms should be present. Some may confuse this pulse with one indicating pregnancy, but I am afraid that I cannot agree with such a diagnosis."

A maidservant who had been attending Chin-shih said, "The doctor is right in every detail. . . ."

. . . So saying he gave the prescription to his son, who in turn gave it to a servant to have it filled.

Tsao Hsueh-chin, Dream of the Red Chamber
(New York: Doubleday, 1958), pp. 79–81

Professor's coupling: "This is a case of sarcoidosis. Which is to say, this patient is a man who has something wrong with him, a disorder of unknown etiology and uncertain course but with sufficient signs and symptoms and pathology in common with other such cases to warrant the class name sarcoidosis, a name, however, which serves

204

as nothing better than a shorthand method of speaking of an ill-defined illness."

Medical student's coupling: "This is a case of sarcoidosis. *Which is to say, the patient is assigned to the disease-class* sarcoidosis *Platonically." The patient is understood to participate in a higher reality than himself, namely, his disease. Later the student will refer to the patient by some such sentence as, "I have a case of sarcoidosis on the third floor."*

Patient's coupling: "This is a case of sarcoidosis. *I have been invaded by an entity, a specter named sarcoidosis."*

Walker Percy, The Message in the Bottle
(New York: Farrar, Strauss, and Giroux, 1975), pp. 180–181

The subject of this chapter and the next is cognitive and communicative transactions between healers and patients. Although I will discuss healers, they are *not* the primary concern, and consequently I will devote little space to them. The overwhelming distortion in medical anthropology, resulting from several decades of research, has been one in which healers were studied in isolation as the central component of medicine in society. More recently, the distortion has been reversed by studies which deal almost exclusively with patients, but neglect the crucial health care *transactions* as the central subject for clinically oriented anthropological research.

The paradigm of practitioner-patient relationships is derived from the clinical orientation of medicine in the West. This component of the medical model, while facilitating cross-cultural clinical comparisons, may distort the reality we wish to describe. For example, it invites the assumption that practitioner-patient transactions are dyads, as is most common in contemporary professional medicine in the West. But in Taiwan, as in many other societies, the practitioner-patient interaction usually involves family as well as the sick person. It is most often not a dyad. Also, the illness may be attributed to more than just the sick person. In Taiwan, as we have seen, the entire family may be labeled sick or inharmonious and treatment directed to it or to key family members. In folk practice the afflicted individual may not be the focus of clinical care and may

not even be present during clinical transactions. A close relative may consult a specialist, bringing some of the sick person's
clothing, or relatives and friends may give the fortune-teller an
individual's eight characters (*pa tzu*), specifying his time of
birth, to inquire about the influence of fate on the course of his
illness and its treatment. In most situations of this kind that I
have witnessed, the healer dealt with his clients as if they were
patients. He explained to them and for them, performing rituals that were meaningful to them. That is, he gave care to
people other than the sick person: advice, support, technical
and symbolic therapies. The folk healers held the view that illness in such cases directly influenced family and social relationships. They responded by treating those relationships and
family members.

Most clients in folk practice are females. Folk healers often
are asked by them to treat the problems of other (usually male)
family members. But they may consider that the real patient
is actually the woman before them. Her problem may be her
concern for another sick person. Even when the ostensibly sick
person is present, it is not uncommon for the folk healer to
direct most of his attention to the mother or other female relatives who have accompanied him. In this way a folk healer
seems to consider that his therapy is principally meaningful for
the female relative of the sick person. When I made follow-up
visits in such instances, it was usually that "other" person on
whom the treatment had had the greatest impact. Mothers frequently told me *they* felt better and even that their offspring
were better, when in fact the "patient" reported no improvement. These mothers evaluated the folk healing practices to be
effective, while their children often refused to do so or stated
that they were ineffective. This was particularly evident when
the patients were better educated and more modern in orientation than their mothers.

The danger in using a concept like that of doctor-patient interaction is that it invites the imposition of Western medical
views of clinical reality. I hope to avoid this bias. In a separate
section at the end of the following chapter, I will outline a different model of the clinical encounter between patient and family. Here, I will comment upon family-practitioner relationships for each type of patient-practitioner interaction I examine.

CATEGORIES FOR COMPARING THERAPEUTIC RELATIONSHIPS

A substantial impediment to the development of more discriminating cross-cultural comparisons among healing systems is the absence of generally agreed upon criteria for determining similarities and differences. To remedy this problem I will set out five more or less discrete categories that I employ in comparing practitioner-patient transactions. Some of these categories are based on materials that I have discussed in earlier chapters. Others are derived from my reading of the anthropological and cross-cultural literature on healing and from my own field research. Together they represent what I take to be the most adequate criteria we presently possess both for framing cross-cultural comparisons and for systematically collecting ethnographic data. For any type of practitioner-patient interaction, then, we can determine its:

1. Institutional Setting (i.e., specific location in a given health care system's sectors and subsectors)

2. Characteristics of the Interpersonal Interaction
   a. *Number* of Participants
   b. *Time* Coordinates (i.e., whether it is *episodic* or *continuous*, the expected average length of treatment, the amount of time spent in each transaction, the time spent in communicating or in explaining)
   c. *Quality* of the Relationship (i.e., whether it is *formal* or *informal* with respect to etiquette, type of social role— primary, secondary, tertiary, emotional distance, restricted or elaborated communicative code, nature of transference and countertransference; whether it is *integrated* into or *divorced* from everyday life experiences and ongoing daily activities)
   d. *Attitudes* of the Participants (i.e., how practitioners and patients view each other, particularly if they hold mutually ambivalent views of the other)

3. Idiom of Communication
   a. *Mode* (i.e., psychological, mechanistic, somatic, psychosomatic, sociological, spiritual, moral, naturalistic, etc.)
   b. *Explanatory Models* (i.e., shared, openly expressed,

tacit, or conflicting; whether the EMs are drawn from single, unified belief systems or fragmented, pluralistic ones)

4. Clinical Reality
    a. *Sacred* or *Secular* (indigenous or Western)
    b. *Disease-Oriented* or *Illness-Oriented*
    c. *Symbolic* or *Instrumental* Interventions
    d. *Therapeutic Expectations* (i.e., concerning etiquette, treatment style, therapeutic objectives, and whether these are shared or discrepant)
    e. Perceived *Locus of Responsibility* for Care (the individual patient, family, community, or practitioner)

5. Therapeutic Stages and Mechanisms
    a. *Tripartite Organization* or Other Structure
    b. *Mechanisms of Change* (i.e., catharsis, insight, psychophysiological, social, etc.)
    c. *Adherence, Termination, Evaluations of Outcome* (i.e., shared or discrepant assessments of satisfaction, efficacy, cost-effectiveness)

We can describe the concrete details of a given practitioner-patient relationship for each of these categories, or we can use them to compare different therapeutic relationships. And we can discuss their practical implications. Although not exhaustive of all issues relevant to clinical relationships, these categories should enable us to determine their universal and culture-specific aspects, whereas the ethnocentric and medicocentric categories of biomedical practice or psychoanalysis or behavioral medicine cannot.

In this chapter I examine two types of sacred Chinese folk healing relationships, shaman-client and *ch'ien* interpreter-client interactions, in terms of these five analytic categories; in the next chapter I do the same for Chinese-style physician-patient, Western-style doctor-patient, and family-patient interactions. These categories cannot cover all aspects of clinical practice. Hence, I have included concretely detailed descriptions of practitioner-patient transactions that I observed and recorded in the field in the hope that this ethnographic material will provide the reader a richer, more complete picture of clinical transactions and, at the same time, point out additional issues for cross-cultural research that are not yet adequately conceptualized by this analytic framework.

HEALERS IN TAIWAN: SOME GENERAL CONSIDERATIONS

Strikingly impressive among healers of all types in Taiwan is what might be called the kinship basis of the healing role. Healing in traditional China was frequently an hereditary occupation, and this has been carried over into the ideology of health care systems in contemporary Taiwan. If practitioners do not possess an elaborate genealogy of healers in their families, they often manufacture such medical genealogies in order to conform to the health care systems' ideology and thereby attract patients. Many patients told us that a practitioner from a family with at least three generations of practitioners was more likely to be well-qualified and might even possess secret remedies not available to other practitioners. In many traditional societies (Loudon 1976: 27–28), healing appears to have an hereditary distribution which functions as a means of transmitting esoteric knowledge, ceremonial practices, and other valuable "property" to kinsmen. The same purpose seems to be served in Taiwan.

Although kinship ties among healers are not nearly as prominent as they were in the past, they still are much more extensive in Taiwan than in the United States. More than 75 percent of all the practitioners we studied could point to specific family members who were healers. Interestingly, relatives often did not belong to the same healing tradition. For example, almost half of the Chinese-style doctors I interviewed, most of them middle-aged men, had younger family relations (both men and women) who were training in or had already graduated from Western-style medical schools. Several of the middle-aged *ch'ien* interpreters and shamans had nephews or cousins who practiced or were studying Chinese-style or Western-style medicine. Often I was told by such middle-aged practitioners that they would have become Chinese-style or Western-style practitioners themselves had those alternatives been open to them. Both practitioners and lay people ranked being a Western-style doctor as more desirable than being a Chinese-style doctor, which in turn was ranked as more desirable than being a folk practitioner. Educational background and socioeconomic status were important determinants of which healing role an individual entered, but family background seemed to be crucial in determining if a person became a healer at all.

Not infrequently we found kinship networks among healers being used as referral systems. At times, they had clear financial significance. For example, a primary care practitioner sent his patients to have laboratory tests performed at or buy drugs from companies owned by relatives. The kinship network has the potential to maximize patient referrals and to improve the competitive status of its members. The apprentice-based form of medical training common among Chinese-style and folk practitioners also can have the same effect, since teachers send patients to their students and vice versa. Apprentice-based training is organized on the Confucian master-disciple paradigm and involves pseudo-kinship relationships. Given the press of competition among a very large and diverse body of practitioners for a relatively limited supply of private patients, the kinship and apprentice networks probably still possess economic importance.

Closely tied to this phenomenon is the widespread view that healing activities of all sorts are potentially profitable family businesses. It is common in Taipei, as I shall demonstrate below, to find small Chinese-style and Western-style clinics and hospitals, and small temples where *ch'ien* interpreters and shamans practice, run as family businesses. Father and grandfather may be healers; mother and daughters may be assistants or nurses; sons or cousins may manage the financial affairs; other relatives may prepare and sell medicines or sacred healing paraphernalia. And as we shall see, a given family medical business may contain different medical traditions (for example, family members who are Chinese-style doctors and other family members who are Western-style doctors), though this is less common than family medical businesses organized strictly around a single healing tradition. These cases further illustrate the importance of financial considerations for studies of healers in Taiwan.

Practitioner-Patient Interactions 1: Shaman-Client

Taiwan's shamans are part of a great Asian tradition of shamanism that includes Japan, Korea, and Okinawa and that, in the past, extended across the vastness of China through various central Asian peoples into what is now the Soviet Union and connected up with similar traditions in Tibet. Ancient Chinese texts contain frequent mention of *wu* (shaman), and that tradition seems to have been part of Chinese culture in all areas. In modern times it seems to have been an especially active tradition in Fukien province, where most Taiwanese trace their ancestry. Probably at no time in Taiwan's past have there been as many shamans as now. This is attributed to both an upsurge of folk religion as the only tolerated expression of Taiwanese nationalism and the financial success of shamanism in present day Taiwan. It is not possible to accurately calculate their number, since they are not registered. By estimates that I made in the field, there must be at the least 800 practicing shamans in Taipei alone, though for years officials in Taiwan claimed shamans could only be found in rural villages. Informants have estimated that Shuang-Yüan District's oldest section may have as many as 50 shamans in fairly close proximity to one another.[1] The phenomenon of urban shamanism reflects the massive rural to urban migration of Taiwan's population.

The word for shaman in Taiwan is the Hokkien term *tâng-ki*, which means literally "divining youth." The popular ideology has it that young men or women are chosen by gods to manifest the gods' wish to "save the world." This is revealed via trance, at which time the god "speaks through" the entranced shaman. The ideology also states that a shaman is poor and

---

1. For reports on Taiwan's shamans, see Ahern (1976), Gallin (1966), Gould-Martin (1976), Jordan (1972), Kleinman (1976), Kleinman and Sung (1976), Li (1972), Liu (1974, 1975), Tseng (1972, 1976), and Wang (1971). Shamanism in Singapore and Hong Kong is dealt with in studies by Elliot (1955) and Myers (1974), while DeGroot (1972) reviews shamanism in ancient China and describes shamans in late nineteenth-century Amoy. Some writers use the term "spirit-medium" rather than "shaman." But in Taiwan at least, it comports with anthropological usage to call *tâng-ki*s shamans, inasmuch as they are divinely inspired or possessed healers. There are other sacred folk experts in Taiwan who function solely as mediums for communicating with ancestral spirits. These individuals (frequently women who practice in temples but sometimes visit clients' homes, *ang-î*) do not engage in healing and usually cannot be described as "divinely inspired or possessed." Hence it is more accurate to refer to them as "spirit-mediums" and to reserve "shaman" for *tâng-ki*s.

usually illiterate; that he is often cured of an otherwise incurable illness (usually physical) by his god, who thereafter establishes a Confucian style master-disciple relationship with him that the shaman cannot end by himself if he wishes to keep his health; that he suddenly finds himself, often against his will, spontaneously trancing and able to cure "miraculously" individuals with sicknesses previously thought to be incurable; and that the shaman remains ignorant of what happens when he is in a trance. The shaman does not "charge" a fee, but the client "donates" a gift to the shaman for the god. The shaman often refers to himself as the "child" or "son" of his god.

It is not the shaman who heals, but the god. And healing is in fact his chief activity. Half to three-quarters of all shamanistic consultations deal with health problems. The rest of the consultations include personal, family, and business questions. In each the god is asked to be instrumental in resolving life problems. Revealing people's fate and treating bad fate are other important activities, but most frequently shamans in Taiwan see acute disruptive interpersonal crises requiring immediate intervention. Illness that breaks out of the family context of control is precisely such a problem. And, therefore, from a biased medical and psychiatric perspective, shamans function as indigenous crisis intervention experts. At least five of the twenty-five shamans I have had the privilege to study agreed with this description once I had replaced the "person" with the "god" as active force. That is, the god is seen as a healer. The _tâng-ki_ recognizes illness as the most common and often the most difficult problem he treats. Both the shaman and his clients look upon healing as an appropriate, and in fact the most appropriate, venue for the demonstration of the practical efficacy of their religious beliefs.

I studied shamans by obtaining introductions to their shrines and by attending several sessions as an observer before asking permission to interview them, their assistants, and clients. After that we systematically interviewed clients before they consulted the shaman, observed their interactions with the shaman, and later visited them at home, at which time we asked them to evaluate the care they had received. Many shamans are quite suspicious of visitors, especially Mainlanders or foreigners. They fear publicity, which is almost always negative.

Sacred Folk Healers

Taoist priest who is also a shaman, bone-setter, and drug store proprietor (see pages 67–68)

Entranced *tâng-ki* "fire-walking" during a healing ritual

Tâng-ki entering trance

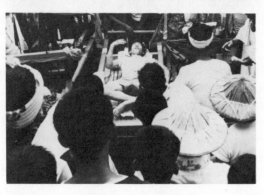

Entranced *tâng-ki* lying on a bed of nails during a festival

Shamanism is a cultural metaphor that Taiwan's elite class does not consider consonant with the image of social development. Similarly, traditional Confucian scholars in China over the centuries felt shamanism was inconsistent with Confucian values and the People's Republic of China sees it as a superstitious vestige of capitalistic feudalism incompatible with Maoist socialism. Moreover, since they make a considerable amount of money, *tâng-ki*s rightly fear the tax agents and the police. Only on one occasion, however, was I denied permission to enter a shrine. Otherwise, shamans generally went along with nearly everything I burdened them and their clients with. In several cases, shamans took an active part in the research: they allowed us to put our tape recorders on the altar table; they encouraged clients to cooperate and permit us to perform follow-up home visits; and they had their assistants make sure that we did not misinterpret their words and actions. But in no case did a shaman provide us with a "real" life history. What we obtained were stylized accounts that followed all the key points of the popular ideology concerning what shamans *should* be like. All the *tâng-ki*s we studied came from lower-class backgrounds; most possessed only rudimentary education or were illiterate; four-fifths were men; all were from rural villages.

Of the twenty-five shamans I observed, I had the opportunity to interview personally and evaluate the mental status of ten. None exhibited any evidence of significant psychopathology nor gave any history of major psychiatric problems. Most were rather remarkable individuals, who possessed strong personalities and many adaptive coping skills. They were adept at quickly assessing and managing life crises and personal difficulties, were as effective at interpersonal communication as at ritual manipulations, and were recognized as such by neighbors and clients. Shamanistic healing clearly demands personal strengths and sensitivities incompatible with major psychopathology, especially chronic psychosis. Thus my findings argue against the view that shamanism provides a socially legitimated role for individuals suffering from schizophrenia or other severe psychiatric or neurological disorders.

Shamans in Taiwan frequently come from extremely poor families, sometimes where one or both parents died when the shaman was still young. They subsequently are identified as helpful, "good," understanding individuals by neighbors and others in the community but are seen not to have a direction open for their advancement and not to have much family support. Through a variety of circumstances, shamanism is made available to them by their social network as a means to succeed, as a "gift" that the shaman *repays* through his service (the popular ideology holds that the shaman "serves the people"). The shaman is expected to be "successful" on behalf of his god, the community, and himself. Achievement orientation, then, is a prerequisite for shamans, who are always in the process of building a newer and bigger shrine (or home) and who are not hesitant to advertise the efficacy of their gods' healing powers.

Most shamans obtain training from older and experienced Taoist priests or other shamans. They are taught how to control trance behavior and about herbs and Chinese medicine, which they frequently prescribe. They are taught how to perform seemingly (and at times actually) dangerous activities at festivals: lacerating themselves with swords, sitting on a bed of nails, walking over fires of coals or spirit money, climbing up sword ladders, holding boiling oil in their mouths, burning themselves with incense sticks, etc. Those activities frequently involve "tricks of the trade," but some are nothing else than frenzied performances of self-mutilation, e.g., when *tâng-kis* slice open their scalps or tongues in order to obtain blood for rituals. But shamans also learn, especially by observing other shamans, how to speak to clients and how to respond to everyday problems, including commonly occurring illnesses. They learn, for example, not to treat acute trauma or any other serious, acute health problem that looks like it might eventuate in death; if they do treat these problems, they also refer patients for appropriate medical attention. Nor will they treat violent psychotic behavior or chronic psychotic disorders. They learn to extricate themselves from these situations without damaging the popular ideology that the gods are powerful therapists. They can do this in a number of ways, the simplest of which is to define an illness as from "within the body," rather than from "gods, ghosts, or ancestors," and therefore outside the boundaries of sacred healing. This maneuver is compatible with the pragmatic orientation we have seen their clients bring to Taiwan's plural healing traditions.

215

We shall visit the shrines of several Taipei *tâng-ki*s. Instead of focusing on the *tâng-ki*, we shall examine the interaction between *tâng-ki* and client. That should give us a sense of the social reality established in the therapeutic relationship the patient enters and participates in when he visits the *tâng-ki*.

Most *tâng-ki*s' shrines are small and resemble the one described below. The *tâng-ki* usually sees clients daily, either in the afternoon or evening. He generally works with several assistants, who are responsible for registering clients, providing them with incense, translating the *tâng-ki*'s words, which may be unintelligible to laymen or simply inaudible, offering additional advice and comments, collecting money, and taking care of the shrine. Not infrequently, one or more of the assistants are family members of the shaman. During the séances, which last from 30 minutes to several hours, the *tâng-ki* enters into and remains in a trance. When he comes out of his trance, it is the sign the treatment session has ended. While in trance, the *tâng-ki* may sing and act out the role of the god possessing him. Before and after the trance, the *tâng-ki* denies any special knowledge or powers. He professes amnesia for his behavior while entranced. During the trance, the *tâng-ki* may inflict wounds on tongue, head, or back to obtain blood in order to write charms. But serious self-mutilation is reserved for special occasions, such as a feast in honor of the shrine's chief god. In some shrines, the *tâng-ki*(s) may use a "god's chair." This is a small chair swung back and forth by one or more *tâng-ki*s or assistants, which writes the god's message in unintelligible characters on the altar table, where they are interpreted by an assistant. While in trance the *tâng-ki* will write charms, conduct short treatment rituals—such as exorcism of possessing demons or transfer of the patient's sickness to a "substitute" (*the-sin*) which is usually a straw or paper image, prescribe herbs or Chinese medicine, and carry on a dialogue with the patient. In the course of a single session, the *tâng-ki* may treat anywhere from two or three to more than thirty clients. Most clients are lower-class, and women outnumber men three or four to one.

*Tâng-ki*s function within the context of the broad syncretic beliefs that constitute Taiwanese folk religion (a mixture of popular Taoist and Buddhist beliefs). However, some shrines, especially where the *tâng-ki* has formed a cult, use special terms and elaborate idiosyncratic ideas. But for the most part, *tâng-kis* work with shared popular beliefs concerning the influence of ghosts, gods, and bad fate on sickness and other personal and family misfortunes (e.g., business, marriage, or school problems). *Tâng-kis* may specialize in certain rituals and even in the treatment of particular kinds of problems (e.g., childhood diseases). Usually *tâng-kis* make use of a relatively small number of rituals, five to ten, which vary somewhat in each shrine and which are used to treat specific sets of problems. Rural and urban shamans differ in many respects. The former, in general, spend more time with each client and engage in more elaborate rituals and in more self-mutilation. Unlike most urban shamans, they may earn their living from other kinds of work, such as farming, and do not earn large amounts of money from their ritual activities. Since rural shamans usually know their clients well, their treatments are more sensitive to interpersonal problems than those of urban practitioners. Laymen's views of shamans, especially in urban areas, tend to be highly ambivalent, believing that shamans are able to cause illness via sorcery as well as treat it, and are just as often hucksters and charlatans as selflessly serving the people. Patients, however, will often travel great distances to consult shamans (or rather their gods) who are believed to be specially effective healers. Thus, it is not uncommon in Taipei to find peasants from rural areas who have journeyed to the city for treatment; similarly, village shamans may be visited regularly by the urban relatives of their village clients. There is a tendency for laymen to consider those shamans "powerful" who are "far away," particularly those who practice in famous temples to which pilgrimages are regularly made or whose festivals are renowned. These *tâng-kis* are most prevalent in the areas of Taipei and of Taiwan that are believed to be centers of the oldest and most traditional Taiwanese culture. But it is also true that urban *tâng-kis* often establish a close relationship with their neighbors, who may support, help run, and regularly attend the nearby shrine on their street. Indeed, such local shrines may function as sites for many family and social network activities, only some of which are "religious."

The first shrine I visited was typical: it was a small room attached to a temple, poorly ventilated, almost airless, hot, packed with thirty clients (including children and infants). Most of the clients were middle-aged women and young mothers from the lower-class. In the center of the room was a large, impressive altar upon which were placed the small painted wooden figures (josses) that represent the shrine's gods. The chief god in this shrine was Ong-ia-kong (the plague god, see Gould-Martin 1976). It was late afternoon.

The *tâng-ki*, a middle-aged man with a red sash tied around his waist (symbolizing, like the ritual blood and self-mutilation, his *yang* powers) and a prominent scarred area on his scalp where he has repeatedly performed ritualistic self-laceration, now possessed by his god, was singing in a falsetto copied from Taiwanese folk opera. He had spent five to ten minutes each with several cases. The assistant announced the next case: a middle-aged man, poorly dressed, unshaven, appearing deeply troubled, surrounded by his family members. The *tâng-ki* did not know this man or his family, as was true of most of his cases and those of other urban *tâng-ki*s. But, like me, he had had an oportunity to observe this client before the séance began and had heard his family talking to other people in the shrine about his problem. The man appeared deeply depressed, and the family had told people in the shrine that he had been this way ever since he suffered severe business losses several months before. The client reported to the *tâng-ki* many physical complaints, including lethargy, insomnia, weight loss associated with loss of appetite, headache, palpitations, dry mouth and difficulty swallowing, and gastrointestinal symptoms, including constipation. He also briefly mentioned his business reverses and admitted to feeling anxious (*fan-tsao*) about them. At no time did he mention any word for depression, nor did his family members, but in the background people were whispering, *"mên"* (depressed).

The *tâng-ki* spoke: "You have too many symptoms. Don't worry about them and your health so much. You are certainly *depressed* [emphasis added], since you have had bad fate in your business and lost much money. That is caused by your younger brother's ghost, who is giving you trouble now." [The *tâng-ki* had asked the client in detail about his family and had learned that two family members, including this younger brother who died as a youth in a fire, had died without leaving descendants who could worship them.]

The *tâng-ki* told the client the ghost was "hungry" and had to be appeased by being "fed" with ritual foods and worshipped at the family altar. He talked with him in a supportive way, encouraging him to get back to his work and family responsibilities. Twice the shaman told jokes. The second time, the client smiled. (It was the first time his troubled expression had changed since he arrived.) The *tâng-ki* prescribed Chinese medicine and advised the client's wife that she had to prepare this medicine by steaming it with a specially prepared chicken dish, which was to be given to the patient several days each week. Then the *tâng-ki*'s tone changed from a supportive one to an authoritarian voice that sounded stern and commanding: "Surely if you do what I tell you, if you take the medicine and appease the ghost, you will get better! You will have no more symptoms!" The *tâng-ki* finished by writing charms for the patient and by performing a brief ritual to treat the patient's bad fate. (From this point on I will use "client" and "patient" interchangeably. Chinese-style and Western-style doctors use the term "patient," *ping-jen*; folk practitioners use the term "client," *k'e-jen,* literally, "guest".)

The assistant told the patient his fate would no longer be bad. He re-explained much of what the *tâng-ki* had said to the patient and his family. They then passed on to another assistant, who gave them a prescription for Chinese medicine based upon the *tâng-ki*'s song. (They were also told where they could purchase this medicine, a Chinese pharmacy not very close to the shrine but owned by the *tâng-ki*'s cousin.) Before the family left the shrine and while the *tâng-ki* went on to treat several other cases, they talked with other clients for more than 30 minutes. They received additional support and encouragement. Someone told them: "Now you know what should be done. The god has made it clear. You shall soon be better. Surely your fortune will change." Although the shaman-patient encounter lasted only 20 minutes, the patient and his family spent several hours in the shrine. Before leaving the patient retold his story several times: each time he referred to himself as "depressed." This profoundly depressed man looked so much better when he left that I could not recall any case that I had treated or observed when the treatment had such a noticeable and immediate effect. Nor did I again encounter as dramatic a therapeutic response in this or other shrines.

Unfortunately this patient was lost to follow-up, and I do not know if his affect steadily improved or worsened. Since he had all the biological symptoms of the depressive syndrome, I would not be surprised if the treatment response did not last. But even so, that should not diminish our respect for the skilled way that this therapist treated this case or for the contribution made by the ethos in the shrine to the patient's care.

There are many ways to interpret what happened in this case. We could invoke, and properly so, the non-specific psychotherapeutic factors that obtain in practitioner-patient interactions. We also might stress the healer's warmth, empathy, supportive techniques, or his authoritarian approach. I purposely have not detailed the ritual symbolism, but this could be examined as an example of the efficacy of symbols (see Kleinman 1975d and Chapter 9). We need not bother with the actual effect (if any) of the Chinese medicine, which was not used during the session. More pertinent is the group support given him by the assistants, other clients, and the patient's family. Like virtually all folk healing activities, this was a public event. Not only the supportive response of people in the shrine but also their presence when the patient spoke about his problems may have reinforced whatever catharsis occurred and the persuasive aspects of the care. The danger here (and in studies of healing in general) is that there are so many possible explanations.

Instead of these, let us bring to bear the theoretical framework advanced above: the social reality of clinical care and its special cultural construction in this society and in this particular shrine. Like the great majority of patients with depression in Chinese culture, this patient did not admit to being depressed. Rather he presented physical complaints, some of which were biological concomitants of his primary affective disorder. His concern was with these and with the business failure he had suffered. Not only is it unlikely that he had ever openly expressed his depressed affect before, but it is also unlikely that his family had ever confronted him with what was such an obvious but psychoculturally dangerous problem. To have done so would have caused great embarrassment, made the patient (the family head) lose face, and gone against the Chinese cultural rules governing emotional communication and behavior that I reviewed in Chapters 4 and 5. Indeed, had this patient seen a Chinese-style or Western-style doctor, he almost certainly would have received the culturally appropriate label of neurasthenia, even if they tacitly diagnosed and treated his depression, so that he could occupy a socially legitimated medical sick role rather than a highly stigmatized psychiatric sick role.

With this in mind, we can appreciate that here was an instance in which the healer provided the patient with an explanation, which the shrine socially endorsed, that allowed him to recognize his problem for what it was and at the same time provided an appropriate cultural model that could be used to treat it. That the patient used the word "depressed" to refer to himself was of great significance. The god told him he was depressed and, what is more, gave him a supernaturally meaningful explanation, one that the patient could understand and to which he would know how to react. The god also sanctioned the business reverses in the most culturally appropriate way by blaming them on bad fate. And the *tâng-ki* provided treatment for the hungry ghost, the bad fate, and even for the physical complaints, which he discounted and reassured the patient he need not worry about, but which he treated nonetheless, with the prescription for Chinese medicine. The therapist's explanations were sanctioned both by their sacred source and by the social ethos of the shrine, where explanations such as "bad fate" and "hungry ghosts" were more real than biological phenomena, where each explanation was linked to a treatment and the more treatment given the better, but where you could not simply diagnose and not treat or place responsibility for treatment on the patient alone. Moreover, the *tâng-ki's* explanation incorporated the only piece of family history that touched on a potential source of tension, the brother who died in childhood. In Taiwan such a death would be seen as a potential source of family troubles. Sickness and other misfortunes would bring out this tension and would raise the question of whether the trouble was due to this ancestor's vengeful ghost. Here the *tâng-ki* made shrewd use of this piece of information in lieu of knowing more about what other specific tensions might be found in this family. This tactic made good psychological sense as well, because, as the eldest brother who had failed in managing the family business, the client may well háve been blaming himself, among other things, for being less capable than his younger brother, who might have helped out or taken over the responsibility for the family's economic success, were he alive. I have seen this happen in similar cases, and perhaps the *tâng-ki* had as well. Therapeutic success was achieved by the insight this indigenous practitioner had into the kinds of culturally constituted concerns that were likely to be causing problems for the client and his family during this sickness episode. His assessment, and the interventions it led to, may have been somewhat off the mark, but, like clinicians everywhere, he was working with probability, not certainty, and in this case knowledge of common lay expectations and fears in Taiwanese culture was virtually all the *tâng-ki* had available to work with.

It is important to see the *tâng-ki*'s explanations as anchored in this shrine's particular social reality. There was really nothing exceptional about the therapist's use of these ideas; they are basic concepts in sacred folk healing in Taiwan and are widespread popular beliefs. (Of course, the *tâng-ki*'s skill came in communicating all of this to the patient in a clinically effective way.) Therefore, they are explanations that convey personal and social meaning to the patient, his family, and the other people in the shrine. Whereas the label "depression" could not be used by the patient or his family, it could be used by the god. It is unlikely that the patient would have accepted this diagnosis as readily elsewhere. Many patients attending the Psychiatry Outpatient Clinic at National Taiwan University Hospital do not accept this label when it is applied by a psychiatrist. Nor could a psychiatrist sensitive to these issues have given the same explanation in the clinic and gotten away with it. Not even the *tâng-ki* could have the same impact outside the appropriate setting. (I was told that on several occasions shamans were invited onto the psychiatric ward to treat patients but did not have beneficial effect.) When these explanations are lifted out of the social context they are embedded in, they seem trite and flimsy, because they have lost the compelling meaning that results from their sacred status. They do not amount to much in an academic seminar room. The power of the explanation is precisely that social reality, the culturally constructed clinical world, that functions as the "real world" for shaman and patient. In this sense, it was the clinical reality, not the clinician, which was effective.

Several weeks later the same *tâng-ki* treated an obese, elderly female who had returned again and again to his clinic for a multiplicity of seemingly endless and usually vague and different physical complaints. I diagnosed this lady as suffering from hysteria. She also had been using the services of a number of Chinese-style and Western-style doctors. In the United States, such "chronic functional" patients are the bane of medical clinics. They do not do well in psychotherapy, since it is the somatic complaints, not psychological issues, they wish to talk about. In Taiwan, such patients are part of an enormous group of cases of somatization that may account for as much as 50 percent of all general medical practice. This patient had spent 20 minutes telling everyone in the shrine about her complaints and remarking that the Chinese medicines the *tâng-ki* had given her had been of no help. She clearly was delighted (just as some patients with chronic functional complaints are in medical clinics in the United States) at demonstrating that nothing could help her problems, and there was no end to the physical problems she could report. Before the séance began, the *tâng-ki* was clearly irritated, and I found myself responding in much the same way:

Client: "I wish to ask about my illness."

Tâng-ki: "You are so fat who will believe you have illness. You want to eat; you want everything to go smoothly and be easy."

Client: "I feel discomfort."

Tâng-ki: "This year is very unlucky for you. Mind your own business, don't mind others'. Don't quarrel with others. Recently, you get angry with people too easily. Do you know this?" (The *tâng-ki* had heard the woman criticize her husband and children and also gossip about her family problems before the séance.)

Client: "I didn't know. I am thinner than before." (The client began to relate a long list of symptoms, but the *tâng-ki* interrupted and prevented her from going on by singing loudly.)

Tâng-ki: "To be thinner is better for you."

Client: "Do I have pain in my abdomen?"

(See below. It is believed an entranced sacred folk practitioner in Chinese culture should be able to tell the client his symptoms without asking questions about them, because of the god's reputed ability to "see" them. The popular ideology similarly holds that a Chinese-style doctor can tell symptoms from the pulse alone. The client is challenging the *tâng-ki* to demonstrate this skill.)

Tâng-ki: "Not only pain in the abdomen. You have many other symptoms. I won't tell you. I will prescribe medicine for you. I won't tell you about your other symptoms so that you don't worry so much about your illnesses."

Client: "I had pain yesterday and could not walk. . . ."

Tâng-ki: "I know! I know! Even now you feel like you don't want to walk."

Client: "Do I have pain in the stomach? I have taken so much medicine for my stomach problems."

Tâng-ki: "Finished! Finished! You shouldn't take stomach medicine because your symptoms will go to other places from now on."

(The patient had been acting in her usual fashion, listing one problem and about to go on from there, but she was taken aback by the *tâng-ki*'s remark. First she seemed embarrassed, and then she laughed. The *tâng-ki* sang out the prescription, indicating the session had ended.)

This example illustrates a group of patients who annoy clinicians worldwide. Though annoyed by her behavior, the *tâng-ki* recognized that complaining too much about symptoms (hypochondriasis) was one of her problems. He responded by giving her a prescription. Not to have done so would have been to act "unprofessionally." The god is expected always to provide treatment. The *tâng-ki* managed this difficult case with considerable skill. I have observed other *tâng-ki*s, and also Western-style and Chinese-style doctors, who performed less well under similar circumstances. He was aided by the socially constructed reality in which the god can get away with calling the patient fat, criticizing her faults, and even implying strongly at the end that she would purposefully defeat the treatment. No other clinical consultations in Taiwan legitimate such behavior. If a physician said these things, the patient would be outraged. Furthermore, several times the *tâng-ki* caused his audience to laugh at the patient, and this eventually helped the patient laugh at herself. When the session ended, the patient bantered lightly with other clients and assistants, criticizing

224

herself for worrying excessively about her health. Although I doubt that this session had a lasting effect, I also doubt that the patient will return to this shrine in her habitual style, though she might do so elsewhere. Modern psychiatry has little to offer such a patient and therefore cannot criticize the *tâng-ki* for his way of treating her psychopathology and chronic abuse of the sick role. Chinese culture, by readily permitting claims to physical illness, works against treatment of this particular disorder.

Transcripts of two short *tâng-ki*-client transactions will further illustrate the kinds of therapeutic communication that occur in these interactions.

> Client [a young mother with a six-month-old infant who is crying in her arms]: "The baby can't sleep well and cries too much."
> *Tâng-ki*: "Fever?"
> Client: "No!"
> *Tâng-ki*: "Caused by the fetus god! Give the baby one charm to eat and put the other under the baby's crib. No problem. Your baby will be well soon. If there is fever, go to a doctor."

Here the *tâng-ki* made a common triage decision. Fever with irritability and sleep disturbance in infants is usually a sign of infectious disease requiring medicine. Without fever, the problem is appropriately treated in the shrine. In straightforward cases, such as this one, the *tâng-ki* may not give any explanation. He may not even give the problem a name (i.e., soul loss, possession, being "hit" by or colliding with a ghost, or bad fate caused by the fetus god). He merely states the cause: the fetus god, who is believed to reside in changing locations in the house of a newborn child, often in the child's bedroom, and who family members must be careful not to disturb, lest it retaliate by making the child sick. The fetus god is implicated as a cause of sickness in infants almost as frequently as "fright" with "soul loss," so that simply mentioning the name, as the *tâng-ki* did, was enough to explain the problem to the mother. But the *tâng-ki* also reassured the mother that it was not a serious problem. He recommended medical treatment if fever developed, thus educating his client about complications and anticipating her concerns. No ritual was performed, and when

225

I asked an elderly assistant if the client might have desired to have one performed, he told me: "For young people it doesn't matter so much. Most don't even understand what the names of the rituals mean."

Few people we interviewed in *tâng-ki*s' shrines, except cult members and elderly devotees, understood the special terms or the symbolic meaning of the rituals; they understood only the most commonly applied explanatory models. Moreover, fully half the *tâng-ki*s and assistants we interviewed, when asked to explain specific folk concepts and rituals, were clearly unable to do so, even though they fully comprehended our questions. They demonstrated either confusion or ignorance about the theoretical dimensions of their practice. This was more true of urban than rural *tâng-ki*s. Several urban *tâng-ki*s invented special symbols that held no meaning in Taiwanese culture. And on two occasions, *tâng-ki*s gave accounts of ritual meanings that contradicted what they had told us at other times. The lack of detailed appreciation of the symbolic meanings of healing rituals by some clients and *tâng-ki*s impressed me that it is dangerous to assume symbolic healing is a major mechanism of the efficacy of shamanistic and other sacred folk care, unless it can be documented for a given case that such a mechanism is in fact operating. Such documentation should include evidence either that a particular psychophysiological effect was produced by a particular symbolic stimulus or that, for particular patients and patient-practitioner relationships, specific cultural symbols held therapeutic significance. Indeed, in the absence of the former, only when such significance can be demonstrated in actual case studies should the researcher employ the efficacy of symbols as an explanatory hypothesis.[2] As McCreery (1978) notes, *effective* meaning in healing rituals needs to be strictly distinguished from *potential* meaning. In that all healing rituals are, from an anthropological perspective,

2. This simply states in stronger terms the distinction I made earlier between "indirect" and "direct" socio-somatic effects. Unless one has physiological evidence of a "direct" socio-somatic effect, psychological evidence of an "indirect" effect is necessary to avoid appeal to an explanatory principle whose validity otherwise can neither be established nor refuted. See Chapter 9 for an analysis of a mechanism mediating symbolic efficacy that seems to operate regularly in shamans' shrines.

saturated with cultural meanings, this analytic distinction is crucial if we are to determine when symbolic meanings actually exert specific therapeutic effects.

> Client [elderly woman holding a man's shirt and pants in her hand]: "My husband's sick. He has heart disease and is being treated at a hospital. Will he get better?"
>
> *Tâng-ki* (after performing a ritual with the clothing and writing charms): "He has a serious sickness, but he will get better. Don't worry so much! His fate is not good but it will change. I will make his fate better. If his fate is bad then the doctors cannot cure him. These charms are for you. Give two to your husband to eat, and eat two of them yourself. That will help him. Don't worry!"

This case was typical of many I witnessed. The *tâng-ki* recognized the husband's sickness and the wife's concern, and he treated both. Not only did he give the wife support, but he reinforced her belief that she could do something to help her husband. About one-fourth of illness episodes I observed in *tâng-kis'* shrines involved treatment of a surrogate brought by a female relative. As in the above case, the *tâng-kis* responded as if the relative was the patient. The psychosocial benefits derived from this kind of substitute treatment probably include assuaging guilt and relieving frustration as much as reducing anxiety. Part of the reduction of anxiety must stem from carrying out specific ritual acts that are held to be efficacious. Even if the client does not believe strongly in the rituals, performing them establishes the fact that the client has tried all available treatment alternatives. Furthermore, as we shall discuss in Chapter 9, healing rituals have a *performative efficacy* (Tambiah 1973) for the individuals who take part in them. That is, they are held to be effective if they are properly performed. One problem attending such surrogate therapy is that the sick person (usually an adult male family member) may not be willing to take part in treatments recommended by the *tâng-ki*. As a result, these treatments may at times precipitate family arguments. In some cases, informants report hiding charms in the sick person's clothes or food. The sick person may have no idea that his female relatives have gone on his behalf to a *tâng-ki*. It is not uncommon to find that a husband has prohibited his wife from visiting a *tâng-ki*; consequently, she must go secretly,

227

alone or accompanied by female friends or relatives. The brevity of this interaction also suggests that much of the care in shamanistic healing occurs both before and especially after consultation with the *tâng-ki,* whose therapeutic recommendations are implemented in the shrine and by the family and social network.

While admiring the utility of *tâng-kis'* practices, we should also observe their negative aspects. *Tâng-kis* perform under difficult restrictions. They do not obtain a full history, and the popular ideology argues that they should be able to divine the symptoms. If they were in a village where they knew their clients well, perhaps it would not matter so much. But in many cases in an urban setting, they are unable to obtain the facts they require to use effectively the explanations and interpersonal manipulations available to them. They do not act consistently. Lacking follow-ups, they have no clear notion of what works and what doesn't. And they do not possess adequate technical interventions. Perhaps one of their most vexing problems, however, also relates to the social reality established in their shrines. Shamans sometimes employ explanatory models that mix beliefs from the sacred folk tradition with beliefs from Chinese and Western medicine. Their clients may not understand certain of these concepts when used in this alien context. For most clients, the supernatural explanations are more compelling and more "real." Yet, at times *tâng-kis* have informed me they would like to make more use of the others. One of them justified this to me by saying "that is what the patient [his word] needs." But *tâng-kis'* clients may have little faith in non-supernatural EMs, and using them may weaken their commitment to sacred EMs. Some *tâng-kis* recognized this problem and were sensitive to the related problem that their clients possessed varying degrees of belief in their practices. A few *tâng-kis* astutely observed that lack of faith influences compliance and treatment outcome. Problems like these would become sharper if there were an attempt to incorporate shamans into Taiwan's official medical system and to train them to integrate traditional and modern EMs and therapies. Such an integration, moreover, might undermine the clinical reality that contributes so importantly to their therapeutic success. This potential hazard should be looked for wherever sacred folk practitioners are introduced into professional health care services. It conceivably could render such integrations ineffective or worse.

Most *tâng-ki*s I have studied, when they deal with sick people, focus on *illness* as the central problem and try to bring to bear whatever they believe will have an effect. I have caught shamans in seeming contradictions, making use of ambiguities, illogicalities, and even blatantly false (from their standpoint) ideas. This is not surprising to me; as a clinician, I have done some of this myself when I thought it indicated. It is part of the explanatory patchwork that sometimes is effective, other times ineffective. But in the shaman's practice, it is not brought under the self-critical scrutiny that it can be, though usually is not, in scientifically based clinical care.

For example, on two occasions in the same afternoon, I observed a *tâng-ki* consult with ladies complaining that their husbands were causing them problems. In the first case, a 35-year-old mother of two complained that her husband had girlfriends, wasted money on gambling, and was infrequently at home. She had responded with anger; when he returned, she would scream at him, and they would then fight. The *tâng-ki* inquired if she and her children were supported by her husband and learned that he supported them quite well. He then reminded her that this was important. He told her her husband had terrible fate this year, but it would change next year. She had to be patient. She should not scold him since his behavior was beyond his control, and he was not responsible for it. After learning that she had a uterine coil for contraceptive purposes, he (the god) told her to have it removed and to have another child. I thought this was a remarkable example of making good clinical use of cultural sensitivities, which led the *tâng-ki* to encourage intimacy in a culturally sanctioned manner (which, as follow-up later revealed, had a positive effect in this case) and in so doing to act in the client's best interests, while espousing, as is typical of shamans, a culturally conservative viewpoint (strengthen family bonds).

My delight, however, turned to disappointment in the second case, which reveals some of the limitations of shamanistic healing. A 45-year-old Taiwanese mother of eight, looking pale, fatigued, and chronically ill, complained that her husband (a Mainlander who had retired from the army) refused to work but would not let her take time off or stop her taxing labors selling vegetables in order to follow her physician's orders and get plenty of rest. This client was as shocked as I was by the *tâng-ki*'s advice that she too should remove her uterine coil and have more children. When we visited her at home, we found her living in terrible poverty with a tremendous workload: caring for young children; acting as the breadwinner for the family; suffering an irresponsible husband who made it clear he had no intention of working and who himself entirely consumed his pension payments; and trying to keep her diabetes under control. She had been further upset by the *tâng-ki*'s advice, which seemed to her (as it did to me) unhelpful and dangerous. I have seen other *tâng-ki*s have more ruinous effects, but not often. The great strength of this form of care, its culturally constituted clinical reality, also is its great weakness. It makes it unlikely that this type of care (at least, as it is now practiced) can be readily integrated into modern health care services. I have already noted that an incompatibility between sacred and professional EMs also casts doubt on the feasibility of integration. But there are other problems, including the fact that *tâng-ki*s believe their gods cannot be told what to do and not do by Western-style doctors and that they show an evident disinterest in learning modern medical or psychiatric concepts and practices. My prediction is that, for these reasons, *tâng-ki*s will not become Taiwan's "barefoot doctors," just as they apparently have not filled this or other modern medical roles in the People's Republic of China.[3]

A well-known and previously studied (Wang 1971) shrine

3. In the summer of 1975, as I have remarked, the government began to crack down on *tâng-ki*s and other unlicensed healers. Police and legal action was accompanied by almost daily newspaper articles attacking "witch doctors," "superstition," etc. This press campaign excoriated persons in temples for acting like unqualified doctors when they ministered to patients. They were charged with dangerous practices aimed at cheating clients. This campaign played upon the ambivalent popular view of healers. Since Taiwanese folk religion is one of the few tolerated signs of Taiwanese ethnicity, the attack on folk healers had indirect political significance. Needless to add, it was strongly supported by the professional medical organizations. By the summer of 1978, there was no evidence it had significantly reduced folk healing, though it may have reduced unlicensed professional medical practice. De-

ciding to enforce the laws and stimulating the press campaign are signs of the negative view the ruling elite has of shamans and other folk healers; these activities also must have reinforced some of the negative aspects of popular sentiment about *tâng-kis*. On the other hand, the indirect political attack on Taiwanese nationalism could have had the opposite effect. This attempt to suppress sacred folk healing, which apparently has petered out, indicates that, though sacred folk healers are in fact a major component of Taiwan's *functioning* health care systems, they are not likely to receive a place in the officially endorsed and controlled orthodox system of care.

I had the opportunity to ask 10 shamans, 15 sacred folk healers of other kinds, and 25 Chinese-style doctors whether or not they wished to become part of the officially sanctioned medical system by being integrated in some way with Western-style health professionals. Whereas four-fifths of the Chinese-style doctors answered this question affirmatively, only one shaman and two other sacred folk healers agreed. Although this was a casual survey whose results should not be assumed to represent the sentiments of all indigenous practitioners in Taiwan accurately, I believe the differences are striking enough to warrant extrapolation. It would seem obvious from this casual survey that Chinese-style doctors, who are secular professionals with their own bureaucratic system of licensing, pharmacies, clinics, and hospitals, are generally in favor of some form of integration, which would not represent a radical departure from their present status under government sanctioning as an autonomous professional therapeutic system. Moreover, since many of these practitioners candidly informed me that Chinese medicine was in their view a second-class system of care when compared to Western-style medicine, whose practitioners they believed had higher status, greater income, and more patients, Chinese-style doctors clearly have some specific gains they wish to achieve from integration. Similar to Taylor's (1976) observations on indigenous practitioners in the Punjab, the only Chinese-style practitioners I talked with who had very substantial numbers of patients and correspondingly high incomes and reputations were the ones who were personally against integration. They pointed out to me that they had little to gain from such change, and they intimated fear that they had much to lose.

Shamans and other kinds of indigenous healers (fortune-tellers, *ch'ien* interpreters, and geomancers), who are presently unlicensed and, therefore, unregulated and in some instances practicing illegally, expressed the fear that integration would be of no benefit but instead of substantial harm to their practices. These folk healers did not believe they would be given status equal to Western-style doctors. They were almost all suspicious that the chief purpose of integration would be to reduce the number of patients they saw and thereby to reduce their incomes. And several shrewdly suggested that since Western-style doctors looked down upon them, integration would mean that they would be controlled by competitors whose interest lay in putting them out of business. A major fear of these indigenous healers was that their earnings would be brought under the supervision of the tax authorities, who would take away their financial gain.

231

near National Taiwan University, where a resourceful *tâng-ki* has developed a cult with more than 100 followers, reveals more about the therapeutic significance of the clinical reality constituted in shamanistic practice. Half of the followers attend each night's séance and sleep in the shrine. Nearly two-thirds of the cult members exhibit trance behavior regularly. Of these, five or six are females who themselves are able to heal while possessed by their gods and would be considered *tâng-ki*s in other settings. These women, as well as many of the other female cult members, are middle-aged or elderly mothers who leave their families each night to pray, induce trance, and sleep in the shrine. The *tâng-ki* encourages this behavior by telling cult members that if they do not come nightly to the shrine their tutelary gods will become angry and the symptoms that brought them to the shrine in the first place will return. A research assistant and I were able to interview and perform mental status evaluations on ten of these women. We found most of them had remarkably similar life histories: born and raised in poor farm villages or market towns; early marriage with subsequent migration to Taipei; relatively impoverished circumstances requiring them to work as maids, laundresses, and laborers in what they now refer to as "the sea of bitterness" (*k'u-hai*); major family problems involving marital discord and/ or strife with in-laws; histories of chronic non-specific physical complaints as well as conversion reactions, dissociation states, and eruptions of hysterical behavior. Some women had suffered short-lived psychoses without sequelae, perhaps best regarded as hysterical psychoses. Several had histories of sexual promiscuity. In behavior, most of the cult women I interviewed were dramatic and quite egocentric. They were unusually emotional, impulsive, and coquettish for women in this Chinese cultural setting. Some of these labels were applied to them by family members, many of whom were unhappy with their membership in the cult and especially with the fact that they slept overnight in the shrine. To my mind, these women combined hysterical personalities with somatization and hypochondriasis quite suggestive of hysteria. For them the role of cult member was preferable to the chronic sick roles they had occupied, and, indeed, none were still seeing doctors or going to hospitals and clinics. In place of the sick role, these women can be seen "performing" nightly at the *tâng-ki*'s shrine, where they trance and heal clients. Their trance behavior involves a great deal of physical exertion. They jump around, sing, act out the characteristics of the gods who possess them, and at times tremble and shake violently. At other times, their activities take on clearly sexualized forms. Perhaps most impressive of all is the release of strong affect while entranced, which, except for the expression of anger, is otherwise so unusual in Taiwanese society.

This cult structures the experience of its members in an adaptive manner by providing legitimate roles for behavior that had been labeled deviant. Whether we call this healing or not, it causes impressive psychosocial gains, including loss of symptoms, improvement of family problems, and personal satisfaction in role performance (gains so significant to these women's families that they accepted, albeit grudgingly, their frequent absence from home and failure to perform their routine functions as wives and mothers). Thus, at least for some of its members, the cult offers a therapeutic milieu to relieve minor mental illnesses, related interpersonal problems associated with the strain between desired and actual social role, and the chronic frustration a wide discrepancy between the two produces. The client moves from a disvalued to a valued role, which Lewis (1971) has shown to be characteristic of folk healing cults, decreasing strain and frustration, which in turn modifies the conditions fostering reactive mental illnesses. Again, as Lewis demonstrated, hostility is appropriately channelled and released, both as anger directed at those the patients hold responsible for their problems (i.e., by sleeping in the shrine contrary to cultural norms and the expectations of family members, who, though they tolerated this behavior, were annoyed and burdened by it) and as dissociated dysphoric affects in trance.

Tâng-kis differ in a number of ways. Some spend more time communicating with clients; others spend more time performing elaborate ritual activities. Some have many clients and earn a great deal of money; others remain poor both in numbers of clients and money. Some are charismatic; others are unimpressive. Some have cults; others do not. Some specialize; others do not. But almost all the ones I observed shared one particular clinical characteristic: they were skilled at responding quickly to exigent intra- and inter-personal *crises*. An example from another *tâng-ki*'s shrine will demonstrate this.

Well before the séance began, while clients were still assembling and the *tâng-ki* was sitting smoking unobtrusively in a corner, a handsome woman in her early forties rushed into the shrine. She was extremely distraught and paced back and forth. Occasionally, she sobbed. At first, her speech was very rapid and incoherent. From the moment she entered, all eyes focused on her. At last, with angry curses she began a lengthy monologue. A thief had broken into the secret place where her money was kept and had taken most of it. All the doors of the house were locked. She suspected the thief was someone they knew well. The client broke into sobs and wails. Other clients began to talk to her softly. They tried to comfort and console her, but she seemed to be inconsolable. While this was happening, the *tâng-ki* quickly entered his trance. Before he tranced, he said loud enough for her to hear: "The thief has no guilt." Other people told her the thief has no conscience. Someone said: "Why did you put it all in one place?" The assistant told her: "Don't be too sad in the loss of your money. It must have some meaning."

Although many others were ahead of her, the *tâng-ki*'s assistant called her as the second case. The *tâng-ki* began to speak, but the client questioned him repeatedly, sometimes angrily. Finally, the *tâng-ki*'s voice and bearing became much more authoritarian. He commanded her to silence. Then he told her: "It is not the gold and money that matter. This is a very bad year for your fortune."

> Client: "I know the god knows who did it. I know I won't get the money and gold back. But the thief also took something from my ancestors that I want to get back."
> *Tâng-ki*: "Forget the money and gold. You must lose it. If you didn't lose it, then something else very bad would happen to you. The things are gone . . . you will not get them. They are lost. But more important is your fate this year. You must do something about that. I will help you." (The *tâng-ki* went on to inform her that the thief was a person close to her and that he stole her things after unlocking the door and then locking it again.)
> Client: "Is the thief a relative or a neighbor?"

The *tâng-ki* at first did not respond, then he replied the thief would receive a great punishment. The session ended when the *tâng-ki* performed a ritual to "repair" the client's bad fate. The *tâng-ki* spent hardly ten minutes with this client. That is more than twice the time he spends with most cases, however, and there were more than twenty other clients waiting. Other clients and his assistant helped translate and interpret. The *tâng-ki* sent the god's soldiers (mythical figures) to search for her money, and he gave her many charms. His assistant refused to receive any money even for the incense she had burned, the only time I saw him refuse payment.

This is not a case of illness, yet it represents a universal clinical task. The clinician must respond quickly to crises. His knowledge, his sources of power, his personality, the clinical relationships he establishes with patients, the social context in which he practices are all used to cope with such immediate problems which threaten the patient and his family. Illness and other personal and social crises are "dis-orders" that undermine personal and social order. They threaten the routines of daily living. Clinical consultation helps to restore order.

In exigent problems such as this, just as in diseases that cannot be cured, the construction (or reordering) of cultural meanings may be all that therapy (and efficacy) consists of. Here the *tâng-ki* applies one of the most powerful interpretations in his armamentarium: the idea of fate. This idea is not limited to the *tâng-ki*'s shrine; it is widely diffused in the popular culture in Taiwan. But by applying it in that very special setting, the concept acquires greater meaning than when employed in the family context. At the same time, by crystallizing around the problem one of the most profound sources of explanatory power in Chinese culture something can be done to cope with this difficult psychosocial stress. Again, this is only one of several different coping strategies used to manage this particular crisis. The client also received considerable social support and sanction to reveal her anguish. After the session several people in the shrine offered her practical advice about what to do next.

*Tâng-ki*s use the concept of a family's bad fate to shift the locus of a problem from a person or situation to the whole family and to attribute the cause to an external source. This explanation also argues that whatever has happened is a substitute for something worse that otherwise would have occurred. As a result, what we find is not simply a redefinition of a personal problem in social terms. This EM may dissolve the problem entirely by defining events as a preventive measure for unspecified but much worse trouble. By alerting the family to its bad fate, the difficulty at hand becomes an occasion to correct this condition so that the family's future affairs will prosper. This displacement may function as an important psychosocial coping strategy. Even if it is not convincing for a client, it may convince others in the family. Bad fate is one of the most troubling concerns in Taiwan's popular culture, and for many families, it is as convincing an explanation as there is. Another case illustration can further clarify how *tâng-ki*s employ this ubiquitous EM.

> Client [an obese elderly woman]: "Problems with my son. He plays too much . . . wasting our family's money on gambling, alcohol, prostitutes." (The client goes on at length to condemn her son's behavior angrily.)
>
> *Tâng-ki:* "Don't be so angry at him! By acting like that he is saving you! You and your husband have very bad fate. You could die from fate. By wasting your money, your son is saving you from that fate. Now you shouldn't do anything until the middle of the 7th (lunar) month. After that you will have a new fate. Then you can tell your son to stop playing around. Explain to him his behavior then is useless; it will not help you any longer. But until then leave him alone. Don't be so angry at him. And don't worry so much about the money. You know you have plenty of money."

The irony of going to a *tâng-ki* with a problem only to be told that it is "saving" one from a much worse problem is not lost on clients. This explanation is sometimes met with disbelief, astonishment, and even laughter, but after the surprise has worn off, it is usually accepted as an appropriate explanation. Like beliefs in gods and ghosts, it is coded into Taiwanese popular thought as a basic orientation to life problems. Bad fate is a component of the natural world, just as are gods and ghosts. The germ theory and belief in the "magic bullet" effect of antibiotics are not viewed as more real. Among secularized middle-class clients, bad fate in the abstract may be scorned as a superstition; but when applied to a specific case it is usually taken to heart as a real possibility. Consequently, this is not an explanation to be proffered or received casually. When employed in the highly charged ethos of the shaman's shrine, it is a remarkably powerful communicative device. For example, I have seen *tâng-kis* appeal to it to assure compliance.

> Client [middle-aged female]: "My health is still bad."
> *Tâng-ki:* "Did you take the medicine I gave you?"
> Client: "No!"
> *Tâng-ki:* "Your fate is very bad. You might die! Did you know that?"
> Client (clearly shocked by these words): "No, I didn't know."
> *Tâng-ki:* "Why didn't you take it? If you don't take it as I tell you to, you will never get better. You will always have symptoms. Nothing will help you. But if you take what I prescribe, you will get well soon."

Although the potential for abusing this explanation by trivializing it and applying it without justification seems enormous, Taiwanese clients, even though they are often aware of its potential abuse, are rarely willing to dispute that bad fate is the cause of a particular problem. It is simply too important a possible cause to be discounted. Moreover, there are effective treatments for it, so that from the pragmatic standpoint commonly employed by patients, it is sensible to obtain treatment for bad fate as one among several possible causes of any sickness or misfortune, even when it does not appear to be the most likely cause. Since certain folk healers tend to emphasize different explanations, people who are specially receptive to this explanation can select a healer who is most likely to diagnose it. Alternatively, if the problem persists and if bad fate has not yet been implicated, they can seek out healers who are likely to apply this label. Bad fate as an EM involves a special logic. It brings into play the logic of corresponding harmonies and inharmonies (Jordan 1972; Porkert 1974). Thus, when we observe it being applied, it is essential to recognize that this non-scientific logic may be responsible for the selection of evidence and the advocacy of a line of argument that, from the standpoint of Western models of causality, is patently "illogical" and false. Because the logic by which EMs are used is determined by the same clinical reality supporting those EMs, a patient may switch between the indigenous logic of corresponding harmonies and the single causal trains of scientific logic as he moves between the clinical realities where these modes of thought are sanctioned. In the *tâng-ki*'s shrine the former is frequently more compelling than the latter. Bad fate represents, then, not just culturally constructed content in a universal clinical communicative process, but also cultural shaping of the norms governing that process. Similarly, cultural differences between clinical realities are more than simply differences in content. They can involve structural differences as well, including differences in logic and even in perception.

In this section I have presented examples of shaman-client interactions to illustrate what is salient about them. I will now summarize these features in terms of the analytic categories outlined at the beginning of the chapter.

Categorization of Shaman-Client Transactions: A Summary

1. Institutional Setting: Shaman-client transactions in Taiwan occur in the folk arena of care and belong to a large and diverse subsector of religious folk healing.

2. Characteristics of the Interpersonal Interaction

a. The *number* of participants includes several key female family members and often other members of the family or social network along with the *tâng-ki*, his assistants, and other clients and their families. The sick person usually attends the therapeutic séance but need not be present. Female clients outnumber male clients three or four to one.

b. Shaman-client interactions may be *episodic or continuous*. In our sample, half of these therapeutic relationships were organized solely around particular illness episodes. That is, clients presented only once or several times for treatment of a specific health problem, and transactions with shamans were limited to this sphere. But the other half of shaman-client interactions involved the treatment of sickness episodes in the context of an ongoing relationship with the shaman and his shrine. That relationship existed prior to the onset of the sickness episode and continued after it had subsided. Even while sickness was present, the shaman-client relationship dealt with other religious and interpersonal questions. Indeed, minor sickness episodes at times simply presented an occasion for family members to pray and socialize in the shrine or to consult the shaman about other matters.

Time spent in treatment setting: usually up to several hours and rarely less than an hour.

Time spent consulting with entranced shaman: (mean time) 7 minutes 15 seconds (range: 1 minute to 29 minutes 20 seconds).

Communication time: (mean time) 5 minutes 4 seconds (range: 1 minute 10 seconds to 11 minutes 9 seconds).

Explanatory time: (mean time) 4 minutes 12 seconds (range: 30 seconds to 8 minutes 15 seconds).

c. Shaman-client interactions consist of both *formal and informal* phases. Consultation with the entranced shaman is a formal relationship which shares similarities with other practitioner-patient relationships as well as with other non-medical transactions of a formal kind. In all of these interactions language and behavior more or less follow the stylized Confucian rules of etiquette. There is a noticeable social distance between client and shaman, who typically relate in a master-student (disciple) mode. The verbal interchange itself is marked as a special event separated from routine social transactions. Usually this exchange uses polite speech, titles or other special terms of address and even on occasion an argot. Both the "time" and "space" coordinates of the relationship are sacralized. But most of the time spent in the shaman's shrine is characterized by informality. Clients and their family members socialize among themselves and with the assistants and even with the unentranced *tâng-ki*, much as they would with neighbors and friends. Their language and behavior is informal. These two types of interpersonal transaction are strikingly different. But both can be assumed to have therapeutic effects, as several of our examples illustrate. Also both types of therapeutic relationship, like most in Taiwan, are public occasions. Personal and family problems are presented in public, and treatment decisions are open to public commentary. The public character of such healing relationships obviously influences therapeutic communication and clinical style.

The shaman-client relationship, furthermore, is *holistic*.

Sickness episodes are placed in a broad range of human miseries and are related to everyday life events and experiences (e.g., financial difficulties, personal loss, typical family tensions, like that between daughter-in-law and mother-in-law, and the ubiquitous frustrations and disappointments associated with human deprivation and struggle). As a result, the shaman-client relationship builds upon the family's and the *tâng-ki*'s view of sickness as threatening an integral part of day-to-day living.

d. The shaman-client relationship is characterized by reciprocally *ambivalent attitudes*. The *tâng-ki* is viewed as powerful, and it is believed that he works on behalf of the community. Patients are often deeply appreciative of his god's therapeutic successes. But he also is envied and distrusted for his financial success and occasionally feared for his reputed power to engage in sorcery or otherwise cause individuals to become sick. On the other hand, the *tâng-ki* views the patient as both an opportunity to demonstrate his god's powers and obtain financial rewards and as a threat to his (and his god's) skills and reputation as a healer. Follow-up visits in chronic sickness reveal the tensions associated with this mutual ambivalence: *tâng-ki*s clearly feel pressed to explain why treatment failure does not signify that their gods are ineffective, while patients occasionally feel equally pressed, in spite of the inhibiting fear of offending the gods they have come to propitiate, to challenge the *tâng-ki*'s motivation and skills.

3. Idiom of Communication

a. The *idiom* articulates personal problems in the combined cosmological, sociological, and somatic language of the popular culture. Psychological and psychosomatic *modes* of communication, as we have seen, are not used.

b. Shaman-client transactions, for the most part, consist of *shared EMs* that are *openly expressed and negotiated*. For this reason, and also because more time is alloted to communication, these transactions lead to less frequent and less marked conflicts over the nature and significance of the problem and the appropriate treatment than occur in professional practitioner-patient transactions. When such conflicts in beliefs and values occur, they sometimes result from discrepancies between esoteric sacred EMs employed in the shrine and the modern secular EMs patients increasingly bring to the shrine. This creates problems for younger, better educated, and more Western-oriented individuals, many of whom find shaman-client transactions unacceptable for just this reason. As a consequence, these relationships predominantly involve older, less educated, and less Western-oriented clients.

4. Clinical Reality

a. The peculiar clinical reality structured in shaman-patient transactions draws upon its *sacred* nature for much of its efficacy. The entranced *tâng-ki* is believed to be a god who can see problems that are hidden from men and who can effect cures that are beyond the powers of doctors. Faith in the gods' powers and in the efficacy of ritual surely contributes significantly to the placebo and psychotherapeutic effects of the shaman-client relationship. Conversely, the sacred nature of this relationship, as we have seen, limits the extent to which it can be "rationalized" as part of a secular organization of health care. Belief in the gods' powers to "see" the cause of sickness interferes with the full elicitation of a symptom history, and belief in their own therapeutic efficacy reduces the *tâng-kis'* options in referring patients to other treatment agencies. These beliefs may seriously hamper the therapeutic effects of the *tâng-ki*-client relationship and may yield untoward outcomes. The point requiring emphasis is that the sacred clinical reality constructed in this practitioner-patient relationship is the source of its therapeutic strengths *and* weaknesses. We will observe a similar phenomenon when we examine the clinical realities constructed in other health care relationships, secular as well as sacred, which equally serve ideological interests that have both therapeutic and non-therapeutic effects.

b. Shaman-client transactions center on the psychosocial concomitants of sickness (*illness problems*). Experiential, behavioral, family, and financial problems associated with sickness (and other life stress) are recognized and man-

241

aged. There is no exaggeration when I describe these relationships as creating a structure of personal and social meaning. This is reflected in the responses patients and family members frequently make after the entranced *tâng-ki* has interpreted their problems: "Now we understand!" "Ah, it is now clear!" "Surely that is it!" "So that is why!" "This is of course what it means!" The *tâng-ki* explains *why* affliction has occurred. Along with common cosmological sources of trouble, such as bad fate and ghosts, his explanations implicate common human sources of trouble: envy, greed, hate, lust, willfulness, and so forth. These explanations are intended to help people recognize and understand particular psychosocial problems so that concrete plans can be fashioned to resolve them. Not only does the *tâng-ki* give practical advice, he also provides support and sanctioning for implementing plans in practical action.

c. Both *symbolic and instrumental* therapeutic interventions are utilized. Patients expect to receive both, and shamans expect to provide both. This aspect of the clinical reality established in shaman-client transactions differs from that found in interactions with other practitioners, which is organized around either symbolic or instrumental treatment, but usually not both.

d. *Therapeutic expectations* include the rules of etiquette outlined above in our discussion of the quality of the shaman-client relationship (2c), the therapeutic objectives and interventions just described, and a treatment style that integrates prayer, ritual acts, and explanatory exchanges— as illustrated by the case vignettes. These expectations, though tacit, are commonly shared by shaman, clients, and families.

e. The *tâng-ki* does *not* view himself as most responsible for his clients' care, nor do they view him in that light. Both regard the family as the *locus of responsibility* for the client's care. The *tâng-ki*-client encounter works on the assumption that for a given sickness the *tâng-ki* may not be the most appropriate treatment resource and alternative forms of treatment may be necessary. Unlike relationships with Western-style doctors, there is no pretense that this relationship contains all of the therapy the patient will receive or that it must organize the rest of his care. It is appropriate to talk about other types of treatment, and shamans and clients routinely do so.

5. Therapeutic Stages and Mechanisms

a. Healing passes through *three stages*: first, the problem is provided with a culturally legitimated name; then that cultural label is manipulated as a symbolic form external to the patient; finally a new label (e.g., "cured," "well," "no problem") is sanctioned.

b. Even the brief case illustrations I present suggest that there are several mechanisms of change, especially psychophysiological, interpersonal, and cultural ones.

c. In general, shamans and clients share similar assessments of outcome. Adherence (compliance) with the prescribed treatment regimen seems to be high (though this still needs to be documented statistically), and there usually is no uncertainty or disagreement about when treatment should terminate.

The subjects outlined in this section are taken up again in detail as the main topic of Chapter 9.

In Taiwan one hears people say that bad fate and bad health need to be "supplemented" or "patched" (*pu; pó*) (cf. Gould-Martin 1976: 129). This is an apposite metaphor to apply to clinical work. Something tears (body, mind, family bonds) and must be patched; the patch itself (sacred and/or secular healing intervention) is a local cultural and social artifact, the meanings and techniques at hand; the act of patching (treating, relieving suffering, coping with crises) is more important than the composition of the patch; and the social construction of clinical reality is the thread that fixes the patch to the fabric (lesion, person, family, etc.) This image can be appropriately applied to several of the shaman-patient interactions described in this section, and it may be useful for studying other practitioner-patient relationships as well. We will now turn to another traditional type of clinical patchwork.

PRACTITIONER-PATIENT INTERACTIONS 2: *CH'IEN* INTERPRETER-CLIENT

In most temples of any size in Taiwan, there are *ch'ien* or fortune papers. These contain one's personal or family fortune, usually expressed by vague fragments of archaic poetry with obscure classical allusions. Often the *ch'ien* paper is divided into separate sections, or there are different *ch'ien* papers, covering the major subjects people ask the temples' gods about: health, business, marriage, children, and so forth. The system of using *ch'ien* begins with a person praying to the god(s), then throwing divining blocks until they fall in such a way as to indicate that the god has agreed to let the individual ask about his fate. Since each person must first select a bamboo stick with a number on it before casting the divining blocks, he uses that number to obtain a fortune paper with the same number. For most people these *ch'ien* papers are virtually uninterpretable. Therefore, they turn to specialists, generally old men with some connection to the temple, who sit in a prominent booth in the temple and interpret the *ch'ien*. These men sometimes make use of books, which contain the *ch'ien* along with commentaries on them (cf. Hsu 1976).

Ch'ien interpreters are one of several kinds of specialists who practice divination. Shamans often use the eight characters associated with a person's year, month, day, and hour of birth to divine his fate. Fortune-tellers use the same technique, or others using the classic text, *I Ching* (Book of Changes). Astrologers, physiognomists, and geomancers all read fate from different sources. Their interpretations are considerably more than categorical or arbitrary statements. They use essentially random events like the throw of divination blocks or the blind selection of a numbered bamboo stick to answer problems where the ultimate causes and course of events are unknown or uncontrolled (Aberle 1966). The power to order reality is thus objectified by attributing it to a disinterested procedure. Through these divinatory acts, furthermore, immediate clinical problems, whose natural course and probable response to treatment until recently were highly uncertain, are linked to cosmic systems (e.g., the movements of the constellations, numerical and calendrical systems, etc.) remote from the uncertainties of everyday life, whose probabilities can be precisely calculated and are believed to describe outcome accurately. These constructions are the basis for prediction and control (Young 1976).

Fortune-telling and *ch'ien* interpretation accomplish many of the same ends as do psychotherapy and supportive care (see

Tseng 1976). They reduce anxiety, bolster morale, affirm models of behavior, give practical advice, and help in solving concrete problems. They help clients to integrate past events and to anticipate future problems, and they reduce personal fears and a family's sense of threat in making necessary decisions. They can also be described, following the EM model, as cognitive and communicative transactions between differing explanations of clinical reality. An aspect of this source for their efficacy is the "performative efficacy" that results from their ritual use in sacred healing (Tambiah 1973). The calculation of fate may be effective simply because the performance, appropriately conducted, legitimates the assertion of its efficacy, regardless of its empirical effects.

Although *ch'ien* interpretation is supposed to be objective, most *ch'ien* interpreters report that they do not transmit a reading that is utterly bad. They either lessen the impact of the reading by a careful choice of words, or they ask the client to choose another *ch'ien* paper, telling him that he has not followed the rules correctly. A few *ch'ien* interpreters say that they draw upon their sense of the person and his problem to interpret the *ch'ien*, sometimes changing a bad fate into one that is less unfortunate or even slightly favorable. Even if a bad fortune is transmitted, and in fact many are, it will be interpreted in terms of the client's particular situation. When really bad readings are given, the client is shown how he can respond by having his fortune treated (made better) by going to a shaman or a priest or ritual expert. One group of *ch'ien* interpreters asks the client for his age and date of birth before revealing the fortune. They use that information to determine his fortune by another method, then select for the client either the better reading or the one they feel is better suited to his problem. When expressed, however, the fortune is read as if it came directly from an objective rendering of the contents of the *ch'ien* paper, which confers on it the god's sanction. One *ch'ien* interpreter confessed to us that he frequently paid no attention to the *ch'ien* paper whatsoever but interpreted solely on the basis of what he felt would do the client most good. *Ch'ien* interpreters frequently give culturally conservative advice based on experience with similar problems and astute assessment of a situation. Although the body of information they work with is limited, they may break the rules by asking about the client's personal and family history. They are not supposed to give practical advice or information, but nonetheless they routinely do so. Since the reading is public, other clients and onlookers are encouraged to add additional commentary, advice, and support. Some *ch'ien* interpreters told me since they know which problems were common to people of different ages, sex, and social and educational background, they knew from the onset what was likely to be troubling their client and what might be helpful to hear.

Although women still predominate (approximately two to one), *ch'ien* interpreters see both middle-class and lower-class clients, as well as people of all ages. Consultations average only two-and-a-half minutes each, though some may take five minutes or more, but almost all of this time is devoted to communication, particularly to offering an explanation.

Ch'ien interpreters are middle-aged or elderly men. Most are literate members of the lower class who have retired from work or now only work part time and who have family or friendship ties to the owners of the temple. They often receive a small stipend from the temple. A few of the elderly interpreters whom I interviewed, however, claimed that they received no financial recompense but did this work for altruistic reasons, as a substitute for the boredom of retirement, and as a way of making themselves useful to the temple, where they spend much of their time socializing with friends and neighbors. *Ch'ien* interpreters do not receive fees or gifts from clients. They are viewed popularly as fairly low-level temple employees who perform a needed but routine, almost mechanical, service. They are not thought to possess any special power and, therefore, are not regarded with the same awe and fear as are shamans. As a consequence, their interpretations are treated as less authoritative, sometimes questioned, and not infrequently discarded in favor of readings of the fortune by sacred healers of higher status. Nonetheless, one commonly hears *ch'ien* interpreters appreciated as men of experience who possess both a wide practical knowledge of the everyday world and an understanding of the folk religious system that makes them a source of useful advice about secular as well as sacred responses to life problems, including sickness. When I asked informants about *ch'ien*, most failed to mention the *ch'ien* interpreter at all, as if he were regarded as a taken-for-granted part of the natural process of seeking and obtaining a fortune.

Below are *ch'ien* consultations from several different interpreters. They speak for themselves, using explanatory models to "patch" problems in which the chief concern is not elegance and consistency of theory but practical utility in interpreting difficulties. Illogicalities, contradictions, and even frank dissimulation may be part of these explanations, if they are deemed necessary. This practical clinical reasoning aims to be convincing and relevant to a concrete and often exigent human problem.

> *Ch'ien* interpreter: "What is the problem?"
> Client [a lower middle-class woman about 35 years-of-age]: "Marriage. The man has a concubine."
> *Ch'ien* interpreter: "Don't marry him. The *ch'ien* says not to marry."
> Client: "I'm already married to him. Should I separate?"
> *Ch'ien* interpreter: "Do you have children?"
> Client: "Yes."
> *Ch'ien* interpreter: "Does he give you money?"
> Client: "Yes, he gives me at least half the money."
> *Ch'ien* interpreter: "Then don't separate from him. It is not good to separate."

This culturally conservative advice appears to be the opposite of what is written on the *ch'ien*, but seemed to make sense in this case. And after the client left, people standing around the interpreter as well as my research assistants approved his remarks.

> *Ch'ien* interpreter: "What is your question?"
> Client [attractive, healthy-looking girl in late teens appearing anxious and worried]: "Health."
> *Ch'ien* interpreter: "Is the person you ask about young or old? She (he uses the indefinite third person: he/she) will recover quickly."
> Client: "She has stomach upset."
> *Ch'ien* interpreter: "How does she treat it?"
> Client: "She uses patent medicine."
> *Ch'ien* interpreter: "If it is not serious, she should watch her diet. Also worrying too much can make this worse. She should worry less. Does she vomit?"

247

Client: "No."

Ch'ien interpreter: "She should not use patent medicine but go to a doctor (Western-style) for a check-up and take X-rays."

Client: "She always uses patent medicines rather than going to doctors."

Ch'ien interpreter: "Patent medicines are not good. She should go to a doctor to make sure it is not serious and to get a full check-up. Is this person married yet or not?"

Client: "Not yet married."

Ch'ien interpreter: "Then she should take care of this now before she gets married. When she gets married she will be busy and there will be no time to go to the doctor, and she will need all of her strength."

At the end of this interview several things happened: they both switched from the third person and directly referred to the client herself as the person involved. The *ch'ien* interpreter told a joke and the client laughed; she was noticeably less anxious and troubled than at the start of the interview. She left smiling and seemed relieved. Since medical care is relatively expensive in Taiwan, people avoid going to doctors, and deciding to go to a doctor is often a large decision. Here the client had that choice made for her.

Client [a middle-aged female asking about her daughter's fate for marrying. In this society this is a complex and divisive question, since parents still try to arrange marriages for their children and claim that marriage occurs between families, not individuals, but children increasingly demand to arrange their own marriages or hold "veto power" over their parents' selections. Nowadays parents usually have to agree to the choices their children make.]

Ch'ien interpreter: "Does your daughter have a boy friend yet?"

Client: "Yes. A friend introduced this man to her."

Ch'ien interpreter: "Does your daughter agree with him or not? If she agrees, then you come back to ask again."

Client: "My daughter won't say anything. She has no opinion about it."

Ch'ien interpreter: "You can make a decision only after your daughter has agreed. This *ch'ien* says . . . 'not suitable.' Maybe that's the reason why your daughter does not give her opinion. You can tell her that the god here said 'not right yet.' What's your opinion?"

The client did not answer but went off smiling as if she appreciated this interpretation.

> Clients [Several relatives have come to ask about the fate of health of another family member. They look concerned.]
> *Ch'ien* interpreter (looking at the *ch'ien*): "It is not good. What do you specifically want to ask about?"
> Clients: "This relative is a man with liver disease. Our family would like to send him to Japan to cure this disease. We wish to ask if it is good to send him to Japan?"
> *Ch'ien* interpreter: "It's fine to send him to Japan. To change doctors if the patient is not improving is good for the patient."

This interpretation actually runs counter to the *ch'ien*, which should have been interpreted as *no* in this case. The *ch'ien* interpreter, however, obtained the same impression my research assistant obtained, namely, that the family members were looking for a positive answer to sanction their desire to send this family member to Japan.

Of course, sometimes patients resent the *ch'ien* interpreter's obtrusion into the supposedly impersonal mechanics of interpreting the *ch'ien*.

> Client [middle-aged, middle-class housewife]: "Family's fate."
> *Ch'ien* interpreter: "Is there a particular problem?"
> Client: "No."
> *Ch'ien* interpreter: "Why do you want the fate read then?"
> Client (angrily): "You are not supposed to ask questions. Just tell me what the *ch'ien* says."
> *Ch'ien* interpreter (also in an angry tone): "You have done the whole thing wrong. Go back and get another *ch'ien*."

This is an instance of a communicative problem, rare in our observations of *ch'ien* interpreters, perhaps due to the *ch'ien* interpreter's crude questioning or to the impatience of a testy client. It also reflects polarized views of the *ch'ien* interpreter's task and as such can be analyzed as an instance of conflict between two different versions of this special form of clinical reality.

Several other case examples will illustrate the *ch'ien* interpreter's function as a culture interpreter who gives culturally conservative advice and supports traditional behavioral norms. These cases additionally demonstrate the thin line between psychosocially sensitive advice and trivial platitudes across which each of the cases threatens to shift. The examples also disclose that *ch'ien* interpreters sometimes simply provide a sanctioned EM as authoritative advice, without eliciting or negotiating with client EMs. However, more commonly, they do enter into transactions with the EMs of their clients.

> *Ch'ien* interpreter: "What is the problem?"
> Client [a 13-year-old girl]: "Fate."
> *Ch'ien* interpreter: "Study hard! Be diligent!" (In Taiwan, education, which is extremely competitive, is the major vehicle for upward social mobility, and considerable pressure is placed on children to succeed academically.)
> Client: "I don't study."
> *Ch'ien* interpreter: "How is it you don't study?"
> Client: "I graduated from primary school, and now I work. I want to be a hairdresser. Is my fate good or bad?"
> *Ch'ien* interpreter: "Do it well! Be good tempered!"

The client left. She seemed satisfied, and she told us her fate was good for the job she wished to do, even though the *ch'ien* interpreter had not really told her what her fate was. The traditional moral exhortations were not nearly as significant for her as was the implication of good fate for undertaking the type of work she wished to do.

> Client [middle-aged woman]: "Family's fate."
> *Ch'ien* interpreter (after inquiring about the various members of the family): "Your fate and your husband's fate are not so good, but your children's is good. A couple should consult with each other. Don't do things emotionally, then both of you will be happy and you will do well."

> Client [a young wife]: "What is the fate of my husband's business?"
> *Ch'ien* interpreter: "How old is he?"
> Client: "27."
> *Ch'ien* interpreter: "Strive hard. This year is all right. It will be worse next year. Help him!"

> Client [a 22-year-old girl about to leave home to work in another town]: "Fate." (She explains her situation.)
> *Ch'ien* interpreter: "It is not good to leave your home. You should write home regularly. Don't go out with people you don't know. Be patient and careful!"

Client [a 26-year-old girl]: "Marriage."

Ch'ien interpreter (after learning about her age and present status as a single female, older than the average premarital female): "Marry!"

Client: "But I have several boyfriends. Which one should I marry?"

Ch'ien interpreter: "A girl who is 26 years-of-age should marry. Decide on one of them. Don't hesitate!"

I have been generally impressed with the positive effects of *ch'ien* interpretation, though there are some negative effects as well. Especially in regard to health care problems, we see that *ch'ien* interpreters do not have nearly enough information about the case to work with, possess limited knowledge of modern health care, must come up with an answer in an absurdly short time, and tend to refer patients only for sacred healing rituals or for Chinese-style medicines. Indeed, one commonly finds the name and address of a specific Chinese pharmacy listed at the bottom of the *ch'ien* paper. (The pharmacy's owner probably donated money to the temple or perhaps donated the *ch'ien* paper itself.) For example, in one case, a mother asked what she should do about the chronic tonsillitis of her 20-year-old daughter. She was told that her daughter's fate was bad and that she also was suffering from "fright" and needed a ceremony performed to "call back the soul" and make her fate better. In fact, the girl had a serious chronic illness (probably chronic hepatitis), and the tonsillitis represented an intercurrent infection. This interpretation delayed appropriate treatment. The *ch'ien* interpreter is not trained to make appropriate triage decisions when he deals with diseases. In another case, a pregnant woman went to a *ch'ien* interpreter with symptoms suggestive of hypertension and perhaps early toxemia. The *ch'ien* interpreter referred her to a Chinese pharmacy, saying that Western medicines were dangerous to take in pregnancy. While that may be generally true, certain Western medicines are effective in maintaining pregnancy and treating some of its more serious problems, including the one she was suffering from. Moreover, Chinese medicines can produce abortion and other untoward effects in pregnancy (though these are rare), but this is not recognized in the popular culture, nor by folk healers or Chinese-style doctors. Fortunately, many patients go to several different kinds of practitioners (including Western-style doctors) in succession or simultaneously. Clients commonly go to more than one *ch'ien* interpreter with the same question in order to obtain the answer they desire. That allows them to choose the advice they think most pertinent and best suited to their interests and at the same time enables them to receive cultural sanctioning for that advice.

Ch'ien interpreters' contributions to the non-professional medical referral system are of such significance that another example is worth describing. Frequently, they simply tell the client which direction is most auspicious for him to take in search of a specific kind of practitioner or whether his fate and that of the practitioner he wishes to choose are compatible. But, as the following case reveals, they may at times do more than that. Here we see a *ch'ien* interpreter give detailed medical advice and prescribe a course of action. Other times *ch'ien* interpreters confirm for their clients the health care seeking actions they have initiated or plan to take in the future. By doing that *ch'ien* interpreters provide cultural sanctioning for health choices extending beyond the folk arena of care and thereby instruct clients in the popular culture ideology of their health care system, an ideology *ch'ien* interpreters are legitimated to interpret. In other words, as a culture interpreter, the *ch'ien* interpreter is also a health care system interpreter. He gives culturally conservative advice based on the popular sector's beliefs about treatment choices. The following case shows that he is a healer as well, inasmuch as he prescribes a course of treatment and intends his communications to have therapeutic effects.

> Client [a pregnant mother with her two-year-old child in hand, who has come to the *ch'ien* interpreter at the temple of Pao-sheng-ta-ti, god of medicine, which is renowned for its "medicine *ch'ien*," to inquire about treatment for her symptoms]: "I am dizzy, my heart pounds, and my throat feels uncomfortable. What medicine should I take?"
>
> *Ch'ien* interpreter: "This is the wrong *ch'ien*!" He indicates to us after the client has left that the *ch'ien* she gave him contained information which was not medically helpful. He instructed her, before she went to get another *ch'ien*, exactly where to go to select one. Before she returned, he told us the new *ch'ien* would be much more helpful.

Client: "Here is another."

Ch'ien interpreter: "This is good for mild sickness, not for severe sickness. If you have a bad sickness you must go to a Western-style doctor; if it is mild, you can go to the Chinese pharmacy down the block and buy the medicine written on this *ch'ien*. It is dangerous to take Western medicine when you are pregnant, but you can take Chinese medicine. Your symptoms are mild. They are common in pregnancy. You can take the Chinese medicine. The pharmacist at the Chinese pharmacy can tell you more about your problem if you ask him. But if your symptoms don't improve, you must go to a Western-style doctor to make sure your sickness is not serious. Do you understand?"

Client: "I understand."

The client then asked the *ch'ien* interpreter several more specific questions about her problem. He told her that besides being due to pregnancy, her symptoms probably were due to a mild upper respiratory infection. She agreed. But she added that if her symptoms did not improve, she would only go to a Chinese-style doctor, since she feared taking Western medicine while pregnant. The soundness of this course of action was confirmed by several young mothers and middle-aged women waiting in line behind the client. They listened attentively to this transaction and periodically signalled their approval of the *ch'ien* interpreter's advice. (On other, less frequent, occasions, I have seen such a circle of prospective clients and family members do just the opposite: indicate that they disagreed with the *ch'ien* interpreter and even argue with him and give alternative advice.) They asked the *ch'ien* interpreter further questions, and he responded to them and in so doing gave additional information to his client. The client departed to buy the Chinese medicine, but not before the *ch'ien* interpreter had advised her to eat properly, rest, not tax herself with too much housework, and take vitamins. She told us that many friends and relatives had told her that this temple's "medicine *ch'ien*" were effective. She expected the medicine to cure her symptoms. If it didn't work, she planned to follow the *ch'ien* interpreter's advice. She told us that, even though she had had the same course of action in mind before consulting the *ch'ien* interpreter, she felt much better knowing that he recommended those choices and actions. She left us saying that after visiting *ch'ien* interpreters, she would feel less anxious about deciding what to do about a health problem.

Note that the *ch'ien* interpreter relieved the client's anxiety and helped her decide how to respond to her symptoms by giving her advice about *secular* health care that was specially sanctioned by the *sacred* context of his practice. This is one of the strengths of his practice. *Ch'ien* interpreters need not, and often do not, mention their temples' gods. But the *ch'ien* paper itself symbolizes the sacred source of therapeutic efficacy clients are seeking. The secular advice meets the practical orientation of most clients. This combination constitutes the unique clinical reality of this type of indigenous practice.

Finally, as Tseng (1976) has noted, *ch'ien* interpretation is a major source of indigenous psychotherapy in Taiwan; indeed, it is probably the most widely resorted to form of talk therapy. The popular ideology holds, of course, that it is the written words, the characters on the *ch'ien* paper, that are effective. But, as our examples disclose, it is the communication between *ch'ien* interpreter and client that is the chief psychosocial intervention and the main source of efficacy. Although this relationship is cast in the traditional Confucian master-disciple, teacher-student form, it tends to be less formal, more permissive, more open to verbal give and take, and, as in several of our examples, associated with practical advice. In this respect it is more like supportive psychotherapy than the other major indigenous treatment forms.

A contemporary functional equivalent of *ch'ien* interpretation, to my mind, is the personal and medical advice column in virtually every newspaper in Taiwan. Here again a short, concrete, usually culturally traditional and sometimes socially sensitive, but almost always practical, answer is provided for personal and interpersonal problems. Of course, the sacred canopy has been taken away. But numerous students whom I have spoken with, whose secular, modern, Western orientation keeps them away from the *ch'ien* interpreter's counter and who do not have the psychotherapist's office available to them, use these newspaper columns much as their mothers and grandmothers use *ch'ien* interpretation.

The illustrations of *ch'ien* interpreter-client interactions, like the examples cited for *tâng-ki*-client interactions, underline the therapeutic importance of practitioner-patient communication. In these clinical relationships, communication functions to convey information, confirm or change client explanatory models, provide practical advice, persuade clients to a particular course of action (e.g., a particular health care decision), give psychological support, transmit and reaffirm traditional cultural values, help diminish or resolve social tensions, and perform various other therapeutic tasks. Additionally, it can be seen that the transactional process is crucial to clinical care, even though *ch'ien* interpreters can be as one-sided in these clinical dialogues as their modern professional medical counterparts. For the *ch'ien* interpreter, like the *tâng-ki*, therapeutic power stems in part from a balance between sensitivity to their clients' ideas and the authoritarian confirmation or disapproval of these ideas. Although less true for the *ch'ien* interpreter than for the *tâng-ki*, therapeutic communication is dominated by the practitioner, a phenomenon found in the other practitioner-patient interactions we shall examine and characteristic of many other cultures. What sets indigenous communication off from that of Western medical practice is not the tendency toward authoritarian, practitioner-dominated communication, which both share, but the sensitivity to client EMs and the use of psychosocially meaningful explanations. This is not nearly as much a function of the personal attributes of the healers, which vary greatly, as a consequence of the culturally prescribed clinical reality associated with these indigenous therapeutic interactions.

Categorization of Ch'ien *Interpreter-Client Transactions: A Summary*

The *ch'ien* interpreter-client relationship contains many of the elements that were previously cited as characteristic of the *tâng-ki*-client relationship, but there are also some important differences:

1. Institutional Setting: one component of the temple-based religious healing subsector in the folk sector of Taiwan's health care system

2. Characteristics of the Interpersonal Interaction

a. *Number:* Other clients may comment openly on the interaction, which is a public one, but this relationship is more nearly limited to practitioner and client than is the relationship with a *tâng-ki*. In 150 of these interactions I observed in Taipei, 91 were dyadic, 36 were triadic, and only 23 involved three or more members of the client group.

b. The *ch'ien* interpreter-client interaction is *episodic, not continuous*. Only 15 of 50 consecutive interactions I observed in one large temple in Taipei and 23 of 100 consecutive interactions I observed in four small temples in the same city involved individuals who had some continuing relationship with the *ch'ien* interpreters or the temples, or who viewed the consultation as leading to further care for the presenting problem from these practitioners or their temples. The mean time for these therapeutic interactions was 2 minutes 25 seconds (range: 12 seconds to 10 minutes 11 seconds), of which virtually all the time (mean: 2 minutes 15 seconds, range: 10 seconds to 9 minutes 57 seconds), was taken up in practitioner-patient communication. The mean time devoted to explaining was 1 minute 55 seconds (range: 5 seconds to 9 minutes 13 seconds), so that the proportion of explanatory time for this therapeutic interaction was highest among the various kinds of indigenous and Western-style practice I observed.

c. The *ch'ien* interpreter-client interaction is *less formal* than the *tâng-ki*-client consultation, but it is still based on the master-student paradigm, and there is *no alternation between formal and informal modes*. In spite of these differences, like *tâng-ki*-client relationships, *ch'ien* interpreter-client relationships deal with sickness as part of a *broad array of human problems* and relate it to everyday life events and experiences.

d. Since *ch'ien* interpreters do not charge a fee or receive a personal gift and therefore do not derive a direct profit from their interactions with patients, it is not surprising that there is *little evidence of ambivalence* on the part of their clients. Similarly, since *ch'ien* interpretation seldom challenges the efficacy of their gods, *ch'ien* interpreters do not view clients ambivalently, as either an opportunity to prove their gods' powers or a threat to those powers.

3. Idiom of Communication.

a. This relationship is conducted in the *idiom of the popular culture*. Cosmological explanations regarding fate are joined with common-sense sociological interpretations and moral guides to behavior. Although a somatic articulation of problems is still more common than their psychological expression, this relationship sanctions commonsense psychological interpretations of personal problems to a much greater extent than do other indigenous therapeutic transactions in Taiwan.

b. *EMs* are generally shared, routinely expressed openly, and frequently negotiated. The *ch'ien* interpreter supports lay EMs that are based on the popular culture's traditional belief system.

4. Clinical Reality

a. *Ch'ien* interpreters generally take a more dispassionate approach to their clients than *tâng-ki*s, and their interpretations are treated less reverently than are those transmitted by *tâng-ki*s. While there is no doubt that the *ch'ien* interpreter participates in a sacred clinical reality, that clinical reality is less extensively charged with sacred meanings than is the one in which the *tâng-ki* participates.

b. *Illness problems* are the chief target for therapeutic interventions. Explanation is quite obviously the core clinical task. It is principally concerned with diagnosis, choice of treatment, and prognosis. But, as we have seen, psychosocial support is provided, anxiety is assuaged, quite practical advice is supplied, and the client is morally exhorted.

c. Therapeutic interventions, except for practical advice, are mostly *symbolic;* somatic therapies are recommended less frequently than in the *tâng-ki*'s shrine.

d. *Therapeutic expectations*, in the main shared by practitioner and client, turn on the fact that the *ch'ien* interpreter is viewed less as a therapist and more as a diagnostician and prognosticator who divines sacred writ but does not directly tap sacred sources of therapeutic efficacy.

257

Consequently, less is expected from the relationship by both parties, less emotion is invested in it, and, as our examples illustrate, less therapeutic effect (and probably also less toxicity) is obtained.

e. The *ch'ien* interpreter neither views himself nor is viewed by his clients as *most responsible for care*. Clients and their families view him as a culturally legitimated translator and advisor. The *ch'ien* interpreter characteristically helps patients choose a primary therapist and therapy, most commonly a sacred folk healer but occasionally a professional practitioner.

5. Therapeutic Stages and Mechanisms

a. Unlike healing rituals and *tâng-ki*-client transactions, *ch'ien* interpretation *does not pass through three distinctive stages*. It is best thought of as immediate problem solving in a question and answer format.

b. *Mechanisms of change*, which appear to involve psychological, social, and cultural processes, are discussed in Chapter 9.

c. Although I did not collect specific data on this point, it is my impression that *adherence* to the prescribed medical regimen is less than in treatment by shamans. Rarely did clients express *dissatisfaction* with this form of care. For the most part, practitioner and client *evaluations of outcome* were consistent. Termination was unproblematic and was believed to follow immediately upon transmission of the interpretation and fielding of subsequent questions. Occasionally, busy *ch'ien* interpreters did not provide clients with ample time to raise questions about their interpretations and, at least once, this precipitated a minor dispute. Case follow-up almost never occurs.

8

Patients and Healers:
Transactions Between Explanatory
Models and Clinical Realities
*Part 2: Professional Practitioner-Patient
and Family-Patient Relationships*

PRACTITIONER-PATIENT INTERACTIONS 3:
CHINESE-STYLE PHYSICIAN-PATIENT*

In this section and the next, I will describe observations
in the offices of Chinese-style and Western-style practitioners.
I worked out my own clinical formulations for a number of
cases side by side with Chinese-style physicians and then compared my evaluation with theirs. I will include several of these
exercises to show our different clinical constructions of the
same sickness episode.

Chinese medicine differs from Western medicine in its theories, diagnostic system, treatments, and in the social reality
of clinical practice. As a clinician I found that many, but by no
means all, of the 25 Chinese-style doctors whom I observed
more than casually took a clinical approach to their patients
that I readily understood. Although the Chinese medical concepts they employed were remote from my own orientation,
when a sick person presented before us, I discovered that abstract medical theory was translated into a practical clinical
method that, though still considerably different from my own
perspective, paralleled the translation I made of medical scientific theory into actual clinical strategies. We both made use
of clinical concepts that were transforms of theoretical concepts, and despite markedly different approaches to *disease,*

*See note on p. 310.

which the Chinese-style doctors viewed as their chief interest, we both frequently approached *illness* as an important concern, an orienting problem that focused our quite different systems of knowledge and action around the life crises caused by sickness and that forced us to search for immediate solutions (admittedly, Chinese-style doctors would more often treat these illness problems with somatic rather than psychosocial interventions). These mutually shared aspects of clinical practice were undeniable and were as impressive to some of the Chinese-style doctors as they were to me.

The differences were also clear. If trance and charms symbolize the social reality of *tâng-ki*s' clinical practice, and if *ch'ien* paper and the negotiated interpretation of fate symbolize *ch'ien* interpreters' work, then taking the pulse and, especially, writing out the characters for lengthy, compound prescriptions are the core symbols of practice in Chinese medicine. That practice is not conducted in a temple, of course, but in a doctor's office, often one that is part of a Chinese pharmacy. But it is not what we think of in the West by the term "doctor's office." There is virtually no equipment, unless the Chinese-style practitioner uses acupuncture or bone-setting techniques, which most Chinese-style doctors in Taiwan do not use. There is a desk and on it a small cushion, usually old and dirty, where the patient places his hand and wrist. Often the desk is out in the open, across from the counter of the Chinese pharmacy in which it is located. If it is not in a pharmacy, then it is either in an open area in the midst of a single room that functions as both waiting room and consultation room, or it may be in a separate area blocked off by a screen or a wall from the waiting area. Often it is in as public a place as the settings where *tâng-ki*s and *ch'ien* interpreters ply their clinical trades. Thus, patients tell (and expect to tell) their tales of illness and receive treatment in front of other patients. This clinical "set," which Chinese patients bring to doctors' offices, plays an important role in what is said and what is suppressed. And it reflects certain basic cultural differences in the definition of bodily complaints and treatment as "private" or "public" concerns.

The offices and pharmacies of Chinese-style practitioners open directly into the street, just as do most Chinese businesses and temples, their fronts completely open without door or wall. A few private Western-style practitioners' offices do the same, but most houses of Western medicine are closed to the busy commercial streets. They are walled off and are hence more remote and more formal. Similarly, although the popular image is that of a Confucian scholar, most Chinese-style practitioners in Taipei are members of the lower middle-class and practice more like local businessmen and shopkeepers. Their Western-style medical colleagues, by contrast, are middle-class and often upper middle-class professionals and live in a different social world from that of their patients. Even though Chinese-style doctors usually do not maintain so wide a social distance from their patients, they do establish a wide distance between the knowledge they hold and that held by their patients. The ancient medical classics and the books passed down in the family containing "secret prescriptions" that stand behind their desks mark this intellectual boundary.

Most Chinese-style practitioners I interviewed believed their patients knew very little about Chinese medicine. As a result, unless a patient asks, they rarely explain about cause, pathophysiology, or course of illness. They may not even name the illness. What they do is to give patients detailed prescriptions. For most patients coming to Chinese-style doctors, that is all that matters. The prescription is what gets them the mixtures of Chinese medicinal agents, mostly herbs, that they view as the source of efficacy *and* meaning in Chinese medical practice.

In a typical case a patient (people of all socioeconomic classes, levels of education, and both sexes go to Chinese-style doctors) walks in and sits down at the doctor's desk. He rolls up his sleeve and places first one arm and then the other on the doctor's small cushion. He may describe a complaint but frequently does not. He may say something about the effect of his treatment if he is returning for a follow-up visit. While the Chinese-style doctor spends several minutes taking the pulse at each wrist, they sit in silence. The patient looks around at the calligraphy mounted on the walls, which represents testimonials of satisfied patients and moral exhortations from the Confucian classics. At the same time, the physician is examining the patient's face—making an assessment of color, odor, type of hair; looking at the eyes and perhaps also the tongue.

The doctor then asks questions. For a Westerner this is the

strangest part of Chinese medical practice and the Chinese-style doctor-patient interaction, because these questions seem so bizarre and often seem to have nothing to do with history-taking. In Chinese culture, as we have remarked, the popular medical ideology holds that the skills of a clinician are demonstrated by his ability to ascertain what is wrong from the pulse and perhaps from a few short questions. The fewer the questions the better. A great doctor need ask nothing. Thus, for a clinician the pressure is on from the outset to make as rapid a diagnosis as possible and to do so with the smallest amount of information he can get away with. For obvious reasons, however, experienced clinicians do nothing to discourage patients from talking about their problems and try to obtain the crucial aspects of the history through a small number of questions that cover the chief problems they associate with each age group, sex, and life style.

The mean time of 200 Chinese-style doctor-patient interviews I observed is 7 minutes 35 seconds, as against under 5 minutes for most routine private Western-style doctor-patient interchanges in Taiwan. At least half of the Chinese-style interview is spent in silence, while the Chinese-style doctor reads the pulses of the patient. The verbal interchange, lasting a mean time of 3 minutes and 10 seconds, as against 1 minute and 45 seconds in the Western-style interviews, is completely one-sided. The Chinese-style doctor is the authority. He asks the questions. Virtually the only thing he explains is how the patient should take the medicine he is given and what foods he may or may not eat. Yet the Chinese-style doctor still spends more than double the time of his Western-style colleagues explaining to patients (a mean time of 1 minute 47 seconds against a mean time of 40 seconds).

Moreover, unlike Western-style doctors, the Chinese-style doctor will answer questions. If the patient wants a fuller explanation, he will give it. If the patient has a specific question about the theory behind the practice, he will attempt to explain it to him. If the patient mentions psychosocial problems accompanying his symptoms, the Chinese-style doctor will inquire about them, explain their significance, and suggest how medicine, diet, and other somatic interventions are likely to affect them. Some Chinese-style doctors will allow the patient

Shaman-Client Transactions

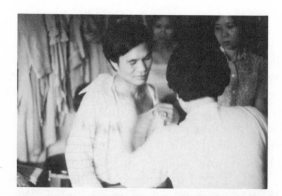

Tâng-ki "blistering" client's skin

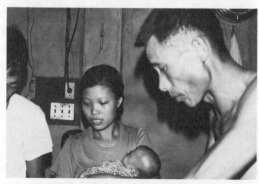

Tâng-ki consulting with clients

Tâng-ki "calling back the souls" of an infant suffering from "fright"

Client throwing divination blocks to obtain god's consent before consulting *tâng-ki*

and the family to ventilate their anxiety. They may offer them support and practical advice and perhaps, if they know them well, even help them decide how best to resolve family, job, and other interpersonal problems. Yet, most often, Chinese-style doctors rely on somatic and not psychosocial interventions to manage illness problems. The Confucian paradigm governing the Chinese-style doctor-patient relationship assures that most patients do not challenge this treatment style, even if they disagree with it, and do not expect the Chinese-style doctor to talk to them as a friend or equal, unless they belong to his family or social network. Indeed, their expectation is that his secret knowledge, somewhat higher social status, and emotional distance are signs of his therapeutic power and, therefore, are an essential part of the doctor-patient relationship. Chinese-style doctors as a group tend to be more concerned with keeping up traditional appearances than Western-style doctors, and their patients expect them to behave that way.

When Chinese-style doctors explain to patients, they transform traditional concepts into modern forms. They usually do not use terms such as *ch'i, yin/yang, wu-hsing* (Five Evolutive Phases or Elements), or *wu-tsang* (Five Body Spheres or "Orbs"), but rather use words commonly employed in the popular sector that can be applied in a modern idiom, frequently an idiom from Western-style medicine. Even when they use classical Chinese medical terms, they frequently employ them with Western medical logic or translate them into Western medical idiom. Thus, *huo*, fire, is used in the Western sense of inflammation, not in its classical Chinese medical sense, where it denotes a type of internal hot energy, *huo-ch'i*. Instead of talking about a state of imbalance between the interrelated *functions* of the internal organs (*wu-tsang*) as responsible for a pathological excess of energy, *huo-ch'i ta* —a central idea in Chinese medicine which Chinese-style doctors often use in formulating a clinical problem—they talk to their patients about "liver fire" or "stomach fire" or "brain fire" in the modern scientific sense of a specific organ lesion. They do this both because they feel this is what their patients can understand and because they themselves have begun to combine their concepts with those from modern scientific medicine.

Chinese-style doctors tend not to be confused by talk of coronary artery insufficiency, viral pneumonia, metabolic and hormonal abnormalities, metastatic hepatoma, and the like, although these are not found in Chinese medical theory. They have developed practical translations from Western terminology to Chinese terminology, and vice versa. However, since they are not systematically schooled in medical science and since translations tend to be haphazard, misconceptions and miscommunications abound.

On the other hand, there is much in Chinese medicine that patients don't understand, and Chinese-style practitioners appreciate this. For example, one of the most important concepts in Chinese medicine is *ch'i* (vital breath or energy). As I have already noted, in our survey of 125 families in Taipei, 90 percent had no idea what this term meant. Only a few people understood its classical medical significance in terms of the normal flow of *ch'i* through the body's organs and channels, its pathological significance when blocked, and the relationship of the body's *ch'i* to the *ch'i* found in the earth and the cosmos.

As we have noted, patients in Taiwan possess packages of information that are strange combinations of traditional and modern ideas about illness. Chinese-style practitioners seem to have a much better sense of this than Western-style practitioners. Yet most Chinese-style doctors I observed rejected popular and folk medical notions, such as ghosts, geomancy, bad fate, and astrological beliefs. These were regarded as superstitions. In talking with their patients about folk and popular beliefs, Chinese-style practitioners, while sometimes disparaging these ideas, tend on the whole to be less intolerant of them than Western-style doctors. Patients recognize this and, therefore, are more likely to tell Chinese-style doctors their real beliefs, though they will not reveal these ideas to them nearly as readily as they will to sacred folk practitioners.

Chinese-style doctors also possess unusual packages of knowledge, packages that combine modern scientific ideas with Chinese medical notions and even certain folk ideas with Chinese medical concepts and that contain different versions of Chinese medical theory. Since most Chinese-style practitioners have studied under a kinsman or some other "master," have read one or two medical classics but not others, and have followed one particular school of orally transmitted clinical knowledge, their conceptual systems frequently differ considerably. For example, acupuncturists follow the ideas in the *Huang-ti nei-ching* (Yellow Emperor's Classic of Internal Medicine), while herbalists tend to follow the ideas in the *Shang-han lun* (Treatise on Cold Disorders), in which the concept of the *wu-hsing* (Five Elements or, following Porkert, Five Evolutive Phases) so central to the *Nei-ching,* is not used at all. This is well beyond the focus of this chapter: I merely wish to stress that Chinese-style doctors vary considerably. Besides different knowledge bases, some are more theoretical and others more practical (indeed, I worked with a few who hardly paid any attention to theory at all); some use many Western concepts, others hardly any; some are skilled professional clinicians, while others are not nearly so experienced and adept.

One of the most skilled was Dr. Lim, a 60-year-old Chinese-style doctor who reminded me of certain experienced, skilled, warm, and quite pragmatic modern medical doctors (usually family practitioners) whom I have encountered (not all that frequently) in our own society. Let us sit in while Dr. Lim treats several cases. Realize as we watch Dr. Lim that he keeps full records of his cases, that he believes, "most patients who come to Chinese-style doctors nowadays come with minor illnesses or chronic illness," that he has considerable regard for the efficacy of Chinese medicines and feels Chinese and Western medicine complement each other, and that he knows many of the patients he sees will not return and that they consider themselves and their families, not him, primarily responsible for their care.

> Patient [a middle-aged woman with a hoarse voice who has recently had an operation on her nose by a Western-style practitioner. She has been to see Dr. Lim before but he cannot locate her chart]: "I still have a problem with my nose. I took Western medicine, and it caused stomach discomfort."
>
> Dr. Lim (who is feeling her pulse during this interchange): "How long ago did you have your operation?"
>
> Patient: "Three months ago. I still have treatment. One nostril is all right, the other is not good."
>
> Dr. Lim: "Since you know which side is bad, you can buy a type of Japanese medicine that you can put on locally with cotton. You can treat yourself and take medicines. That will get you better. You have inflammation of the tissues of your nose. (Here he used the Western medical terminology.) You treat

yourself and take the medicine, and the inflammation will get better. The tissue itself will shrink."

Patient: "Now I'm still taking the Western medicine for the inflammation."

Dr. Lim: "If your stomach cannot tolerate the Western medicine, then only take the Chinese medicine. Take it with five parts of the white section of large onions, and eat hot (in temperature) food not cold food. Do you yourself boil the medicine or does someone else?"

Patient: "Me."

Dr. Lim: "When boiling the medicine, breathe in the steam. If it is too hot then stop for a while, then breathe it in again. If you do this the tissue in your nose will gradually shrink. It takes about two months to cure sinusitis with difficulty breathing."

Patient: "I still have some discharge from my nose."

Dr. Lim: "Do you go to an ENT doctor (he means the Western medical specialist) to have your nose washed?"

Patient: "Yes. I have gone."

Dr. Lim: "After having the nose washed you can treat yourself."

Patient: "I always go back to have my nose washed. Still my nose feels uncomfortable inside."

Dr. Lim: "You can treat yourself for that. Maybe the ENT doctor didn't cut out all the tissue."

Patient: "The operation took two hours. The doctor showed me the tissue. The operation was on both sides."

Dr. Lim: "If he cut out the tissue completely then there should be no more problem. Was part of the surgery done in the throat?"

Patient: "Yes. Why am I still hoarse? What is the medicine for?" (Dr. Lim has begun writing out the prescription.)

Dr. Lim: "Medicine is for letting breath get through the blocked nose. From the time of the operation until now, have you had tonic with wine?"

Patient: "No."

Dr. Lim: "If not, it is all right. I was afraid you had taken tonic."

Patient: "Since the inflammation of the nose is not cured, I cannot have tonic."

Dr. Lim: "Take this prescription for one week. Then the nose will get better."

In this case I think anyone familiar with general medical problems can follow Dr. Lim and feel that what he does is fairly similar to what a Western-style doctor might do, although certain of his questions and recommendations relate only to Chinese medical beliefs (e.g., the prohibition on taking tonic and the diet he recommended to accompany the Chinese medicine). Most of the time Dr. Lim spends less than one minute talking to patients (including asking questions). Thus, this case is atypical. Moreover in other cases, Dr. Lim's conceptual model is quite different from that of modern medical science, and consequently his questions and his entire approach become much more difficult for a Western doctor to follow and are at variance with modern medical diagnostic evaluation.

Patient [a tall, thin, chronically ill-appearing middle-aged man]: "I have great difficulty swallowing sputum."

Dr. Lim (who is looking into the patient's throat): "You have a white spot on your throat. How about the medicine I gave you last time?" (Patient did not answer.)

Dr. Lim: "Indigestion?"

Patient: "Ah?" (He indicated he could not hear Dr. Lim's question because of the loudness of the pharmacy's TV showing the funeral procession for Chiang Kai-shek.)

Dr. Lim: "Pain?"

Patient: "I can't digest. Also have a little difficulty breathing."

Dr. Lim: "How about urine?"

Patient: "At beginning clear, now white. Stool is too soft."

Dr. Lim: "Kidney is weak. Stomach is not well."

Patient: "I had some fever before."

Dr. Lim: "Your kidney has some fire. Do you do heavy labor?"

Patient: "I drive a bicycle truck." (This is very strenuous activity.)

Dr. Lim: "Some pressure is on the lower part of your body."

Patient: "I am not strong enough to use my feet to pedal. That causes my stool to be soft too."

Dr. Lim: "Dream much?"

Patient: "At first no dreams. When dawn comes, I will dream. Medicine could be somewhat stronger!"

Dr. Lim: "Pass gas?"

Patient: "No gas. I have an ache in the side of my neck."

Dr. Lim: "How about nausea?"

Patient: (I could not hear his reply.)

Dr. Lim: "Bad taste in mouth?"

Patient: "I still have a bad taste. Difficulty swallowing. Can these symptoms be treated altogether?"

Dr. Lim: "No! Step by step." (Dr. Lim begins to palpate the patient's abdomen.) "Feel any pain?"

Patient: "No pain, but I can feel something uncomfortable. Powdered medicine doesn't work so well. Medicine I took before made my urine white."

Dr. Lim: "I suggest three days medication this time." (He then wrote out a new prescription.)

I did not follow Dr. Lim's reasoning in this case. After the patient had departed, when we reviewed the case together, he described the patient's problem in terms of traditional Chinese medical concepts that linked it to a particular prescription but did not explain it as a disease or single syndrome. Nor could I decide what was wrong, since I could not do a physical examination or laboratory tests. I would want to determine if a chronic disease was present as well as define more clearly the white spot in the throat, which I perceived as an acute local problem (pharyngitis) responsible for the difficulty swallowing and perhaps also for the difficult breathing and the fever. I could not convince Dr. Lim of the importance of doing this, just as he could not convince me of the validity of his approach. His questions were limited to his diagnostic and treatment concerns, and those were totally foreign to the framework I used and the concerns I had. I needed to elicit different information in order to test my own hypotheses about what sickness this patient was suffering from. Here we find a basic conflict in conceptual models. But there also are obvious differences in therapeutic style. For example, though I realized rules of etiquette governing Chinese medical practice encouraged Dr. Lim not to repeat questions the patient either didn't hear or hadn't satisfactorily answered, my Western medical orientation made me feel dissatisfied with such an obviously incomplete evaluation. The case points up the conflicting values built into divergent clinical constructions of reality. Not only did I fail to understand Dr. Lim's approach, but I felt strongly he was wrong and was giving this patient inadequate care.

In another case, a middle-aged lady complained of stiffness in the neck and headache. Dr. Lim spent only five minutes with this patient and during that time asked his usual questions to evaluate the reputed functions of the five interrelated organs comprising the *wu-tsang*'s internal functional system. I could not relate his concerns to my own. I was wondering if the case was one involving an acute viral illness, early signs of a neurological disorder, the sequelae of hypertension, or somatization with anxiety neurosis, depression, or hysteria. Nor could I determine what was wrong (using my conceptual framework) based on the information he had gathered (using his conceptual framework).And I felt that not only did I have to ask an entirely different set of questions, but that my evaluation would be valueless without a physical examination. In other cases, when Dr. Lim and I both took the patient's pulse, we often disagreed about what it empirically demonstrated. We were trained to assess it differently. I could recognize few of the fine distinctions he made. He was dissatisfied with the small number of pathological pulse signs I recognized, few of which were pathognomonic in my view and most of which required confirmatory evidence from other physical and laboratory tests. Our different theoretical systems led to different clinical observations about what we both believed to be "hard" empirical evidence.

However, in most cases Dr. Lim and I were in general agreement on the problem (arthritis, low back pain, measles, hepatitis, etc.). But we did not agree on what was to be done about it. This kind of disagreement is fundamental unless the observer shares the expectations and beliefs of the culturally constructed world of clinical practice. Dr. Lim would have shared my uneasiness had he watched me practice. But this is not completely fair. Dr. Lim has a niece who is an internist in the United States, and frequently he told me that scientific medical reasoning was more accurate and inclusive than his own conceptual approach. Most Chinese-style doctors I met felt this way. Thus, in the confrontation of Chinese and Western medicine, the Chinese-style cognitive framework appears less adequate (for certain problems) than the Western scientific orientation; and it is changing by attempting to absorb elements from Western medical science (although not systematically). This is a view shared by Chinese-style and Western-style doctors and patients. From what I observed, it appears to be as true for the People's Republic of China as it is for Taiwan. Even where I witnessed herbs, acupuncture or other traditional Chinese therapies employed by Western-style doctors in China, rarely was the traditional theory used, unless it was essential for prescribing a specific treatment. Instead these practices were applied empirically within the Western medical framework. Frequently in Taiwan and generally in the People's Republic, the clinical behavior of Chinese-style physicians I observed likewise approximated Western medical professional norms more than traditional indigenous ones.

Other Chinese doctors in Taiwan labeled diseases with indigenous diagnostic terms that meant a specific entity to themselves and their patients but held no biomedical meaning: *yin/yang* imbalance, summer fever, kidney insufficiency, "cold" disorders. These labels led to specific remedies. They structured the experience of illness and the course of care for the patient as well as for the physician. Western-style practitioners could neither diagnose nor threat these problems in the terms they are understood by patients and Chinese-style doctors. Much of the social reality of Chinese medical practice is a shared (even if only superficially shared) framework for assessing symptoms, categorizing them, and applying treatment, which patient, family, and doctor use. This is usually not the case in Western medical practice in Taiwan. The importance of Chinese medicine derives not so much from the practice of Chinese-style doctors, as from its incorporation into the popular cultural code as a set of strategic categories governing the behavior of patients and popular health care practices.

Many patients complain that Chinese-style doctors do not explain enough to them, take too little time, sometimes use medical labels they cannot understand, and show insufficient "caring" interest in them. These same complaints are applied to Western-style doctors, but with much stronger criticism. Dr. Lim convincingly demonstrated to patients his professional competence, his concern for them as sick people whom he wished to help, and his ability to give them agents that were sometimes empirically effective. (His pharmacopeia contains ephedrine and dozens of other effective drugs, as well as prednisone, a modern addition compounded with many traditional Chinese medicines when they are packaged as pills and powders.) But he often can be faulted for not explaining much to his patients. From a psychiatric standpoint, he and many of his colleagues do very little psychologically oriented practice, although sometimes they give general support and practical advice for life problems. Indeed, Dr. Lim doesn't consider psychological disorders "real" illnesses. He has a somato-psychic rather than a psychosomatic viewpoint, one in which physical problems can produce psychological problems but not vice versa. Here again he and his colleagues depart from the Chinese medical classics, in which psychological factors, as also environmental and bodily causes, are listed as causes of sickness. He has recently begun, however, as have several other Chinese-style doctors I know, to see psychological stress as a potential cause of certain disorders. Ironically, this insight is not the result of a closer reading of the Chinese medical classics but has been acquired from popularization of Western psychological ideas. Patients do not expect Dr. Lim to ask them directly about their personal and social problems, and he does not do this, even though he is willing to listen to their psychosocial complaints when they are raised. Why then do so many patients come to him and his fellow Chinese-style doctors with somatization of primary psychological problems, just as they go to Western-style doctors with the same problems? They do not routinely obtain from these professional practitioners the kind of sensitive psychocultural responses that *tâng-ki*s and *ch'ien* interpreters give them, though they occasionally obtain such help, nor do they seem to expect it. Instead, they go to doctors to get herbs or injections for their reputed efficacy in treating symptoms *and*, in their somato-psychic viewpoint, potential illness problems as well, and also to obtain legitimation for a medical sick role for minor psychological problems. Patients are aware that for help that is more personally and socially meaningful, professional medical care (Chinese and especially Western) is not the right clinical reality; therefore, they visit *tâng-ki*s and *ch'ien* interpreters. They go to Chinese-style and Western-style doctors when they want more potent technical interventions than they can get in the social context of folk medical care. As we have seen, they often do both together. This is a split in the traditional functions of clinical care, which has usually included in the same setting (and practitioner) both technical remedies and social and personal meaning for the experience of illness (see Kleinman 1974a). This split, then, does not simply reflect the difference between modern and traditional medicine in societies undergoing rapid modernization and Westernization; it also results from the medical pluralism and functional differentiation of societies containing separate indigenous healing traditions.

In closing this section, I shall refer to other *styles* of practice in Chinese medicine. Some Chinese-style doctors go out of their way to cultivate traditional values: long fingernails; scholars' gowns; calligraphy and paintings (their own and others') on the walls of their offices; discourses on medical theory to patients; formal etiquette and language; and so forth. Others, especially acupuncturists, go to great lengths to appear like Western-style doctors: they wear white laboratory coats; use blood pressure devices and other modern medical equipment; take symptom histories along modern medical lines; send patients off for X-rays, blood tests, and urinalyses. In one case I am familiar with, a father who is a Chinese-style practitioner runs a large clinic that employs his two sons, who are Western-style doctors, internists well-trained in treating liver and kidney diseases. The father sees all the patients first. He has several nurses (trained in Western-style nursing schools) who perform urinalyses and blood tests. If patients have demonstrated abnormalities, they are sent to his sons for Western-style treatment; if they have no demonstrated pathology, they are treated with Chinese medicine. These different versions of practice point to an aspect of health care in *urban* Taiwan that requires emphasis, the marked competition by a large number of practitioners for a limited supply of patients who can afford to pay. The styles described have obvious appeal to different groups of patients in that pool. As such, they can be regarded in part as economically motivated strategies for competing successfully in this special sphere of commercial life. Certain styles of practice also imply that Chinese medicine in Taiwan is more like the practice of Ayurvedic medicine in India than like the widely-propagated image of Chinese medical practice in the People's Republic of China, since in Taiwan the modern trappings of traditional Chinese medicine signify its lower status when compared to Western medicine, certain of whose surface symbols it borrows so as to improve its professional image, in the eyes of both many patients and many of its practitioners. One wonders if a less romantic assessment of the status of Chinese-style medicine in China would disclose a similar, but less pronounced, difference in status.

The following transcripts of Chinese-style doctor-patient

transactions should serve to support certain of the general points I have made about this form of clinical reality and to extend our appreciation of EM interactions.

> Patient [46-year-old female]: "I had a tumor removed surgically from my uterus three years ago. I was fine until the last few months, when I began to have red and burning eyes. I thought this was a side-effect of the Western medicine I take for my female problem, but when the (Western-style) doctor discontinued it, the symptoms did not go away. Other Western medicines (she enumerates them) have not been helpful. I still think this is a side-effect of the Western medicine. What can I do?"

> Chinese-style doctor (after taking a lengthy symptom and drug history): "I don't think this problem is due to a side-effect of the medicine or your female problem. It sounds to me like an allergy. It is your own reaction, maybe to spicy foods, seafood, or something else you have been eating. Or maybe it is caused by the soap you use. For one week do not eat these things, and don't use soap or take hot spring baths. I will give you a medicine that may be of help. It will strengthen you. But to cure you we must get rid of whatever is irritating you and causing this abnormal reaction."

Although the doctor is a Chinese-style practitioner, the concepts and even the words he uses are entirely from Western medicine. Note that he responds to the patient's EM both by politely disagreeing with her ideas about cause and by advancing his own explanation (allergy), which he describes simply and forcefully. He successfully negotiated with the patient, and when she left she not only took the medicine and said she would follow the rest of his treatment regimen, but also remarked that she thought his explanation was a good one and was probably correct. This case is *atypical* of most Chinese-style doctor-patient interactions, but it is a good example of one type of practice where the Chinese-style doctor's concepts and approach are strongly influenced by Western-style medicine. The example is also somewhat atypical because of this doctor's unusual communicative skills.

> Patient [a 20-year-old housewife, looking pale and tired]: "When I breathe there is pain in my chest. My eyes are always tearing."

274

Chinese-style doctor (who, after taking the patient's pulses, began to write out a prescription): "Take this medicine. Steam it with pork. How much rice do you eat?"

Patient: "Is the medicine also good for my eyes?"

Chinese-style doctor (not looking at patient, but putting final touches on his lengthy prescription, which will be filled by his assistant who is working behind the pharmacy counter on the other side of the room): "Yes!"

This transaction, which took less than two minutes, is typical of many I have witnessed in Chinese-style practice. The Chinese-style doctor simply takes the chief complaint and his reading of the pulse and then comes up with a prescription. He does not name the problem for the patient. His explanation is limited to telling the patient how to prepare and take the medicine and includes a few words on her diet. Diet is viewed both as a treatment and as a potentially major influence on the medicine. I was disturbed by the patient's pallor, which suggested anemia, and by her chief complaint, which sounded like pleurisy. The Chinese-style doctor told me he did not share these concerns, since the patient's pulse had been diagnostic of a special type of *yin/yang* imbalance for which he possessed an excellent medicine. He would not tell me more about the medicine nor the specific name of the disorder. It was a problem for which his family for generations had possessed a special remedy. He told me the medicine was known to no other Chinese-style doctors, since it had never been published or talked about. Patients knew that he possessed it and knew it was effective, he said, but that was all they knew. Such secrecy is still frequently found in Chinese-style medical practice but is reputed to have been even more common in the past. It is a salient aspect of Chinese medicine's clinical reality, one that exerts an influence on the expectations of patients as well as on the behavior of practitioners. This patient, for example, was no more surprised by the secrecy than she was by the dietary recommendations. The latter represented the practitioner's concern not only for the influence of diet on the efficacy of the medicine he prescribed, but also, as he told me, for the patient's malnourished appearance. Prescribing medicine that must be taken with special foods so as to increase its efficacy is also a culturally sanctioned way of assuring a more adequate diet (e.g., increasing protein intake), as this practitioner well knew. This limited use of explanation is found in almost half of all Chinese-style medical consultations. Ten percent of those we observed involved no explanations at all. The appeal to *secret* knowledge and drugs easily lends itself to quackery and even fraud, a problem patients and practitioners are not unaware of.

> Patient's mother [a young mother with her three-year-old son, who is experiencing enuresis, which is the reason they are returning to this Chinese-style doctor for further treatment]: "He doesn't like to take medicine with wine as you prescribed because of the smell. If he eats cold (temperature) food, he makes urine too frequently."
>
> Chinese-style doctor: "Does he like to take powdered medicine?"
>
> Patient's mother: "Powdered medicine is inconvenient to prepare."
>
> Chinese-style doctor: "Then what kind of medicine does he like to take?"
>
> Patient's mother: "He prefers pills."
>
> Chinese-style doctor: "It would be easier if he would take powdered medicine, we don't have the medicine he needs in pills. Couldn't you steam powdered medicine with rice, then he would eat it?"
>
> Patient's mother. "He won't take it."
>
> Chinese-style doctor: "He is a child, how would he know the difference? If he takes the powdered medicine, he will be cured. He shouldn't eat beans and dried bean curd, bean sprouts, noodles made of green bean flour. He shouldn't eat too spicy foods."
>
> Patient's mother: "What about sweet foods."
>
> Chinese-style doctor: "He shouldn't eat sweet things. Give him powdered medicine and tonic; they will strengthen his constitution."
>
> Patient's mother: "All right. If you say he should take powdered medicine, I will give it to him. Is it expensive?"
>
> Chinese-style doctor: "No! Not expensive, because it is children's medicine. It will be good for him. Patent medicine would not be effective, because it does not contain these ingredients. Some people only want cheap medicine. It will not help. Make sure you give him tonic (ginseng). It will keep him from getting sick too often."

This interchange, which is longer than most in Chinese-style practice, illustrates the tendency of such transactions to focus on the details of how to prepare and take Chinese medicines. Chinese-style doctors concentrate their explanations on this subject. That underlines the medicine as the most important component of Chinese medical care and as the focus of concern of patient and practitioner. Patients sometimes complain of the difficulty in preparing Chinese medicine. Although this mother said her son preferred pills, it is likely she preferred them as well, because they are easier to administer. Chinese medicines take a long time to prepare and are more difficult to administer. Tonics, as in this case, are frequently prescribed for strengthening the patient's constitution and for preventing sickness. On the whole, the doctor exhibited patience and skill in communicating with this young mother, whose anxiety is reflected by the number of questions she asked. Western-style transactions similarly tend to focus on treatment. This pattern of clinical communication is not specific to Taiwan or Chinese culture. Much the same happens in our own society.

Patient [very anxious middle-aged female]: "Menstrual difficulties. Also, when I eat hot (symbolically hot) foods, I get headaches. When I eat cold (symbolically cold) foods, I vomit up a whitish material. I have no appetite. When I bend to sweep the floor, I get pain in my back. I feel *suan* in my joints. Sometimes I hear a ringing noise in my ears. I have lost weight. There is no taste in my mouth. Tonic gives me problems. I think all of this was caused by not getting enough nourishment when I was younger and going through my seven deliveries."

Chinese-style doctor (who has smiled at the patient throughout her report of complaints, shaking his head in assent, while silently examining her pulses): "I know. We have talked of these problems before. Here is a prescription."

Nothing further was said. The patient filled the prescription and left. The doctor told me that the patient's problem was "summer fever," a problem associated with an excessively hot and weak constitution, too many pregnancies, poor diet, overwork, and excessive worries. Hot days would make it worse. The prescription, he claimed, was specific for this disorder. I asked if the patient could be suffering from a psychological problem. He said no, and rejected the diagnosis of hysteria when I explained it. Here again we see minimal explaining, emphasis on the somatic and social, not the psychological, and sole concern with the provision of a medicinal agent as a specific remedy. Both patient and doctor discount the value of talk as a therapy. Both see medicine as capable of curing the entire set of symptoms, which, though different in nature, are assumed by both to be manifestations of a single underlying problem. Once the prescription has been written, the clinical encounter is brought to a close. Although I felt the patient was probably suffering from hysteria, I could not assess this case in such a short time frame and without adequate tests. But the Chinese-style doctor had seen the patient several times before for the same complaint, and, therefore, this brief encounter should be viewed as an isolated moment in an ongoing course of care. Such a course of care perhaps should be thought of as a continuing conversation between doctor and patient, in which the interaction between EMs can only be studied over many doctor-patient encounters. The conversation is supported by the clinical reality and in turn helps maintain it.

This case also illustrates the quality of time in Chinese-style medicine. There is less of the urgency and immediacy found in Western-style practice. The practitioner is generally slower in his response, and the patient expects the medicine to work slowly, requiring many return visits. Time is felt to be working on the side of the doctor, in contrast to Western-style practice, where it is commonly regarded as working against him. These distinct views of time are an important difference in the clinical realities that characterize Chinese-style and Western-style medical practice.

> Patient [middle-aged male]: "I have a cough and pimples around my mouth."
> Chinese-style doctor (after asking patient to open his mouth and examining the patient's mouth and throat): "You have a red throat. Liver weakness is causing your problems. The functions of your organs are out of harmony because of that. Do you have stomach ulcers or other problems?"
> Patient: "No! Can you give me medicine for this problem?"
> Chinese-style doctor: "Yes, but you must take it regularly for some time."

The patient repeated the doctor's explanation and the prescription several times, as if to make sure he had not misunderstood. This explanation is typical of the more "traditional" explanations given by Chinese-style doctors. The doctor used classical medical terms and implied a logic of functional harmony and balance, rather than one involving an organ specific lesion. But even here some Western terms were also used, and the throat examination was more like a Western-style examination than the traditional Chinese-style examination of the tongue and breath. About one-fourth of all Chinese-style medical explanations we recorded were similar to this one. Characteristic of this kind of explanation is that the doctor explains local symptoms as caused by an underlying disorder that must be treated for the local symptoms to disappear. This is the "radical cure," rather than symptomatic treatment, which is expected of Chinese-style doctors. Patients obviously value highly the Chinese-style doctor's ability to see beyond the manifest to the hidden disease process. Thus, they are not usually put off when told they have a more general problem they can neither see nor feel. In particular, patients believe the pulse will reveal hidden information to the Chinese-style doctor. It will tell him about a hidden aspect of the natural world, just as the _tâng-ki_'s divination will reveal the gods and ghosts belonging to the "unseen order" as aspects of the natural world. Consequently, patients are not greatly surprised when the Chinese-style doctor informs them that their pulse reveals the disease is still present, even if they are symptom-free and feeling well. An essential component of all clinical realities in Chinese culture, then, is that the clinician will be able to "see" and treat aspects of the natural world that are not apparent to the patient, who lacks the special knowledge and skill to deal with them. Obviously, this aspect of indigenous clinical realities was easily adapted to the practice of Western-style medicine, which also implicates natural processes that only a clinician can apprehend.

Several additional points about Chinese-style doctor-patient transactions are worth noting. The more traditional contemporary practitioners of Chinese medicine still analyze cases in terms of the classical _cheng_, or "manifestation types" (Agren

1976). They are used because the system of medicinal prescriptions is based upon them. To prescribe a given Chinese medicine, you must know the *cheng* for which it is used. The types are not usually disclosed to patients, the great majority of whom do not know them. Increasingly, Chinese-style doctors have worked out ways of circumventing these categories and have begun to work with a small number of problems (understood in both Western and Chinese diagnostic terms) which are simply known by the names of the prescriptions used to treat them, which also have been limited to a relatively small functional group. This clinical shorthand is creating a syncretic, clinically applied system of medical theory and treatment, and is also responsible for simplifying and limiting the number of indigenous Chinese medical concepts and treatments. The Sinologist or medical historian looking at the contemporary practice of Chinese medicine in Taiwan might well wonder whether this version of tradition should be called Chinese medicine. Regardless of how we label the extensive changes, what we are describing is what practitioners and patients in Taiwan call Chinese medicine. Many patients and families we interviewed were unaware of these changes and of the fact that classical Chinese medicine was a far more original and developed system than the professional Chinese medicine presently functioning in Taiwan.

One result of these changes are the Chinese-style practitioners who exploit the public by claiming that they possess secret remedies for cancer, serious heart disease, dense stroke, renal failure, and various other terminal conditions. They are called charlatans by other Chinese-style and Western-style physicians. Yet, they may provide the terminally ill and the dying with hope and support, and they are willing to deal with the frustrating tangle of life problems that surround terminal care and intractable disability, whereas Western-style doctors often abdicate the healer's role when faced with problems that no longer respond to technologically based cure. This group of practitioners poses sharply the serious ethical and legal questions that surround traditional medical practice in the contemporary world, but have not yet received the attention they deserve from ethnomedical researchers and public health planners.

Like their Western-style colleagues in Taiwan, Chinese-style doctors, when they manage life-threatening illness, explain virtually nothing to the patient. They aim their remarks at the family members whose job it is to support the patient. For example, they tell the family, not the patient, that he is suffering from cancer or that the treatment of a serious illness has been unsuccessful. This is viewed neither by patients nor by practitioners as an ethical dilemma. It is simply accepted as a sanctioned feature of both types of professional medical practice. Since the family, not the patient, commonly makes crucial decisions about treatment of serious sicknesses, the patient does not see himself as needing such information. I never witnessed a case of terminal illness in Taiwan where this widespread practice seemed to create problems for patient care or for the patient himself, but I can appreciate how it might produce such problems. Certainly, it fundamentally alters clinical communication, replacing patient-practitioner with practitioner-family and patient-family transactions as the chief vehicle of clinical communication and the chief source of therapeutic actions. In the cases I studied, this transformation (which is not a radical one in Taiwan, since patient-family and practitioner-family communication often are an essential part of care there) tended to have major benefits for terminal patients, who were never isolated from family nor cut off from their contexts of meaning and support. This aspect of the management of dying within health care systems in Chinese culture provides the different clinical realities in those systems with a powerful therapeutic approach. In contrast with the management of dying in health care systems in the contemporary West, which is notorious for being poorly handled and frequently maladaptive, the Chinese cultural approach is striking, as are traditional cultural approaches in many other societies that also encourage and support the family context of dying.

An undesirable effect of the Westernization of indigenous Chinese medicine is that Chinese-style doctors discontinue certain highly adaptive traditional practices, including those mentioned above, in order to appear more like their Western-style counterparts. It is difficult to predict what lies ahead for Chinese-style medical care in Taiwan. The thrust of the modernization process is ever pushing it in the direction of becoming a second-rate form of Western medicine, as Ayurvedic medicine appears to have become in India and perhaps also osteopathy in the United States. Communication with patients is an indicator of these changes. It registers the increasing use of Western medical concepts and idiom, as well as a shift toward copying Western medical indifference to and lack of skill in performing this core clinical task. It also registers many problems that appear to result from syncretism in the course of medical modernization.

One Chinese-style practitioner I studied in detail, Dr. Ao, managed to combine Chinese and Western ideas and practices in a syncretic clinical approach that seems quite effective and reminds one of the success Chinese culture has usually shown in developing syncretic systems in response to foreign influence. Dr. Ao is a 55-year-old man who owns a large Chinese pharmacy and specializes in the treatment of women's and children's diseases. He has read modern medical textbooks on obstetrics and gynecology and pediatrics. He has a good knowledge of modern contraceptives and their side-effects. He knows about the anatomical and physiological changes of pregnancy and menopause. He knows a great deal about early child development and spends time advising young mothers how to care for children. He uses both Western and Chinese medical concepts and makes frequent referrals to modern hospitals and laboratories. He does not claim to possess herbs that can cure cancer, something that many Chinese-style doctors claim. He recognizes the limitations of his treatment, something most Chinese-style doctors do not. He diagnoses and frequently treats both hysteria and depression, which makes him much more psychologically sophisticated than most Chinese-style *or* Western-style doctors in Taiwan. He has created a clinic atmosphere that seems to combine the best of both systems, and he is virtually the only Chinese-style doctor I know who has successfully done this. Clearly, he is an intelligent man who wanted to practice the best clinical medicine he could. This has led to a large clinical practice that has brought him considerable wealth. (He has visited the United States three times, including visits to several major university medical centers.) He is the exception that proves the rule: the clinical reality structured in the clinics of most Chinese doctors is quite different from the world of Western-style medicine and from the successful syncretism practiced by Dr. Ao.

Categorization of Chinese-style Practitioner-Patient Transactions:
A Summary

Compared to the other forms of indigenous practitioner-patient relationships in Taiwan, Chinese-style physician-patient interactions can be summarized as follows:

1. Institutional Setting. Chinese medicine occupies a special indigenous subsector of the professional sector of Taiwan's health care systems.

2. Characteristics of the Interpersonal Interaction
    a. *Number*. It is customary for most patients to be accompanied by family members or friends, so that most therapeutic relationships involve triads or quadrads (132 out of 200 cases observed).
    b. These relationships are most often *episodic* and only occasionally *continuous*. Unlike Western-style doctor-patient relationships, which occupy two or three treatment sessions for the same illness episode, Chinese-style doctor-patient relationships usually extend over a longer period, weeks to months. Although they are not ongoing in the context of a wider relationship that extends beyond particular sickness episodes (168 of the 200 cases I observed were either first visits or in several cases revisits following a separation of years), as are half of *tâng-ki*-patient interactions, they involve more continuous care than do most Western-style doctor-patient relationships or *ch'ien* interpreter-client transactions.

    Mean time for consultation: 7 minutes 35 seconds (range: 3 minutes 15 seconds to 32 minutes 43 seconds)
    Mean time for clinical communication: 3 minutes 10 seconds (range: 20 seconds to 15 minutes 12 seconds)
    Mean time spent in explaining: 1 minute 47 seconds (range: 0 to 6 minutes 25 seconds)

    c. These are *formal* relationships that do not alternate with an informal phase. The degree of formality varies; in general, these relationships are less formal than Western-style doctor-patient interactions or the formal phase of *tâng-ki*-client relationships. Several of the relationships I observed, however, were among the most traditionally formal of all interpersonal interactions I witnessed in Taiwan.

There usually is no attempt to relate health problems to a wider array of human misfortune or to integrate them into the context of everyday life, except in those instances where patient and practitioner either belong to the same social network or have a long-standing therapeutic relationship.

d. Chinese-style doctor-patient relationships are usually *not characterized* by *ambivalence*. But the recent increase in fees due to the worldwide popularity of Chinese medicine has surfaced resentment about the commercial success of some Chinese-style practitioners.

3. Idiom of Communication
    a. *Mode*. Communication takes place in technical, professional idiom that is not accessible to most patients. But, unlike Western-style doctors, Chinese-style doctors at times translate their conceptions into popular terms more or less understandable to the laity. The explanatory language tends to be functional rather than mechanistic, somato-psychic rather than psychosomatic, and avoids sociological, psychological, and cosmological terminology. Resort to naturalistic and moral expressions is frequent. But Chinese-style physicians and their patients are increasingly importing the metaphors of Western medicine into their communication.
    b. EMs most often are *not shared,* and patient and practitioner views of clinical reality are often substantially different and may conflict. But such discrepancies and conflicts are less frequent and severe than those found in Western-style practitioner-patient relationships. Explanations rarely take into account psychosocial issues, and "meaning" is provided largely in terms of Chinese medical theory or an amalgam of Chinese and Western medical concepts.

4. Clinical Reality

a. The clinical reality structured in these relationships is *secular,* yet it draws upon traditional Chinese beliefs and values. Chinese-style medical relationships are not entirely dependent upon this clinical reality for their therapeutic effects, though it probably is responsible for the placebo response, but the conflicting views of clinical reality that these relationships at times engender do have negative therapeutic consequences.

b. Chinese-style physician-patient interactions are principally oriented to *disease problems* as defined by the physician. But *illness problems* are not infrequently managed as well and are much more often considered than in Western-style medical practice.

c. Therapeutics is almost entirely *instrumental;* symbolic therapies are only occasionally employed. Somatic therapies were used in all cases I observed and were believed by most Chinese-style doctors to treat psychosocial as well as physical problems.

d. *Therapeutic expectations* are illustrated by the case vignettes. Most Chinese-style doctors cultivate a traditional treatment style; some, especially those who specialize in acupuncture, cultivate a modern Western treatment style. Patients of the latter have occasionally expressed to me discrepant treatment expectations. But most patients in Chinese medical care whom I interviewed held the same traditional treatment expectations as their physicians.

e. Chinese-style physicians do not view themselves as *most reponsible* for their patient's care, nor are they viewed in this way by their patients. They view patients or families as most responsible for minor problems, but families alone are regarded as the locus of responsibility for serious medical problems.

5. Therapeutic Stages and Mechanisms

a. Chinese-style medical practice regularly exhibits a *tripartite organizational structure.*

b. Physiological and psychophysiological *mechanisms of change* predominate. Psychological and social change is less commonly observed to occur.

c. It is the impression of several anthropologists working in Taiwan that patient adherence and satisfaction are higher for Chinese-style medicine than for Western-style medicine and highest of all for sacred folk healing. But systematic ethnomedical studies of patient and practitioner evaluations of outcome are only now being initiated and have not yet generated the data needed to answer this question. I have observed conflicting patient and Chinese-style practitioner assessments of treatment outcome but less frequently than in Western medical practice in Taiwan. Conflicting views of the appropriate time to terminate Chinese medical treatment are common, since for most patients the prescribed treatment regimen is lengthy and expensive and physicians routinely use changes in the pulse rather than symptom change as the basis for determining when to end treatment.

PRACTITIONER-PATIENT INTERACTIONS 4: WESTERN-STYLE DOCTOR-PATIENT

Chinese patients in Taiwan believe Chinese medicines contain the power of the indigenous Chinese medical tradition. Those who know herbs and other medicinal agents do not bother to go to a Chinese-style practitioner but self-administer them. Similarly, in the popular cultural view, injections are the essence of all that is powerful in Western medicine. These two therapeutic agents symbolize the distinctive clinical realities created and sustained by patients and practitioners. In the popular ideology recorded in our family-based interviews, Chinese medicines are seen as cumbersome and crude in form, difficult to prepare, slow to work, but delicate and without danger in their actions and resulting eventually in a "radical" or complete cure. On the other hand, Western intramuscular and intravenous injections are viewed as stream-lined, ultra-modern, and quickly and easily administered. They are believed to be extremely powerful with dangerous side-effects but working immediately to cure symptoms or not at all. These deeply ingrained beliefs help determine expectations and evaluations of clinical practice.

In the popular view (and this is a view clinicians are sensitive to and admit being unable to resist), going to a Western-style doctor, no matter what the problem, should eventuate in symptom improvement after two or three visits (over not more than two or three days) or something is wrong—with the doctor and his treatment. Even educated people describe Western medicine as "the magic bullet." And in Taiwan, it is practiced in line with this metaphor.

In fact, antibiotics (the original and perhaps only magic bullets) were the *technological intervention* that had the largest visible impact on the practice of medical care in Taiwan, as in many other developing nations. (Nutritional, social, and economic changes, of course, had a far greater impact on health in Taiwan, as in China and most of the world [Kleinman 1973c], but this is overlooked by lay people and practicing doctors.) Along with intravenous hydration, antibiotics had a significant impact on treating the chief killers of infants and children, the pneumonia-diarrhea complex of diseases, though social change and public health practices were essential here as well. Antibiotics also were dramatically effective in adult infections, some of which previously had been deadly. But this metaphor has been carried over to all aspects of medical care in Taiwan, including many areas where it is absolutely the wrong image, such as in the management of chronic diseases, in the treatment of disorders of the elderly, and in the care of mental illness.

This is the popular perspective, and it is a compelling social reality, especially for doctors in private practice. As odd as it sounds, of the 300 cases we observed in the clinics (private and public) of Western-style practitioners, fewer than one-fourth failed to receive injections of one sort or another. There is a strong financial motive here. In Taiwan, as we have already noted, practitioners *only* get paid for treatment. Most doctors (Chinese-style and Western-style) provide their own medicines—sold in small pharmacies on their premises. If a practitioner gives the patient a prescription to be filled elsewhere, he does not get paid; the pharmacy where it is filled does. If a practitioner gives the patient medicine to take orally, he gets paid, but less than if he gives the patient an injection. Furthermore, giving an injection is giving the patient the message that you are offering him the best treatment you possess. Consequently, almost all medicinal agents that can be given by injections are so administered. That includes medicines—vitamins, mild sedatives, antipyretics, anti-inflammatory agents, medicines used in the long-term management of chronic illnesses like hypertension, etc.—for which there is no good clinical reason to administer parenterally and good reasons *not* to administer in this way, since it may increase the incidence of dangerous side-effects and can add complications of injections, like iatrogenic infection. (Indeed, epidemiologists are now investigating this as a possible source of the high incidence of infectious hepatitis in Taiwan.)

Many Western-style doctors told me this was a dangerous, quite unnecessary practice, but one they could not relinquish given the "realities" of clinical care in Taiwan. They feared the loss of income and patients. Since referral by satisfied patients is how most patients in Taiwan get to doctors, it is not surprising that doctors fear going against such expectations. There is some preliminary evidence from my work that the few doctors studied who do not follow this ideology have not been seriously affected by their deviant clinical practice. But doctors clearly are part of this social reality and are responding to its ideology and the fears that ideology generates.

The practical effects can be perilous. Almost every case of hepatitis (no matter how mild) that I saw in the offices of private-practicing Western-style doctors was receiving intravenous saline or dextrose in water. These treatments were absolutely unnecessary in most of these cases. Worse still, they might have helped spread hepatitis to other patients, nurses, and the practitioners themselves. Much the same treatment is given to run-of-the-mill cases of enteritis, again for poor clinical reasons. ECT (electroconvulsive therapy) is the supposedly magic bullet of psychiatry and is administered excessively and in situations where it is of doubtful value.

Probably owing to this practice, over the past decade or so penicillin reactions increased greatly, including some deaths from penicillin allergy. In some of these cases the only reason penicillin was given was because the patient had fever and bacterial infection was a possible, though not very likely, cause. Medical-legal litigation followed swiftly on the heels of these deaths. Awards have been relatively high, and that has terrified practitioners, since there is no malpractice insurance. Some doctors have had to go into bankruptcy to pay off these claims. Even where suits have not been filed, families have taken a traditional Chinese approach of bringing the corpse in its coffin into the practitioner's office until the claims are met. This has had a disastrous effect in the last few years. Private physicians now fear treating any case who might die. They turn down cases of pneumonia and many other kinds of acute medical problems. Managing chronic illness has come to mean being prepared to "dump" the patient into a hospital before the patient dies. Moreover, recourse is now made hardly at all (outside hospitals) to penicillin, which has become a fearsome symbol to physicians though it remains an excellent drug if properly used, but instead to a vast array of "new" antibiotics—many of them with severe side-effects, but ones less immediate than penicillin's. The fear of suits and the large numbers of suits virtually have brought private major surgery to a halt. ENT has overnight become a medical subspecialty, since its surgically trained practitioners fear performing surgery. This has put an enormous burden on government and military hospitals, especially the National Taiwan University Hospital, which carry most of the load of major surgery and the care of the acutely or dangerously ill. The current clinical reality of Western-style medical practice is thus working against the best interests of patients and doctors and against good medical care. It also illustrates how sociopolitical and economic factors help determine the features of clinical reality.

But there is much more to culturally constructed Western-style clinical reality in Taiwan. Of the two hundred-fifty patients my research assistants and I observed in *private* Western medical practice in Taipei, with the exception of emergency visits, most got to see the doctor for 2 to 3 minutes. During that period there was barely time to express fully the chief symptoms. Virtually nothing was explained to the patient, unless he/she asked. This varied by education and social class. Upper middle-class patients and patients who were professionals or students did get explanations; laborers and semiliterate or illiterate housewives got none. When explanations were given, they were limited and in terms either too technical or too abstract for patients to make much sense of. Even more than Chinese-style doctors, Western-style doctors regarded patients as essentially ignorant. As others have shown (Ahern 1976; Gale 1976), if you ask a question in the Western-style doctor-patient interview, you most likely will be ignored or given an inadequate answer. Patients realize this and do not ask questions. Over a two-day period in observing 10 hours of doctor-patient interactions involving five Western-style doctors in private practice and fifty patients, I calculated a mean time of 40 seconds spent explaining to patients (in transactions that lasted a mean time of 3 minutes and 15 seconds), and one-fourth of these patients heard no explanations at all. What was explained was on the order of "You need several shots; that will make you better." Seventy-four percent of these patients when interviewed afterwards were unsatisified with the care they received because they were told so little. Of those almost all said they had definite questions to obtain specific information about their illnesses and treatments which they did not ask because they felt intimidated in the doctors' presence. That sense of intimidation is especially strong because of the traditional Chinese behavioral pattern of enforced politeness and subservience in the presence of "superior" individuals. Patients frequently bow to doctors, and in one instance I saw an old man get on his knees and kowtow to a doctor who was angry at him.

Practice in government and military hospitals is not much different from what I have described for private medical care. It holds less, but still to some extent, for practice in the local university hospital, where many excellent physicians are faced by a stupendous work load. Because, as has been noted, patients in Taiwan see the National Taiwan University Hospital as the court of last resort, large numbers of patients attend its clinics, even from distant areas. For example, two interns, two residents, and one senior psychiatrist see four to twelve new cases and usually more than fifty and on some days more than one hundred return cases each morning four days per week. These include "problem" cases referred for careful evaluation. In such a setting only the most severe and immediate problems can be effectively managed, and there is essentially no time to talk with the patient about personal, social, and less immediate or severe problems or to do more than a cursory psychiatric evaluation. This is a great handicap for modern psychiatric care, and it is not surprising that less severe cases will go instead for care to traditional practitioners. With hardly any psychotherapy available, the disenfranchised patient is the better educated and more modern and Western in orientation, because he is often unwilling to see a *tâng-ki* or *ch'ien* interpreter. I have seen cases of masked depression, for example, who were excellent candidates for short-term psychotherapy, but for whom none was available. Many of these were college graduates who refused to consider my suggestion that they go to a local temple or a particular *tâng-ki*, because they had rejected folk beliefs and no longer viewed these traditional sources of care as a serious option.

At the same time, in medical clinics as many as 50 percent of all cases may be suffering from primary psychological or social problems with secondary somatic symptomatology. There is little possibility that serious cases can get the psychiatric treatment they require in those clinics, because their culturally constituted clinical ethos systematically enforces the medical sick role and makes no provision for psychological treatment. This also works against the use of effective biological agents for mental illness, as in cases of masked depressions—a large segment of this patient group—who frequently would respond to anti-depressant therapy, but who go unidentified.

This clinical practice has an interesting effect on how patients evaluate Western-style medical care. I compared several groups of patients with respect to their evaluations of the care they had received: twenty-five patients in the clinics of private Western-style doctors; twenty-five patients in the general medical clinic at the local university hospital; twenty-five psychiatric outpatients at the same institution; and twenty-one patients seen by *tâng-ki*s, including twelve seen consecutively by one *tâng-ki*. All were interviewed at home with the same questionnaire and by the same interviewers. Patient satisfaction for all of the Western-style groups ran between 30 and 35 percent. Patient satisfaction for the shamans' group was 85 percent. This is a complex problem, because patient samples were small and not precisely matched. Most patients in the Western-style group complained of lack of sufficient time and explanations. Most patients in the shamans' group stressed the importance of meaningful explanations. I reported these findings at the local university hospital, where they were received with polite laughter as demonstrating the obvious: "Obviously if we had more time, we would explain more." This is not in fact the case: it is the expectations of clinicians and patients that lead to this situation. I observed Western-style doctors on many occasions who had much time and only one or two patients but still behaved *as if* there were no time and they were overwhelmed with patients. The patients did not demand different behavior from their doctors under these circumstances. Under the same circumstances, Chinese-style doctors do spend more time talking with patients.

These findings need to be balanced against other facts before conclusions are drawn about health care in Taiwan.[1] Notwithstanding these health care problems, the standard of care and the availability of care in Taiwan are much higher than in most Southeast Asian countries. Many of the problems described are relatively minor when compared with the fact that in Chinese

---

1. Before comparisons can be usefully drawn between health care in Taiwan and in the People's Republic of China, we need to have the results of field studies in the People's Republic comparable to those reported for Taiwan both here and elsewhere (Kleinman et al. 1976). Because we presently lack such research, it is simply not possible to draw conclusions about clinical practice in the People's Republic along the lines outlined in these chapters.

I have referred sparingly in this and other chapters to observations made during my visit to the People's Republic of China in June 1978 as a member of the "Rural Health Care Delegation" of the Committee on Scholarly Communication with the People's Republic of China, because these impressions, unlike the findings from my research in Taiwan, were necessarily hurried, superficial and unsystematic. Although I was struck by certain impressive similarities with Taiwan—such as the high prevalence of somatization in primary medical care, the use of "neurasthenia" to socially legitimate psychological and interpersonal problems, the practice of Chinese medicine as part of a theoretical framework dominated by Western medical concepts and terms, the extremely limited role of psychotherapy in outpatient psychiatric care and of management of the psychosocial problems of illness behavior in both Western-style and Chinese-style outpatient medical care, and obvious discrepancies between how patients construe and use local health care systems and how professional planners and practitioners believe they are used— I was unable to pursue these issues beyond their surface resemblances to what I had documented in Taiwan. The differences between health care in these two Chinese societies were at least equally impressive, though even harder to assess. For example, self-care in the family and social network is discouraged in favor of treatment by barefoot doctors or health aides. Al-

society before 1949 there was virtually no modern medical care outside of the large cities. Furthermore, the quality of care has improved as physicians have received better clinical training, despite the emigration of 1,500 doctors to the United States and other countries. Finally, some of the problems are not limited by any means to Taiwan but are found in other Asian and developing countries and in the United States. For example, the failure to spend sufficient time with patients and to provide adequate and meaningful explanations seems to be almost uni-

---

though there still appears to be recourse to self-care, it was reported much less frequently among 138 outpatients I interviewed with Professor David Mechanic in provincial, county, and commune hospital clinics and production brigade health stations in six north and south China provinces than in our Taiwan research (cf. Chapter 6 above). But I am certain that the presence of local health officials in the institutional setting of care must have constrained many patients from admitting to self-care practices because they knew these were officially discouraged. In support of this surmise, when Professor Mechanic and I, along with other members of our delegation, walked unaccompanied into several production teams for "sightseeing" and casually inquired about self-care practices as part of polite conversation, we elicited much higher utilization rates for these popular health care activities. Similarly, though sacred folk healing is branded as a "feudal superstition" and said to be virtually non-existent, I am not sure if this claim is anymore valid than the one made to me before I commenced my research by public health officials in Taipei that shamans could not be found in that city. This suspicion is supported by reports from refugees in Hong Kong, who aver that some sacred folk religion practices survive, albeit clandestinely. We simply do not know, then, to what extent this component of health care systems continues to function in the People's Republic of China, nor do I think the health authorities know. Have certain sacred folk care functions been taken over by recent innovations? For instance, do the ubiquitous "small groups" serve "psychotherapeutic" as well as political functions? Because we cannot conduct ethnomedical research in the People's Republic, we simply cannot answer these questions. More importantly, we now know that earlier visitors' reports of health care delivery there may well be romantic fictions that present a serious distortion of a much more complex and difficult to evaluate reality. How do we make sense of even such taken-for-granted issues as barefoot doctors and the integration of Chinese and Western medicine? At the very moment that the WHO is pointing to these developments as examples for health care delivery systems in the Third World generally, are we not beginning to hear the Chinese themselves speak of them with slight embarrassment and the intriguing proviso that these are transitional developments on the road to a more technologically sophisticated system of care? It is these sorts of things that have restrained my natural desire to make more comparisons between Taiwan and China.

versal in professional biomedical practice throughout the world. In research with Dr. Thomas Hackett at the Massachusetts General Hospital, I found this to be a large problem, about which physicians tended to be insensitive in spite of the concern of their patients. Our findings suggest that this problem had a detrimental effect on the care these patients received.[2] The question is inescapable, then: are modern physicians socialized in clinical practices that have systematically negative effects on the human aspects of care?

In Taiwan, strange as it may seem, it is difficult to talk to psychiatrists and physicians about the impact of Chinese cultural factors on illness and care. Not that they disbelieve this influence but it is not as interesting to them as the biological perspective they have acquired in the course of medical training. Again and again, I pointed out to psychiatry residents and interns how Chinese culture influenced the behavior of their patients in obvious and clinically important ways. And again and again, I was disheartened to learn that more "real" to them than this direct clinical experience was what they read about psychiatric problems from American textbooks. For example, when cases of schizophrenia in which possession states occurred were presented at the Psychiatric Case Conference, residents were much more interested in learning about the World Health Organization concept of what schizophrenia was than in trying to figure out why schizophrenia in Taiwan, though capable of being diagnosed by Western standards, still differed in presentation from schizophrenia in the West.

The psychiatry and internal medicine presently practiced in Taipei are based almost entirely on models developed in the West, as if the patients and the cultures were the same. Why has so little attention been given to masked depressions and somatization in Taiwan when clearly they are such tremendous problems? Because they are not major interests in the psychiatric frameworks developed in the West.[3] The same is true of

2. Cases illustrating such problems are presented in Kleinman (1975a).

3. The fact that patients with somatization and masked depression have not been a major concern of modern psychiatry does not mean such patients are not to be found in the West. Indeed, they are found in large numbers in the United States and elsewhere, especially among ethnic minorities and the lower social classes. This disinterest is chiefly due to psychiatry's pre-

the small amount of attention devoted to hysterical psychoses and culture-bound disorders. It has been estimated that by the year 1980 almost one out of four people in the world will be Chinese, half of the world's population will be Asian, and more than three-fourths will be non-Western. Yet, it is likely that psychiatry in those populations will be based then, as it is now, on concepts developed almost entirely in the West in research and treatment with Western populations. This is a product of the bias built into the clinical reality created by modern scientific medicine (in Taiwan and the United States), which legitimates for its practitioners a professional perspective and behavioral style that routinely ignores cultural differences.

A few transcripts of Western-style doctor-patient communicative interactions in Taiwan should further illumine the nature of clinical reality in Western-style medical practice.

> Patient [a 25-year-old woman appearing pale and feverish]: "I have pain when I urinate, and the urine is discolored."
> Western-style doctor (after examining the patient carefully for 10 minutes): "I think you need injections. Have you seen anyone else about this problem?"
> Patient: "Yesterday I went to a gynecologist. He told me I have a urinary tract infection. He gave me medicine and told me to come back. But the pain didn't go away, so I decided to go to someone else."
> Western-style doctor: "All right, here are two shots: one for pain and one for the infection. You can either go back to the other doctor or come back here for another shot."

Although the amount of time spent with the patient was well above the average time Western-style doctors spend with patients, this case illustrates the potentially dangerous effects Western-style medical practice may have. No attempt was made to take a urine culture to document the presumed infection. This occurred not because the doctor negligently failed to think of it, but rather because his past experience indicated that

occupation in the past with psychologically minded patients (educated, middle-class members of the mainstream Western culture), who best fit the psychoanalytic program's commitment to "insight" therapies. Recently rekindled psychiatric interest in the psychiatric problems of patients in general medical settings promises to correct this deficiency and is itself an example of a shift in the social construction of clinical reality in modern psychiatry (cf. Eisenberg 1976).

it was very unlikely the patient would return, and, therefore, the information from the culture would be useless. The patient, following popular culture beliefs about Western medicine, expected Western drugs to work immediately or not at all, as demonstrated by her response to the gynecologist's treatment. The same orientation would determine her response to this doctor, as he well knew. Therefore, he gave her the choice of returning to whichever doctor she chose. But he did not give her a diagnosis or tell her what medicines he was injecting her with. The likelihood is that both doctors administered different antibiotics. The danger lies in administering single doses of antibiotics, since this can make the infection resistant to antibiotics and potentially can result in failure to control the infection, while it exposes the patient to allergic reactions and side-effects from several drugs. Who should be blamed: patient or doctor? From our perspective, neither are responsible. The potentially dangerous treatment is the direct result of the interplay between popular and professional Western-style views of clinical reality, as was detailed at the beginning of this section.

> Patient [a middle-aged, lower-class man]: "I have a bad taste in my mouth, swelling of my gums, congestion in my nose. Perhaps I have *huo-ch'i ta?*"
> Western-style doctor (a young ENT specialist): "You don't have fever, so you don't have an upper respiratory tract infection. I will give you a shot for it. It will make you better."
> Patient: "Good."

This interchange, typical of the one or two sentence exchanges that precede the ever-present "shot" in Western-style practice, is interesting in several respects. The patient interprets his complaints as *huo-ch'i ta*, and, indeed, they are characteristic of that category as it is popularly used in Taiwan. But most often in Western-style practice, patients will not use this term, since they are aware it is not part of Western medical vocabulary. The doctor responds by translating *huo-ch'i ta* into what he wrongly believes is its Western medical equivalent, fever. Here is a clear example of clinical miscommunication based on distinct medical idioms. Though the patient didn't agree with the doctor's reasoning that because there was no fever, there was no *huo-ch'i ta*, he later told me that he felt too intimidated to contradict the doctor and also thought perhaps the doctor knew something he didn't. The mistake he made was to use a term that was appropriate for the clinical reality of folk or Chinese-style practice but not for Western-style medical care. Most patients do not seem to make this mistake. They often provide what they believe is a Western medical equivalent of *huo-ch'i ta*. The doctor, on the other hand, not only failed to understand what the patient meant by this term, which his older colleagues almost certainly would not have done, but the little he explained to the patient was in a technical idiom—"upper respiratory tract infection"—that the patient could not understand. (In fact, the patient's first question to us was what this term meant and whether it was dangerous or not). Again we see a potentially serious communication problem—which may affect whether the patient returns and follows the treatment regimen—due to the physician's failure to translate the biomedical concept into an idiom the patient could comprehend. This is a common source of clinical miscommunication easily understood in terms of our model of tacit conflicts between doctor and patient EMs.

There are, of course, exceptions to the generally poor quality of clinical communication and minimal time spent with patients that characterize most Western-style doctor-patient encounters. Of the twenty-five Western-style doctors I systematically studied and the more than fifty others I casually observed in practice throughout Taiwan, only two physicians demonstrated real interest in and skills at clinical communication. Both were unabashedly intrigued by psychosomatic relationships. Both lamented the pressure of practice, which prevented them from spending additional time with each patient. Both believed that supportive psychotherapy could be given in the context of primary medical care and attempted to do so with small number of patients suffering from somatically masked psychological problems and psychophysiological disorders. I present a transcript of a clinical interview one of them took part in. This is wholly unlike most Western-style doctor-patient encounters, but is a good illustration of what is feasible even in the inhospitable circumstances of Western-style clinical reality. The reader doubtless will detect things that could be improved in this doctor's clinical communication, but it should be remembered that it is very much better than 95 percent of the transcripts of Western-style transactions in Taiwan we possess. Not surprisingly, this doctor's patients were high compliers and scored equally high on our patient satisfaction scale.

Patient [middle-aged, chronically ill woman in a return visit]: "The doctors at the hospital told me I needed an operation for my problem, but they didn't say why, and I don't want one."

Western-style doctor: "How is your back now?"

Patient: "Getting worse."

Western-style doctor: "And your walking?"

Patient: "Bad. I can hardly walk at all."

Western-style doctor: "You need a corset for support. But even that will not cure you. The operation would help you a great deal. It is not dangerous. The doctors at the hospital are experts. They want you to have it so that they can straighten your back, which will enable you to walk better. I spoke with them. And I fully agree with them. Did they scare you?"

Patient: "Yes. They said it could be dangerous. Why should I have it if it is dangerous?"

Western-style doctor: "Just as I thought. They do that sometimes. They didn't mean to scare you. Any major surgical procedure is potentially dangerous, but there is no special danger in your case. The doctors at the hospital want to make sure you know there is a slight risk. They also want you to know that not every operation is successful. But look at yourself. You can hardly walk. You are in pain. The best medication we can give has been of no help. Don't you think it is worth trying?"

Patient: "Perhaps you are right."

Western-style doctor: "Anyway you are too weak to have the surgery for several months. We need to build up your strength. You can decide slowly. Don't worry, we would not schedule the surgery for next month."

Patient (who laughed because the following month is when "hungry ghosts" are believed to leave the underworld and travel to this world, where they are blamed for causing serious problems, thus making the month inauspicious for any important venture): "I am worried because my eldest son is in America. Perhaps I will not live long enough to see him again. My husband does not have insurance or very much money for my treatment. My other sons are in school. My eldest daughter has had to start work cooking for other families. . . ."

Western-style doctor: "We have talked about these problems before. They are real, but you should not worry so much about them. I told you before what the surgery would cost, and you agreed you could afford it. What are you most worried about?"

Patient: "I don't know why I worry so much."

Western-style doctor: "What is bothering you now? You look upset."

Patient: "My daughter is over 25 and still not married yet. She has no boyfriend and no prospect of marrying."

Western-style doctor: "She is old enough to find a boyfriend herself. Why don't you suggest this to her. That is all you need do. We should have an X-ray of your back again to see if you need a cast. That would be better support than a corset. But it would be more troublesome than surgery. Surgery would be best. If you agree to have it, I could arrange for you to have it at the National Taiwan University Hospital with a famous professor who specializes in such operations. I will speak to your husband about the cost. Don't worry so much. If you have problems, you can discuss them with me and with your husband and friends. Don't hesitate to talk about them. If you keep things locked up inside, it will affect your disease and make the treatment take longer. After you take the X-ray (tomorrow or the next day) come back to see me the following day. The X-ray will be of your back and side, it will not take long."

By the standards of Western-style medical transactions in Taiwan, this is a remarkable interview. I don't think I need to dissect it line by line. The doctor spends about 15 minutes talking with the patient. He reassures her about the surgery, carefully explaining why it is essential. He points to her major complaints as the reason why the surgery is necessary. He removes some of the reason for her fear. He sets out a course of action, but leaves it to the patient to decide. He deals with economic and family concerns. He listens to the patient, and encourages her to talk about problems on her mind that are, strictly speaking, not medical, but that he relates to her disorder in a psychosomatic framework. He comments on her concern about her daughter and gives her advice and support, albeit perfunctory. The doctor, in passing, shows his sensitivity to popular fears about "hungry ghosts" and removes any fear the patient might have that her surgery might be performed on such an inauspicious occasion. He subtly elicits his patient's

EM and negotiates with it. Neither he nor the patient mention the name of her disorder. This is no accident. She is suffering from tuberculosis of the spine, and tuberculosis is a highly stigmatized disease label in Taiwan. The doctor was sensitive to this. He was also aware of the patient's need for privacy and, unlike the vast majority of clinical encounters in Taiwan, arranged to speak with her in a room with a closed door, so that his other patients were not present to inhibit their talk. Lest the reader wonder if this interview was purposely arranged to impress me, I should add that this was one of ten interviews recorded for this practitioner, all of which demonstrated his interest and skill in clinical communications, though admittedly this was one of the more impressive ones. All, by the way, were recorded in three very busy half-day sessions in his private clinic. Furthermore, interviews with patients disclosed that this doctor frequently engages in exchanges such as the one described. Indeed, he is well-known in his district of Taipei for his "compassion," willingness to talk, and skill in explaining. Ironically, his Western-style colleagues, in a telling comment, refer to him, in an attempt to be disparaging, as "the folk doctor."

Because the last example is so atypical, I shall end our description of Western-style doctor-patient transactions with other cases that are more characteristic of Western-style clinical communication in Taiwan.

> Patient [a 20-year-old, male college student suffering from a severe case of nephrotic syndrome]: "How am I doing?"
> Western-style doctor: "All right. Your blood and urine tests are the same as last time." (He then goes on to ask the patient about specific symptoms.)
> Patient: "When will I be able to return to school?"
> Western-style doctor: "We shall see. I'm sorry I have to go now. I can't answer any more questions. Why don't you speak to the nurse."

This patient was deeply dissatisfied by this interview. Because the doctor was a well-known specialist who had been following his case over several months, he felt unable to change doctors.

Furthermore, he knew from experience most Western-style doctors would behave in a similar way. The patient was terrified by his disorder. He had read that one could die from it. He had been trying for several weeks to learn from his doctor how serious his disease was and what the prognosis was. He could not make plans. And his family members were unable to get more information out of the doctor than he had. In six sessions, the doctor had merely reviewed his laboratory tests and prescribed medicines or diet. On no occasion had he been willing to tell the patient the prognosis. Nor had he responded to the patient's very evident fear. When I finally asked this doctor why he did not answer the patient's questions, he told me: "The patient's questions don't matter. He is ignorant of medical concepts. All he has to do is listen to me and follow my advice. Nothing is gained from talking with him, except getting him to take the medicine properly and follow the right diet. It is much more important to study the laboratory findings. They show what is *really* (my emphasis) going on inside his kidneys." There is no need to comment on these remarks other than to highlight them as a remarkably frank expression of the "veterinary" tendency of the biomedical approach, an approach that this doctor could so callously employ only because it is sanctioned professional medical behavior.

> Patient [42-year-old lower-class woman]: "My stomach hurts."
> Western-style doctor: "Is it dyspepsia?"
> Patient: "I don't know. Could you prescribe a cheap medicine and keep the cost of the treatment down?"
> Western-style doctor: "The medicine is expensive. There is no cheap drug. You must change your diet. Eat more meat. Do less work. Take a shot and a drug by mouth."
> Patient: "Okay."

The patient received an injection and a bottle of pills. After leaving the doctor's office she told us she was disappointed and would not return to see him again. She was angry that the treatment was so expensive. She asked us if we knew the name of her sickness or what it was due to, and she expressed disappointment that the doctor had not told her about these things. "But how could I ask such a big man these questions?

301

He would laugh at me," she added. She said she had expected to receive an examination or tests and could not understand why she had not received them. Bitterly, she complained that if she were not poor, the doctor would have spent more time with her, been more helpful, and carried out the necessary tests. Many of the patient's complaints were justified. This doctor's care was poor in a number of respects: the medical work-up was minimal; he failed to clearly define her disease problem; and he also did not help her with her illness concerns—the cost of the medication and her anxiety over the nature and cause of the disorder. He gave her no prognosis or support. He used a technical term that she did not understand. He did not specify the exact kind of diet. His suggestion about meat neither made medical sense nor was feasible given the patient's limited financial resources. He did not tell her what kind of medicine she was receiving, why he was prescribing it, and whether she needed to return or not. He gave her no opportunity to ask questions. Moreover, from beginning to end of the interview, he remained distant from the patient, making the distinction in their social status painfully apparent. Although the patient was critical of the doctor to us and said she would tell friends and neighbors not to consult him, she admitted that many Western-style doctors were like this: "What can one do? None of them tell you very much. They show little regard for you. You are lucky if they spend two minutes with you. They don't care about the expense."

Complaints such as these are generic for the practice of Western medicine in Taiwan, especially in private clinics and with lower-class patients. The complaints are of problems systematically produced, to a lesser or greater degree, by its clinical reality. That version of clinical reality, which is in fundamental, though usually tacit, conflict with popular views, is characterized by concern for disease rather than illness, technical interventions rather than communication, financial reward more than effective patient care, and by the specific problems depicted in these transcripts. As we previously indicated, these professional "interests" and many of the problems they give rise to in Taiwan are found in many other societies, including our own. They account for both the successes *and* the failures of biomedicine's clinical reality.

Categorization of Western-Style Practitioner—Patient Transactions:
A Summary

Western-style doctor-patient relationships can be summarized in the following terms.

1. Institutional Setting. Biomedical subsector of the professional sector of Taiwan's health care systems.

2. Characteristics of the Interpersonal Interaction
   a. The *number* of participants was more than two in half of the transactions I observed, since the patient was frequently accompanied by family members or friends who stayed with the patient while he was examined and who entered into discussion with the doctor, often to a greater degree than the patient. But dyadic relationships are more frequent in Western medical practice than in Chinese medical care or in shamanistic healing, and Western-style doctors talk about the therapeutic dyad as if it were the norm.
   b. The great majority of transactions I observed involved *episodic* patient contact. Less than one-fifth consisted of continuous relationships with the same Western-style doctor.

   Mean time for consultation: 3 minutes 15 seconds (range: 45 seconds to 18 minutes 35 seconds)
   Mean time for clinical communication: 1 minute 18 seconds (range: 23 seconds to 4 minutes 55 seconds)
   Mean time spent in explaining: 40 seconds (range: 0 to 3 minutes 32 seconds)

   c. These relationships are *formal,* unless the patient and practitioner belong to the same social network. Western-style doctor-patient relationships are *not holistic* but instead are narrowly focused on a mechanistic view of bodily dysfunction that divorces sickness from everyday experience and from other human problems.
   d. These relationships contain strongly *ambivalent* feelings. Patients obviously appreciate the powers of Western therapies but deplore the "inhuman" quality of care and criticize doctors for not empathizing with them. Western-style doctors are thought to be principally interested in

financial gain, and it is commonly remarked by patients that they are the wealthiest people in Taiwanese society. Western-style doctors also hold ambivalent feelings about their patients, who are valued as sources of income and "interesting" problems but feared for their propensity to initiate medical-legal suits.

3. Idiom of Communication

a. Most Western-style doctors communicate in a technical, professional, Western idiom that is not readily accessible to most patients. This idiom is mechanistic and somatic; it does *not* use psychological, sociological, or spiritual terms. The somatic idiom is clearly congruent with Chinese cultural norms, but the technical, mechanistic idiom is not.

b. In general *EMs* are *not shared*. They tend to be neither openly expressed nor negotiated. Tacit conflicts between EMs are frequent and have negative therapeutic consequences. The only time biomedical EMs are translated into popular explanations is on those rare occasions when patients either challenge the doctor's EM or balk openly at the prescribed treatment. To cope with these infrequent outbursts and also at times to enforce compliance, I have observed doctors employ moralistic and even religious arguments.

4. Clinical Reality

a. Western-style clinical reality is *secular*. Although it is suffused with Western values, it also draws upon traditional Chinese norms. Even more than Chinese-style medical relationships, Western-style doctor-patient interactions do not depend on their clinical reality for their efficacy, but, as several of our examples illustrate, the clinical reality they construct often yields negative therapeutic consequences.

b. Western-style medical practice is oriented to *disease problems* as defined by the doctor. Illness problems are infrequently considered, and little attention is given to provide psychosocial interventions to manage such problems.

c. Therapeutics are almost entirely *instrumental;* symbolic therapies are rarely used.

d. *Therapeutic expectations* are well illustrated by the case vignettes. Discrepancies concerning etiquette, treatment style, and therapeutic objectives occur more frequently in Western medical practice than in indigenous therapeutic transactions.

e. Western-style doctors often view themselves as *most responsible* for their patients' care and criticize families for playing too large a role in the care of patients. In cases of serious sickness, they deal with the family rather than the patient. But in other instances, their transactions center to a greater extent on the sick individual than do the other therapeutic relationships I have described.

5. Therapeutic Stages and Mechanisms

a. Western-style doctor-patient relationships commonly do not move through the three therapeutic stages found in indigenous healing rituals.

b. Physiological, psychophysiological, and psychological change can be demonstrated to occur routinely. But Western-style doctors pay much more attention to the first than to the other two. While both social and cultural change also may occur, they are much less frequent than in indigenous practice and rarely attract the interest of Western-style doctors.

c. For the above reasons, patient and practitioner evaluations of outcome are often divergent. The latter attend to disease problems but not illness problems, while the former attend to illness problems more than disease problems. As I have repeatedly noted, patient adherence to the prescribed medical regimen is much less than in the other therapeutic relationships, while patient and family dissatisfaction with care tends to be greater. Termination does not often provoke open conflict, since most patients do not return after two or three treatment sessions. But uncertainty about the appropriate time to terminate is common among patients, and doctors cannot regularly plan on patients remaining in treatment for an optimum course of care. The imprecise termination point of psychotherapy and its lengthy course become particularly serious treatment issues for even Westernized Chinese patients.

PRACTITIONER-PATIENT INTERACTIONS 5:
FAMILY-PATIENT TRANSACTIONS

It may appear strange to some to consider the family as a "practitioner" and to add family-patient interactions to our list of practitioner-patient interactions. Taking into account, however, that 73 percent of all sickness episodes recorded in the Taipei survey described in Chapter 6 were treated solely in the context of the family, there is nothing at all strange about looking upon the family as practitioner. Indeed, in most societies it would appear to be by far the most active form of clinical practice. We know unfortunately little about family-patient interactions, but what we do know suggests that they differ from other kinds of health care relationships in several important ways. Based on our family interviews and follow-up of a small number of sickness episodes treated in the context of the family, I shall venture a tentative outline of salient features of family-patient transactions. Although the following remarks are restricted to therapeutic interactions in the context of the family, I believe they apply to lay health care transactions in general.

1. Institutional Setting. A distinctive family subsector of the popular (lay) health care sector of Taiwan's health care systems.

2. Characteristics of the Interpersonal Interaction.
    a. These therapeutic relationships are usually *not dyadic* but instead involve interactions between the patient and his family members acting as a small group—what John Janzen (1977) calls the lay (or kinship) "therapy management group." The family "therapy management group" (perhaps a more accurate term would be the family "health management group") provides the setting within which most health and health care-related decisions and actions take place. The group's decisions determine whether the patient will enter professional or folk care, whether he will stay in a particular kind of extra-familial care or switch to

306

an alternative therapeutic relationship, and how adherence, termination, and evaluations of outcome will be handled.

b. Family-patient transactions are *continuous* rather than episodic relationships, occurring over a longer period of time than other health care transactions, and representing only one of a large number of social functions in ongoing family relationships. Communication and explaining also occupy a greatly expanded time frame. Care encompasses the entire course of sickness and is integrated into the daily routine of family affairs.

c. These relationships are *informal* with respect to etiquette. They are embedded in undifferentiated primary social roles and, hence, are characterized by intimate affective ties, a restricted communicative code (cf. Bernstein 1971), and intense transference and countertransference reactions (cf. Balint 1957). This contrasts sharply with folk and professional therapeutic relationships, where there are highly differentiated tertiary social roles, either an elaborated or specialized communicative code is used, and affective ties and transference/countertransference are less intense. Informality does not necessarily mean that there is less tension in family health care transactions. Indeed, sickness frequently heightens already existing family tensions or creates new ones. Negative social values associated with certain types of sickness (e.g., epilepsy, tuberculosis, venereal disease, mental illness) may make family-patient interactions maladaptive, as in the pathetic case of the young woman in a mental hospital who was expelled from her family, as described in Chapter 6. But in general, family care appears to be less stressful for patients than are the more formal and foreign environments of folk and professional practice.

Sickness is dealt with as one of a range of human "troubles," inseparable (and often not separately categorized) from everyday life events and experiences.

d. Typically, family-patient transactions are *not characterized* by the same kind of *ambivalent attitudes* found in shaman-client and Western-style doctor-patient relationships. But inasmuch as all primary relationships involve both strongly positive and strongly negative affective responses, ambivalence as defined psychoanalytically is doubtless found in all patient-family transactions.

3. Idiom of Communication

   a. Illness and care are articulated in the *idiom* of the popular culture. That idiom draws on somatic, sociologic, cosmologic, moralistic, and naturalistic terminology. It does not normally present psychological or mechanistic accounts of causality and cure, but it does utilize somatopsychic and, less frequently, psychosomatic concepts. These communicative transactions are an integral part of the ongoing conversation between family members that results from and sustains the family's social reality.

   b. *EMs* tend to be *shared* and *openly discussed*. It is my impression there are less frequent and less marked communicative conflicts than occur in other practitioner-patient relationships, but conflicts still may occur and can be accentuated by existing family tensions. Generational differences in modern Western versus traditional Chinese orientation—in education, religious affiliation, role expectations, and in past experience with the health care system—suggest that family members in Taiwan's increasingly pluralistic society draw on different systems of health beliefs, and that conflicts between their EMs may well increase in the future.

4. Clinical Reality

   a. Among the rural population and lower class and lower middle-class urban dwellers, clinical reality often combines *secular and sacred* components. But for the educated middle class, it is increasingly secular. The family's orientation to health care is pragmatic. As noted in Chapter 6, there are many determinants of family health care seeking choices and behaviors, but a principal one appears to be the family's prior experience with the health care system.

   b. Although family-patient transactions are interested in both symptom change and the meaning context of sickness, they tend to be much more concerned with the management of *illness problems* than with disease problems.

Included in the former category are: financial and work-related problems, personal and family perceptions of stress and coping responses to it, moral questions, and many other related problems in day-to-day living. Care is *holistic* inasmuch as it encompasses health, health maintenance, and the entire illness trajectory from initial labeling of symptoms and choice of treatment alternatives to evaluation of therapeutic outcomes.

c. Treatment regularly includes both *symbolic and somatic* therapies.

d. *Therapeutic expectations* are characterized by the preceding descriptions of characteristics of the interpersonal transaction, idiom of communication, and clinical reality.

e. The family commonly interacts with other practitioners, and in many cases *family-practitioner interactions* are as important as and occasionally more important than patient-practitioner interactions. Indeed, this relationship should be analyzed as a distinctive therapeutic transaction. The *family* is regarded as *most responsible* for the patient's care, but individual autonomy of family members in health decisions varies with their age and status in the family and with the family's degree of modernity. Responsibility for the entire course of sickness and care is a major factor distinguishing family-patient transactions from other health care relationships, most of which are fragmentary and oriented to a single aspect of care.

5. Therapeutic Stages and Mechanisms

a. Family-patient relationships cannot be generally described in terms of a *tripartite therapeutic organization*, but particular relationships involving the treatment of particular sicknesses may exhibit this structural characteristic.

b. Psychological, physiological, social, and cultural change all can be demonstrated to occur, and commonly they are interrelated and occur together.

c. Too little is presently known about adherence, terminations, and evaluations of outcome in family-patient transactions to support generalizations. But it is my impression that conflicts regarding these questions are less frequent than in other therapeutic relationships, though they do occur.

These characteristics obviously are strongly affected by family patterns in different societies and among different ethnic groups in the same society, as the Chinese and American comparisons I have drawn demonstrate. Taken together, they suggest why patient-family transactions are the most difficult health care transactions to describe accurately. If we think of EMs, the difficulty becomes obvious. When are we to record such transactions? There is no precise time when they occur, nor do they end with the finality of a healing ritual or a modern clinical consultation. EM exchanges are going on all the time. What is decided at one time, may be reversed somewhat later until a course of action emerges. This is why I am unable to present transcripts of recordings of patient-family interactions. How are such ethnographic descriptions to be conducted? Until that question is resolved our knowledge of this crucial relationship will remain incomplete and derivative, and systematic comparisons will be infeasible.

We must develop methods for systematically comparing and evaluating the culturally constructed realities of clinical care that I have impressionistically sketched in this chapter and the preceding one. Such a comparative study calls for integrating anthropological and clinical methods in an interdisciplinary field project. It should become a central objective both for clinically oriented medical anthropologists and for clinicians interested in forging an anthropological medicine and psychiatry. That such a venture is required, regardless of the evident limitations of these chapters, is certain, even if the forms it will take remain uncertain.

NOTE: Since few of the transactions I observed followed the orthodox format of classical Chinese medicine, I do not describe here what Sinologists regard to be the "ideal" clinical transaction. Nor do I review the classical concepts and style of practice of Chinese medicine, because it goes beyond the scope and purpose of this book. Instead I present a few salient characteristics of how most Chinese-style doctor-patient relationships are actually conducted at present using the clinical categories described above to compare this relationship with others so as to inform us *not* about Chinese medicine per se but about therapeutic relationships generally. Agren (1976), Porkert (1974), and Sivin (1975) present historical, "internalist" accounts of ideal-type Chinese medical practice that contrast with our "externalist," comparative perspective. To sharpen the contrast between Chinese and Western modes of medical praxis and make readers consider both the practical and ethical implications, I intentionally present my observations as a Western-style clinician confronting a different therapeutic system.

9

The Healing Process

The study of indigenous healing may be important to the general anthropologist for the light it throws on a particular culture. It may be important to the medical anthropologist in understanding a given society's system of health care. But the cross-cultural investigation of indigenous healing holds further significance for the medical anthropologist. Here the interest of the medical anthropologist is virtually the same as the chief concern of clinicians who pursue cross-cultural research. They seek to elucidate universal and culturally particular features of the healing process, and they wish to compare indigenous healing with modern medical and psychiatric care.

The chief research questions are straightforward and have been known for some time: Is indigenous healing effective? If so, how? What role do cultural factors play in bringing about that efficacy? How does the efficacy of indigenous healing compare with that of modern clinical care? What does that comparison tell us about the nature of the healing process? And can we learn anything that might be practically applied either to the solution of the extraordinary problems besetting contemporary health care or directly to the treatment of sickness in different societies?

Yet, while the questions are clear, the answers are not. What we now have are impressions, anecdotes, unsystematic findings, and strong opinions. The material I present below, lim-

This chapter is a revised and expanded version of an earlier paper, A. Kleinman and L.H. Sung: Why Indigenous Practitioners Successfully Heal? Follow-up Studies of Indigenous Healing in Taiwan, presented at the Medical Anthropology Workshop on The Healing Process, Michigan State University, April, 1976, to be published with the workshop's proceedings in Social Science and Medicine.

ited as it is, nonetheless represents the only attempt I am aware of to follow systematically patients treated by indigenous healers in order to determine, first, if a particular form of indigenous healing is effective, and, then, how it might work. In attempting to answer these and the other questions listed above, I have tried to avoid using ready-made explanations, such as the time-worn and essentially unproven psychoanalytic theories that (to my mind) have introduced so much obscurantism into this subject. Instead, I present the complex issue of how we evaluate therapeutic efficacy as *the* central problem in the cross-cultural study of healing. The explanations I propose for understanding how indigenous healing (as described in this chapter) works are anchored in the theoretical framework already discussed.

At the outset I draw attention to the inadequacy of our present understanding of the healing process. This is, in part, a function of the early stage we are at in medical anthropological research and theory. But it also results from an enormous distortion in clinical research and theory. For researchers in clinical medicine, healing is an embarrassing word. It exposes the archaic roots of medicine and psychiatry, roots usually buried under the biomedical science facade of modern health care. It suggests how little we really know about the most central function of clinical care. It resonates too well with the criticisms leveled by patients and consumers generally at modern health care. It raises questions that deal with human values, and meanings not easily reduced to technical problems that can be answered with simple biological explanations. And it strips away the illusion that biomedical research is the only scientific approach to health care problems. Instead, the question of healing makes it apparent that much of clinical science can only be approached from the perspective of social science.

SETTING

The *tâng-ki* whose patients I report on in this chapter practiced in Taipei, not far from the campus of the National Taiwan University. He was a 47-year-old Taiwanese family head who worked as a bank teller during the day and had been practicing as a *tâng-ki* seven nights each week for several decades. He was somewhat atypical for several reasons, some already mentioned when I described members of his cult in Chapters 5 and 7, but his therapeutic results were similar to those of other *tâng-ki*s I studied. He was atypical because he had a large cult, with perhaps as many as fifty regular members and at least another fifty occasional members. Unlike most *tâng-ki*s' shrines, many of the members of his shrine actively tranced, and several of them functioned as healers in their own right. The *tâng-ki* engaged in less ritual activity than most other *tâng-ki*s I observed, and he also had less verbal interaction with his clients while he was entranced then did other *tâng-ki*s, but he was the most charismatic of all the healers I studied in Taiwan. On most nights he spent less than five minutes with each case, and on busy nights he spent about two minutes with each case, which was less time than other *tâng-ki*s spent with their clients. The *tâng-ki* had elaborated his own philosophical system and the cult had its own ideology. Like other *tâng-ki*s with cults, he actively recruited new cult members from his patients, telling them that the most effective therapy was for them to be possessed (demonstrated by trance and jumping or dancing) and that preventing recurrences of their problems required regular attendance at his shrine, which assured protection from the shrine's many gods. Again like other *tâng-ki*s I have described, much of the healing in his shrine went on outside the *tâng-ki*'s interaction with patients and involved the therapeutic milieu of the shrine. I have already described the relatively large number of middle-aged women with hysteria (following the diagnostic criteria in Woodruff et al. 1974: 58–74) who received treatment in the shrine with documented benefit.

The shrine itself was called the "Saintly Emperor's Palace." The chief god was San-tien-hsia, but there was some ambiguity as to who this god really was. The term is sometimes used in Taiwan to refer to Lo-chia-kong (Mandarin, Li-na-tsa), a popular god in Taiwan's folk religion and one commonly associated with *tâng-ki*s and with healing. But members of the shrine claimed the name referred to the third son of the Jade Emperor (Yü-huang-ta-ti; Yü-huang-tai-tzu), San-tai-tzu, whom they called the third tien-hsia. They differentiated this chief god from Lo-chia-kong, who also was worshipped in the shrine. This uncertainty over the person of the chief god was associated with similar uncertainty about the meaning of special terms used in the shrine's healing rituals and new concepts elaborated by the *tâng-ki* in the shrine's unique ideology. The *tâng-ki* recognized this ambiguity and seemed quite willing to tolerate it. On several occasions, he presented his belief system with obvious contradictions of prior statements he had made. On no occasion that we witnessed were such contradictions openly discussed. The *tâng-ki*, his assistants, and the cult members seemed not to be concerned by uncertainties and even errors concerning the cosmology and its ritual applications. The *tâng-ki*'s explanations, as emended by his assistants, were taken as authoritative, but, in general, the practical efficacy of the shrine's gods and social interaction between cult members were treated with much more concern than were niceties of theory and ritual symbolism.

The shrine's altar was filled with small statuettes (josses) representing dozens of gods, in addition to the shrine's chief god, from the pantheon of Taiwanese folk religion. The *tâng-ki* could be possessed by any of the gods, whereas each cult member usually had only one "master" (the god who possessed him/ her) and at most several. When possessed, cult members were said to demonstrate some of the well-known characteristics of the gods possessing them, e.g., anger, compassion, healing skills, gifts of tongues, etc. The gods' personality traits were believed to carry over into and influence cult members' behavior when they were no longer entranced and even when they were not in the shrine. The *tâng-ki* was called the "master" of the shrine, and cult members referred to themselves in Confucian terms as his "sons." The positive virtues of the shrine's cult were repeatedly contrasted with the outside world, the "sea of bitterness" *(k'u-hai)*, which was said to be filled with personal and family problems, inharmonious, threatening, and constantly producing sickness and other misfortunes. The shrine's syncretic and idiosyncratic cosmology held that there were three levels of gods, with the shrine's gods at the highest level. The cult member moved upward in his affiliation with gods until his "master" was one of the gods on this highest plane.

Healing sessions began at night, seven days a week. They lasted from just after dinner until the early hours of the morning. The shrine had one large room which could hold about thirty people comfortably and a large altar table and altar. It opened to the street along one entire side, and cult members and clients commonly spilled over onto the street. Each night there were ten to thirty new patients and at least twenty to thirty cult members, and frequently more. The shrine's activities could be divided into two parts: the hour or so when the *tâng-ki*, entranced, formally consulted with new clients and performed ritual treatments, and the rest of the time, during which cult members and clients informally socialized but also prayed and tranced.

When cult members were actively trancing, it was a wild and colorful scene, a drama charged with passionate and sometimes frenzied activity. Informants described it to me as one of the most exciting experiences they had ever witnessed or participated in. This must have been especially true for lower-class mothers and grandmothers, ordinarily trapped in the physical confines and daily routines of their homes. Cult members did not merely trance: they danced, jumped around, sang, exhibited glossolalia, gave voice to strong emotions, and sometimes engaged in activities with strong sexual overtones. For example, men and women touched and massaged each other; they jumped around together; women rubbed the inside of their thighs and men exhibited rapid thrusting movements of the pelvis; at times the ecstatic frenzy of the trances resembled orgasmic behavior. All of this was very unusual public behavior in Taiwan, unsanctioned in any other place. In their trance and normal interictal states, cult members, as we have noted, were expected to display behavioral characteristic of the gods who possessed them. Some were "saintly" Buddhas; others, irrepressibly impish "Monkeys"; still others, sagelike or warlike. It was not unusual to see individuals, while entranced, express both in words and non-verbal behavior sadness, anger, fear, and other deeply felt emotions. Cult members told me they felt relieved and happy after trancing. Many appeared exhausted following several hours of repeated trance. At the beginning of each healing session, and off and on throughout the night, there was much socializing between cult members and also with members of their families who often accompanied them.

New clients registered with one of the *tâng-ki*'s assistants when they first entered the shrine. They gave name, address, problem, and the eight characters (*pa tzu*) associated with their birthdate. The last was used to calculate their fate. Each new client burned incense and prayed, asking one of the gods (often the shrine's chief god) about his problem. The client threw divination blocks to learn if the god would answer his question. After the divination blocks indicated the god's consent, the client waited for the *tâng-ki* to enter his trance and for the assistant to call him for the formal consultation. The *tâng-ki* might ask a question or two but usually did not. Most frequently a client volunteered some information about the problem that brought him to the shrine. The god speaking through the *tâng-ki* informed the client what was causing his problem. He then prescribed various therapies: he gave the client ashes to drink or charms to eat or wear, and sometimes he prescribed herbs or Chinese medicines or dietary therapy. At the end he pronounced the client cured or ordered him to return regularly to the shrine and become possessed (indicating that a god who wished to possess him was causing his problems). His explanations of the nature and etiology of the disorder as well as his therapeutic advice, similar to examples cited in Chapter 7, frequently mixed sacred folk, classical Chinese, popular, and even Western medical ideas. The two most common rituals he performed each took less than one minute. In one he would write a charm in the air over the client, which was believed to transfer power to the client and drive away bad spirits or ghosts. In the other, he rapidly moved his hands in front of the client from head downward to mid-body and from feet upward to mid-body. He then grasped at the space over the mid-body and made a throwing motion as if he were throwing something to the ground. This ritual signified the client was cleansed of bad spirits and ghosts. Sometimes, the *tâng-ki* would massage middle-aged and elderly clients.

After spending five minutes with the *tâng-ki*, the client would return to his seat in the shrine. There he would sit quietly— meditating, praying, or resting. The client would remain in the shrine for several hours. During that time he would be treated by several cult members, who, during their trances, massaged him, gave him further divine advice, and attempted to get him to trance and/or jump. Other cult members, who were not entranced, would give the client and the family members who

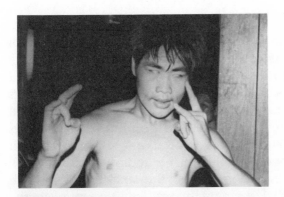

Tâng-ki possessed by a god

Cult member, possessed
by a god, healing clients
(see page 346)

Client in trance with members of shaman's cult
(see pages 230–233, 315)

Cult member in trance (see
pages 230–233, 315)

had accompanied him friendly and reassuring advice, often of a quite practical problem-solving nature, or they would ask them to tell their stories. Clients and family members would disclose full accounts of their problems to sympathetic listeners several times at least in the course of an evening. They might be given certain things to do, such as burning large amounts of spirit money to propitiate a god or an angry ancestral spirit or buying special foods to offer to the gods, which they will later take home to eat. Sometimes, the *tâng-ki* and his cult members would direct their treatment activities more to the oldest or most responsible-looking female family member accompanying the client than to the client. Not infrequently, female family members brought articles of clothes of sick family members, usually adult males and children, as surrogates for the *tâng-ki* to treat.

On seven consecutive nights in this shrine, there were one hundred and twenty-two new clients: fifty-four (45 percent) came seeking treatment for sickness; thirty-three (27 percent) came to have their fate determined and bad fate treated; twenty-four (19 percent) came because of business or other financial problems; and eleven (9 percent) came with questions concerning personal and family problems. More than three-fourths of the clients were lower class, two-thirds were female, and all were Taiwanese. Slightly more than one-fourth of the cases were young children or infants. Of the sickness complaints, by far the most common problems were acute, but not severe, upper respiratory or gastrointestinal disorders, probably viral. Chronic disorders such as low back pain, arthritis, and chronic obstructive pulmonary disease were present, but more prevalent were chronic, non-specific complaints labeled "functional" or neurasthenia by Western-style doctors, which to me represented somatization with depression, anxiety neurosis, hysteria, or other psychological or social problems. Most infants came with a history of irritability, poor sleep pattern, and prolonged unexplained crying. Such cases were diagnosed to be suffering from "fright" and were treated, as was previously described, with a ritual that called back the soul that was believed to have been frightened away. A client might spend anywhere from the equivalent of 50¢ to $5.00, depending on the treatment he received and the amount of incense and spirit money he had to burn. These charges were comparable to, but usually somewhat less than, charges in Western-style doctors' and Chinese-style doctors' offices. Nonetheless, they were considerable expenditures for many lower-class families.

We attempted follow-up evaluations of nineteen consecutive clients treated for complaints of sickness over a three-night period in this shrine. Several patients were interviewed before their interaction with the _tâng-ki;_ most were not. All patients were visited at their homes two months after their initial visit to the shrine. Follow-up interviews could not be completed with seven cases: two gave wrong addresses; three refused to be interviewed; two had moved to addresses too far away to be followed. Of the twelve patients who were interviewed at home (see Table 9) one (case 3) gave very brief answers to most of our questions and refused to answer some of them, and another (case 4) had been treated at the shrine many times before and was the only return patient in our sample. All the others were new patients. Each patient was interviewed with the same format and questions. Each interview took at least 30 minutes and often much longer.

We asked patients to evaluate their treatment in the shrine. Was it effective or not? To what did they attribute its efficacy (or lack of it)? Had they experienced symptom or behavioral change? Why did they evaluate their treatment as effective (or not)? We asked if their improvement could have been the result of the natural course of the sickness, and we explained what this meant since most did not understand "natural course of sickness." We asked them about intercurrent treatment from other health care agents for the same problems. We obtained brief histories of the onset and course of their disorders and attempted to work out our own assessment of patients' current physical and psychosocial status. Our evaluations were limited because we were unable to perform physical exams, blood tests, X-ray examinations, or psychological tests, either initially or at time of follow-up.

Besides the analysis of the follow-up evaluations of these twelve cases, we add a full description of another case. That patient, Mr. Chen, was examined by us at some length before he was treated by the *tâng-ki*. We also observed some of the treatment he received at the shrine, which lasted over many sessions, and we were able to follow Mr. Chen's course at home and at the shrine over a period of two years. We present his case in order to fill out the necessarily superficial presentation of the other cases. We feel justified in focusing special attention on this particular case, because it is typical of many other cases we studied in both indigenous and Western practice in Taiwan. It also provides us with an opportunity to discuss several salient issues in clinical practice in Taiwan, issues that hold considerable cross-cultural significance. Finally, I shall report follow-ups on several patients treated by another *tâng-ki* in Taipei, which lend support to findings from this particular shrine.

I need to raise several points of caution: our sample size is obviously very small. However, there are virtually no other follow-up studies of indigenous practice; and, importantly, these findings are in line with our findings from studies of other indigenous healers and our impressions from observation of large numbers of patients treated by *tâng-ki*s. Nonetheless, it is likely our results are skewed toward more positive evaluations of healing, since it is reasonable to assume that the clients who refused to be interviewed were more likely to evaluate their treatment negatively. However, even with these cautions in mind the results are striking.

As we see in Table 9, ten of twelve patients (83 percent) reported (or their family members reported) at least partially effective treatment. Six patients (50 percent) regarded themselves or were regarded by family members as completely cured. Only two patients (17 percent) are listed as treatment failures. One evaluated her treatment a failure, but her mother felt the treatment would have been effective if tried for a longer period of time. The father of one child evaluated his daughter's treatment at the *tâng-ki*'s shrine completely ineffective and implied that it had allowed her sickness to worsen. Nonetheless, an 83 percent rate of cure (even partial cure) is impressive and would seem to be evidence in favor of the efficacy of this indigenous practitioner's treatment. Or is it?

It is fascinating that of the ten patients whose treatment was evaluated by themselves or family members to be effective, one

Table 9

Follow-up of Cases Treated at a Shaman's Shrine

Case	Presenting Health Problem	Symptom Change	Behavioral Change	Other Treatment	Patient's Evaluation	Patient's Attribution	Our Evaluation	Tâng Ki's *Evaluation* & Attribution
1.	25-year-old mother with (1) chronic rhinitis; (2) upper gastro-intestinal (GI) complaints; (3) acute sensation of numbness in head. Neurasthenia diagnosed in past. Now an occasional cult member.	+ (3) complete, (1) and (2) partial	+ Feels happier	+ (1) and (2) being treated by Western-style doctors and self-medication (Still takes medicines)	+ Partially effective	God and doctor effective	Hysteria with secondary somatic complaints, (2) and (3). Complaint (1) is mild chronic disorder. Somatization decreased and psychological status improved.	Cure. A god wishes to possess patient. Advice to attend shrine regularly.

Table 9 (cont'd.)

Follow-up of Cases Treated at A Shaman's Shrine

Case	Presenting Health Problem	Symptom Change	Behavioral Change	Other Treatment	Patient's Evaluation	Patient's Attribution	Our Evaluation	Tàng-Ki's Evaluation & Attribution
2.	54-year-old mother with mild chronic lower GI complaints of 20 years' duration. Past history of multiple non-specific somatic complaints. Now a regular cult member who trances and jumps around.	+	+ Better spirits	+ Long-standing treatment in Western-style medical clinics and self-treatment. (Now no longer uses either)	+ Effective	God effective	Hysteria and chronic functional GI complaints. Severe family problems. Somatization has ended and psychological status improved. Family problems improved.	Cure. A god wishes to possess patient. God may test her again, requiring additional ritual treatment and daily participation in cult.
3.	10-year-old boy brought in by mother because he does not listen to her, behaves badly, and does not study hard enough. No symptoms. Mother thought problems might be due to illness or bad fate.	No symptoms	+ Listens to his mother, behaves better, studies harder	None	+ (Mother's evaluation)	God effective	No sickness. Behavior problem with related family and school problems. Behavior improved and family problem improved.	Cure. (? attribution) Ritual treatment.

4. 18-year-old female with paralysis and deformities due to infantile polio. Occasionally brought to shrine by family for "exercise," because she enjoys trancing, and for god's help. Poor family, could not afford rehabilitation therapy. Patient also has mild mental retardation.	−	+	None	+ Slightly effective, makes muscles stronger and patient feels better	God effective (Mother has doubts.)	Chronic physical and psychological incapacities. Psychological and family gains from treatment at shrine.	Partial cure. He told them long before that the god could not cure this kind of problem completely. (? attribution) Advice to attend shrine regularly and trance.
5. 31-year-old married man with chronic pain in throat. First treated by Western-style doctor, then by Chinese-style doctor, then by *táng-ki*. Patient has history of psychophysiological complaints and anxiety problems.	−	+ Partial (Still has some pain)	+ Took Western and Chinese medicine. Western doctors said it was pharyngitis.	+ Partially effective	Both god and medicines effective	Most likely pharyngitis 2° upper respiratory infection (URI) or chronic irritation from cigarette smoking. Possibility of psychophysiologically based complaint.	Cure. (*huo-ch'i ta*) Treated patient with ritual, ashes to drink, and herbs.

Table 9 (cont'd.)

Follow-up of Cases Treated at A Shaman's Shrine

Case	Presenting Health Problem	Symptom Change	Behavioral Change	Other Treatment	Patient's Evaluation	Patient's Attribution	Our Evaluation	Tâng-Ki's Evaluation & Attribution
6.	61-year-old female with hypertension and chronic aches and pains. The latter got better, but patient became increasingly weak and short of breath. She is a regular cult member of shrine. Patient has long history of chronic functional complaints.	– Worsening of symptoms	+ Feels happier	+ Treated by Western-style doctor for her hypertension and still takes medicine.	+ Partially effective (patient). (Husband did not think it was effective.)	God effective	Hypertension with worsening congestive heart failure and inadequate medical treatment. History and mental status consistent with hysteria.	Cure. Requires repeated ritual treatments and regular attendance at shrine because god keeps testing her with symptoms.
7.	1-year-old infant brought by its parents because of fever and cough of five days' duration.	+	+	+ Went to two different Western-style doctors over five days. Injections of antibiotics. Did not go back after visit to shrine.	+ (Parents)	Father: god; mother: god and doctors effective.	URI. Cure. Either spontaneous remission or secondary to antibiotics.	Cure. (? attribution) Treatment: ashes, charms, ritual for calling back the soul.

8. 4-month-old baby with transient irritability and restlessness with poor sleep pattern. No fever or specific symptoms. Mother thought it was "fright." Asked to have baby's soul called back. If there were fever, she would have taken baby to doctor.	+	+	None	+ (Mother)	God effective.	Transient colic or mild viral symptoms. Spontaneous remission.	Cure. Fright. Treatment: ritual for calling back the soul.
9. 3-month-old baby brought by grandmother to shrine for treatment of URI.	+ Partial (Still has symptoms of URI)	−	+ Parents took baby to several Western-style doctors for injections.	+ (Grandmother and parents)	God (grandmother); doctor and god (parents) effective.	URI. Partial improvement. Natural course of illness or secondary to antibiotics.	Cure. (? attribution) Treatment: ashes, charms, rituals

Table 9 (cont'd.)

Follow-up of Cases Treated at A Shaman's Shrine

Case	Presenting Health Problem	Symptom Change	Behavioral Change	Other Treatment	Patient's Evaluation	Patient's Attribution	Our Evaluation	Táng-Kî's Evaluation & Attribution
10.	2-month-old baby with poor sleep pattern and frequent crying. No fever or specific symptoms. Grandmother took her to temple for treatment of "fright" by calling back the soul.	+	+	None	+ (Grandmother) (Parents are uncertain)	God effective.	Transient colic. Spontaneous remission.	Cure. Fright. Treatment: ritual for calling back the soul.
11.	22-year-old single female with depressed affect and suicidal thoughts. Long-standing personal and family problems. Brought to shrine against her will by mother.	–	–	+ Has been treated by Western-style and Chinese-style doctors. Has seen a psychiatrist once but refuses psychiatric care. Family supports her in this.	– Patient; mother feels Chinese medicine and _táng-kî_ would be effective if tried longer.	Nothing has been of help. (Daughter admits to "mental stress." Mother says it is a physical problem causing depression.)	Depressive syndrome, acute. Long-standing severe personality problems (borderline personality). No treatment has been effective.	Cure. Treatment: ashes, charms, rituals. Problems caused by a "ghost" that "hit" the client and was driven away by charms and rituals.

| 12. | 6-year-old girl with flank pain, fever, discolored and bloody urine. Girl's symptoms got progressively worse while she was at shrine. | − (Worsened at shrine.) | − | + After girl became worse at shrine, parents took her to hospital, where she was treated as inpatient. | − (Father's evaluation of shrine. He said doctor was effective.) | Doctor effective, "god is useless for disease" (father). | Acute renal disorder (could have been pyelonephritis). Patient's condition worsened at shrine. Now resting after one month of modern medical treatment. | Cure. (? attribution) Ritual treatment |

reported no symptom change at all, one infant and one adult experienced only minimal symptomatic improvement, and a fourth patient actually experienced worsening of her symptoms. Two of these patients experienced some behavioral change (they felt psychologically better after being at the shrine), but the other adult did not and the infant gave no sign of such change. Furthermore, in several cases (e.g., 6, 10, and 11), there was some discrepancy between different family members' evaluations of whether or not the *tâng-ki*'s treatment had been effective. These cases raise a serious question about how evaluations of therapeutic efficacy are made. Clearly the patients positively evaluated their care for different reasons. In some cases symptomatic change was the chief determinant, while in others behavioral change was most important. For example, cases 4 and 6 experienced no symptomatic change but derived psychological benefits and probably also social benefits (e.g., they got out of the house, away from family problems, socialized with friends, enjoyed the shrine's exciting atmosphere, etc.) from their treatment. Other patients explained to us that negative evaluations of their treatment in the shrine might prejudice the gods, whose favors they were seeking, against them and thereby worsen their disorders. Some patients apparently could not bring themselves to challenge the *tâng-ki* and the cult members, who had repeatedly and emphatically told them they were cured. Indeed, in this shrine and others, if one asks patients to evaluate their treatment while they are still in the shrine, immediately after being treated, one obtains uniformly positive evaluations. That is why home visits at a later date are necessary. In case 1, certain problems improved, while others did not, but the overall impression was one of effective treatment. We have not exhausted all the issues surrounding these evaluations of the efficacy of healing. They illustrate the special criteria patients use to evaluate their treatment. These criteria differ among patients and even among family members. They are quite different from those we employed, as a comparison between our evaluations and patient evaluations demonstrates. Such a comparison also reveals differences in criteria indigenous and modern professional practitioners employ to evaluate therapeutic success. It is worth noting that no patients were willing to state definitely that the natural course of the disorder was responsible for their improvement, and most had no understanding of "natural course of sickness" or "spontaneous remission" until we explained these terms. The popular ideology holds that all significant sicknesses must be treated if they are to improve, and, correspondingly, that remission is always due to therapy.

The *tâng-ki* essentially regarded all of these cases as cured (at least in part), since those who returned to the shrine told him that they were, while those who were not helped did not return, which he took to mean they had been cured and saw no reason to return. Furthermore, cure also meant to him that the cosmological agencies causing these problems were appropriately treated, and this he felt had happened in each case. In the cases of "fright," he evaluated cure not so much by the condition of the infants as by the responses of their mothers. Here alleviating the distress of a key family member was a criterion of cure.

Our evaluations suggest that the question of efficacy in this patient sample is a good deal less certain. To begin with, *what* was effectively treated? In one case we had a naughty child who (to our minds) was suffering no sickness at all. Effective treatment of a sickness may be a similarly irrelevant concern in the two cases of "fright." These infants may have had some minimal, self-limited sickness but just as likely were cranky or "colicky" for reasons having nothing at all to do with sickness. Several patients seemed to be suffering from self-limited disorders (possibly viral syndromes) that probably improved spontaneously as part of the natural course of such disorders. We thought that two, and possibly three, of the patients were suffering from somatization. Their somatic complaints were secondary manifestations or symbolic expressions of underlying psychological disorders or social problems. Evaluation of therapeutic efficacy in these cases depends on what happens to the underlying psychological and social problems. In the two cases with hysteria, treatment in the *tâng-ki*'s shrine seemed to be at least partially successful. Finally, several patients who reported symptom relief were receiving other therapies, including Western drugs known to be effective for their specific symptoms. Thus, from our perspective, only a few of the cases seem to provide evidence in favor of the efficacy of this indigenous form of healing. We do not find conclusive evidence to show that a single case of biological-based disease was effectively treated by the *tâng-ki*'s therapy alone.

It is of particular interest that the only patients who did not evaluate their treatment to be effective both suffered from severe acute disorders, one somatic and one psychological. This is an important point we shall return to in the Comments.

Findings from our other studies support these results. For example, on two other consecutive evenings in this shrine, there were sixteen cases who presented with health problems. Fifteen involved somatic complaints, compared with eleven out of twelve in our study. The sixteenth patient was suffering from catatonia, but the treatment was organized around a relatively minor skin lesion which she had rather than for her major mental disorder. (The *tâng-ki* told us he could not cure severe or chronic mental illnesses.) Here is further evidence for somatic preponderance among complaints treated by this indigenous healer. And we have evidence to show that all forms of indigenous practice in Taiwan principally see patients who complain of somatic symptoms. This holds for modern clinical care as well. Even in the Psychiatric Clinic of the National Taiwan University Hospital, 70 percent of patients with documented psychiatric disorders initially complained of somatic symptoms (Tseng 1975), as we noted in Chapter 4. This underlines the fact that most psychological care in Taiwan is disguised as the treatment of somatic problems. Clearly, patients in this *tâng-ki*'s shrine receive care that has an effect on their behavioral problems, though this is not acknowledged openly. Instead their psychological difficulties are legitimated, and eventually treated, via medical sick roles.

Of the fifteen cases mentioned above, four had chronic cardiac and chest diseases, six had mild or moderate viral-like, self-limited disorders, and five were experiencing somatization. Of the last group, two suffered from anxiety neuroses, and three had major family and other interpersonal problems. These findings are supported by analysis of one hundred cases we followed who were treated by different kinds of indigenous practitioners. Ninety percent were suffering from: (1) non-life-threatening, chronic diseases in which management of psychological and social problems related to the illness were the chief concerns of clinical management; (2) minimal, self-limited diseases; and (3) somatization. The last group accounted for almost 50 percent of cases. The overwhelming majority of these cases were satisfied with the indigenous care they received and believed it to be at least partially effective. However, most cases with severe acute diseases in this sample were not satisfied with indigenous care and did not believe it to be effective. Indigenous care, then, is effective for certain kinds of problems but not for others. Intriguingly, in our research in Taiwan, about half the case loads of private Western-style doctors were made up of the same kind of disorder that was preponderant in the practices of indigenous practitioners: somatization. And almost another quarter of their patients suffered from problems in groups (1) and (2) above. But here we found patient satisfaction to be considerably less and evaluations of efficacy no better. The major difference is in the treatment of severe acute disorders, where Western-style practitioners are rated by patients as very effective, whereas, as we have already noted, indigenous practitioners are thought not to be effective.

These evaluations fit with patient choice of treatment. Among the one-hundred fifteen families in Taipei questioned about specific sicknesses experienced in the preceding month (described in Chapter 6), it was reported that virtually all adult problems were first treated at home, but, thereafter, severe acute disorders were most often brought to Western-style doctors, while chronic disorders were more frequently brought first to indigenous healers and then to Western-style doctors. Self-limited sicknesses and somatization cases tended to end up more frequently in the treatment settings of indigenous healers than in the clinics of Western-style doctors, though obviously many were brought to Western-style doctors as well. We should expect that patient expectations follow the same logic: patients and families do not expect indigenous healers to be as effective as Western-style doctors in the treatment of severe acute sickness, whereas they expect the reverse for chronic and minimal health problems. It is also likely that practitioners are aware of these expectations and in some way incorporate them into their treatment practices.

Two further findings are worth reporting: Of one hundred cases treated by indigenous healers, at least three had negative effects on the patients' diseases. In two cases, patients with severe hypertensive cardiovascular diseases were ineffectively treated while there was progressive worsening of their congestive heart failure. Both cases were delayed from receiving effective care because of indigenous treatment. In another case, an indigenous healer ineffectively treated a young girl with severe acute hepatitis and in so doing delayed her from receiving adequate diagnosis and potentially life-saving therapy. In our experience, however, such situations were distinctly unusual: most patients who suffered from serious disorders for which there was effective modern biomedical treatment and no effective indigenous treatment, but who were receiving indigenous treatment anyway, were also receiving the appropriate modern treatment from Western-style doctors whom they consulted at the same time. Families of patients and most (but, unfortunately, not all) indigenous practitioners whom we encountered were generally quite sensitive and knowledgeable about those disorders for which indigenous treatment was clearly ineffective but for which modern biomedical treatment was effective. Nonetheless, this problem remains a disturbing and potentially dangerous issue.

Finally, on several occasions we met patients with chronic incapacity (e.g., hemiplegia from cerebrovascular accidents or paralysis secondary to infantile polio, as in case 4 above) and even terminal diseases (e.g., hepatic carcinoma) who had been discharged from modern health care facilities as untreatable and who were receiving active treatment from indigenous practitioners. These patients, and their families, reported that they felt psychologically better and experienced active social lives in place of vegetating existences because of indigenous care. This was definitely true of three patients with hemiplegia following stroke who were treated in the therapeutic milieu of this *tâng-ki*'s shrine.[1] This is an extremely important but frequently unappreciated aspect of healing.

FOLLOW-UP OF PATIENTS TREATED BY ANOTHER *TÂNG-KI*

Six additional consecutive cases treated for health problems by another shaman in Taipei also received follow-up evaluations. Findings from those cases add impressionistic support to the findings from a single shrine described above.

In Table 10 we see that all the patients, or in the case of small

---

1. A full description of this *tâng-ki* and his cult is found in Wang (1971).

children, the mothers, evaluated the *tâng-ki*'s treatment as at least partially effective. Half reported complete cures. The *tâng-ki* evaluated all six patients as cured. My evaluation again revealed a very different set of determinants: natural remission of minimal, self-limited health problems in cases 1, 2, 3 and 4; somatization of underlying interpersonal and psychological problems with no demonstrable improvement in case 6; and a chronic medical problem with partial improvement due either to natural remission or, more likely, to professional medical treatment in case 5. Half the cases received treatment from other practitioners, which may have contributed to their response. All cases, except the infants, reported behavioral change (feeling happier or experiencing significantly less "dis-ease"). Symptom change was partial or minimal in two cases, and less than complete in a third. None of the six patients experienced a severe acute medical or psychological disorder, and only one suffered from a severe chronic sickness.

None of these patients fully understood the concept of natural or spontaneous remission, and none used it to evaluate the *tâng-ki*'s treatment. But five patients said the god (*tâng-ki*) was only one of the factors responsible for cure. Almost all the patients demonstrated a pragmatic orientation toward sacred folk healing: they reasoned it should be tried along with any potentially effective secular treatment. What was important was getting better, not discovering what was responsible for getting better. All available treatments that might be of help should be tried. Interestingly, two patients changed *tâng-kis* because they were initially dissatisfied with their treatment, in part owing to the *tâng-ki*'s unsatisfactory relation with them and in part owing to the lack of improvement. That is, they experienced neither symptom change nor behavioral change in the shrine of the first *tâng-ki* they consulted. Cases 2 and 3 placed more emphasis on behavioral change than symptom change in evaluating the outcome of their treatment, and cases 5 and 6, who experienced only partial symptom change, evaluated their treatment as at least minimally effective because of their behavioral response.

The Case of Mr. Chen

Mr. Chen, our patient, is a 44-year-old married Hakka male. He is a lower-middle-class master woodworker with a primary

Table 10

Follow-up of Cases Treated at Another Shaman's Shrine

Case	Presenting Health Problem	Symptom Change	Behavioral Change	Other Treatment	Patient's Evaluation	Patient's Attribution	Our Evaluation	Tàng-Ki's _Evaluation_ & Attribution
1.	4-year-old girl with low grade fever of several days' duration.	+	?	Mother took patient to a Western-style doctor twice, where she received injections of antibiotics and antipyretic pills.	Complete cure. Change in weather and bad fortune responsible for sickness.	Both Western-style doctor and god were effective.	Viral URI, natural remission.	Cure. Ritual treatment of bad fortune enabled medicine to be effective.
2.	28-year-old mother of four young children with non-specific, intermittent, relatively mild chest discomfort of several days' duration.	+	+	No other treatment. Patient not sure if pains in chest were an illness or not. She asked _tàng-ki_ about them after going to shrine to have her fate divined. They lasted for several weeks, then disappeared.	Cure	God was effective, but patient admitted there was not much of a health problem to treat.	Minor, transient, nonspecific chest wall symptoms, spontaneous improvement or simply no longer attended to as a problem.	Cure. _Huo-ch'i ta._ Ritual treatment, charms, and lotus root juice used to lower body's excessive heat.

3.	65-year-old widow with non-specific backache and tired feeling of one day's duration.	+	+	No other treatment.	Cure. Backache and fatigue disappeared after leaving shrine.	God effective.	Nonspecific ache in back without significant underlying pathology. Natural remission of symptom, or patient no longer attending to minimal complaint.	Cure. (? attribution) _Tâng-ki_ massaged patient's body and gave charms.
4.	7-month-old male infant with rash on buttock.	+ (Significant but not complete)	?	Mother also used salve from Western pharmacy. She believes disturbing fetus god in bedroom by driving nail into wall may have caused baby's rash. That made baby susceptible to soul loss and also "medical disease" such as diaper rash.	Almost complete cure. Claims to feel psychologically reassured after taking baby to shrine.	God and medicine effective. Must obtain treatment from both.	Diaper rash, improved by keeping skin dry and applying topical medication, modern and traditional.	Cure. (? attribution) Ritual performed to "call back the soul." Charms given. Herb medicine given to be applied in bath.

Table 10 (*cont'd.*)

Follow-up of Cases Treated at Another Shaman's Shrine

Case	Presenting Health Problem	Symptom Change	Behavioral Change	Other Treatment	Patient's Evaluation	Patient's Attribution	Our Evaluation	Tâng-Ki's Evaluation & Attribution
5.	35-year-old married woman with chronic breast cysts over past five years.	+ (Partial)	+	Surgery, Western and Chinese medicines, application of herbs prescribed by friends and relatives, and treatment from several *tâng-ki's*.	Problems caused by breast-feeding and taking medication to aid in breast feeding.	Significant improvement. All treatments have contributed to efficacy. "One must try everything."	Chronic suppurative cystic disease of breasts in partial remission, owing to surgery, antibiotics, and hygienic practices, but might also be natural remission in chronic disease.	Cure. Ritual performed to treat offended god and herbs prescribed for topical use and for ingestion.

6.	30-year-old mother with insomnia, lethargy, headaches, nausea.	(Partial)	+	+	Discontinued birth control pills. Went to see several *tâng-kis*.	Partially improved. Health problems caused by conflict with husband and by birth control pills.	Perhaps due to help from *tâng-ki*, perhaps due to improving relationship with husband.	Somatization secondary to marital problems and reactive depression. Birth control pills may have been responsible for headache and nausea, which disappeared after pills discontinued. No evidence that marital problems and depression have been successfully treated.	Cure. (Complete cure to follow regular attendance at shrine.) Problem caused by marital strife and birth control pills, which produced neurasthenia and *huo-ch'i ta.* Recommended patient discontinue contraceptive pills, relate better with husband and friends, and use charms to treat herself and, secretly, her husband, too.

school education who lives with his wife and five children in a poor but newly developed urban district on the edge of Taipei. He came to this shrine (his first visit here) to be cured of a chronic recurrent illness. He was introduced to the shrine and its *tâng-ki* by several of his neighbors who belong to the *tâng-ki*'s cult, including the *tâng-ki*'s chief male assistant and the chief female healer in the cult, both of whom, like Mr. Chen, belong to Taiwan's Hakka minority.[2] Mr. Chen's neighborhood includes more than one hundred people who have been treated at this shrine; as a result, he has heard a great deal that is positive about the shrine. He knows dozens of individuals who claim to have been cured by this *tâng-ki*'s chief god.

Mr. Chen complains of a vague sensation of discomfort in his chest: "a feeling of pressure or tension." He feels as if his chest muscles are snapping apart. He also complains of being very troubled or anxious (*fan-tsao*). He describes this feeling as both a psychological and physical one, a disturbing sense of inner tension which he feels is located in his chest, where it produces

2. Approximately 17 percent of Taiwan's 16 million population are Chinese who speak the Hakka dialect and are identified as a distinct subgroup: the Hakka (*k'e-chia jen*, "guest people"). The Hakka are ethnic Chinese who once lived in northern China and who long ago migrated from there to the south, primarily Kwangtung province. From there many migrated to Taiwan. They are considered to be one of the most culturally traditional Chinese groups with a strong ethnic identity. They tend to be endogamous and reside in their own communities. Taiwan has several large areas that are predominantly Hakka, but in Taipei and other large urban communities there is now considerable intermarriage with Taiwan's predominantly Hokkien-speaking population. However, in the past these two groups frequently fought each other, and even now bitter feelings remain. Many of my Hokkien-speaking informants held the following ethnic stereotype of the Hakka: more achievement-oriented, more intellectual, more filled with their own sense of importance, more close-knit, more concerned with cleanliness, and more traditional in beliefs and customs than the Hokkien population. These views are portrayed in negative terms with resentment for what are seen as the "strengths" of the Hakka culture (the Hakka similarly hold "negative" stereotypes of the Hokkien). Of interest, many Hokkien people have an impression (one I share) that Hakka are overrepresented in the medical profession (Western and Chinese).

As I noted in Chapter 6, the number of Hakka subjects in our survey of family illness beliefs and practices was too small to determine if there were any statistically significant differences between them and Hokkien subjects, but we did receive the impression that there were many similarities in how they viewed and responded to sickness episodes.

a physically discomforting sensation which he also experiences as a general nervousness and worry. Even so, he makes it clear that his preoccupation is with the physical components, which he takes to be primary. These include feelings of general weakness, malaise, and tension in the back of his neck. His is a physical illness, he tells us. But he admits his symptoms either start or worsen when he is worried about business or family problems. As his symptoms worsen, he worries increasingly about his health problem: What kind of illness is it? Can it be cured?

Mr. Chen's illness first began sixteen years before. He was living alone in Taipei trying to establish a woodwork business. Business was poor, and he was suffering serious financial problems. He felt lonely and unhappy. He worried a great deal about failure. His symptoms began at that time. Chinese-style and Western-style medicines were unhelpful. He eventually left Taipei and returned to his family's home in a Hakka region in Taiwan. There he consulted four Western-style doctors, none of whom was able to diagnose precisely what ailment he was suffering from. A Chinese-style doctor told him that his problem was caused by "working too hard and worrying too much," that this in turn caused a pathological excess of hot energy (*huo-ch'i ta*) from his lungs, liver, and heart to "rise up" into his chest, where it "inflamed the nerves." This diagnosis impressed Mr. Chen because it could explain both the chest discomfort and the tension. From that time on he considered himself suffering from *huo-ch'i ta*. This problem he associated with an excessively "hot" physical constitution, a tendency to irritability and anger, and a variety of non-specific complaints that he had had. He quite literally could feel heat rising up in him when he was worried, and burning "like a fire" beneath his sternum, just as the popular ideology says it does. He could see how it then affected his chest and his "nerves."

Although the Chinese-style doctor diagnosed his illness, he was unable to cure him with Chinese medicine. This led Mr. Chen to seek advice from a fortune-teller who told him (as he already feared) that he had "bad fate." The bad fate, said the fortune-teller, following the very well-known line of explanation in Taiwan we have previously examined, was responsible not only for the illness but also for the inability of the doctors and the medicines to cure the illness. When his fate changed (and the fortune-teller predicted it would change, though he could not specify exactly when), then Mr. Chen would experience good fortune generally and, specifically, his illness would be cured by doctors or medicine. The fortune-teller went on to report the "true cause" of his client's problem: an ancestor—one from the underworld who was not being worshipped by his/her descendents—was "bothering" him. The fortune-teller advised Mr. Chen to find out which ancestor it was, so that he could properly propitiate him/her.

Mr. Chen told me this information had a tremendous effect on him. He immediately realized that the ghost haunting him might very likely be his biological mother. She and his father had divorced when he was four-years-old. Even though his mother had asked him to come to see her when she was dying and to worship her as an ancestral spirit after her death, his father had prohibited him from doing so, a prohibition that Mr. Chen implied had been a chronic source of worry. Mr. Chen confirmed this impression by throwing the divination blocks to indicate the god's answer was "yes." Knowing, then, that it was indeed his mother's ghost that was troubling him, Mr. Chen prayed to her, offering her meats and wine. He asked her to release him from his illness and in turn prayed that her soul would be released from suffering in the underworld. Ten days later his symptoms disappeared entirely. Mr. Chen was convinced he had been cured by following the fortune-teller's advice.

For the next ten years he remained essentially free of this problem, although he recognized a tendency to worry about his affairs much more than others did. The full-blown disorder recurred again when his wife developed a strange, incapacitating neurological disease and he was once more in a bad financial situation. Both problems worried him greatly. His wife's malady slowly departed over the course of a year, and after she regained her health and their financial situation improved, his symptoms also disappeared. He and his wife attributed the effect of the medicines to the gods' help. Mr. Chen came to the conclusion: medicines could only cure mild or "bogus" illness, while the gods alone could cure "true" illness.

Over the past six years Mr. Chen's symptoms waxed and waned. Three years ago Western-style and Chinese-style medicine, with which he self-medicated himself, failed to attenuate an exacerbation of his illness. However, after visiting a famous temple in the south of Taiwan and consulting its _tâng-ki_, Mr. Chen felt greatly relieved. Both his chest discomfort and anxiety improved. One year ago he again returned to that temple, owing to a recurrence of his symptoms, and again improved. On neither occasion did Mr. Chen trance, nor had he ever done so before. He would sit quietly in the temple, resting and praying: slowly he would feel less tense and his chest discomfort would also lessen.

Recently Mr. Chen's panoply of symptoms returned. They appeared at a time when Mr. Chen's business was at a crucial stage, one that he believed could lead to either failure or success. Western and Chinese medicines proved ineffective. Western-style doctors diagnosed neurasthenia, which he accepted as the name of his problem and believed to be a physical disorder. But they, as well as the Chinese-style doctors he consulted, were unable to relieve his symptoms. All X-rays and blood tests done at this time were normal.

In response to his fear that his business would fail, leaving him unable to support his family and exposing him (and his family) to the ridicule of friends and neighbors (who "would laugh at me"), Mr. Chen became increasingly anxious, stayed awake at night, and felt irritable and frustrated during the day. He became preoccupied with his somatic complaints. Although he talked to family members and friends about those symptoms, he could not talk about his anxiety and fears with anyone.

Finally, because nothing else worked, he consulted a fortune-teller who told him he had bad fate that was the cause of his sickness and his business worries. Because of this advice, Mr. Chen returned to the temple in the south of Taiwan, which twice before had brought him relief. There he met members of the Taipei *tâng-ki*'s cult and the *tâng-ki* himself, who were on a pilgrimage to the south. Just deciding to go to this temple had made Mr. Chen feel better. He felt confident he would be protected by the temple's god. While at the temple in the south, the *tâng-ki* from the Taipei shrine told him: "You have no problem! You should rest quietly at my shrine when we return to Taipei. Wait! The god will come to you."

Mr. Chen's symptoms did not disappear, but they did improve. After returning to Taipei, he immediately went to the *tâng-ki*'s shrine. (Note that he did this even though it, like the pilgrimage to the south, cost him precious time from his work, which he usually carries out seven days a week for at least ten, and often more, hours per day.) After arriving at the shrine (his first visit), Mr. Chen quietly sat off in a corner surrounded by his friends and neighbors, including the *tâng-ki*'s chief male assistant. They told him that he would be better after eating charms and sacred ashes which were being specially prepared for him by the *tâng-ki*. His friends frequently reassured him.

They repeated the *tâng-ki*'s advice, which Mr. Chen already had memorized, "You have no problem! You should rest quietly. Wait! The god will come to you." Every few minutes, other members of the *tâng-ki*'s cult, usually people from Mr. Chen's neighborhood, came up to him and gave him encouraging advice. They told him about their own cases and how they were healed here. They told him that he, too, would be healed. They related to him stories of clients with problems either similar to his own or much worse, who were cured in this shrine. While he swallowed the charms the *tâng-ki* had prepared for him, they smiled and said: "Ah! Surely now it will not be long until you are better." During all this time the *tâng-ki* had not "officially" consulted with Mr. Chen. But he looked over at him every few minutes, when he was not entranced, and smiled, shaking his head affirmatively. Mr. Chen told me that he expected to be cured and that he believed one of the *tâng-ki*'s gods would make his illness go away.

Relevant History

There is no history of mental illness in Mr. Chen's family. With the exception of his present problem, Mr. Chen's health has been excellent. Repeated physicial examinations have never disclosed any significant abnormalities. Both his biological father and foster mother believed strongly in folk religion and frequented the shrines of local *tâng-ki*s. As a child Mr. Chen accompanied them. Mr. Chen and his wife note that he has always worried excessively. Neither sees this in itself as a problem. Only his physical complaints are referred to as an illness.

Initial Mental Status Examination

When I first met Mr. Chen at the time of his initial visit to the shrine, before he had been treated by the *tâng-ki*, I carried out a full mental status examination. That examination revealed marked anxiety, but no other significant abnormalities. Motor behavior, orientation, speech, and thought structure and content were not remarkable. He did not appear depressed and gave no history of experiencing the somatic concomitants of depression. He was preoccupied with his chest discomfort and frequently rubbed or pointed to his chest. He was circumspect with his answers and did not give full replies to questions about his family and personal history.

Mr. Chen showed only quite limited insight into (and interest in) the psychological sides of his illness, favored a somato-psychic rather than a psychosomatic causal sequence, and was relatively unsophisticated in his use of psychological terms. He turned most questions about affect and beliefs into responses about somatic complaints. When questioned about intimate aspects of his personal life, he gave vague replies, actively suppressed most private information, and elaborated hardly at all beyond the words used in the questions he responded to. He was unable to define even his anxious and worried feelings much beyond the non-specific term he used for them (*fan-tsao*). In all of these regards, he was like the Chinese patients described in Chapters 4 and 5.

In summary, Mr. Chen presented no evidence of psychosis. He did demonstrate considerable anxiety and pronounced somatic preoccupation; however, historical evidence and laboratory and clinical support for a primary organic etiology were lacking. Since I was unable to perform a physical examination or laboratory tests, the history and mental status exam had to suffice as the basis for formulating a diagnosis. My impression was (and still is) that Mr. Chen suffered from an acute exacerbation of a chronic anxiety neurosis stimulated by certain psychosocial stressors, principally financial and business concerns. The same stressors had precipitated several other acute anxiety attacks. These episodes, including the present one, involved somatization as a secondary manifestation of his primary psychological problem.

Treatment in the Tâng-ki's Shrine

Although Mr. Chen spent more than four hours in the shrine at the time of his first visit, the *tâng-ki* spent very little time with him, less than ten minutes. He was one of approximately ten new cases the *tâng-ki* treated while in his trance. The *tâng-ki* saw Mr. Chen after the latter had been at the shrine for more than two hours. The assistant called out Mr. Chen's name, date, day, and time of birth, and his problem: "health problem." The entranced *tâng-ki* spoke authoritatively. He (the god) reiterated his former advice, stressing the point about the desirability of Mr. Chen coming to the shrine as often as possible. He then told Mr. Chen that his problems were due to the shrine's chief god, who was troubling Mr. Chen because he wished to become Mr. Chen's master. Once Mr. Chen "allowed" the god to possess him, he would become his disciple, and his complaints would go away entirely. Furthermore, the god would protect him (as

343

long as he served the god as a faithful disciple by attending regularly at the shrine) from further episodes of this illness and would reward him with good health, long life, a large, prosperous family, and success in business. But Mr. Chen must be patient.

The *tâng-ki* wrote out sacred charms for Mr. Chen. He scooped up some ashes from the large incense pot on the altar table. Both of these were wrapped up by his assistant and handed to Mr. Chen, who was instructed to eat them. Then the *tâng-ki* took his writing brush and several burning incense sticks in his right hand and made passing movements before Mr. Chen as if he were writing a charm over his body.

The *tâng-ki* told Mr. Chen to return to where he had been sitting and again to sit quietly and rest. The *tâng-ki*'s last words were repeated several times: "You have no problem!" This is a special expression used in this shrine to indicate that the client will receive the god's full therapeutic efficacy and will be healed. Mr. Chen did not understand the special meaning of this term at the time of this visit to the shrine. Before Mr. Chen returned to his seat, the *tâng-ki* wafted incense and perfumed resin around his head, something that he does to encourage trance behavior. (The incense and resin give off strong aromas which make many people feel lightheaded and nauseated. There is no evidence, however, that they contain any hallucinogens or psychoactive drugs.) The chief male assistant encouraged Mr. Chen to let himself relax and to allow the god to possess him.

Compared with his treatment of other cases, the *tâng-ki*'s behavior with Mr. Chen was much less dramatic. He kept his powerful voice low. He did not perform any of the elaborate, impressive, or frightening ritual activities that he frequently performs. And he made no attempt to focus the concern of his large audience on Mr. Chen, a strategy he sometimes employs in difficult cases. This treatment was much quieter and more private than most I witnessed in this shrine.

In fact, most of Mr. Chen's "therapy" during this first visit was provided by the milieu not the *tâng-ki*. As we have seen, he received support from friends. When he returned to his seat in the rear of the shrine, his friends and neighbors again formed a small group around him. They told him he would now certainly be cured. They suggested he close his eyes, relax, and try to trance. They also told him not to feel disappointed if he was unable to trance the first night, since for one to trance and jump is like an infant "growing up and learning first to sit, then to crawl, stand, and finally walk." Mr. Chen did not trance that evening. He sat quietly in his chair, his eyes often closed, trying, as he later told me, to "meditate." He returned home well after midnight. Mr. Chen reported feeling slightly better after this first night's treatment. He was confident that he would be completely cured, although he could relate no evidence to support this self-assessment. His symptoms were still present. "Somehow I feel better," he said.

Mr. Chen returned to the *tâng-ki*'s shrine each night for one week. Thereafter, he returned almost every night for several months, failing to attend only when he was engaged in important business and family obligations. After the second night in the *tâng-ki*'s shrine, he reported feeling a great deal better, and he claims to have felt completely well after the third night there. Neither evening did the *tâng-ki* formally treat him. The second night one of the female cult members, herself in trance, actively treated him. She forced him (much against his wishes and to his clear embarrassment) to jump about with her, but he did not trance. On the following night, the cult's chief female healer placed her hands on him, massaging and slapping his arms, legs, and chest. (These movements are believed to help drive out evil influences from the body. This is one of the very few socially legitimated occasions when men and women can touch each other's bodies in public.) Again, he was led away from his chair and forced to jump. That night he tranced, or so he tells us. (It is impossible to be sure if a trance is authentic or sham behavior.) He flung himself around the shrine violently and eventually collapsed to the floor exhausted after about 15 minutes. He then lay on the floor, not asleep but apparently unable to move, for a similar period of time. When he threw himself on the floor, sweat was pouring off his face; his shirt was completely wet and sticking to his skin; and he was momentarily the focus of attention of the many people in the shrine. While he jumped, he copied the actions of the shrine's many trancers, who themselves copy the stylized movements of characters in Taiwanese folk opera. But Mr. Chen's behavior was considerably less controlled and more violent than that of the experienced cult members, who told us that he would learn in time how to control his trance behavior. Recalling his first trance, Mr. Chen stated that he heard people talking near him and did not feel as if the god was possessing him. He kept his eyes closed but neither hallucinated voices nor images inside his head. Nor did he experience depersonalization or deluded thoughts. He could remember nothing else. He felt physically exhausted after coming out of the trance, but he described this sensation as pleasurable and associated it with a significant decrease in anxiety and in preoccupation with his symptoms.

Mr. Chen attributed special healing powers to the handsome, middle-aged Hakka woman, his neighbor and the shrine's chief female healer, who along with the *tâng-ki* were the two most charismatic figures in the shrine. Her master was "Monkey," a deified folk hero in Chinese culture, who is reported to possess many magical powers, regarded as clever and cunning, and referred to by the *tâng-ki* as "he who finds out all secrets."[3] Her healing skills were highly valued in the shrine and were well known to Mr. Chen before he came. Mr. Chen told me that she had cured "hundreds" of sick people, and he cited several impressive examples. He attributed most of his therapeutic improvement to her. She told him he must come back to the shrine each night. At the time of his first trance, she told him he was cured. Since that time he had returned to the shrine regularly but had only tranced and jumped on several other occasions. Most of the time he sat quietly in the shrine and meditated or spoke with friends. During each of his visits, the *tâng-ki*'s chief male assistant spoke with him at length. They talked softly, sometimes laughed, but never were overly serious or somber. This assistant was a very large man who acted deliberately and calmly, with a soft smile, radiating warmth and confidence. His slow, methodical movements and quiet speech and Buddha-like smile created a model that was the very opposite of anxiety. He was a close neighbor of Mr. Chen's and had known him for many years. They frequently sat together at the shrine sharing cigarettes. Mr. Chen talked to this assistant about his life problems in a relaxed way, and in return the assistant gave him advice and encouragement, while explaining to him the meaning of the shrine's rituals and beliefs. They would sit together for 45 minutes to an hour, and even more. Most of the time they were silent or exchanged polite and quite superficial remarks. Mr. Chen's motor behavior and speech became noticeably less quick and intense in the assistant's presence.

Since his initial visit to the shrine, Mr. Chen had taken no medication. He had not gone to consult other shamans or other

---

3. The shrine's *tâng-ki,* an extremely shrewd person, assigned me this same tutelary god, "Monkey," making sure that my research assistant and I were aware of this epithet.

kinds of healers. He believed that his illness had been cured and that the cure was the result of the shrine's chief god, whose faithful disciple he had become. These beliefs were confirmed by the *tâng-ki*, his assistants, and the shrine's cult members.

Follow-up Interviews

Mr. Chen's subjective evaluation: The first follow-up interview with Mr. Chen took place five days after his initial visit to the *tâng-ki*'s shrine and two days after he first tranced. My research assistant and I visited him at his home. We spent most of a Sunday morning talking with him. We also spoke briefly with his wife and children. Mr. Chen first reported to us: "I feel better . . . I have been cured." He said both the feeling of discomfort in his chest and his feeling of tension had disappeared. Whereas before his chest discomfort often was provoked by hard physical work, it had not bothered him for the past several days, in spite of the fact that he had been working very hard. He repeated to us that he had felt slightly better after his first night at the shrine, much improved after the second night, but only after the third night there did he feel completely better. He still remained worried about his business and financial concerns (but no longer about his health). But he distinguished these worries from the marked tension he had been feeling. He did not feel as if his responsibilities have been lessened or transferred to the shrine's god; indeed, he listed them in full for us, but he was more confident now that he could successfully cope with them. He repeated again and again his cure was "strange"; it could not be explained by him or by us. The god had cured his health problem; now he himself had to work out his business problems.

Mr. Chen stated emphatically that the medicines he had previously taken had had no effect on his illness. The *tâng-ki*'s shrine's chief god had changed his "fate" as well as healed his "body" and would continue to "protect" him as long as he attended regularly at the shrine. He also believed he must continue to abstain from eating symbolically hot foods, since these would provoke his already overly "hot" constitution and produce a "hot" illness. Mr. Chen ended his comments by telling us the *tâng-ki*'s shrine had made him forget about everything else, including all the "problems" that had been bothering him so severely. Just being there, he said, made him stop worrying and begin to feel calm and reassured. If he started to feel tense and become preoccupied with his worries during the daytime, he tried to fill his thoughts with images from the *tâng-ki*'s shrine,

347

and then he felt better. He concluded: "If you don't think about things troubling you, then you have no problem." Mr. Chen's wife and older children agreed with the things he told us. They too believed he was better and attributed his improvement to the *tâng-ki*. His wife cautioned him, however, to continue taking medicine as well, so that he obtained the combined effect from the treatments of both "god and man."

Objective Evaluation: To my research assistant and me, Mr. Chen looked considerably more relaxed, much less outwardly anxious, and less troubled and distressed than at the time of our initial evaluation. His voice was stronger, and he was more assertive in answering questions. Unlike our first meeting, he maintained eye contact, did not glance away, smiled fairly frequently, and had generally good communicative rapport. He carried himself with more confidence. These behavioral changes were as striking to my research assistant as they were to me.

Mental status examination was remarkable only because it revealed no significant anxiety. Mr. Chen also denied any physical complaints. We observed him hard at work and relaxing with his family. In both situations he acted entirely appropriately, displaying almost none of the signs of anxiety that were so pronounced five days before.

My overall impression was that he demonstrated no significant psychopathology and that his former anxiety had been largely, and perhaps entirely, relieved, while his physical symptoms were no longer present. Although much of this evaluation perforce was based on Mr. Chen's own subjective assessment, all the evidence was consistent in supporting his own contention that his treatment had been successful.

Further Follow-up Evaluations: Almost three weeks after this first follow-up visit, I saw Mr. Chen again at the *tâng-ki*'s shrine. He looked much the same as when we first met: restless, quite anxious, and preoccupied with his troubles. Although he reported feeling well, he also admitted he still occasionally suffered from discomforting feelings of tension in his chest, along with fatigue and malaise. He remained worried about his business. (To me he seemed a good deal more troubled than at our first follow-up visit.) He told me he came to the shrine almost every night. As soon as he arrived, he felt better: calmer and less tense. By 11:00 p.m., when he arrived home, he was able to go directly to sleep and slept soundly until his usual time for awaking. Mr. Chen told me that though his anxious feelings still occasionally returned, they were less severe than before. Moreover, by concentrating on the shrine and "filling my mind with things concerning the shrine," Mr. Chen claimed to be able to exert some self-control over these daytime bouts of anxiety. He felt especially "good" and even "happy," when he was able to trance and jump about at the shrine in the evenings. His wife encouraged him to go to the shrine regularly because he seemed to be better after he returned home, whereas he got worse if he failed to go to the shrine, and if he delayed departing for the shrine, he would feel a strong urge to go. He reported no significant change in his business. During the day he now saw much more of those neighbors who also attended the shrine.

One week previously the shrine's congregation had made another pilgrimage to a shrine in the south of Taiwan. Mr. Chen accompanied them. Before they departed, he felt a painful lump in his throat, and had difficulty swallowing. He also had a night cough. His feeling of tension returned and was quite severe. He was deeply concerned about his health again. He bought both Chinese and Western medicine, which the pharmacists prescribed for his symptoms, but neither was effective. He somewhat reluctantly told the _tâng-ki_ about the recurrence of his problem. This was the first time he had formally consulted the _tâng-ki_ since his first visit. The _tâng-ki_ replied that the god was testing Mr. Chen's patience. He told him: "After you are able to trance and jump regularly, which you are not yet able to do, you will get better." During the trip to the south, the _tâng-ki_, his chief male assistant, and some of Mr. Chen's neighbors who belong to the cult spent much time with him. The evening they returned (four days before this interview), Mr. Chen's physical symptoms disappeared, though he remained anxious.

Before going on this two-day pilgrimage, Mr. Chen's business had become very active. He felt under much pressure to finish his work; moreover, he wanted to finish it before he left on the journey. At the last moment, he almost decided not to go. But his friends and neighbors persuaded him. They told him the pilgrimage was more important for him than his work, which he could finish after he returned. His wife supported this view. At the shrine they visited, Mr. Chen did not trance, but he felt less tense. Indeed, he told us he had had "a good time" on the trip.

During this interview, I was impressed by the obviously high level of Mr. Chen's anxiety, this time in the absence of physical complaints. Unlike the previous follow-up visit, he sat in the shrine without closing his eyes and meditating. He exhibited no signs of trance. Instead, he constantly looked around to gaze momentarily at different people, occasionally took a nervous glance at his watch, and, on the whole, revealed himself to be quite uneasy and easily distracted. Although he did not formally consult the *tâng-ki*, he spoke with him from time to time when he was not in his healing trance. The chief male assistant sat by Mr. Chen's side for most of the evening, talking slowly, occasionally smiling in a relaxed and easy-going style which contrasted sharply with Mr. Chen's behavior. Although no special attention was focused on Mr. Chen, members of the cult frequently stopped to ask him how he felt, offered encouraging words, and stayed to talk with him if he showed a desire to do so. Finally at 10:30 p.m. he closed his eyes, meditated, and seemed to sleep for a few minutes. Just before he departed, Mr. Chen rose and shook hands with the *tâng-ki* and his chief male assistant. He seemed less anxious than earlier in the evening, laughed aloud at a funny story the *tâng-ki* told those around him, and warmly exchanged formal words of courtesy as he left. To my mind, Mr. Chen was suffering a recurrence and being treated for it.

Three months later, we again interviewed Mr. Chen at the shrine. This was the evening of a local festival celebrating the birthday of one of the shrine's gods. About 100 people crowded into the shrine and presented offerings of food to the god. It was noisy. Many people, in trance, were jumping about. There was much socializing going on.

Mr. Chen was with his wife and their youngest child. He told us emphatically that he no longer suffered from an illness. At times he still got a sensation in his chest, but it only lasted for a few moments. His business had been doing well. Outwardly he showed no anxiety. He smiled easily, and he talked to me at length with considerable competence and ease. He did not point to or rub his chest. He was quite well-dressed and appeared (just as he purported to feel) prosperous and happy. His wife, who also seemed unconcerned, agreed with her husband's statements about himself. Later in the evening, Mr. Chen went into a trance while sitting on a stool: He rapidly turned his head from side to side, with his eyes and mouth closed and with both hands slapping his thighs. This lasted for about five minutes. He did not get up and jump or sing with the many other cult members who did so throughout the shrine. After coming out of his trance, his face was covered with sweat, and he smiled broadly at his three-year-old son. From what I could gather from Mr. Chen, his wife, and others at the shrine, he had been free of signs and symptoms of anxiety for several months and also had not complained of physical discomfort.

One month later, several days before I left Taiwan, I paid a final visit to this shrine. Again, it was the time of a festival. There was much noise and excitement. Most of the *tâng-ki*'s cult were present, as were some of their families, well over one hundred people. Mr. Chen appeared much as he had at our last meeting. He was relaxed and obviously enjoying himself. I did not observe any signs of anxiety, and he neither reported those nor physical complaints to me. He told me he felt well. He reaffirmed that his old illness, "neurasthenia" he called it, was no longer a problem. Indeed, from the time of our last encounter until now, he had experienced no difficulties at all. He had become an active member of the cult, and was assisting with the moving of furniture and ritual objects. Mr. Chen was now part of the shrine's "therapeutic milieu." He even talked with several new clients, offered them support, and, in one instance, told his own story as an example of the chief god's efficacy. He spoke as if his problem had long since ceased to trouble him. With this new client, he talked of his "new life" as a member and contrasted it with the sufferings of his former existence in the "sea of bitterness." Everyone around him agreed that Mr. Chen had indeed been cured. I wanted to question him at length, but he told me he was embarrassed to talk about "bad things" when things were now so "good" with him, his family, and his business. And he reminded me talking of such things could tempt fate, anger the god, and thereby induce a change in fortune. At that moment the *tâng-ki* came by and told us: "Is it not enough Mr. Chen is well? Must you trouble him more? He is cured! The god cured him. What more do you need to know?" Neither he nor Mr. Chen would answer any further questions. My research assistant performed a seven-month follow-up visit, at which time she found Mr. Chen to be unchanged. He was, and had been through this time, free of somatic complaints. He did not appear anxious and denied experiencing any acute anxiety attacks. Mr. Chen was still an active member of the *tâng-ki*'s cult.

Our last follow-up evaluation of Mr. Chen took place two years after his initial visit to the shrine. By that time he had become an important and much respected member of the *tâng-ki*'s cult, assisting the *tâng-ki* in treating patients who attended the shrine, especially Hakka patients. He entered into trance nightly, singing and dancing and jumping, and had almost as much authority as a healer as did the _tâng-ki_'s chief female assistant. From what my research assistant could learn, Mr. Chen appeared to be free of his former symptoms.

COMMENTS

The follow-up cases I have reported illustrate the many difficulties surrounding cross-cultural evaluations of treatment outcome. First, field studies of indigenous forms of clinical care place certain constraints on the analytic tools the researcher can use to evaluate illnesses and treatment responses. It would have been helpful in these cases to have carried out our own physical examinations, given certain psychological tests, and reviewed X-rays, EKGs, and blood test results, but none of this was feasible. On the other hand, studies that have attempted to do this have drastically altered the treatment situation, so that what they ended up studying was not actual indigenous practice. Second, as I have pointed out, almost all anthropological assessments of therapeutic efficacy dispense with follow-ups entirely and rely simply on the subjective report of the patient, almost immediately after he is treated, or on the ethnographer's independent judgment. Both approaches are inadequate. Anthropologists usually do not possess the training to make such assessments (and when they make them usually fail to specify how these assessments were made). Treatment outcome simply cannot be evaluated immediately after treatment since, for reasons already mentioned, most patients are constrained to affirm at least some level of therapeutic success while they are still in the treatment setting. And such assessments give no sense of the effect over time. Furthermore, in most situations it remains unclear what sickness is being treated. Obviously, a chronic recurrent illness, like Mr. Chen's disorder, needs to be studied for a considerable period of time to be certain of the nature of the problem and to examine the effect of therapy on its course and to rule out spontaneous remissions.

To make much of a single case, or a single series of cases, is particularly dangerous. Although Mr. Chen's case is one of many I have followed in a similar way, generalizations based

352

on independent cases (even a fairly large number of them) can be quite misleading since strong bias operates in indigenous treatment settings to select unrepresentative cases—those with more impressive illness manifestations, dramatic treatments, and immediate response. This is why consecutive or randomly selected cases need to be studied. Retrospective studies (which make up much of the literature) are notoriously unreliable, but even prospective evaluations, such as in Mr. Chen's case and the others recorded, can be unreliable because there are so many important variables that are difficult to control: type of disease, severity, type and magnitude of illness problems, intercurrent stress, prior treatment, concomitant treatment by other kinds of practitioners, etc. If comparisons are to be made with other types of treatment, patients clearly must be carefully matched. And, of course, there is a strong observer bias. Almost everything in the treatment setting encourages the researcher, like the patient, to affirm the success (even in quite limited terms) of treatment.

These problems usually make it impossible to carry out rigorous studies of indigenous healing that are comparable to the best studies of treatment outcomes in modern medical settings both in the United States and elsewhere in the West (Frank 1974b; Luborsky et al. 1975; White et al. 1961; White 1973). In Taiwan, such scientifically rigorous studies can be carried out at the National Taiwan University Hospital's Outpatient Psychiatry Clinic, where only a small fraction of cases are treated, but not in shamans' shrines, fortune-tellers' offices, and *ch'ien* interpreters' temples, where the great majority of cases are treated. When the treatment intervention is psychotherapy (modern or traditional), the problem of determining outcome even in a modern treatment setting is, of course, considerable (Frank 1974b; Luborsky et al. 1975). All of which leads me to argue, not against doing such studies, but for recognition of their serious limitations. For example, in the follow-up study of twelve consecutive cases, our results were almost certainly skewed toward more positive evaluations of treatment, as I mentioned, because we were unable to complete follow-up with seven cases, three of whom refused follow-up. It is reasonable to assume for these three cases that their evaluations were not positive. It has been my general experience, moreover, that patients treated by indigenous practitioners tend to resist follow-up interviews much more than do patients studied in Western medical practice. Research fits better (although not always very well) with the expectations of patients treated by modern professional medical practitioners than with those who seek indigenous treatment, especially sacred, temple-based treatment. I have already pointed to some of the difficulties resulting from subjective patient evaluations of the efficacy of healing. Different criteria for evaluating treatment are used, and these in turn differ from those used by practitioners and the researcher.

These concerns make it necessary to confront a vexing yet basic question: What is healing? Clearly, it is a somewhat different thing for patient (and perhaps family), practitioner, and researcher. Indigenous practitioners in Taiwan believe most cases are successfully treated, since few return for treatment, and they believe failure to return is a likely sign of treatment success. This runs directly counter to the popular patient viewpoint that you don't return to the same practitioner if you derive no therapeutic benefit. For the practitioner, as was discussed, treatment may be directed at the female family member(s) who usually accompanies the patient or who comes with the illness problem of someone else in the family. Hence, successful treatment in part means success in treating the female family member(s), rather than the sick person. By the sacred folk healer's explanatory model, illness may be due to bad fate or possession either directly causing sickness or interfering with treatment. Therefore, successful treatment means appropriately treating the fate or expelling the god or ghost possessing the client, which should lead to symptom relief (in his theory), but at times (for various reasons that he can list) does not. In such a case, the *tâng-ki* may claim partial or complete cure even in the absence of symptom change, although he will either predict such a change for the future or explain that another problem has been encountered that first must be "cured." Practitioners of shamanistic and other temple-based healing in Taiwan are usually quite clever at explaining therapeutic failure in such a way as not to imply that their gods' healing powers have been inadequate. Chinese-style doctors use the pulse both to diagnose illness and to evaluate if the patient has re-

turned to a harmonious state of bodily functioning. They sometimes will tell patients who feel entirely better that they are still
ill, since the underlying problem has not been completely
treated. I have seen Chinese-style doctors tell patients that
even though their symptoms have not "yet" improved, their
pulse indicated treatment had been effective. Of course, this
very same process occurs all the time in Western medicine,
where the physician may attribute cure or improvement to
measured changes in blood chemistry and other physiological
measures of the body in the absence of overt clinical signs of
improvement. For patients, these discrepant practitioner assessments may present significant problems that cause them
to leave treatment or fail to comply; but many seem to accept
these views as part of the medical mystique, the medical expert's special understanding of the problem and its treatment.
In the terms of our theoretical framework, this is an example
of the EM entailed by the social structural position of the practitioner in the health care system providing criteria for the evaluation of therapeutic outcome determined by the beliefs and
values that EM represents. Obviously this can lead to significant conflicts in the evaluation of therapeutic efficacy.

Similarly, for the shaman, symptom relief in the absence of
complete ritual treatment to expel an evil spirit or, for the
Chinese-style doctor, symptom relief in the absence of a return
to harmonious balance of *yin/yang*, hot/cold, or the five elements may not be cure, no matter what the patient says. But
these niceties usually are explained only to the researcher,
because for most indigenous practitioners resolving the chief
psychosocial issues constituting the illness experience is the
central task of care.

Treatment, we remarked above, can be directed at either or
both aspects of a given health problem: the *disease* or the *illness*.
Seen from this perspective, either or both may be successfully
treated. Problems in clinical care seem to arise when the practitioner is concerned only with "curing" the *disease*, and the
patient is searching for "healing" the *illness*. Indigenous folk
practitioners in Taiwan seem to be generally more sensitive
than Western-style doctors to treating *illness*, especially the
personal and social problems it gives rise to. From the perspective of the Western medical profession in Taiwan, indig-

enous healers are viewed as dangerous, however, because they cannot define the *disease* in scientific terms and fail to treat it, which could have potentially disastrous results for patients. And our follow-up study suggests that this is precisely why indigenous healing fails with certain patients, albeit a small number.

From the patient perspective, however, disease and illness are usually not distinguished. Most of the time patients are concerned with symptom relief together with treatment of psychosocial problems produced by the stress of illness. For most patients this includes a need for explanations of their health problems that are personally and socially meaningful and that usually requires that the practitioner explain the illness. Indigenous practitioners (especially sacred folk practitioners) in Taiwan seem to be remarkably skilled at giving meaning to the experience of illness and, through that and other means, producing a behavioral and experiential impact, whether they change symptoms or not. Western-style doctors, both in Taiwan and the West, seem to have considerable difficulty in doing this. Part of the problem may be that indigenous practitioners are better at eliciting patient views of the nature and significance of their problems, the nub of which often concern this very issue, whereas Western-style doctors perform this clinical task quite poorly, when they do it at all. But as we shall see there is more to the problem than this.

For the researcher, the disease/illness dichotomy creates a special difficulty. Which aspect of sickness does he study? When he evaluates outcome is it the "curing" of disease or the "healing" of illness or both? Most anthropological writing is unclear on this point. But so is most medical and psychiatric writing. I contend that future research should evaluate both the efficacy of treating disease and the efficacy of treating illness. This would represent a major contribution from anthropological field work, and almost certainly would substantially alter our understanding of therapeutic efficacy.

Thus far we have observed why the question of healing (and its evaluation) is so complex. The cross-cultural perspective highlights the difficulties. In concluding this section, I shall return to Mr. Chen's case and the other cases we followed in order to examine in detail some of the problems we heretofore have discussed only in general terms.

From a psychiatric perspective, Mr. Chen's disorder—his anxiety neurosis—was chronic with recurrent acute episodes. Therefore, there were times when it was quiescent and times when it was fulminant. Then what do we make of our evaluations of his treatment? At the time of our first formal evaluation, five days after the initial treatment in the shrine and three days after the apparently definitive treatment (as Mr. Chen described it) and while he was still receiving therapy, both Mr. Chen's subjective evaluation and our objective evaluation pointed to a significant therapeutic response. Were this our only follow-up, we no doubt would have been tempted to evaluate Mr. Chen's therapy as entirely effective: Mr. Chen seemed to be cured of his somatic and psychological symptoms. But three weeks later, his status was much as it was at the time of our initial evaluation. Was this due to incomplete therapeutic effect, the natural course of a chronic disease with periodic remissions and exacerbations, or an acute decompensation owing to specific psychosocial stress, in which the chronic disease played a minor role and still might be regarded as improved since he had psychological symptoms without somatization? This is a problem for clinical judgment. But the evidence suggests that, whereas the shaman's treatment may well have played a significant role in Mr. Chen's rapid recovery from the acute anxiety reaction he was suffering from initially (though this also may have been part of the waxing and waning course of his illness), the return of acute anxiety three weeks later was most likely an acute recurrence of his disease. That is, seen from the vantage of three weeks of therapy, the chronic course of Mr. Chen's disease seemed unaffected by treatment, though once again we have some evidence to support the claim that treatment in the shrine had at least partially ameliorated another acute episode (by having an effect on somatization). Our evaluations at three-month, five-month, seven-month, and two-year intervals were consistent with therapeutic success, because Mr. Chen was asymptomatic and without significant signs of anxiety. But could we make such an assessment and be sure that what we were seeing was not simply the course of his disease, which merely had not produced an acute recurrence yet? This is a difficult question that might be answered by subsequent follow-ups, although some patients with this disorder can go years between acute episodes, but even they usually demonstrate significant levels of anxiety in the interictal period. Thus, Mr. Chen seemed to have had a therapeutic effect, but we cannot be entirely sure.

From Mr. Chen's perspective and that of his wife, older children, and friends, there was absolute certainty that he had been cured by the time of our last four follow-up visits. Mr. Chen was convinced that he was cured at the time of our first follow-up visit. In fact, even when his symptoms recurred and his treatment became more active, he felt that he was essentially cured but that (as the *tâng-ki* suggested) the god was testing him as part of a final trial before his sickness would disappear entirely. The *tâng-ki*'s view also followed this line of reasoning. Mr. Chen's wife's concern on one occasion that he continue taking his medicine and the approach of the *tâng-ki*'s chief male assistant (who knew Mr. Chen much better than did the *tâng-ki*), who gave him a kind of supportive psychotherapy focused on reducing his anxiety, both suggested a realization that Mr. Chen was suffering from a chronic sickness or constitutional tendency that had to be kept in check by continued treatment. In fact, some cult members described Mr. Chen's anxious personality as part of his long-term problem. And in this respect too, the *tâng-ki*'s advice that he must return to the shrine regularly was a sign of the recognition of the need for chronic care. Mr. Chen himself seemed to adopt this view at the time of our second follow-up visit, when he explained to us how evening visits to the shrine were able to relieve anxiety building up over the course of the day.

But a major discrepancy remains. Mr. Chen and the *tâng-ki* were convinced his disorder has been cured. I am not convinced and suspect that treatment may not have altered the chronic course of his disease, as it is defined by my psychiatric explanatory model. (But I do read the clinical evidence as suggestive that treatment in the shrine did have an effect on the acute episodes of anxiety Mr. Chen experienced.) Was Mr. Chen cured? The *tâng-ki* and Mr. Chen say: yes. I am tempted to say: perhaps not. The question again turns on what is meant by cure. Mr. Chen's symptoms went away, his chronic anxiety appeared to be controlled, and he had received and incorporated a personally and socially meaningful explanation of his illness. By the definition of "healing" I gave above, he was effectively treated. In this sense, it does not matter if cure has been brought about by the shrine or a non-specific placebo effect or natural course of the disorder. Put differently, Mr. Chen's *illness* has been successfully treated, but not his *disease*—at least not yet. My prediction is that his symptoms will recur. But I also predict that they will go away again, as in the past, but perhaps more rapidly than in the past while he is treated at the *tâng-ki's* shrine. The acute illness will continue to recur (and remit) as long as the chronic disease exists.[4] But to demand evidence in support of the successful resolution of the disease may be quite unfair, because even with appropriate modern psychiatric care (tranquilizers plus psychotherapy) it is also unlikely the disease would entirely disappear.

This viewpoint leads onto treacherous ground. Anxiety neurosis is not an entity but an explanatory model. Within the medical explanatory model I employ, it makes sense to talk of it in terms of sickness and healing. These terms also seem appropriate because they are used by Mr. Chen, his family and friends, the shaman, and the other indigenous and Western practitioners Mr. Chen consulted. That is, they make cultural sense. But I could employ other explanatory models from whose perspective these terms do not make sense. This would be true of the explanatory model of social deviance, which would view Mr. Chen as undergoing societal labeling for a non-medical deviance as part of a process of social control; it also would be true of the explanatory model of existential psychiatry, which would see Mr. Chen's problem as a life-problem, not a disease or an illness. Behavior therapy's explanatory model might or might not regard this as a disease/illness but could look at it simply as an example of conditioned dysfunctional behavior requiring extinction. Other field workers, such

4. A three-year follow-up by me in the summer of 1978 confirmed these predictions. Although Mr. Chen appeared unchanged from our two-year follow-up, he admitted that every few months he would experience a slight recurrence of his former symptoms. However, after trancing in the shrine these complaints would rapidly come under control. He demonstrated no significant anxiety, but rather heightened self-assurance and self-competence. Mr. Chen obtained obvious pleasure from his leading role in the cult and from the sense of personal efficacy that resulted from mastering his anxiety and playing a therapeutic role in the shrine.

as anthropologists not concerned with medical issues, might use EMs that study Mr. Chen solely in terms of change in social role and status. Finally, a different popular cultural explanatory model in Taiwan might regard Mr. Chen as suffering from sin, not illness, and obviously, in other cultures, other popular explanatory models might view his problem in still different ways.

As with sickness, so with healing. It only makes sense to talk of healing from the perspective of certain explanatory models. Even when this concept is used, it can be, as we have seen, one thing in one model and something quite distinct in another. From the theory advanced in this book, healing on the cultural level is not so much a result of the healer's efforts as a condition of experiencing a fit between socially legitimated forms of illness and care within the cultural context of the health care system. Cultural healing is a necessary activity that occurs to the patient, and his family and social nexus, regardless of whether the patient's disorder is affected or not, as long as the sanctioned cultural fit is established. The health care system provides psychosocial and cultural treatment (and efficacy) for the illness by naming and ordering the experience of illness, providing meaning for that experience, and treating the personal, family, and social problems that constitute the illness. Thus, it "heals" the illness, even if it is unable to effectively "cure" the disease. In Mr. Chen's case, we see this very thing happening.

Let us offer a provisional and seemingly paradoxical conclusion: Mr. Chen's disease was not effectively treated; Mr. Chen's illness was effectively treated. Mr. Chen's health care system, not the shaman and not his shrine, was responsible for that efficacy. That is, Mr. Chen's illness was healed by the cultural construction of clinical reality. In that sense, the shaman and his shrine cannot do anything but heal Mr. Chen's illness and the illnesses of others like him, who are prepared to participate fully in the cultural reality of the shrine and accept its explanatory models and whose personal and social problems are effectively dealt with there. The same holds for patients who actively and fully participate in the cultural reality of any form of clinical practice (indigenous or modern) in which their illness is treated by the provision of personal and social meaning for the illness experience and the clinical resolution of personal and social problems constituting illness as a human experience. It is striking to realize, however, that this kind of cultural healing is *least likely* to occur in the health care institutions of modern professional medicine, whose clinical reality is so constructed as to discourage this most traditional type of healing of illness from happening, at the same time that it strives to maximize effective treatment of disease.

It is also essential to recognize that, just as healing can be studied on the social and cultural level, it can and must be studied on behavioral and physiological levels as well. Healing may occur on any or all of these analytic levels, and evaluations of therapeutic efficacy should take each of these into account.

Why do indigenous practitioners successfully heal?

Based upon the material presented, I draw the perhaps surprising conclusion that in most cases indigenous practitioners must heal. Why? As we have seen, indigenous practitioners primarily treat three types of disorders: (1) acute, self-limited (naturally remitting) diseases; (2) non-life threatening, chronic diseases in which management of illness (psychosocial and cultural) problems is a larger component of clinical management than biomedical treatment of the disease; and (3) secondary somatic manifestations (somatization) of minor psychological disorders and interpersonal problems. The treatment of disease plays a small role in the care of these disorders. Therapeutic efficacy for these problems is principally a function of the treatment of the psychosocial and cultural aspects of the illness. The indigenous practitioner usually (but not always) is exceptionally well poised to maximize psychosocial and cultural treatment of the illness. He may not be competent in most cases to control severe, acute diseases effectively. In our sample of twelve cases treated by the *tâng-ki* who treated Mr. Chen, only the two cases of severe, acute physiological and psychological diseases led to negative evaluations of indigenous treatment by patients and families. Of the six patients treated by another *tâng-ki*, none suffered from severe, acute disease, and none evaluated the care as ineffective. From our standpoint, the case of the patient with progressively worsening congestive heart failure in the first series of cases is an example of ineffective

361

indigenous treatment, regardless of the patient's positive evaluation of the treatment. The cases of infants with infectious diseases who were being treated both by indigenous and modern professional practitioners suggest that families in Taiwan are quite sensitive to this issue. They go to Western-style doctors for the control of potentially life-threatening diseases, diseases that Western medicine is particularly effective in treating, and to *tâng-ki*s for personally and culturally meaningful treatment of illnesses. They do not go to Western-style doctors for the treatment of "fright," which is a cultural illness, but to practitioners who are poised to apply the culturally sanctioned treatment for that illness.

What we have said is not meant to imply that indigenous therapy is ineffective against all severe, acute and chronic diseases. In fact, it may exert placebo or direct effect upon such diseases. For example, in the case of Mr. Chen, the therapeutic milieu of the *tâng-ki*'s shrine may have provided him with effective psychotherapy, not only for the treatment of his illness, but perhaps also for his underlying disease. We know that different forms of psychotherapy seem to work for a wide range of mental disorders (Luborsky et al. 1975). The universal therapeutic components of psychotherapy (Frank 1974b) seem to be present in many modern and traditional forms of healing (Tseng 1976). Thus, there is much in favor of the argument that indigenous forms of psychotherapy may effectively treat certain psychological (and perhaps also psychophysiological) diseases. Moreover, recent research on the physiological effects of meditation, behavior therapies, biofeedback, and placebos suggests a number of different ways by which indigenous therapies may affect biologically based diseases. The epidemiological web causing and sustaining physiological diseases not infrequently includes key psychosocial factors; indigenous healing may at times work to affect such diseases by altering those factors. And, in the Chinese case, certain (though usually quite few) of the medicines used by indigenous healers (e.g., ephedrine) are pharmacologically active agents that have a specific effect on physiological processes.

But our argument is that providing effective treatment for disease is *not* the chief reason why indigenous practitioners heal. To the extent that they provide culturally legitimated treatment of illness, they *must* heal.

The equally surprising corollary of this argument is that in most cases modern professional clinical care *must* fail to heal. Why? Because most of primary care in general medical practice is made up of the same types of disorders found in indigenous practice (Stoeckle et al. 1964). Thus, the majority of cases require successful treatment of illness for there to be therapeutic efficacy. But the modern professional practitioner is trained to ignore illness systematically as part of his exclusive interest in the recognition and treatment of disease. He is taught to *cure*, not *to care* (Eisenberg 1976). This profound distortion of clinical work is built into the biomedical training of physicians. It succeeds in the application of biomedical technology to control disease, a less common but crucial clinical function, while it founders on the psychosocial and cultural treatment of illness, which is a much more common clinical function. Failure to heal illness is not articulated in the health professional's system of evaluating the efficacy of healing but is articulated in patient non-compliance and dissatisfaction, subsequent use of alternative health care facilities, poor and inadequate care, and medical-legal suits.

The fact that many primary care physicians do heal most of the time is a function of their clinical skills in treating illness as well as disease, by which they overcome the profound limitations and distortions of the biomedical approach dominating modern health care. What is needed in modern health care systems, in developing and developed societies, is systematic recognition and treatment of psychosocial and cultural features of illness. That calls for a fundamental reconceptualization of clinical care and restructuring of clinical practice. If appropriately trained, the modern health professional (not necessarily a physician) can effectively and systematically treat both disease and illness, whereas, in many instances, indigenous healers can neither systematically nor effectively diagnose and treat disease.

A mechanism by which social and cultural context
mediates the healing process

The habitual (and frequently unproductive) way researchers try to make sense of healing, especially indigenous healing, is by speculating about psychological and physiological mechanisms of therapeutic action, which then are applied to case material in a truly Procrustean fashion that fits the particular instance to putative universal principles. The latter are primarily derived from the concepts of biomedicine and individual psychology. There are a number of large problems associated with this tactic. It opens up a Pandora's box of explanations of potential mechanisms of healing but does not provide a method to decide which, if any, are applicable to a given therapeutic approach. Since healing, like all human behavior, is overdetermined, this type of analysis produces considerable confusion and makes a shambles of comparisons. Second, it pays insignificant attention to social and cultural processes as compared with biological and psychological processes. Since the argument of this book is that the health care system transmits and expresses the effects of cultural meanings and social structural arrangements on physiological and psychological processes, such an analysis is useless for making sense of healing as a *function of* health care systems and for understanding the role of social and cultural forces in the healing process. By reducing healing to the language of biology, the human aspects (i.e., psychosocial and cultural significance) of healing are removed, leaving behind something that can be expressed in biomedical terms, but can hardly be called healing. Even reducing healing to the language of behavior, which is the ploy of many psychological and psychiatric investigators, leaves out the language of experience, which, as we have seen in this chapter, is a major aspect of healing. Furthermore, it is the *relationships* between different analytic levels (i.e., cultural, social, psychological, physiological) that are of special significance for understanding the healing process and for making cross-cultural comparisons, yet these crucial interactions are precisely what the reductionistic approach to healing avoids.

Sickness is best regarded as semantic networks (culturally articulated systems) that interrelate cognitive categories, personal experiences, physiological states, and social relationships. Healing, viewed from that perspective, involves the same semantic networks. Biomedical and psychiatric reductions make it impossible to study healing from this cultural standpoint. In the preceding section of this chapter, we analyzed the major means by which indigenous healers in Taiwan successfully heal from within our model of sickness and healing as a cultural system. In so doing, I believe we gained a broader and more inclusive appreciation of the healing process. In this final section, I shall attempt to deepen that appreciation by examining a social and cultural mechanism that appears to mediate healing. Future studies might attempt to delineate significant similarities and differences between this therapeutic mechanism and those found in other treatment settings in other health care systems.

Healing through the provision of culturally constituted and socially sanctioned behavioral models and symbolic meanings

Much of the necessarily disguised psychotherapeutic treatment in the *tâng-kis'* shrines we have studied would seem to work by providing behavioral and explanatory (experiential) models, strongly legitimated by the shrines' culturally constructed and socially mediated clinical reality, that are the opposite of those maladaptive and malfunctioning ones previously held by Mr. Chen and other patients. The switch in models and metaphors is from negatively valued, anxiety-laden ones to positively valued, adaptive ones reflecting personal mastery over anxious feelings, along with control of related behavioral and physiological manifestations and rise in social status. For example, the calm, sure, unflappable behavior of the *tâng-ki's* chief male assistant was the virtual opposite of the anxiety-ridden behavior afflicting Mr. Chen. And Mr. Chen's improvement would seem to involve modeling his behavior on that of the Buddha-like chief male assistant, who often was able to calm him during several hours in the shrine. This is a straightforward example of social learning reinforced by the behavior of other cult members toward Mr. Chen, which also aimed at assuaging his anxiety, and by the higher social status he gained as he moved up the social hierarchy in the shrine. The methods of anxiety management operating in the shrine included the following: sitting quietly and meditating; talking calmly with others and receiving their support; focusing attention away from intrapsychic and interpersonal concerns on to somatic complaints, cosmological causes, and other "external" issues, including displacement of interest to the shrine's activities and the behaviors and problems of others; trance with sanctioned release of strong (and frequently dysphoric) affects without subsequent memory or responsibility for them; and, ultimately, full membership in the cult with concomitant rise in social status and self-esteem. Since anxiety, in one or another form, is perhaps the most common problem affecting clients of indigenous practitioners (even if it is usually secondary to sickness or other problems), these methods for coping with anxiety are frequently resorted to and are of considerable importance in indigenous treatment in Taiwan, and doubtlessly in most other societies. Providing personally and socially meaningful explanatory models for sickness and its treatment, as we saw in Mr. Chen's therapy, is effective, at least in part, because such EMs help reduce anxiety and related dysphoric affects that are generated as the psychosocial (in our terminology, "illness") problems of sickness.

This mechanism might operate in the following way. Individuals with minimal somatic symptoms, it is now recognized, will label those symptoms as sickness under conditions of psychosocial stress associated with the induction of significant anxiety. In many, if not most, cases these symptoms are nonspecific, minimal, and transient. They do not bespeak serious disease. Indeed, where individuals perceive some psychological or social reward from occupying a sanctioned sick role, these symptoms represent illness in the absence of disease. Therapeutic response in these cases obviously will follow upon removal of the psychosocial stressor and reduction in anxiety. Much the same happens where somatic symptoms reflect tensions in interpersonal (family, friendship, job, community) relationships. In such cases, which I would contend make up by far the largest single category of health problems treated by practitioners of all kinds, treatment of the secondary anxiety state is responsible either for actual symptom change or for change in perception of symptoms to the degree that they are no longer labeled as sickness and seen as a threat. For such cases we would expect the social and cultural healing mechanism we are describing to be a powerful and perhaps specific treatment intervention. It is probable that this mechanism is also commonly at work in family-based care and in popular health care generally. If so, it is in the best interests of society and its practitioners to see this type of healing mechanism rationalized and properly used. It represents the most appropriate treatment for many patients, a large number of whom will otherwise end up in professional care, where they are viewed as an unnecessary burden on limited facilities and where the care they receive may lack this specific treatment mechanism.

It is now also recognized that reduction in patients' anxiety and related dysphoric affects is an important determinant in the successful treatment of many physiological and psychophysiological problems. In this way, this mechanism can play a role in curing disease. We can similarly hypothesize that it should contribute importantly to the placebo response, which, it has been argued, involves the establishment of a context of meaning that supports expectant faith in the efficacy of a therapeutic agent (Brody 1977). Obviously, it will have particular significance in the management of psychological disorders. In social terms, these culturally constructed adaptive models transform deviance into socially accepted and approved behavior; hence, they play a potentially crucial role in societal management of deviance, as the collective experience of the cult members with hysteria described above seems to document. Such a therapeutic mechanism, then, can affect disordered biological, psychological, and social levels of experience singly or in concert.

Returning to the treatment of Mr. Chen in order to spell out more fully how this mechanism works, we saw that the *tâng-ki* offered a behavioral model of effective power which contrasted sharply and, we would argue, "therapeutically," with Mr. Chen's feelings of inferiority, incompetence, ineffectiveness. That model was further reinforced because it was sanctioned as the shrine's Confucian behavioral paradigm. It was how the "master" of the shrine behaved toward his "disciples," and it symbolized ideal father-son, teacher-student, superior person-inferior person, healer-patient relationships. It was how cult members, such as the chief female assistant—who themselves have been successfully healed—behaved. It was both a model for Mr. Chen and a promise that he, too, would be like them. Much of Chinese culture is concerned, not with the provision of specific rules to govern behavior, but rather with paradigmatic exemplars of appropriate (moral, wise, successful, effective, etc.) behavior. Membership in the cult included learning how to demonstrate and articulate these virtues. That some of the cult members were Mr. Chen's close friends and neighbors and that key ones were members of the Hakka minority to which he belonged could be expected to enhance the power and relevance of the shrine's Confucian behavioral models and the morally articulated affective responses they engender.

Mr. Chen's possessing god was the chief god of the temple, a god known for his power as a healer and described by terms such as "strong," "powerful," "effective." These were the very qualities that Mr. Chen questioned in himself and about which he was most anxious. Here we find a form of metaphoric balancing used therapeutically. Mr. Chen eventually took up some of this terminology. Although he himself never indulged in symbolic associations or pointed to the symbolic aspects of his care, he referred to himself as the god. He spoke of the shrine as "beautiful," "safe," and "good," compared with the world outside ("the sea of bitterness"). For Mr. Chen, on the level of cosmological metaphor, his illness was due to the fact that the god had been troubling him (haunting him, causing bad fate, etc.) in order to get him to become his disciple. That is, the god wanted Mr. Chen to allow him (the god) to possess him. Treatment, or healing, in this idiom meant being possessed by, or becoming, the god. Mr. Chen, anxious, with feelings of inferiority and fears of being incompetent or a failure, was healed (on the level of this cosmological metaphor) by becoming the god who possessed qualities of competence, efficacy, and superiority that precisely balanced his psychological deficiencies and that he desired to possess. In this sense, and in this sense alone, he was provided with a symbolic language that employed a vocabulary of the emotions that opposed his present conditon (illness) and represented an ideal state (health). Treatment (healing) meant movement from his present condition *toward* the ideal condition, from his present behavior toward the ideal behavior personified by the god, from the symbolism of the former to the symbolism of the latter. This fit—even though it was not expressly recognized by Mr. Chen nor stated in such terms in the shrine—with what actually happened (at least from my perspective) and with what was viewed as salient in the treatment (being possessed). It does not suggest some mystical mechanism of symbolic action but a simple behavioral modeling scheme that we can explain in the language of behavioral science, and it involves symbolic forms applied within a traditionally sanctioned Chinese cultural model: Confucian paradigms of moral and successful men who should be copied.

It obviously gained additional persuasive force from group support and a change in social status from personally disvalued sick role to socially valued cult role. What is remarkable about this process is that it was a psychological and social therapy aimed at psychological and social problems in a setting in which the only sanctioned overt terminology for labeling and treating the problem was somatic. Thus, it was a therapeutic model that could not be explicitly acknowledged in the shrine, even if it was tacitly recognized and used as such. But given the realities of Chinese culture—where psychological problems are stigmatized and where their treatment routinely involves deflection into somatic complaints, sanctioned dissociative behavior, and the like—we would expect that indigenous psychological treatments (and to some degree social therapy as well) would have to work in similarly disguised forms if they were to function at all. What we have here, then, is an illness episode in which a primary psychological and social problem presented as a somatic problem, and that somatic manifestation, a symbolic representation if you will, was treated directly, while indirectly the psychological and social issues were treated via a symbolic therapy that did not recognize them as such and, therefore, avoided stigmatizing the patient.

Could this indeed have happened? If it was at work, it had a strong cultural precedent in Chinese systems of healing. Much of Chinese food, diet, and herbal therapies have to do with balancing polar opposites: yin/yang, hot/cold, etc. Together, we might regard them as a culturally sanctioned symbolic therapeutic logic to which the use of behavioral models also belongs. The danger is in pushing the concept of the effectivity of symbols too hard. If we do so in Mr. Chen's case, it reduces our hypothesis to an absurdity. Mr. Chen's condition was regarded as overly hot (symbolically hot). But he accepted neurasthenia as the name of his sickness, even though it was popularly classified as a symbolically cold disorder. Thus, anything he did to balance the former should have produced a greater imbalance in the latter and vice versa. This contradiction simply was not a problem for Mr. Chen or the cult members around him. To them it was not the logical rigor of the theory that mattered, but the use of culturally sanctioned models to name, classify, explain, and treat the disorder. Much of popular and clinical reasoning used in exigent health care problems contains, as we have seen before, illogicalities and contraditions, which neither healer nor patient would accept in a theoretical discussion, but which are applied as part of clinical handiwork because something has to be done and they seem to work.

These symbolic models unquestionably derived their therapeutic power not only from their psychological and cultural "fit," but also through their social application. They were attested to by the social group (the cult), and their acceptance was part of the group's solidarity. Much *time* was devoted to their application, as in Mr. Chen's case, and their reputed success in altering a client's behavior was announced and affirmed by the entire group. The healing rituals and relationships sanctioned the models and also sanctioned their application to the client. That application was an instance of social labeling of behavior, a point I shall elaborate below.

As was underscored earlier, the cult functioned as a "therapeutic milieu." One of its therapeutic tasks was to get Mr. Chen, and patients generally, to accept its explanations of etiology, pathophysiology, appropriate treatment, and efficacy. Mr. Chen was taught to think and act as cured, and when he so thought and acted, his cure was affirmed by the cult. Of course, tertiary socialization into the cult drew upon behavioral patterns learned in earlier socialization experiences in the family and elsewhere in the popular culture. These earlier experiences established the template for his response to the therapeutic symbols and their social application in the shrine.

The social effects of this treatment mechanism extended to Mr. Chen's marital relationship, his business and financial concerns, and his interpersonal transactions generally. It was the same with the female hysterics who had joined the cult. The behavioral and explanatory models they had acquired established new relationships and altered the characteristics of old ones. They were part of a process of social change that affected many aspects of their day-to-day life, only some of which were, strictly speaking, part of their illness behavior. This general process of sanctioned *change* in beliefs, relationships, and roles suggests just how extensive therapeutic effects frequently can be on the social level.

One other aspect of this mechanism of healing requires emphasis: cosmological and other symbolic explanatory models placed Mr. Chen's problem outside (external to) himself and fostered treatment via external manipulation. For example, the logic of systematic correspondence between microcosmic physiological and psychological processes and macrocosmic social and cosmic spheres required that harmonious balance be produced between these levels. In order to do so, the treatment of sickness could not be reduced to simply manipulating an organ lesion or behavioral deviance but required simultaneous efforts to create harmony on each of the levels believed to be involved, which translated into enforced concern for and treatment of "external" cosmological and social relationships as well as personal problems. In each instance of sickness, sacred folk treatment deflects attention from the sick person and his symptoms to his relationships in the family, community, and "hidden" cosmic order. Healing demands external manipulation of these relationships. Morita therapy, an indigenized form of modern psychotherapy in Japan, which was developed to treat somatization and culturally patterned personal and interpersonal problems such as Mr. Chen's, holds that by externalizing the problem *and* the treatment, self-centered attention fixed on the feared complaints is reduced and thereby the problems are significantly lessened (Reynolds 1976). Such "externalized" healing may exert an important effect on care-givers that leads to further therapeutic impact on patients, since care-givers learn to view the problem as no longer present once the external agent has been removed or appropriately manipulated. Thus, they learn to treat the patient as if he is no longer ill and as if he is again occupying his normal social role in spite of any residual experiential or behavioral deviance he may demonstrate. Translated into positive group support, this may well encourage adaptive behavior, while discouraging illness behavior. EMs and treatments that focus attention on the inner person as somehow responsible for the sickness and that require demonstrable internal changes before the patient is viewed as cured might exert the opposite effect: maintaining illness behavior and preventing movement away from the sick role, even in the absence of experiential and behavioral deviance. The former might be regarded as a general, if rarely recognized, strength of non-psychological formulations and treatments of psychological and interpersonal problems, while the latter might be viewed as an untoward effect of psychologically oriented care. If so, this potentially important therapeutic mechanism may be largely unavailable in modern psychiatric care. Ironically, it may still figure in general medical care in contemporary Western (psychologically oriented) societies, and, if so, might be a reason for the continuing large numbers of patients with somatization who go for treatment to general medical settings in these societies.

The therapeutic mechanism I am describing can be pictured in other terms. *Healing rituals move through three separate stages. The sickness is labeled with an appropriate and sanctioned cultural category. The label is ritually manipulated (culturally transformed). Finally a new label (cured, well) is applied and sanctioned as a meaningful symbolic form that may be independent of behavioral or social change.*

The preceding paragraphs outline the behavioral and social features of the healing process as we saw it operate in the case of Mr. Chen. Here I single out its cultural dimension in order to underscore the fact that, while healing may involve the interrelationship of all three levels, it can occur solely as a cultural event, just as it can occur as independent behavioral or social changes. Mr. Chen, and the other patients we followed, were told by the *tâng-ki* that they were suffering from a certain type of disorder. The sickness was named and its cause was stated. During the course of the healing ritual, that label was manipulated in culturally sanctioned ways: it received treatment and was eventually transformed into a new label. The new label (well, cured) was legitimated by the *tâng-ki*, the cult, and the family. That is, the externalized problem took on a special symbolic form in the shrine: first, as a sickness label; then, as a label of successful cure. It was ritually treated, external to the patient and the social interaction, on the level of meaningful symbolic forms. Healing, like illness, was defined and legitimated, within the ideology of the shrine, as a meaningful symbolic form apart from the sufferer. This is what I take Tambiah to mean by the "performative efficacy" of healing rituals (1977). The healing occurs within the set of transformed symbols sanctioned as the explanatory system in the treatment setting. Although the setting I described was sacred folk healing, much the same could and does occur in other treatment settings as I indicated in our categorization of therapeutic relationships in Chapters 7 and 8. Healing can occur in terms of the models or symbolic forms of Chinese medicine or of biomedicine, independent of behavioral and social change. But it is in the tripartite structure and movement of healing rituals that this process of "cultural healing" is most strongly sanctioned.

The nature of healing is plural. It may produce biological, behavioral, and social change. It may occur in isolation. Because of this, evaluation of healing by care-givers and by patient (and family) can be (and often is) discrepant. That is, they may evaluate it on different analytic levels. These different significations of healing have led to confusion among ethnographers. Clinicians have failed to recognize the cultural level of healing, even as they have often failed to see healing as a social activity serving social purposes. Cultural healing is a special dimension of the healing process that anthropology forces us to consider. Structural and symbolic analyses of this aspect of healing are as availing for a general understanding of healing as are functional clinical and social psychological analyses of its other dimensions.

These "lessons" from the shrines of *tâng-ki*s raise questions for a comparative science of healing. Given the multiple levels on which healing occurs, what interdisciplinary methodologies can we use to study the interrelationships between these levels in the healing process? How can we compare indigenous and modern biomedical care with respect to the socially and culturally mediated healing mechanism described in this section? And how can we relate *evaluations of therapeutic efficacy* that examine different analytic levels and that reflect the divergent clinical constructions of reality associated with different health care sectors and roles? This last question leads us back to the hermeneutic problem inherent in ethnomedical research—a problem that we now see is as central to comparative studies of the healing process as we found it to be for comparative studies of illness and clinical communication. It is a sign of the early stage we are at in both medical anthropology and cultural psychiatry that we cannot point to definitive answers for these questions. But the fact that we now ask them is a sign of significant broadening of the problem-frame within which we study healing, as well as recognition that it is unavailing to conceptualize healing in narrower terms.

10

Epilogue:
Implications

What are the chief implications the preceding chapters hold for medical anthropology on one hand, and for medicine and psychiatry on the other?

If medical anthropology is more adequately to frame ethnographic and comparative investigations of sickness and healing in society, it must accept as a cardinal concern the clinical categories and activities I have focused on in this book. It is inconceivable that ethnomedical studies can any longer avoid systematically assessing the nature and significance of clinical praxis, or that they can exclude modern professional health care from cross-cultural comparisons of healing systems. The disappointing progress of theory building in medical anthropology is, at least in part, a result of its failure to come to terms with what I have called "clinical reality" and to examine how it is differentially constituted in diverse social structural and cultural settings. The core clinical tasks of health care systems and the clinical construction of reality provide medical anthropology with an autonomous subject matter, but one that calls for concepts and methods different from those originating in its more traditional concerns with healing in folk religion; with physical anthropological and biomedical studies of disease; and with international aspects of public health.

A major research issue for medical anthropology should be to determine more precisely the universal and culture-specific features of clinical activities. We simply do not now possess valid conceptual frameworks for comparing indigenous and Western forms of clinical praxis, or for testing hypotheses about healing mechanisms, or for precisely determining therapeutic outcome.

A clinical orientation in field studies, furthermore, immediately shows the need for developing interdisciplinary methods, or multi-disciplinary research teams, suitable for investigating the crucial biosocial interactions between the sociocultural and psychobiological sides of clinical phenomena. Cultural reductionism is no better than biomedical reductionism in learning how these interrelationships mediate sickness and healing. Assessments of ethnomedical categories would be more powerful if they were related to assessments of biomedical categories (treated as 'emic' not 'etic' explanations), just as biomedical epidemiologies of disease would be more powerful if they were related to ethnomedical epidemiologies of illness. The investigation of how cultural meanings and norms influence either the perception and expression of symptoms or therapeutic mechanisms has gone about as far as it can without interdisciplinary methodologies that can measure both biological and culture change.

Lastly, only by addressing clinically relevant questions from its unique perspective can medical anthropology exert a practical effect on the practice and teaching of clinical medicine and psychiatry. This could be accomplished either by promoting clinically applied research and teaching in departments of anthropology or by creating clinical anthropology (or clinical social science) groups in schools of the health sciences. The latter, while it is a far more ambitious alternative, also would be likely to have a much more substantial influence on clinical care. Clinical anthropologists and social scientists would receive some practical clinical training to become: (1) more effective teachers of clinicians and of medical anthropologists who would work in clinical settings; (2) able to consult with clinicians on patient care problems involving the kinds of cultural, social structural, family, and communicative issues that I have discussed and illustrated; and (3) better equipped to conduct research on clinically relevant questions. As clinical consultants and teachers, they would be expected to translate and apply anthropological and sociological concepts as practical clinical strategies to resolve concrete problems in patient care and clinical practice. They would, for example, be expected to be experts in identifying illness problems and in formulating and, where feasible, applying illness interventions. Hence, they might consult on problems relating to discrepant ethnic and biomedical beliefs about sickness, or be called in to resolve tacit conflicts in clinical communication, or to negotiate between the family's and the practitioner's treatment objectives. The prescription and delivery of illness interventions are a key clinical task for which the clinical social science consultant could draw upon the social science basis of clinical practice in the same way the clinical pharmacologist draws upon the biological science basis of clinical practice to provide specific disease interventions.

An essential activity for the clinical social scientist is to assess the adaptive and maladaptive aspects of popular health beliefs and practices so as to recommend and implement popular educational programs. This would involve instituting programs to teach patients and families about normal bodily functioning, routine health care problems, useful coping responses, choosing and applying available remedies, and rationally organizing triage decisions about when to refer problems to health professionals, what types of problems to refer, and whom to refer them to. The clinical social scientist might facilitate patient access to and movements between the different sectors and subsectors of health care systems, including preventing or correcting structural conflicts intrinsic to these movements. I have already outlined many issues that would be pertinent for clinical anthropological and social science research. Clearly, implementing this approach would necessitate major alterations in the relation of medical anthropology to the health sciences.

These remarks should not be construed to mean that I am recommending clinical issues become the only or even the major focus of medical anthropology (cf. Dunn 1976; Fabrega 1974; Lieban 1977; Wellin 1977, who review the scope of problems relevant to medical anthropology). But they should become one of its main concerns, which heretofore they have not been.

In analyzing and comparing clinical categories and situations, it is essential that anthropological investigations do not accept the biomedical paradigm as the appropriate theoretical frame for describing and interpreting them.[1] Instead medical anthropology should advance its own ethnomedical paradigm as an alternative, autonomous theoretical frame more suitable for describing and interpreting clinical affairs. The core clinical tasks of health care systems and the clinical construction of reality do not emerge as fields of inquiry from the former but from the latter. It is the latter perspective, not the former, that supports the argument that health planners need to conceive of ways to strengthen the adaptive health care functions of the popular sector by rationalizing and increasing its decision-making and therapeutic roles. And it is the ethnomedical model, not the biomedical model, that shows that change in health care is a function of the interaction between macro-system and micro-system.

Looking backward from a decade or so in future, I think two quite different appraisals of the development of medical anthropology will be possible. One, the more likely, will find that this field became a legitimated, though relatively limited, venue for biomedical research and that it attained the status of a full-fledged research specialty in medical and nursing schools and schools of public health. Its teaching input, especially into clinical fields, would be small. Within anthropology and comparative studies it would be viewed as an outpost of the health sciences, and its own members would see themselves more biomedical than social science researchers. Epidemiological and other biomedical methodologies would have transformed ethnography and comparative cross-cultural studies, making them much more sophisticated statistically and principally con-

1. Recent reviews of medical anthropology disclose a tendency to make tacit use of the biomedical paradigm in order to frame research questions and select methodologies (Fabrega 1974; Lieban 1977; Wellin 1977). The widely recognized and much talked about need for "autonomous" medical anthropological theory, it is hoped, will protect the field from the increasing, if usually disguised reliance on biomedical presuppositions and categories, particularly in the investigation of sociobiological interactions. A strong, self-reflexive cultural analysis program in medical anthropology, even when studying clinically relevant and practical public health issues and even when part of teaching programs and interdisciplinary research projects in the health sciences, would seem to be a specially powerful defense against this tendency, which threatens to remove the "teeth" from the anthropological approach (cf. Kleinman 1977d; Mitchell 1977).

cerned with a problem-frame generated by biomedicine. But medical anthropology would not have created major theoretical models, especially models of the clinical process, nor would it be closely involved with relating cultural analysis to practical issues in health care and public health. To some extent, it would deal with salient clinical problems, like compliance, but from a professional perspective that did not include concern with the popular sector in its own right, only as it related to the professional sector. Routine aspects of clinical care and the everyday context of illness behavior would be of less interest than exotic sicknesses and esoteric healing rituals.

I do not believe such an appraisal will be able to point to major contributions to the solution of large health care and public health problems. And indeed, such problems might not be viewed as "suitable" for this discipline. Furthermore, medical anthropology would focus on ethnic groups in virtual exclusion from mainstream culture in the United States and other Western societies and would limit its international comparisons to the "most traditional" societies. It is likely that it would have erected disciplinary barriers and would not encourage interdisciplinary research.

I need not belabor this description. If it becomes accurate, I will consider it a sad and negative summary of a future almost as unavailing as if medical anthropology had remained the minor subdivision of anthropology, cut off from both the health sciences and practical problems in health care, it had been until a decade ago.

An alternative future contrasts sharply with the foregoing description. If it is achieved, the present will be recognized as the origin of a new conceptual approach to the health field— as the emergence of an independent social science framework for studying health problems. Although medical sociology would have made an important contribution to this conceptual breakthrough, medical anthropology and cross-cultural studies would be recognized as having contributed something very special. By systematically developing cultural analysis, they would have elaborated a new way of conceptualizing sickness and health care quite distinct from the biomedical framework, though in open dialogue with it. That new conceptualization would represent both an epistemologic break and a basic reorientation of clinical practice and teaching. Medical anthropology would contribute importantly to the training of health professionals; it also would study the popular sector in its own terms and might even contribute toward rationalizing and strengthening its role in health and health care. Unlike biomedicine, ethnomedicine would take the context of *meaning* within which sickness is labeled and experienced as its central analytic and comparative problem. For ethnomedicine, the chief problem would be to examine patient, community, practitioner, *and* researcher conceptualizations of sickness. Similarly, if the biomedical model were to become anthropologically informed, it too would recognize that the study of sickness in the setting of everyday experience, because it is at heart a question of how culture affects perceptions and explanations of sickness, is "first and foremost a conceptual study of an intrinsically semantic subject matter. . . " (Crick 1976). That "intrinsically semantic subject matter" would confer on anthropological and related social science investigations in the health field the obligation of widening the biomedical framework to include the sick person's and the practitioner's context of meaning.

In this vision of the future, medical anthropology is seen as a social science in medicine, distinct from the biomedical sciences yet an integral part of clinical science. Major concern would be given to exploiting its unique interstitial position between the social sciences and the health sciences. It would be concerned with fundamental issues in primary care, health seeking behavior, organization and delivery of health services, and public health policy. It would very likely have made practical contributions to those areas, and also would have made theoretical and methodological contributions to anthropology and comparative studies. It would be viewed by anthropologists as an important and independent branch of social anthropology, and substantial numbers of anthropologists would have entered this field—with many fewer appointments in departments of anthropology than in departments in the health sciences. Those in the health sciences would come from special training programs that combined anthropological and health science training with practical teaching and research experiences in primary care, psychiatry, nursing, and various fields in public health. Some medical anthropologists would work as clinical social science consultants in the actual day-to-day practice of health care and public health. But rather than disciplinary concerns, medical anthropology's chief interest would be in applying cultural analysis and cross-cultural comparisons to a wide array of empirical and theoretical questions at the border between health sciences and social science. It would have a strong interdisciplinary orientation. Medical ethnography, while remaining a basic research tool, would include biological and clinical assessments. New techniques would be used to study both psycho- and socio-physiological interactions. A uniquely anthropological approach would have been developed in social epidemiology and in cross-national comparisons in psychiatric epidemiology.

The latter vision of the future is probably less likely to be achieved. It is a vision, however, that is justified by the anthropological and cross-cultural approach explored in this book. It exemplifies the values and aims and powerful potential for change immanent in the cultural analysis program as applied to sickness and healing, patients and healers.

The implications of our study for clinical medicine and psychiatry are equally large. Viewed from the perspective advanced in this book, medicine and psychiatry are not what they appear (and claim) to be. Cultural analysis calls into question their purpose and scope. Seriously rethinking medicine will require a more rigorous and developed analytic framework than I have presented. Provisional as it is, our framework nonetheless makes abundantly clear that medicine as a field of health care problems and medicine as a profession are two completely different things. The modern medical profession claims dominance over the "field of medicine," and its claim is sanctioned by government, but in actual practice it accounts for only a small percentage of what goes on in that field. And, as we have repeatedly pointed out, the biomedical reductionism and technological "fixes" it employs are inadequate to understand *and* treat most problems in health care. Its analytic tools are not self-reflexive and consequently can tell us very little about medicine as a social practice. Its system of knowledge, as we have seen, is as much ideology as science. The sphere of relevance of professional medicine, as now constituted, is almost entirely limited to *disease*. Without significant social science input, even disease does not receive adequate analysis. Furthermore, the medical profession's conceptualization of sickness has disappointingly little to contribute to understanding illness as symbolic networks. Therefore, the everyday context of sickness and treatment falls outside its interest and competence.

The alternatives seem clear. Either the professions of medicine and psychiatry and public health should recognize their profound limitations and markedly reduce their professional claims, or they must be reshaped to include *health* and *illness* and the everyday context of sickness and care within their boundaries. The latter course means that the biomedical framework must be united with the ethnomedical framework in some overarching integration. That integration, which is not available at present, would reshape the medical model to include social and cultural questions and methods and would radically alter the program of the health sciences and the professions that carry it out.

I strongly favor such an integration, even though it will require difficult and long reform, and though there will be extreme problems of professional compliance and conflict over bringing social science into medicine. The alternative is so poor as to be almost unimaginable. It could well produce disastrous results by legitimating a total divorce between biomedicine, on the one hand, and psychological, social, and cultural aspects of sickness and care, on the other. It would transform medicine into a veterinary practice. Doctors would become body technicians. There would be an unbreachable divide between mind and body. The result would be far worse than what exists today; it would be completely unacceptable to patients and also, I believe, to most practitioners, even though it might receive considerable support among biomedical academicians.

Nonetheless, the alternative I favor might entail potentially serious consequences. It could further medicalize society. It could lead to dangerous abuse by the medical profession of its strengthened and extended social functions, e.g., in the areas of social control and economic exploitation. As has so frequently happened in the American health enterprise, reform carried out for the best reasons might produce the worst results. Witness the history of the asylum (Rothman 1971). Such reform would have to be carefully monitored, its effects systematically evaluated. But as I see it, cultural analysis, in forcing us to rethink medicine, leaves us with no other viable alternative. If we do nothing, we are almost certain to see further movement in favor of the other alternative: total separation of medicine as an organized practice from the personal and social context of sickness and care.

In order to effect this integration between social science and biomedical science, the main venue for teaching anthroplogical and cross-cultural materials in schools of medicine should be the clinical clerkships. Teaching input should not be restricted to medical students but, through the creation of the kind of clinical social science I have already discussed, should extend to the period of postgraduate clinical training. Indeed, it is likely that it would have its major impact through postgraduate teaching. Much the same holds for teaching in schools of nursing and public health. Obviously, this calls for a fundamental reorganization of the medical school and postgraduate training curricula. That will require corresponding changes in the allocation of resources (faculty positions, teaching time, research funding).

Undoubtedly, this prospect is responsible for provoking much of the resistance that social science has had to face in health science schools. Such changes pose a significant threat to the way medical education and research are presently organized and to the "interests" that control them. The leaders of biomedicine rightly perceive their domination of academic medicine challenged, their feudal baronies encroached upon. But without such a deliberate shift in resource allocation within medicine, psychiatry, and public health, it is unlikely that anthropological and cross-cultural approaches will exert any significant effect.

Bringing about this far-reaching change will require "outside" influence because the vested professional academic interests are certainly not going to retrench on their own. Kuhn (1970) has shown for the scientific enterprise in general that conflicts between paradigms, and the changes in control of sources of power and prestige they bring about, frequently can only be resolved through sociopolitical action. The conflict between biomedicine and social science in the health sciences is likely to necessitate precisely this kind of resolution. The present differential in power between the two paradigms and the groups gathered around them is enormous. But increased consumer dissatisfaction with health care, widespread criticism of the untoward effects of bio-technology, and governmental attention to problems associated with the social organization of care, all suggest that at least some changes along the lines we have discussed will be forthcoming. However, it is unlikely that these changes will significantly weaken the hold of the biomedical establishment. All that can be expected in the near future is a modest increase in the place of the social sciences in the house of medicine. Nonetheless, even a modest change could have quite far-reaching effects on the way practitioners and patients think and behave, as the model I have proposed for clinical communication suggests.

We are just beginning to witness changes in the health care systems of advanced Western societies and, to a much lesser extent, in developing societies. The inter-sector conflict between popular and professional "interests" is in part reflected in the intra-sector professional conflict between biomedical and social science paradigms. The anthropological and comparative medical materials presented in this book suggest that there will be a significant increase in this conflict in the future. I advocate the desirability of such conflict, inasmuch as it should secure increased space for the social sciences in the professional medical sector.

The task for anthropology in the health field is twofold. First, it must help widen and deepen the non-biomedical cultural perspective on health, sickness, and health care. This includes the need to build a firm foundation for research and teaching concerned with biosocial and biocultural interrelationships that could lead to a new comparative science of sickness and healing to which both biomedical analysis and cultural analysis would contribute. To accomplish this end, cross-cultural psychiatry and other comparative medical studies must be self-consciously transformed into *anthropological medicine and psychiatry*. That is to say, they must frame their research investigations in terms of the ethnomedical model's orientation to the meaning context of illness and health care. Only through such a fundamental transformation will we possess a discipline whose theory and methodology are equal to the task of forging a cross-cultural understanding of clinical categories and praxis. Second, by studying the everyday context of health and sickness in the popular sector, anthropological studies should do more than simply demonstrate the inadequacy of the epistemology underlying the biomedical framework. They should focus attention on the non-professional side of the health field and especially on its positive adaptive features, which deserve to be better understood.

But this book argues for an even more significant change. The logic of the preceding chapters calls for a thorough reappraisal of the popular health care sector. By far most decisions and actions about health and sickness take place in the popular sector. The professional sector of most health care systems is already functioning at near maximum. There is, therefore, every reason to favor rationalizing and strengthening its adaptive functions. Indeed, unless this happens it is hard to visualize how health care systems will be able to meet the tremendous challenges of inflation, population expansion associated with increased consumer demand, relatively much smaller change in numbers and distribution of health professionals, and limits on government and private spending for health and health care.

One solution, albeit a radical one in the eyes of health professionals, is legitimation for much of what presently takes place in the popular sector, followed by efforts to provide necessary information and technical resources to families and social networks, so that appropriate triage decisions can be made and a rational basis for treatment established within the popular sector. Clearly, this would involve profound changes: patients and the laity generally would be delegated much greater autonomy. They would be expected to handle most health maintenance questions and health care practices and would be provided with the knowledge and materials to do so. Health education would be the basis for successfully implementing such a program. It would be systematically organized in schools and in occupational settings and in communities. It would require that people learn about their bodies, that they study normal and pathological physiology and practical therapeutics.

I shall not draw a more complete picture. What I have sketched should suggest what rationalizing and strengthening the health enhancing, health maintaining, and health care functions of the popular sector would entail. Though a logical conclusion from the anthropological perspective, this is heresy from the professional medical perspective, which would see it as a move to undermine the near-total control over the health field it claims and to threaten its economic interests and socio-political power (albeit its ideological argument against such a program would be cast in such terms as the ignorance and potential dangers of consumer practices). Compared to the tremendous struggle this recommendation would set off, the biomedicine/social science debate is minor.

Obviously, the power structure of most health care systems precludes this radical change from happening unless it is mandated by "external" political force. Nonetheless, I would contend that anthropological and sociological approaches to sickness and health care will eventually promote some such revolution of the popular sector. This is part of the threat they pose to the biomedical establishment in the health professions. But perhaps it is also a reason why that establishment wishes to see social science "enter" the health sciences, where it can be better controlled than if it were on the "outside" as an autonomous institution.

This is why the question of biomedical paradigm versus autonomous social science paradigm is so highly charged. Incorporation within the biomedical paradigm would effectively emasculate medical anthropology. To date, I would argue, this has in fact happened. Medical anthropology in the main has either been cut off from practical issues by having its scope restricted to the academic interests of anthropology departments or has followed the positivist, value-neutral biomedical approach within schools of the health sciences that, as we have seen, functions as an ideology supporting the interests of the health professions. It has not overtly challenged those interests, although the materials it works with provide ample support for such a challenge.[2] A jaundiced critic might wonder if

2. This is well-demonstrated in the international health field, where the practical implications of the ethnomedical perspective discussed in this chapter have only recently and in a quite circumscribed way been given serious consideration. Thus, while the question of integrating folk practitioners into

the underdevelopment of the theoretical side of medical anthropology does not serve established interests precisely because it fails to generate an alternative model powerful enough to provide a significant challenge to the reigning biomedical ideology.

In summary, the implications of anthropology for medicine and psychiatry are potentially vast. Clinical anthropological studies are clearly at a crucial juncture. I do not see how there can be any turning back from the issue we are examining. Anthropological investigations force the health professions and society at large to consider fundamental changes in health care systems. These include changes in the structure and functions of the popular sector to greatly enhance its adaptive efficacy. At the same time, they will alter the very nature of health care systems as we presently know them. Consequently, the ethnomedical model's challenge to the biomedical model represents more than a shift in theoretical orientation, important though that is. It calls for a truly radical shift in the way health care in society is organized and practiced. Not the least of its implications is the recognition that only an anthropological medicine and psychiatry are adequate to conceptualize and implement clinical tasks if we are to achieve the full potentialities of a culturally appropriate, humane, integrated practice of clinical care. That is the echo I hope this book sends down the corridors of clinical facilities, health science schools, and anthropology departments.

---

professional health services is presently being discussed, the far larger issue of planning for a rationalized and expanded role of popular health care has not been addressed. Anthropologists have thus far largely failed to present the clinical and public health implications of the ethnomedical model for international health in sharp terms that challenge the supremacy of the biomedical model, even though the latter's shortcomings as a guide to international health are now widely recognized. See Allan Young (1978) and accompanying papers in a special issue of *Medical Anthropology* for examples of how treating seriously non-positivist theories in medical anthropology leads to several potentially important and quite distinctive challenges to the orthodox biomedical program in international health and health care.

Glossary of Selected Terms

(Note: Mandarin terms are italicized; Taiwanese and Cantonese terms are italicized and underlined.)

Romanization	Definition	Characters
ang-î	Taiwanese female spirit medium	尪 姨
chao hun	"call back the soul"; name of a common healing ritual.	招 魂
cheng	manifestation type; diagnostic categories in the classical Chinese medical texts.	證, 証, 症
ch'i, _khì_	vital essence	氣
chieh-ku shih-fu	bone-setter	接骨師傅
chien-k'ang	condition of health	健 康
ch'ien, _chiam_	divining sticks and fortune paper	籤
ching, _kiaⁿ_	fright	驚
ching	seminal essence	精
ching-shen ping	mental illness	精神病
ch'ou-ch'ien	divination by drawing bamboo sticks and reading fortune paper.	抽 籤
chung-i-sheng, _tiong-i-seng_	Chinese-style doctor	中醫生
chung-yao, _tiong-ióh_	Chinese medicine (medicinal agents)	中 藥
fa-shih (wu-shih)	Taoist magician and ritual expert	法師 (巫師)
fan-tsao	troubled, worried, anxious	煩 躁
feng, _fung, hong_	wind	風
feng-shui, _hong-sui_	geomancy	風 水

Glossary

Romanization	Definition	Characters
feng-shui hsien-sheng	geomancer	風水先生
hsi-i-sheng, se-i-seng	Western-style doctor	西醫生
hsi-yao, se-iȯh	Western medicine (medicinal agents)	西 藥
hsiang-mien	physiognomist	相 面
hsiao	filial piety	孝
hsieh-ch'i	invading pathological tendency or agency in Chinese medicine (in folk medicine, a possessing worm or demon)	邪 氣
hsin, sim	heart	心
hsin-ch'ing pu-hao	emotional upset (general, non-specific)	心情不好
hsin-li wen-t'i	a psychological "problem"	心理問題
hû-á	charm or magic character	符 仔
huo-ch'i ta	a pathological excess of inner hot energy in Chinese medicine; a common symptom term amongst contemporary Chinese patients	火氣大
jê, ít, jièt	hot	熱
jen	human heartedness	仁
kan	liver	肝
k'an-ping, koàⁿ-piⁿ	literally "to look at the sickness"; diagnosis	看 病
k'e-chia-jen, kheh-lâng	Hakka ("guest people")	客家人
k'e-jen, lâng-kheh	guest or client	客 人
kuei, kúi	ghost	鬼
k'u-hai	"sea of bitterness"	苦 海
leng, leung, liông	cold	冷
m̄-kaù huet	"not enough blood"	不夠血
mên, būn	sad, depressed, troubled	悶
mi-fang	secret knowledge	祕 方

390

Glossary

Romanization	Definition	Characters
nao-chin	brain nerves	腦 筋
nao-chin pu-ch'iang	brain nerve damage or weakness (a somatization term)	腦筋不強
nan-kuo	sad, troubled	難 過
nei-k'e	internal medicine	內 科
pa kua	Eight Diagrams (Trigrams) from the *I Ching,* used in calculating a person's fate	八 卦
pa tzu	"eight characters" defining the exact time of a person's birth used in calculating his/her fate	八 字
pao	reciprocity	報
ping-jen, pīⁿ-lâng	patient	病 人
pu, pö	supplement, patch, tonic	補
shen	god(s)	神
shen-ching shuai-jo	neurasthenia	神經衰弱
shen-k'uei	kidney deficiency or weakness	腎 虧
shih	wet	濕
shou ching	"catch fright"	受 驚
sien-siⁿ-má	literally "doctor's or master's mother"; a local "wise" woman who performs rituals and administers other treatment	先生媽
suan	sour	酸
suan-ming	fortune-teller	算 命
tâng-ki	"divining youth"; shaman	童 乩
tao-shih	Taoist priest	道 士
t'ien-ming	fate	天 命
t'ou-chung	sensation of heaviness in head	頭 重
t'ou-t'ung	headache or pain in head	頭 痛
t'ou-yün	dizziness, vertigo	頭 暈
ts'ao-yao	herbs	草 藥
tu, tók	poison	毒

Glossary

Romanization	Definition	Characters
tuan-ken	"cut down the root"; radical (as in radical treatment or cure)	斷 根
ut siong	a Taiwanese disease term (see Chapter 2)	欝 傷
wai-k'e	external medicine, surgery	外 科
wei-sheng	health maintenance, hygiene	衛 生
wu-hsing	Five Evolutive Phases, also rendered Five Elements (wood, fire, earth, metal, water and their correspondences)	五 行
wu-tsang	the internal functional system of bodily organs comprising the Five Body Spheres (liver, heart, spleen, lungs, and kidneys)	五 臟
yin/yang, im/iông	female principle/male principle	陰 陽
yu-yü	depression as a symptom (as officially translated in Taiwan)	憂 欝
yu-ping	depression as a disease (as officially translated in Taiwan)	憂 病

Bibliography

Aberle, D.F.
    1966.   Religio-magical phenomena and power, prediction, and control. *Southwestern Journal of Anthropology* 22:221–230.

Adair, J. and Deuschle, K.
    1970.   *The People's Health: Medicine and Anthropology in a Navaho Community.* New York: Appleton-Century-Crofts.

Ader, R., and Cohen, N.
    1975.   Behaviorally conditioned immunosuppression. *Psychosomatic Medicine* 37:333–340.

Adler, H.M. and Hammett, V.B.O.
    1973.   The doctor-patient relationship revisited: An analysis of the placebo effect. *Annals of Internal Medicine* 78:595–598.

Agren, H.
    1976.   Patterns of tradition and modernization in contemporary Chinese medicine. In A. Kleinman et al., eds., *Medicine in Chinese Cultures,* Washington, D.C.: U.S.G.P.O. for Fogarty International Center, N.I.H.; pp. 37–60.

Ahern, E.
    1976.   Sacred and secular medicine in a Taiwan village: A study of cosmological disorder. In *ibid.*; pp. 91–114.

Alland, A.
    1970.   *Adaptation in Cultural Evolution: An Approach to Medical Anthropology.* New York: Columbia University Press.

Anderson, E. and Anderson, M.
    1968.   Folk medicine in Hong Kong. *Etnoiatria* 2:22–35.

Apple, D.
    1960.   How laymen define illness. *Journal of Health and Human Behavior* 1:219–225.

Baker, T.D. and Perlman M.
    1967.   *Health Manpower in a Developing Economy: Taiwan, a Case Study in Planning.* Baltimore: The Johns Hopkins University Press.

Balint, Michael
    1957.   *The Doctor, His Patient, and the Illness.* New York: International Universities Press.

Barclay, T.
    1923.   *Supplement to Carstair Douglas's Dictionary of the Vernacular or Spoken Language of Amoy.* Shanghai: Commercial Press.

Beck, A.
    1971.   Cognition, affect and psychopathology. *Archives of General Psychiatry* 24:495–500.

Bibliography

Beidelman, T.
　1966.　Swazi royal ritual. *Africa* 36:373–405.
Benveniste, E.
　1945.　La doctrine medicale des Indo-Européens. *Revue de L'histoire des Religions* 130:5.
Berger, P.L.
　1973.　Identity as a problem in the sociology of knowledge. In G.W. Remmling, ed., *Towards the Sociology of Knowledge.* New York: Humanities Press, pp. 273–284.
Berger, P.L. and Luckmann, T.
　1967.　*The Social Construction of Reality.* Garden City, New York: Doubleday.
Berger, P. et al.
　1973.　*The Homeless Mind: Modernization and Consciousness.* New York: Random House.
Berlin, B. et al.
　1973.　General principles of classification and nomenclature in folk biology. *American Anthropologist* 75:214–242.
Bernstein, B.
　1971.　*Class, Codes and Control.* London: Routledge and Kegan Paul.
Blacking, John, ed.
　1977.　*The Anthropology of the Body.* New York: Academic Press.
Bowers, J., ed.
　1974.　*Medicine and Society in China.* New York: Josiah Macy, Jr. Foundation.
Brenner, M.H.
　1974.　*Mental Illness and the Economy.* Cambridge, Mass.: Harvard University Press.
Brody, H.
　1977.　"Persons and Placebos: Philosophical Implications of the Placebo Effect." Ph.D. dissertation, Department of Philosophy, Michigan State University.
Campbell, J.D.
　1975.　Attribution of illness: Another double standard. *Journal of Health and Social Behavior* 16:114–126.
Carr, J.
　1978.　Ethno-behaviorism and culture bound syndromes: The case of Amok. *Culture, Medicine and Psychiatry* 22:269–293.
Cartwright, A.
　1964.　*Human Relations and Hospital Care.* London: Routledge and Kegan Paul.
Cassell, E.J.
　1976.　Disease as an "it": Concepts of disease revealed by patients' presentation of symptoms. *Social Science and Medicine* 10:143–146.
Caudill, W. and Lin, T.Y., eds.
　1969.　*Mental Health Research in Asia and the Pacific,* Volume 1. Honolulu: East-West Center Press.

Bibliography

Cawte, J.E.
  1974. *Medicine is the Law: Studies in Psychiatric Anthropology of Australian Tribal Societies*. Honolulu: University of Hawaii Press.
Cay, E.L. et al.
  1975. Patient assessment of the result of surgery for peptic ulcer. *Lancet* 1:29–31.
Chang, Y.H., Rin, H., and Chen, C.C.
  1975. Frigophobia: A report of five cases. *Bulletin of the Chinese Society of Neurology and Psychiatry* 1(2): 13.
Chessick, R.
  1969. *How Psychotherapy Heals*. New York: Science House.
Chiang, Y.
  1952. *A Chinese Childhood*. New York: Day.
Chin, R. and Chin, A.L.
  1969. *Psychological Research in Communist China, 1949–1966*. Cambridge, Mass.: M.I.T. Press.
Chrisman, N.
  1977. The health seeking process. *Culture, Medicine and Psychiatry* 1:351–378.
Church, J.
  1961. *Language and the Discovery of Reality*. New York: Random House.
Cicourel, A.V.
  1973. *Cognitive Sociology*. Baltimore: Penguin.
Clements, F.E.
  1932. *Primitive concepts of disease*. University of California Publications in American Archaeology and Ethnology 32:185–252.
Cohen, A.
  1976. *Two-Dimensional Man: An Essay on the Anthropology of Power and Symbolism in Complex Society*. Berkeley: University of California Press.
Colson, A.C.
  1971. The differential use of medical resources in developing countries. *Journal of Health and Social Behavior* 12:226–237.
Crick, M.
  1976. *Explorations in Language and Meaning: Towards a Semantic Anthropology*. New York: Halstead Press.
Croizier, R.
  1968. *Traditional Medicine in Modern China*. Cambridge, Mass.: Harvard University Press.
Currier, R.L.
  1966. The hot-cold syndrome and symbolic balance in Mexican and Spanish folk medicine. *Ethnology* 5:251–263.
D'Andrade, R.
  1976. A propositional analysis of U.S. American beliefs about illness. In K. Basso and H. Selby, eds., *Meaning in Anthropology*. Albuquerque, New Mexico: University of New Mexico Press, pp. 155–180.

Bibliography

Davis, M.
    1968.   Variations in patients' compliance with doctors' advice. *American Journal of Public Health* 58:274–288.

DeGroot, J.J.M.
    1972.   *The Religious System of China.* Volume VI, Book II, Part V: *The*
    (1890–   *Priesthood of Animism.* Taipei: Ch'eng Wen Publishing Co., pp.
    1910)   1187–1340.

Doi, L.T.
    1962.   *Amae*—a key concept for understanding Japanese personality structure. In R. J. Smith and R.K. Beardsley, eds., *Japanese Culture.* Chicago: Aldine.

Douglas, C.
    1899.   *Dictionary of the Vernacular or Spoken Language of Amoy* (new edi-
    (1873)   tion). London: Presbyterian Church of England.

Douglas, M.
    1970.   The healing rite. *Man* 5:302–308.

Dreitzel, H.P., ed.
    1971.   *The Social Organization of Health.* Recent Sociology No. 3. New York: Macmillan.

Dubos, R.
    1952.   *The White Plague: Tuberculosis, Man, and Society.* Boston: Little, Brown.

Dull, J.
    1976.   Implications of Chinese history for comparative studies of medicine in society. In Kleinman et al., eds., *Medicine in Chinese Cultures,* op.cit.; pp. 669–678.

Dunn, F.L.
    1976.   Traditional Asian medicine and cosmopolitan medicine as adaptive systems. In C. Leslie, ed., *Asian Medical Systems.* Berkeley: University of California Press, pp. 133–158.

Edgerton, R.B. and Karno, M.
    1971.   Mexican-American bilingualism and the perception of mental illness. *Archives of General Psychiatry* 24:286–290.

Eisenberg, L.
    1976.   Conceptual models of physical and mental disorders. In *Research and Medical Practice* (Ciba Foundation Symposium #44). Amsterdam: Associated Scientific Publishers, pp. 3–23.
    1977.   Psychiatry and society: A sociobiological synthesis. *New England Journal of Medicine* 296:903–910.

Elder, R.
    1973.   Social class and lay explanations of the etiology of arthritis. *Journal of Health and Social Behavior* 14:28–35.

Elliott, A.
    1955.   *Chinese Spirit-Mediums in Singapore.* London: London School of Economics Monographs.

Emerson, J.
    1970.   Behavior in private places: Sustaining definitions of reality in gynecological examinations. In H.P. Dreitzel, ed., *Patterns of*

Communicative Behavior. Recent Sociology, No. 2. New York: Macmillan, pp. 73–100.

Engel, G.L.
1977. The need for a new medical model: A challenge for biomedicine. *Science* 196:129–136.

Engelhardt, H.T.
1974. Explanatory models in medicine. *Texas Reports in Biology and Medicine* 32:225–239.

Erasmus, C.J.
1952. Changing folk beliefs and the relativity of empirical knowledge. *Southwestern Journal of Anthropology* 8:411–428.

Evans-Pritchard, E.E.
1937. *Witchcraft, Oracles, and Magic Among the Azande.* London: Oxford University Press.

Fabrega, H.
1971. Some features of Zinacantecan medical knowledge. *Ethnology* 9:25–43.
1972. The study of disease in relation to culture. *Behavioral Science* 17:183–203.
1974. *Disease and Social Behavior: An Interdisciplinary Perspective.* Cambridge, Mass.: M.I.T. Press.
1976. The function of medical-care systems: A logical analysis. *Perspectives in Biology and Medicine* 20:108–119.

Fabrega, H. and Manning, P.K.
1973. An integrated theory of disease: Ladino-Mestizo views of disease in the Chiapas Highlands. *Psychosomatic Medicine* 35:223–239.

Fabrega, H. and Silver, D.
1973. *Illness and Shamanistic Curing in Zinacantan: An Ethnomedical Analysis.* Stanford: Stanford University Press.

Field, M.G.
1973. The concept of the "health system" at the macro-sociological level. *Social Science and Medicine* 7:763–785.
1976. Comparative sociological perspectives on health systems: Notes on a conceptual approach. In Kleinman et al., eds., *Medicine in Chinese Cultures, op.cit.,* pp. 567–587.

Foucault, M.
1965. *Madness and Civilization.* New York: Mentor.
1973. *The Birth of the Clinic: An Archaeology of Medical Perception.* New York: Random House.

Fox, R.
1968. Illness. In D. Sills, ed., *International Encyclopedia of the Social Sciences,* Volume 7. New York: Macmillan, pp. 90–96.

Frake, C.O.
1961. The diagnosis of disease among the Subanun of Mindanao. *American Anthropologist* 63:113–132.

Frank, J.
1974a. *Persuasion and Healing.* New York: Schocken.
(1961)

Bibliography

1974b. Therapeutic components of psychotherapy. *Journal of Nervous and Mental Disease* 159:325–342:

1975. Psychotherapy of bodily disease. *Psychotherapy and Psychosomatics* 26:192–202.

Freidson, E.

1961. *Patients' Views of Medical Practice.* New York: Russell Sage Foundation.

1970. *Profession of Medicine: A Study of the Sociology of Applied Knowledge.* New York: Harper and Row.

Freidson, E. and Lorber, J., eds.

1972. *Medical Men and Their Work.* Chicago: Aldine.

Gale, J.L.

1976. Patient and practitioner attitudes toward traditional and Western medicine in a contemporary Chinese setting. In Kleinman et al., eds., *Medicine in Chinese Cultures, op.cit.,* pp. 195–208.

Gallin, B.

1966. *Hsin Hsing, Taiwan: A Chinese Village in Change.* Berkeley: University of California Press.

Gaw, A.C.

1976. An integrated approach in the delivery of health care to a Chinese community in America: The Boston experience. In A. Kleinman et al., eds., *Medicine in Chinese Cultures,* op.cit., pp. 327–350.

Geertz,H.

1968. *Latah* in Java: A theoretical paradox. *Indonesia* 5:93–104.

Geertz, C.

1973. Thick description: Toward an interpretive theory of culture. *The Interpretation of Cultures.* New York: Basic Books, pp. 3–32.

Giddens, A.

1976. *New Rules of Sociological Method: A Positive Critique of Interpretative Sociologies.* New York: Basic Books.

Glick, L.B.

1967. Medicine as an ethnographic category: The Gimi of the New Guinea highlands. *Ethnology* 6:31–56.

Gonzalez, N.

1966. Health behavior in cross-cultural perspective: A Guatemalan example. *Human Organization* 25:122–125.

Good, B.

1976. Medical change and the doctor-patient relationship in an Iranian provincial town. In K. Farmafarmaian, ed., *The Social Sciences and Problems of Development.* Princeton, New Jersey: Princeton University Press, pp. 244–260.

1977. The heart of what's the matter: The semantics of illness in Iran. *Culture, Medicine, and Psychiatry* 1:25–58.

Goody, J. and Watt, I.

1963. The consequences of literacy. *Comparative Studies in Society and History* 5:304–345.

Bibliography

Gould, H.A.
  1965. Modern medicine and folk cognition in rural India. *Human Organization* 24:201–208.
Gould-Martin, K.
  1976. Medical systems in a Taiwan village: *Ong-ia-kong*, the plague god as modern physician. In A. Kleinman et al, eds., *Medicine in Chinese Cultures, op.cit.*, pp. 115–142.
Gove, W., ed.
  1975. *The Labelling of Deviance.* New York: Wiley.
Gunderson, J. and Singer, M.
  1975. Defining borderline patients. *American Journal of Psychiatry* 132:1–10.
Gussow, Z. and Tracy, G.S.
  1970. Stigma and the leprosy phenomenon: The social history of a disease in the nineteenth and twentieth centuries. *Bulletin of the History of Medicine* 44:425–449.
Halliday, M.A.K.
  1976. *Explorations in the Functions of Language.* London: Edward Arnold.
  (1973)
Hallowell, A.I.
  1955. *Culture and Experience.* Philadelphia: University of Pennsylvania Press.
  1963. Ojibwa world view and disease. In I. Galdston, ed., *Man's Image in Medicine and Anthropology.* New York: International Universities Press.
Harwood, A.
  1971. The hot-cold theory of disease: Implications for treatment of Puerto Rican patients. *Journal of the American Medical Association* 216:1153–1158.
  1977. Puerto Rican spiritism: Description and analysis of an alternative psychotherapeutic approach. *Culture, Medicine and Psychiatry* 1:22–48; 135–154.
Health Statistics
  1974. *Republic of China, Vol. 1: General Health Statistics, 1974.* National Health Administration, Taiwan Provincial Health Department, and Taipei City Health Department.
Helman, C.G.
  1978. "Feed a cold, starve a fever"—Folk models of infection in an English suburban community and their relation to medical treatment. *Culture, Medicine and Psychiatry* 2:107–138.
Holmes, T. and Rahe, R.
  1967. The social readjustment rating scale. *Journal of Psychosomatic Research* 11:213–218.
Holzner, B.
  1968. *Reality Construction in Society.* Cambridge, Mass.: Schenkman Publishing Co.

Bibliography

Horton, R.
  1967. African traditional thought and Western science, 1. *Africa* 37:50–71.

Hsu, F.L.K.
  1949. Suppression versus repression: A limited psychological interpretation of four cultures. *Psychiatry* 12:223–242.
  1971a. Eros, affect and *pao*. In F.L.K. Hsu, ed., *Kinship and Culture*. Chicago: Aldine, pp. 439–475.
  1971b. Psychosocial homeostasis and *Jen:* Conceptual tools for advancing psychological anthropology. *American Anthropologist* 73:23–44.

Hsu, J. and Tseng, H.S.
  1972. Intercultural psychotherapy. *Archives of General Psychiatry* 27:700–705.

Hsu, J.
  1976. Counseling in the Chinese temple: A psychological study of divination by *chien* drawing. In W. P. Lebra, ed., *Culture-Bound Syndromes, Ethnopsychiatry, and Alternate Therapies*. Honolulu: University Press of Hawaii, 1976, pp. 210–221.

Hu, H.C.
  1944. The Chinese concept of face. *American Anthropologist* 46:45–64.

Hughes, C.
  1968. Ethnomedicine. In D. Sills, ed., International Encyclopedia of the Social Sciences, Volume 10. New York: Macmillan, pp. 87–92.

Hulka, B.S., et al.
  1972. Determinants of physician utilization. *Medical Care* 10:300–309.

Hwu, H.G.
  1975. *Doctor and Patient*. Taipei: Hsing Wen Publishing Co. (In Chinese).

Illich, I.
  1975. *Medical Nemesis: The Expropriation of Health*. London: Calder & Boyars.

Ingham, J.M.
  1970. On Mexican folk medicine. *American Anthropologist* 72:76–87.

Inui, T. et al.
  1976. Improved outcomes in hypertension after physician tutorials. *Annals of Internal Medicine* 84:646–651.

Jansen, G.
  1973. *The Doctor-Patient Relationship in an African Tribal Society*. Assen, Holland: Van Gorcum.

Janzen, J.
  1977. "The comparative study of medical systems as changing social systems." Paper presented at the Conference on Theoretical Foundations for the Comparative Study of Medical Systems, National Science Foundation, Washington, D.C., November 21–23, 1976. *Social Science and Medicine* 12(2B):121–130, 1978.

Jordan, D.
  1972. *Gods, Ghosts and Ancestors: Folk Religion in a Taiwanese Village*. Berkeley: University of California Press.

Bibliography

Kagan, A. and Levi, L.
    1974. Health and environment—psychosocial stimuli: A review. *Social Science and Medicine* 8:225–241.

Kane, R. et al.
    1974. Manipulating the patient: A comparison of the effectiveness of physicians and chiropractic care. *Lancet* 1:1333–1336.

Kaplan, B. and Johnson, D.
    1964. The social meaning of Navaho psychopathology and psychotherapy. In A. Kiev, ed., *Magic, Faith and Healing.* New York: Free Press, pp. 203–229.

Kennedy, D.
    1973. Perceptions of illness and healing. *Social Science and Medicine* 7:787–806.

Kerr, G.
    1965. *Taiwan Betrayed.* Boston: Houghton Mifflin.
    1974. *Formosa: Licensed Revolution and the Home Rule Movement, 1895–1945.* Honolulu: The University Press of Hawaii.

Kiev, A., ed.
    1964. *Magic, Faith and Healing.* New York: Free Press.

Kingston, M.H.
    1977. *The Woman Warrior.* New York: Knopf.

Kiritz, S. and Moos, R.
    1974. Physiological effects of social environments. *Psychosomatic Medicine* 36:96–114.

Kleinman, A.
    1973a. Toward a comparative study of medical systems. *Science, Medicine and Man* 1:55–65.
    1973b. Medicine's symbolic reality. *Inquiry* 16:206–213.
    1973c. The background and development of public health in China: An exploratory essay. In M.E. Wegman et al., eds., *Public Health in the People's Republic of China.* New York: Josiah Macy, Jr. Foundation, pp. 5–25.
    1973d. Some issues for a comparative study of medical healing. *International Journal of Social Psychiatry* 19:159–165.
    1974a. Cognitive structures of traditional medical systems. *Ethnomedicine* 3:27–49.
    1974b. A comparative cross-cultural model for studying health care in China. *Studies in Comparative Communism* 7:414–419.
    1975a. Explanatory models in health care relationships. *National Council for International Health: Health of the Family.* Washington, D.C.: National Council for International Health, pp. 159–172.
    1975b. Medical and psychiatric anthropology and the study of traditional medicine in modern Chinese culture. *Journal of the Institute of Ethnology, Academica Sinica* 39:107–123.
    1975c. Cross-cultural studies of illness and health care: A preliminary report. *Bulletin of the Chinese Society of Neurology and Psychiatry* 1(2): 14–18.

Bibliography

1975d. The symbolic context of Chinese medicine. *American Journal of Chinese Medicine* 3:1–25, 1975.

1976. Social, cultural, and historical themes in the study of medicine and psychiatry in Chinese societies. In A. Kleinman et al., eds., *Medicine in Chinese Cultures, op.cit.*, pp. 589–658.

1977a. Depression, somatization and the new cross-cultural psychiatry. *Social Science and Medicine* 11:3–10.

1977b. "Concepts and a model for the comparison of medical systems as cultural systems." Paper presented to the Conference on Theoretical Foundations for the Comparative Study of Medical Systems, National Science Foundation, Washington, D.C., November 20–22, 1976. *Social Science and Medicine* 12(2B):85–94, 1978.

1977c. Comparisons of practitioner-patient interactions in Taiwan: The cultural construction of clinical reality. In A. Kleinman et al., eds., *Culture and Healing in Asian Societies: Anthropological, Psychiatric and Public Health Studies*. Cambridge, Mass.: Schenkman Publishing Co, pp. 329–374.

1977d. Lessons from a clinical approach to medical anthropology. *Medical Anthropology Newsletter* 8(4):11–15.

1977e. Rethinking the social and cultural context of psychopathology and psychiatric care. In T. Manschreck and A. Kleinman, eds., *Renewal in Psychiatry: A Critical Rational Perspective*. Washington, D.C.: Hemisphere Publishing Co., pp. 97–138.

Kleinman, A. et al., eds.

1976. *Medicine in Chinese Cultures: Comparative Studies of Health Care in Chinese and Other Societies*. Washington, D.C.: U.S. Government Printing Office for Fogarty International Center, N.I.H., DHEW Publication No. (N.I.H.) 75-653. Stock No. 017-053-00036. (Note: Although this book carries a 1975 publication date, it was not released until summer, 1976, and therefore the latter date is used throughout the present volume.)

Kleinman, A. and Sung, L.H.

1976. "Why do indigenous practitioners successfully heal? A follow-up study of indigenous practice in Taiwan." Paper presented at the workshop on the healing process, Michigan State University, April 8–10, 1976, to be published with the proceedings of the workshop in *Social Science and Medicine*.

Kleinman, A. and Mendelsohn, E.

In press. Systems of medical knowledge: A comparative approach. *Journal of Medicine and Philosophy*.

Kleinman, A., Eisenberg, L., and Good, B.

1978. Culture, illness and care: Clinical lessons from anthropological and cross-cultural research. *Annals of Internal Medicine* 88:251–258.

Ko, Y.H.

1973. Birth order and psychological needs. *Acta Psychologica Taiwanica* 15:68–80

1974. A study on the effects of psychotherapy. *ibid.* 16:141–154.

Koo, L.C.
1976. "Nourishment of Life: The Culture of Health in Traditional Chinese Society." Ph.D. dissertation, Department of Anthropology, University of California, Berkeley.

Kosa, J. et al., eds.
1969. *Poverty and Health: A Sociological Analysis.* Cambridge, Mass.: Harvard University Press.

Kuhn, T.S.
1970. *The Structure of Scientific Revolutions.* Chicago: University of Chi-
(1962) cago Press.

Kunstadter, P.
1976a. Do cultural differences make any difference? Choice points in medical systems available in northwestern Thailand. In Kleinman et al., eds., *Medicine in Chinese Cultures, op.cit.,* pp. 351–384.

1976b. The comparative anthropological study of medical systems in society. In *ibid.,* pp. 683–696.

Lain-Entralgo, P.
1970. *The Therapy of the Word in Classical Antiquity.* New Haven: Yale University Press.

Lambo, T.A.
1969. Traditional African cultures and Western medicine. In F. Poynter, ed., *Medicine and Culture.* London: Wellcome Institute Publications.

Lamson, H.
1935. *Social Pathology in China.* Shanghai: Commercial Press.

Langness, L.L.
1967. Hysterical psychosis: The cross-cultural evidence. *American Journal of Psychiatry* 124:143–152.

Lazare, A.
1973. Hidden conceptual models in clinical psychiatry. *New England Journal of Medicine* 288:345–350.

Lazare, A. et al.
1975. The customer approach to patienthood. *Archives of General Psychiatry* 32:553–558.

Lebra, W.P., ed.
1976. Culture-Bound Syndromes, Ethnopsychiatry, and Alternate Therapies, Volume IV. *Mental Health Research in Asia and the Pacific.* Honolulu: University Press of Hawaii.

Lee, R.P.L.
1976. Interaction between Chinese and Western medicine in Hong Kong: Modernization and Professional Inequality. In Kleinman et al., eds., *Medicine in Chinese Cultures, op.cit.,* pp. 219–240.

Leff, J.
1977. Cross-cultural studies of emotions. *Culture, Medicine and Psychiatry* 1: 317–350.

Leighton, A. et al.
1968. The therapeutic process in cross-cultural perspective. *American Journal of Psychiatry* 124:1171–1183.

Bibliography

Leslie, C.
  1974.   The modernization of Asian medical systems. In J. Poggie and
          R. Lynch, eds., *Rethinking Modernization: Anthropological Perspec-*
          tives. Westport, Conn.: Greenwood Press.
  1976a. The ambiguities of medical revivalism in modern India. In C.
          Leslie, ed., *Asian Medical Systems.* Berkeley: University of Cali-
          fornia Press, pp. 356–367.
Leslie, C., ed.
  1976b. *Asian Medical Systems.* Berkeley: University of California Press.
Lewis, G.
  1975.   *Knowledge of Illness in a Sepik Society.* London: Athlone Press.
Lewis, I.M.
  1971.   *Ecstatic Religion: An Anthropological Study of Spirit Possession and*
          Shamanism. Harmondsworth, Middlesex, England: Penguin.
Levi, L., ed.
  1971.   *Society, Stress and Disease.* London: Oxford University Press.
Levy, R.
  1973.   *Tahitians: Mind and Experience in the Society Islands.* Chicago: Uni-
          versity of Chicago Press.
Li, Y.Y.
  1972.   "Shamanism in Taiwan: An Anthropological Inquiry." Paper
          presented at the Fourth Conference on Culture and Mental Health
          in Asia and the Pacific, East-West Center. Reprinted in W.P.
          Lebra, ed., *Culture-Bound Syndromes, Ethnopsychiatry, and Alter-*
          native Therapies, op.cit., pp. 179–188.
Li, Y.Y. and Yang, K.S., eds.
  1974.   *The Character of the Chinese: An Interdisciplinary Study.* Nankang,
          Taipei: Institute of Ethnology, Academica Sinica. (In Chinese).
Lieban, R.W.
  1977.   The field of medical anthropology. In D. Landy, ed., *Culture Dis-*
          ease, and Healing: Studies in Medical Anthropology. New York: Mac-
          millan, pp. 13–30.
Lin, T.Y.
  1953.   Anthropological study of the incidence of mental disorder in
          Chinese and other cultures. *Psychiatry* 16:313–336.
Lin, T.Y. et al.
  1969.   Mental disorders in Taiwan, 15 years later. In W. Caudill and
          T.Y. Lin, eds., *Mental Health Research in Asia and the Pacific, op.cit.,*
          pp. 61–91.
Lin, T.Y. and Lin, M.C.
  1977.   "Ethnicity and pathways of patients seeking treatment." Unpub-
          lished manuscript.
Lin, T.Y. et al.
  1978.   Ethnicity and patterns of help-seeking. *Culture, Medicine and Psy-*
          chiatry 2:3–14.
Lipowski, Z.J.
  1969.   Psychosocial aspects of disease. *Annals of Internal Medicine* 71:1197–
          1206.

404

1973. Psychosomatic medicine in a changing society: Some current trends in theory and research. *Comprehensive Psychiatry* 14:203–215.

1977. Psychosomatic medicine in the seventies: An overview. *American Journal of Psychiatry* 134:233–244.

Litman, T.J.
1974. The family as a basic unit in health and medical care: A socio-behavioral overview. *Social Science and Medicine* 8:495–519.

Litman, T. and Robins, L.
1971. Comparative analyses of health care systems—a sociopolitical approach. *Social Science and Medicine* 5:573–581.

Liu, C.W.
1974. *Essays on Chinese Folk Beliefs and Folk Cults.* Monograph No. 22. Nankang, Taipei: Institute of Ethnology, Academica Sinica. (In Chinese.)

1975. The world of the divining youth. *Ethnos in Asia* 3:56–67. (In Japanese.)

Loudon, J.B.
1976. Introduction. In J.B. Loudon, ed., *Social Anthropology and Medicine.* New York: Academic Press, pp. 1–48.

Luborsky, L. et al.
1975. Comparative studies of psychotherapy: Is it true that "everyone has won and all must have prizes?" *Archives of General Psychiatry* 32:995–1008.

Mabry, J.
1964. Lay concepts of etiology. *Journal of Chronic Disease* 17:371–386.

Marsella, A.J.
1977. Depressive experience and disorder across cultures. In H. Triandis and J. Draguns, eds., *Handbook of Cross-Cultural Psychology, Volume 5: Culture and Psychopathology.* Boston: Allyn and Bacon, pp. 30–72.

In press. "Towards a conceptual framework for understanding cross-cultural variations in depressive affect and disorder." Paper delivered to the seminar on psychocultural aspects of ethnicity, School of International Studies, University of Washington, April 18, 1978. To be published in the seminar proceedings.

Mason, J.W.
1976. Emotion as reflected in patterns of endocrine integration. In L. Levi, ed., *Emotions: Their Parameters and Measurement.* New York: Raven Press, pp. 143–181.

Mathews, R.H.
1963. *Mathews' Chinese-English Dictionary.* Cambridge, Mass.: Harvard University Press.

Mauksch, H.O.
1974. A social science basis for conceptualizing family health. *Social Science and Medicine* 8:521–528.

Bibliography

Mauss, M.

1950. Les techniques du corps. In M. Mauss, *Sociologie et Anthropologie.* Paris: Presses Universitaires de France.

McCorkle, T.

1961. Chiropractic: A deviant theory of disease. *Human Organization* 20:20–22.

McCreery, J.L.

1978. Potential and effective meaning in therapeutic ritual. *Culture, Medicine and Psychiatry* 2(4), in press.

McDermott, W. et al.

1972. Health care experiment in Many Farms. *Science* 175:23–28.

McKeown, T.

1965. *Medicine in Modern Society.* London: George Allen and Unwin.

McKinlay, J.

1973. Social networks, lay consultation and help-seeking behavior. *Social Forces* 51:275–285.

Mead, G.H.

1934. *Mind, Self and Society.* Chicago: University of Chicago Press.

Mechanic, D.

1962. The concept of illness behavior. *Journal of Chronic Diseases* 15:189–194.

1972. Social psychological factors affecting the presentation of bodily complaints. *New England Journal of Medicine* 286:1132–1139.

Mendelsohn, E.

1976. Comparative studies in science and medicine. In Kleinman et al., eds., *Medicine in Chinese Cultures, op.cit.,* pp. 659–667.

Messing, S.

1968. Interdigitation of mystical and physical healing in Ethiopia: Toward a theory of medical anthropology. *Behavioral Science Notes* 3:87–104.

Metzger, D. and Williams, G.

1963. Tenejapa medicine 1: The curer. *Southwestern Journal of Anthropology* 19:216–234.

Metzger, T.A.

1977. *Escape From Predicament: Neo-Confucianism and China's Evolving Political Culture.* New York: Columbia University Press.

Meyer, B.F. and Wempe, T.F.

1947. *The Student's Cantonese-English Dictionary.* New York: Field Afar Press.

Mitchell, W.E.

1977. Changing others: The anthropological study of therapeutic systems. *Medical Anthropology Newsletter* 8(3):15–20.

Montgomery, E.

1976. Systems and the medical practitioners of a Tamil town. In C. Leslie, ed., *Asian Medical Systems, op.cit.,* pp. 272–284.

Meyers, J.T.

1974. *A Chinese Spirit-Medium Temple in Kwun Tong.* Hong Kong: Social Research Centre, Chinese University of Hong Kong.

Bibliography

Nakamura, H.
 1960. *The Ways of Thinking of Eastern Peoples.* Tokyo: Printing Bureau, Ministry of Finance, pp. 167–226.

Nash, J.
 1967. The logic of behavior: Curing in a Maya Indian town. *Human Organization* 26:132–140.

Navarro, V.
 1975. The industrialization of fetishism or the fetishism of industrialization: A critique of Ivan Illich. *Social Science and Medicine* 9:351–363.
 1976. Social class, political power and state, and their implications in medicine. *Social Science and Medicine* 10:437–458.

Neutra, R. et al.
 1977. Cultural expectations versus reality in Navajo seizure patterns and sick roles. *Culture, Medicine and Psychiatry* 1:255–276.·

Newman, P.
 1964. "Wild man" behavior in a New Guinea Highlands community. *American Anthropologist* 66:1–19.

Nida, E.
 1974. *Toward a Science of Translating.* Leiden: Brill.

Obeyesekere, G.
 1976a. The impact of Ayurvedic ideas on the culture and the individual in Sri Lanka. In C. Leslie, ed., *Asian Medical Systems. op.cit.,* pp. 201–226.
 1976b. Some comments on the nature of traditional medical systems. In A. Kleinman et al., eds., *Medicine in Chinese Cultures, op.cit.,* pp. 419–426.

Oksenberg, M.
 1974. The Chinese policy process and the public health issue: An arena approach. *Studies in Comparative Communism* 7:375–408.

Park, G.
 1974. *The Idea of Social Structure.* New York: Anchor Books.

Paul, B.D., ed.
 1955. *Health, Culture, and Community.* New York: Russell Sage Foundation.

Pickering, G.
 1974. *Creative Malady.* London: George Allen and Unwin.

Platonov, K.
 1959. *The Word as a Physiological and Therapeutic Factor.* Moscow: Foreign Languages Publications House.

Polanyi, M. and Prosch, H.
 1975. *Meaning.* Chicago: University of Chicago Press, pp. 22–45.

Polgar, S.
 1962. Health and human behavior: Areas of interest common to the social and medical sciences. *Current Anthropology* 3:159–205.

Porkert, M.
 1974. *The Theoretical Foundations of Chinese Medicine: Systems of Correspondances.* Cambridge, Mass.: M.I.T. Press.

1976. The dilemma of present-day interpretations of Chinese medicine. In A. Kleinman, ed., *Medicine in Chinese Cultures, op.cit,* pp.61–70.

Potter, J.
1970. Wind, water, bones and souls: The religious world of the Cantonese peasant. *Journal of Oriental Studies* (Hong Kong University) 8:139–153.

Pouillon, J.
1972 Doctor and patient: Same and/or other? In W. Munsterberger and A. Esman, eds., *The Psychoanalytic Study of Society,* Volume 5. New York: International Universities Press.

Press, I.
1969. Urban illness: Physicians, curers, and dual use in Bogota. *Journal of Health and Social Behavior* 10:209–218.

Public Health in Taipei
1973. Taipei: Taipei City Health Department.

Quesada, G.M.
1976. Language and communication barriers for health delivery to a minority group. *Social Science and Medicine* 10:323–327.

Reynolds, D.
1976. *Morita Psychotherapy.* Berkeley: University of California Press.

Rin, H.
1965. A study of the aetiology of koro in respect to the Chinese concept of illness. *International Journal of Social Psychiatry* 11:7–13.

Rin, H. et al.
1962. A study of the content of delusions and hallucinations manifested by the Chinese paranoid psychotics. *Journal of the Formosa Medical Association* 61:46–57.

Rin, H. et al.
1966. Psychophysiological reactions of rural and suburban populations in Taiwan. *Acta Psychiatrica Scandinavica* 42:410–473.

Rivers, W. H. R.
1924. *Medicine, Magic and Religion.* New York: Harcourt and Brace.

Roazen, P.
1971. *Freud and His Followers.* New York: Knopf.

Rogers, C.
1951. *Client-Centered Therapy.* Boston: Houghton Mifflin.

Rosaldo, M.
1972. Metaphors and folk classification. *Southwestern Journal of Anthropology* 28:83–99.

Rosen, G.
1975. Nostalgia: A "forgotten" psychological disorder. *Psychological Medicine* 5:340–354.

Rothman, D.J.
1971. *The Discovery of the Asylum: Social Order and Disorder in the New Republic.* Boston: Little, Brown.

Bibliography

Rubel, A.
    1964.   The epidemiology of a folk illness: Susto in Hispanic America. *Ethnology* 3:268–283.

Sartorius, N. and Jablensky, A.
    1976.   Transcultural studies of schizophrenia. *WHO Chronicle* 30:481–485.

Saunders, L.
    1954.   *Cultural Difference and Medical Care: The Case of Spanish-Speaking People of the Southwest.* New York: Russell Sage Foundation.

Schmale, A. et al.
    1970.   Current concepts of psychosomatic medicine. In O. Hill, ed., *Modern Trends in Psychosomatic Medicine II.* New York: Appleton-Century-Crofts.

Schutz, A.
    1970.   *On Phenomenology and Social Relations.* Chicago: University of Chicago Press.

Schwartz, L.R.
    1969.   The hierarchy of resort in curative practices: The Admiralty Islands, Melanesia. *Journal of Health and Social Behavior* 10:201–209.

Seijas, H.
    1973.   An approach to the study of medical aspects of culture. *Current Anthroplogy* 14:544–545.

Shapin, S.
    1977.   Scientific states of mind. *Times Literary Supplement* (London), May 20, 1977, p. 613.

Shaver, D.
    1974.   Opticiancy, optometry and ophthalmology. *Medical Care* 12:754–765.

Shryock, R.
    1969.   *The Development of Modern Medicine.* New York: Hafner.

Siegler, M. and Osmond, H.
    1966.   Models of madness. *British Journal of Psychiatry* 112:1193–1203.
    1973.   The "sick role" revisited. *Hastings Center Studies* 1(3):41–58.

Sigerist, H.
    1951.   *A History of Medicine, Volume 1: Primitive and Archaic Medicine.* London: Oxford University Press.

Sih, P.K., ed.
    1973.   *Taiwan in Modern Times.* New York: St. Johns University Press.

Singer, K.
    1975.   Depressive disorders from a transcultural perspective. *Social Science and Medicine* 9:289–301.

Sivin, N.
    1972.   "Folk medicine in traditional China." Mimeographed paper.
    1975.   "Classical medicine and popular medicine in traditional China." Mimeographed paper.

Bibliography

Snow, L.
1974. Folk medical beliefs and their implications for care of patients. *Annals of Internal Medicine* 81:82–96.

Solomon, R.
1971. *Mao's Revolution and the Chinese Political Culture.* Berkeley: University of California Press, pp. 1–133.

Spiro, M.E.
1967. *Burmese Super-naturalism: A Study in the Explanation and Reduction of Suffering.* Englewood Cliffs, New Jersey: Prentice-Hall.
1976. Supernaturally caused illness in traditional Burmese medicine. In A. Kleinman et al., eds., *Medicine in Chinese Cultures, op.cit.,* pp. 385–400.

Spradley, J.P. and Phillips, M.
1972. Culture and stress: A quantitative analysis. *American Anthropologist* 74:518–529.

Stimson, G.
1974. Obeying doctor's orders. *Social Science and Medicine* 8:97–104.

Stoeckle, J. et al.
1964. The quantity and significance of psychological distress in medical patients. *Journal of Chronic Disease* 17:959–970.

Suchman, E.
1965. Social patterns of illness and medical care. *Journal of Health and Human Behavior* 6:2–16.

Sue, S. and Wagner, N., eds.
1973. *Asian-Americans: Psychological Perspectives.* Palo Alto: Science and Behavior Books.

Svarstad, B.
1976. Physician-patient communications and patient conformity with medical advice. In D. Mechanic, ed. *The Growth of Bureaucratic Medicine.* New York: Wiley Interscience Publication, pp. 220–238.

Taiwan's Health, 1972–1973.
1973. Department of Health, Taiwan Provincial Government, Republic of China.

Tambiah, S.J.
1968. The magical power of words. *Man* 3 :175–208.
1973. Form and meaning of magical acts: A point of view. In R. Horton and R. Finnegan, eds., *Modes of Thought.* London: Faber, pp. 199–229.
1975. *Buddhism and the Spirit Cults in North-East Thailand.* Cam-
(1970) bridge, Engl.: Cambridge University Press.
1977. The cosmological and performative significance of a Thai cult of healing through meditation. *Culture, Medicine and Psychiatry* 1:97–132.

Taylor, C.E.
1876. The place of indigenous medical practitioners in the modernization of health services. In C. Leslie, ed., *Asian Medical Systems.* Berkeley: University of California Press, pp. 285–299.

Bibliography

Teichner, W.
  1968. Interaction of behavioral and physiological stress reactions. *Psychological Review* 75:271–291

Thomas, K.
  1971. *Religion and the Decline of Magic*. London: Weidenfeld and Nicholson.

Topley, M.
  1953. Paper charms and prayer sheets as adjuncts to Chinese worship. *Journal of the Malayan Branch of the Royal Asiatic Society* 26:63–80.
  1970. Chinese traditional ideas and the treatment of disease. *Man* 5:421–437.
  1976a. Chinese traditional etiology and methods of cure in Hong Kong. In C. Leslie, ed., *Asian Medical Systems, op.cit.,* pp. 243–271.
  1976b. Chinese and Western medicine in Hong Kong: Some social and cultural determinants of variation, interaction and change. In A. Kleinman et al., eds., *Medicine in Chinese Cultures, op.cit.,* pp. 241–272.

Torrey, E.F.
  1972. *The Mind Game*. New York: Emerson-Hall.

Truax, C. and Carkhuff, R.
  1967. *Toward Effective Counseling and Psychotherapy*. Chicago: Aldine.

Tseng, W.S.
  1972. Psychiatric study of shamanism in Taiwan. *Archives of General Psychiatry* 26:561–565.
  1974. "Folk psychotherapy in Taiwan." Paper presented to the Fourth Conference on Mental Health Research in Asia and the Pacific. Honolulu, East-West Center, March 20–24, 1974. Reprinted in W.P. Lebra, ed., *Culture-Bound Syndromes, Ethnopsychiatry, and Alternate Therapies, op.cit.,* pp. 164–178.
  1975. The nature of somatic complaints among psychiatric patients: The Chinese case. *Comprehensive Psychiatry* 16:237–245.
  1976. Traditional and modern psychiatric care in Taiwan. In A. Kleinman et al., eds., *Medicine in Chinese Cultures, op.cit.,* pp. 177–194.

Tseng, W.S. and Hsu, J.
  1969. Chinese culture, personality formation and mental illness. *International Journal of Social Psychiatry* 16:5–14.

Turner, V.
  1967. *The Forest of Symbols*. Ithaca, New York: Cornell University Press.

Twaddle, A.C.
  1972. The concepts of the sick role and illness behavior. *Advances in Psychosomatic Medicine* 8:162–179.
  1974. The concept of health status. *Social Science and Medicine* 8:29–38.

Unschuld, P.U.
  1976. The social organization and ecology of medical practice in Taiwan. In C. Leslie, ed., *Asian Medical Systems, op.cit.,* pp. 300–321.

Verma, R.L. and Keswani, N.H.
  1975   The physiological concepts of Unani medicine. In Hakim Mohammed Said, *Hamdard: Voices of Eastern Medicine* 18:42–60.

411

Bibliography

Wallace, A.F.C.
  1959. The institutionalization of cathartic and control strategies in Iroquois religious psychotherapy. In M. Opler, ed., *Culture and Mental Health*. New York: Macmillan.

Walser, H.H. and Koelbing, H.M.
  1971. *Erwin Ackerknecht–Medicine and Ethnology*. Bern, Switzerland: Huber.

Wang, C.M.
  1971. "A Folk Doctor and his Cult on Keelung Street in Taipei." B.A. thesis, Department of Anthropology, National Taiwan University. (In Chinese.)

Wartofsky, M.W.
  1974. Organs, organisms and disease: Human ontology and medical practice. In H.T. Englehardt and S.F. Spicker, eds., *Evaluation and Explanation in the Biomedical Sciences*. Dordrecht, Holland: Reidel Publishing Co., 67–83.

Waxler, N.E.
  1974. Culture and mental illness: A social labelling perspective. *Journal of Nervous and Mental Disease* 159:379–395.
  1977. Is mental illness cured in traditional societies? *Culture, Medicine and Psychiatry* 1:233–254.

Wegmen, M.E., Lin, T.Y , and Purcell, E.F., eds.
  1973. *Public Health in the People's Republic of China*. New York: Josiah Macy, Jr. Foundation.

Weiss, J.M.
  1972. Psychological factors in stress and disease. *Scientific American* 226(6):104–113.

Wellin, E.
  1977. Theoretical orientations in medical anthropology: Continuity and change over the past half-century. In D. Landy, ed., *Culture, Disease, and Healing: Studies in Medical Anthropology*. New York: Macmillan, pp. 47–57.

Werner, H. and Kaplan, B.
  1967. *Symbol Formation*. New York: Wiley.

White, K.
  1973. Life and Death and Medicine. *Scientific American* 229(3):23–33.

White, K. et al.
  1961. The ecology of medical care. *New England Journal of Medicine* 265:885–892.

WHO International Pilot Study of Schizophrenia, Volume 1.
  1973. Geneva: WHO.

Whybrow, P.C.
  1972. The use and abuse of the "medical model" as a conceptual frame in psychiatry. *Psychiatry in Medicine* 3:333–342.

Wittkower, E.D. and Prince, R.
  1974. A review of transcultural psychiatry. In G. Caplan, ed., *Child and Adolescent Psychiatry, Sociocultural and Community Psychiatry,*

Bibliography

American Handbook of Psychiatry. Volume 2, Second Edition. New York: Basic Books, pp. 535–550.

Wolf, A., ed.
1974. *Religion and Ritual in Chinese Society.* Stanford: Stanford University Press.

Wolf, M.
1970. Child training and the Chinese family. In M. Freedman, ed., *Family and Kinship in Chinese Society.* Stanford: Stanford University Press.

1972. *Women and the Family in Rural Taiwan.* Stanford: Stanford University Press.

Wolf, M. and Wittke, R., eds.
1975. *Women in Chinese Society.* Stanford: Stanford University Press.

Wolff, R.
1965. Modern medicine and traditional culture: Confrontation on the Malay peninsula. *Human Organization* 24:339–345.

Woodruff, R.A. et al.
1974. *Psychiatric Diagnosis.* New York: Oxford University Press.

Worth, R.
1963. Health in rural China: From village to commune. *American Journal of Hygiene* 77:228–239.

Yalman, N.
1964. The structure of Sinhalese healing rituals. *Journal of Asian Studies* 23:115–150.

Yang, L.S.
1957. The concept of *pao* as a basis for social relations in China. In J. Fairbanks, ed., *Chinese Thought and Institutions.* Chicago: University of Chicago Press, pp. 291–309.

Yap, P.M.
1965. Phenomenology of affective disorders in Chinese and other cultures. In A. De Reuck and R. Porter, eds., *Transcultural Psychiatry.* Boston: Little, Brown.

1967. Ideas of mental health and disorder in Hong Kong and their practical influence. In M. Topley, ed., *Some Traditional Chinese Ideas and Conceptions in Hong Kong Social Life Today.* Hong Kong: Hong Kong Branch of the Royal Asiatic Society.

1974. *Comparative Psychiatry.* Toronto: University of Toronto Press.

Young, A.
1977. Order, analogy, and efficacy in Ethiopian medical divination. *Culture, Medicine and Psychiatry* 1(2):183–200.

1978. "Mode of production of medical knowledge." Paper presented to the Conference on the Transition to Global Health: Rethinking the Western Health Enterprise, Case Western Reserve University, March, 1978, *Medical Anthropology* 2(2):97–121, 1978.

Zborowski, M.
1952. Cultural components in responses to pain. *Journal of Social Issues* 8:16–30.

413

Bibliography

    1969. *People in Pain*. San Francisco: Jossey-Bass.
Zola, I. K.
    1966. Culture and symptoms: An analysis of patients' presenting complaints. *American Sociological Review* 3:615–630.
    1972a. The concept of trouble and sources of medical assistance. *Social Science and Medicine* 6:673–679.
    1972b. Medicine as an institution of social control. *Sociological Review* 20:487–504.
    1972c. Studying the decision to see a doctor. *Advances in Psychosomatic Medicine* 8:216–236.
    1973. Pathways to the doctor—from person to patient. *Social Science and Medicine* 7:677–684.

. Index

Index

Chiropractors, 54; case description of, 103; clinical reality of, 55; illness as focus of, 81

Chrisman, N., 30, 51, 80

Chronic disorders: disease and illness hard to distinguish in, 74; folk healers viewed as more effective than Western-style doctors for treating, 194, 330, 331, 332

Ch'ung (chhiong-tioh), 109, 113n

Chung-i-sheng. See Chinese-style doctors

Chung-yao. See Medicines, Chinese

Clements, F.E., 29

Clinical care, fees for various types of, 13–14n

Clinical clerkships in ethnomedicine, 383

Clinical medicine, anthropological framework for, 381–387

Clinical anthropology, 375–387

Clinical reality, 120, 132; as category in practitioner-patient interactions, 208; in ch'ien interpreter-client interactions, 249, 253–254, 255, 257–258; in Chinese-style doctor-patient interactions, 269, 271, 272, 275, 278, 279, 281, 282–283, 284, 285; and construction of illness and disease, 73; defined, 38–41; differences in, in each sector of health care system, 53; as effective agent in treatment, 222–223; EMs in construction of, 110–111, 237–238; in family-patient interactions, 308–309; and healing efficacy, 360–361; and health care sectors' contacts, 98–101; legitimation of, 44–45; mediated by symbolic reality, 43–44; model of, 42 fig.; at National Taiwan University Hospital, 61–62; patient and practitioner differences in each sector of health care system, 53; power as factor in determining, 52, 58–59; and process of indigenizing professional sector of health care system, 55–56; and professional sector of health care system, 55, 56–59, 61–62; as research focus, 375–377, 378; in tâng-ki-client interactions, 220, 222–223, 224–225, 228–229, 230, 232–233, 237–238, 241–243; in tâng-ki's ritual, 218–223; translation between different definitions of, 53, 58–59, 101–104; in Western-style doctor-patient interactions, 287–294, 295–302, 304–305

Clinical social science, 375–387

Cognitive coping mechanisms, 147–178; American and Chinese compared, 172, 174 table, 175n; case descriptions of, 151–152, 153–155, 156–157, 162–163, 166–168; and creation of culture-spe-

cific affects, 170–171, 173 fig., 177; cross-cultural typologies of, 175n, 176; hypotheses about, 176–178; model of, 173 fig.; social class, education, and life style as determinants of, 172n, 175n; and Westernization, 177. See also Dysphoric affects; Somatization of dysphoric affects

Cohen, A., 43n

Colson, A., 24n

Communicative operations, 71, 82, 83–84, 90–104; in clinical dyad, 111–115, 116–117; EMs in, 104–118; examples, 84–90; interpretive problems in, 101–104; therapeutic importance of, 255. See also Idiom of communication; Labeling illness

Core clinical functions of health care system, 71–83, 120; interpretive problems in cross-cultural comparisons of, 101, 104; as research focus, 375–377, 378

Crick, M., 380

Croizier, R., 17

Cult, 232–233, 370; members, 226, 267, 313, 315

Cultural iatrogenesis, 82

Cultural healing, 82, 360, 373

Culture-bound disorders, 163–165, 294–295

Curing of disease, 82

Dental offices, 2

Depression: case descriptions of, 123–124, 151–159; in China, 76, 148; cross-cultural variation in EMs of, 76–77; and diabetes, 77; difficulties of modernizing Taiwanese in getting treatment for, 291; in Japan, 148; labeling of, as cultural process, 76, 171; research study of, 21–22; as shaped by cognitive coping mechanisms, 161, 171, 172, 176–178; somatization of, 138–142, 151–159, 220; in Taiwan, 138, 291; tâng-ki treatment of, 218–222; in the United States, 76, 138–140, 141, 148, 161

Deuschle, K., 29, 46–47

Diabetes: changing EMs for, 111; and chronic anxiety, 79; as illness and disease, 74

Diet: in clinical practice of Chinese-style doctors, 275–276; in health maintenance of infants, elderly, and post-delivery women, 195; in home treatment, 185–186, 190 fig., 193 fig.

Disease: Chinese cultural patterns affecting, 133–145; Chinese explanatory framework for, 91–92; and chronic disorders,

417

Index

Disease (continued)
74; classical Chinese medical categories for, 86; defined, 72–73; as focus of biomedical model, 381–382; as focus of Western professional health sector, 73–74, 100–101; and fulminant acute disorders, 74; and illness, 72–73, 130; in model of impact of culture on affect, 173 fig.; natural history of, 107; patient focus on, 356; and psychiatric disorders, 74; and psychophysiological disorders, 77–79; problems, 81, 241, 257, 260, 285, 304, 309, 366; research difficulties in evaluating treatment of, 356, 359, 360–361; symptomatology of, as cultural process, 75–80; treatment success criteria, 355–356; Western explanatory framework for, 91–92; without illness, 76

Dissociation of dysphoric affects, 148–149, 150, 154, 155, 163, 172, 174–175 table, 369; by female members of *tâng-ki*'s cult, 232, 233; in hysterical psychosis, 169

Divination, 244, 316. *See also* Ch'ien interpreters; Fortune-tellers

Doi, L.T., 147

Drug abuse, illness and disease models of, 74–75

Drug peddlers, 66–67

Dunn, F.L., 24n, 46, 83

Dying: and indigenous healing, 332; management of, by Chinese-style doctors, 280–281

Dysphoric affects, 36; in Chinese culture, 148–178; dissociation of, 148–149, 150, 154, 155, 163, 169, 172, 174–175 table, 232, 233; impact of culture on, 173 fig.; minimization of, 148, 150, 154, 157, 172, 174–175 table; psychobiological substrate of, 147; shaped through cognitive processes, 147–148; somatization of, 138–145, 149, 150, 151–172, 174–175 table; stress on situational context, 141, 149–150, 151, 152–153, 156–157; trance behavior in management of, 169, 170

Eisenberg, L., 29, 295

Elderly people: family treatment choices for, 183, 184, 185 table; health maintenance of, 195; patterns of health seeking behavior for, 193 fig.; self-treatment of, 183, 187; sickness episodes of, 181–182; traditional pattern of affect among, 177

Electroconvulsive therapy (ECT), 288

Emotions in Taiwanese culture: public vs. private, 136, 138; situational context

of, stressed, 136–138, 141–142; somatic terms for, 135–136. *See also* Somatization of dysphoric affects

EMs. *See* Explanatory models

Engel, G., 73

Engelhardt, H.T., 73

Enteritis, 190 fig., 192 fig.; injections for, 288

Ethnocentrism in study of health care systems, 29, 32

Ethnomedical model, 18–20, 84; implications of, 375–387

Exercise as home treatment, 186 table

Explanatory models (EMs), 104–118, 120; autistic, 162–164; bad fate as, 235–238, 243; change and plasticity in, 109–1 0; in *ch'ien* interpreter-client interactions, 245, 247, 250, 255, 256, 257; in Chinese-style doctor-patient interactions, 274, 277, 278, 284; clinical vs. theoretical, in practitioner's work, 109, 110, 113–114; in construction of clinical reality, 110–111, 237–238; about disease/illness, 72–73; disease as focus of professional practitioner's, 73–74; in family-patient interactions, 308, 310; of folk healers, 354; and idiom of communication between practitioner and patient, 207–208; illness as focus of lay, 73, 74; intra-family differences in, 196–198; logic of, 237–238; metaphoric components in Taiwanese, 108–109; multiplicity of, in concrete cases, 120–133; outcomes of, in practitioner-patient relationship, 111–115, 116–117; popular, pragmatic rationality as basis of, 110, 127; practitioner's, compared to popular, 110; of professional practitioners, 73–74, 354–355; psychiatric, 131–132; questions addressed in, 105–106; research method to elicit lay, 106n; as response to *particular* illness episode, 106–107; and structures of relevance, 107, 108 fig., 110–111; tacit knowledge in, 109–110; in *tâng-ki*-client interactions, 221–223, 226, 228–230, 235–238, 240–241, 242, 366, 370–372; variations in, and evaluation of healing efficacy, 358–360; war metaphors in Western, 107–108; in Western-style doctor-patient interactions, 286–288, 296, 299–300, 302, 304

Fabrega, H., 24n, 25, 30, 33n, 43n

Family: bad fate of, as EM, 235–238; central place of, in Taiwanese culture, 133–135, 138; and construction of illness experience, 72, 73, 179–181; disagreement

Index

Index

family's role in health seeking behavior, 201–202; and indigenization of professional sector of health care system, 56; of indigenous Chinese medicine, 281–283; and transformation of social reality, 37

Montgomery, E., 24n

Morally articulated affect, 177n

Morita therapy, 56n, 159–160, 371

Nao-chin, 144

National Health Service, 61

National Taiwan University Hospital: clinical burdens on, 289, 290–291; clinical reality of, 61–62; fees at, 13–14n; psychiatric clinics of, 16

National Taiwan University Medical School, 12; clinical reality of, 61–62

Naturopathy, 54

Navaho, 81

Navarro, V., 48

Ndembu healers, 82

Nei-k'e, 64

Neurasthenia: in case description, 156; as Chinese label, 128–130, 191 fig.; as EM, 123, 126, 127, 128; as legitimation for sick role, 128–129, 130; as Western label, 129, 130, 190 fig., 191 fig.; in People's Republic of China, 292

Nida, E., 111

Nurses: in Taiwan, 12, 62; in the United States, 54, 55

Obeyesekere, G., 33n, 69n, 93

Ong-ia-kong, 121, 218

Orthopedic surgeons, 81, 103

Osteopathy, 54

Pa kua, 66

P'a leng, 164

Pao, 135, 171

Pao-sheng-ta-ti, 2

Patients, 8–9, 206; EMs of, 105–116, 122–123, 124, 127, 132; in health care system, 24–25, 26. *See also Ch'ien* interpreter-client interactions; Chinese-style doctor-patient interactions; Practitioner-patient interactions; *tâng-ki*-client interactions; Western-style doctor-patient interactions

Pa tzu, 66, 206, 316

Penicillin, 288–289

People's Republic of China, health care system of, 44, 46, 47–48, 292–293n; bone-setters in, 64; campaign against professional dominance in, 57; Chinese-style medicine used by Western-style

doctors in, 270–271; expression of affect in, 137n; external influences on, 46, 47–48; indigenization of, 56, 160n; neurasthenia label in, 128–129; professional subsectors in, 61; Western-style medicine used by Chinese-style doctors, 270–271

Peptic ulcer disease, 81

Performative efficacy, 227, 373

Pharmacies, Chinese, 2, 3, 13, 15 table; compared to herbalist shops, 4, 6; and family decisions on illness, 68; in patterns of health seeking behavior, 188–189 fig.; referrals to, by *ch'ien* interpreters, 251, 253. *See also* Chinese-style doctors; Medicines, Chinese

Pharmacies, Western, 2, 6, 12, 13, 15 table; and family decisions on illness, 68; for infants, 195; in patterns of health seeking behavior, 188–189 fig., 192 fig.; in professional sector of health care system, 62. *See also* Medicines, Western

Physical reality, 28 fig., 41, 42 fig.

Physiognomists, 12; divination by, 244; fees of, 13n; in folk sector of health care system, 3, 66

Pickering, Sir George, 129, 130

Placebo response, 367

Plural life-worlds, 37

Polanyi, M., 57

Popularization, 56

Popular sector of health care system, 50–53, 60, 62–63, 67, 68–69; in Boston, 69–70; disease orientation of lay illness models, in the West, 74; EMs in, 105–110, 115–117; family role in, 68–69, 179–202; frameworks of relevance regarding illness and care in, 81–82; health seeking behavior in, 92–97; idiosyncratic and pluralistic beliefs in, 95–97; illness as focus of, 161; importance of financial aspects in, 67; interrelationships with professional and folk sectors, 59, 97–101, 252; labeling of illness in, 92–97; levels of, 69; and medical anthropology's paradigm, 376–377, 378, 379, 380, 384–386; medical knowledge within, 68–69; medical referrals to, by *ch'ien* interpreters, 252; need to strengthen, 385–386, 386–387n; pragmatic orientation in, 196; semantic network of, 106–107; symptom terms in, 140–145; and valuations of disorders, 199; view of Western-style medicine in, 286–287, 296, 302, 303–304. *See also* Health seeking behavior; Illness experience; Sickness episodes

Porkert, M., 91, 237, 259n

423

Index

Index

Sickness: cognitive appraisal of, 79–80; and disease, 72, 74, 77; and illness, 72, 74, 77; labeling of, as cultural process, 76; lay orientation to, in the West, 74; valuations of, 199. *See also* Disease; Illness; Sickness episodes

Sickness episodes, 181, 182 table, 183–186; adults, 181–182, 183; children, 181–182, 183, 192 fig.; elderly, 181–182, 183, 193 fig.; patterns and cases in health seeking behavior, 188–193 figs.

Sick role: abuses of, 74; changes in, from sector to sector of health care system, 125–126; of children, 186, 194; of children and of adults compared, 186; in Chinese culture, 125; cultural construction of, 119, 125–126; and EMs, 116, 371–372; and internal/external aspects of illness, 371–372; and labeling of illness, 75n; neurasthenia as legitimation for, 128–129, 130; and sectors of health care system, 51, 52–53, 125–126; and social withdrawal, 195; substitutes for, by female members of *tâng-ki* cult, 232–233; variations of, by role in family, 194–195

Sien-siⁿ-má, 195

Sigerist, H., 28

Singer, K., 138

Sivin, N., 97, 143, 259n

Snake shops, 67

Snow, L., 29, 34n, 69n

Social control by health care system, 40, 41, 83, 382–383

Socialization, 41; as internalization of social reality, 36; in therapeutic milieu, 370–371

Social reality: and construction of illness and disease, 73; defined, 35–36, 41; distinguished from other dimensions of reality, 28 fig., 41; health care system as form of, 35, 37–41, 44–45; homogeneity of, in traditional societies, 36–37; medicalization of, 40, 41; pluralization of, in developed societies, 37; transformation of, in developing societies, 37; variations in, 37–38. *See also* Clinical reality; Symbolic reality

Somatic delusion, 162–163

Somatic disease, 77–78

Somatic illness, 77–78; richness of Taiwanese terms for, 135–136

Somatization of dysphoric affects, 119–120, 138–145, 149, 150, 151–172, 174–175 table, 223; adaptive and maladaptive dimensions of, 158–159; 160–161, 163, 164, 173 fig.; class differences in,

in the United States, 172n; and emotional states, 135–136, 138; and family, 157–158; as focus of indigenous healing, 330, 331, 333; and health seeking behavior, 190–191 fig.; psychotherapy complicated by, 159–161; and *tâng-ki* healing efficacy, 369

Somatopsychic disorders, 77–78

Spirit-medium, 211n

Spiro, M. E., 33n, 151

Stroke, 199

Suan, 143, 277

Suchman, E., 31n

Summer fever, 271, 277

Surgery, 289, 298–299

Symbolic reality: as bridge between social and personal environment, 28 fig., 42–43; defined, 28 fig., 41; and disease/illness processes, 79–80; formation and internalization of, 41–42; health care system as form of, 43–45; as mediating sickness and care, 42 fig., 43–44. *See also* Clinical reality; Social reality

Symbolism, efficacy of, in healing process, 220, 226–227, 365, 368–374

Symptomatology: as cultural process, 84–90; and EMs, 125–126; and relation between illness and disease, 75–80

Symptoms, cultural patterning of, 75–80, 138–145

Taipei, 11

Taipei City Health Department, 15

Taipei City Psychiatric Hospital, 16

Taiwan, 10–17; expression of affect in, 133–138; health care system in, 11–17, 60–70; impact of Japan on, 10, 16–17

Tambiah, S.J., 31, 373

Tâng-ki, 7, 12, 158; chronic illness therapy, 88–89, 194, 330, 331, 332; and clients' hysterical behaviors, 169, 170; disorders not treated by, 215, 330, 332, 362; divination by, 244, 316; EMs of, 121, 122, 123, 124, 321–327 table, 334–37 table; in folk sector of health care system, 66, 67–68, 238; government crackdown on, 230–231n; healing as main activity, 212; healing success criteria, 354, 355; ideology of, 211–212, 215, 216–217, 223–224, 228; illness as focus of care, 229, 241–242, 355–356, 360–362; income and fees, 13n, 14n; kinship basis of, 209, 210; and measles therapy, 87–88; not used by Mainlanders, 180; patient satisfaction with, 291–292; and patient's sick role, 125, 126; in patterns of health seeking behavior, 188

Index

Index

United States, health system of: class differences in somatization, 172n; cognitive coping mechanisms in, compared to Chinese, 174–175 table; cognitive systems of sectors compared, 104; external influences on, 48; scope of, 40–41; hysterical psychosis in, 169; phenomenology of depression in, 138–140, 141; popular sector in, 50; professional sector in, 54–55; sectoral interrelationships, 98–99; semantic sickness network in, 144–145

Unschuld, P., 33

Ut siong, 84–87, 92; as culture-bound disorder, 164–165; EMs for, 115–117

Vaccination, 88
Venereal disease, 199

Wai-k'e, 64
Wartofsky, M.W., 111
Wei-sheng, 53
Western-style doctor-patient interactions, 208, 286–306; case descriptions of, 295, 296, 298–299, 300, 301; clinical reality of, 287–294, 295–302, 304–305; compared to Chinese-style doctor-patient interactions, 261, 262, 264, 267–268, 269–270, 277, 278, 283–284, 285, 286; disease as focus of, 304, 305; fast cure and symptom improvement as popular expectation in, 286–287, 295–297; idiom of communication in, 289–290, 293–294, 295–302, 304; institutional setting of 289, 290–291, 303; interpersonal interactions in, 289–290, 291–292, 293–294, 295–302, 303–304; role of injections in, 286, 287–288, 295–296; summary categorization of, 306–310; therapeutic stages and mechanisms in, 305–306. *See also* Western-style doctors
Western-style doctors: absence of understanding of popular EMs among, 116–117; on cause of disorders, 89, 90, 91–92; *ch'ien* interpreters' referrals to, 253; and Chinese-style doctors, 261, 262, 264, 267–268, 269–271; class differences in

resort to, 183–184; and communication of meaning, 101; disease as focus of, 355–356; EMs of, 116–117, 123–124, 128, 130, 132; in family health seeking behavior, 187, 188–189 fig., 190 fig., 191 fig., 192 fig., 193 fig.; in family treatment choices, 183, 184, 185 table, 186; income and fees, 13n, 14n; for infants, 192 fig., 195–196; kinship basis of, 209–210; lay frameworks of relevance for care by, 81; patient satisfaction with, 291–292; patient's sick role for, 125, 126; and polar term logic of patient, 199–200; and popular beliefs about mental illness, 198–199; on popular medical beliefs, 93; in professional sector of health care system, 61–62, 65–66, 303; research study of, 21, 22; resorted to, for acute rather than chronic disorders, 194, 331, 332; statistics on, 12, 15 table; treatment expectations for, 194, 286–287, 295–297; on *ut siong*, 86–87

Wittkower, E.D., 30
Wives, sick role of, 194–195
Women: as clients of *ch'ien* interpreters, 246, 247–248, 249, 250, 252–253; as clients in folk sector of health care system, 196–197, 206; as clients of *tâng-ki*, 216, 218, 223–225, 227–228, 229–230, 232–233, 234–235, 236, 238; health maintenance of, after delivery, 195; pattern of affect, 177; traditional orientation of, 177, 196–197
Wu-hsing, 91, 264, 266, 269
Wu-tsang, 90, 91, 142, 264

Yalman, N., 31
Yen-Ping district, 14, 15, 67
Yin/yang imbalance, 191 fig., 199; as cause of disease, 90–91, 102; as cause of sickness, 90, 275; as EM, 122, 126, 127, 130–131, 139; and illness of children and elderly, 195; usage avoided by Chinese-style doctors, 264
Young, Allan, 244, 387n
Yu-yü, 141

Zola, I.K., 31n, 40, 41

427

Designer: Dave Comstock
Compositor: Chapman's Typesetting
Printer: Publisher's Press
Binder: Mountain States Bindery
Text: VIP Palatino
Display: VIP Palatino
Cloth: Holliston Roxite B53531
Paper: 55lb. P&S offset regular